PFLAUM / STANDARD
38 West Fifth Street, Dayton, Ohio 45402

14-31

William Kuhns

MOVIES IN AMERICA

Photo Credits

Acknowledgment is gratefully made for the cooperation of many persons and organizations in providing photographs to illustrate this book. All the photographs are through the courtesy of the Stills Library, Canadian Film Institute/Institut Canadien du Film, Ottawa, Ontario, or the author's collection (28 stills), with the following exceptions:

American Film Institute Collection, page 99.

Gene Andrewski Collection, pages 12, 13, 48 (Yellow Submarine); 98 and 99 (The Crime Nobody Saw, The Kansan, Gone With the Wind, Margie); 123, 124, and 125 (Gold Diggers of 1937, Busby Berkeley production); 145 (Louella Parsons and Cary Grant); 162 and 163 (Life Begins for Andy Hardy, Out West With the Hardys, Andy Hardy Comes Home).

Brother Alexis Gonzales, F.S.C., pages 240, 241.

Robert Hoekstra, the posters, pages 174-175.

Richard Koszarski Collection, pages 54, 58, 63, 86, 120 and 137 (I Was a Fugitive . . .), 120 and 140 (Life of Emile Zola); 123, 124, and 125 (Wonder Bar, Fashions of 1934); 141, 146, 147, 148, 162, and 163 (Love Finds Andy Hardy, Andy Hardy's Private Secretary); 169, 180.

Loew's Collection, Theatre Historical Society, pages 59, 60 and 61.

Museum of Modern Art, pages 4, 8, 10-11, 23 (Griffith with megaphone); 39, 74 and 75 (The Wind); 108-109, 139, 158 (Nanook with spear); 161 (Robert Flaherty); 197 (High Noon); 198-199 (center photo).

National Film Board of Canada, pages 237, 238, 239.

TIME, Inc., pages 36 and 37; 189, LIFE magazine photo by J. R. Eyerman.

Paul Tucker, page 190.

Donald Wigal Collection, pages 48 (Little Red Hen); 49 (lower left).

Discrepancies in dates given for movies in the copyright notices, in photograph identification, and in the text illustrate a difficulty in "dating" films. It is not generally agreed how a film should be dated, whether by copyright date, completion of production, or release for public showing. Dates on most photographs were supplied by the photo sources.

Book Design: Dan Johnson, Joe Loverti, Tim Potter.

Library of Congress Catalog Card No. 72-86109

ISBN 0-8278-0045-2

Following is a list of the pages where films are illustrated, along with the studios and/or producers who originated the films. A companion volume to MOVIES IN AMERICA, entitled TEACHING IN THE DARK, identifies where many of these films can be purchased or rented.

The Publishers

Page 5 Record of a Sneeze Thomas Edison/6 Dreamy Sweedy © 1914 Essanay/10, 11, 28, 29, 30, 31 The Birth of a Nation © 1915 Epoch Producing/20 The Exploits of Elaine © 1914/15 Pathé Studios/26 Judith of Bethulia © 1913 Biograph Company/33 Intolerance © 1916 Wark Producing/34 Hearts of the World © 1917 Comstock/World/35 Broken Blossoms © 1919 United Artists/38, 44A, 44B, 45A Modern Times © 1936 United Artists/39, 43A The Kid © 1920 First National/40 Shoulder Arms © 1918 First National/42 The Pilgrim © 1922 First National/43B City Lights © 1931 United Artists/45B The Great Dictator © 1940 United Artists/46 The Gold Rush © 1925 United Artists/48 Donald's Dream Voice © 1948   /49 Yellow Submarine © 1968 United Artists/55, 66 Merry-Go-Round © 1923 Universal/58 Don't Change Your Husband © 1919 Art Studios/62, 63 Sunrise © 1927 Fox Film Corp./64, 65 Lady Windermere's Fan © 1925 Warner Bros./67 Foolish Wives © 1922 Universal/68, 69A, 69B, 69C, 70 Greed © 1923/24 Goldwyn Company/71A The Merry Widow © 1925 MGM/71B The Wedding March © 1926/27 Paramount/73 Flash Gordon © 1936 Universal/74, 75A The Wind © 1928 MGM/75B He Who Gets Slapped © 1924 MGM/75C, 75D The Scarlet Letter © 1926 MGM/76 The Scarlet Empress © 1933 Paramount/77 The Devil Is a Woman © 1935 Paramount/78 Underworld © 1927 Paramount/79 The Shiek © 1921 Paramount/81B The Covered Wagon © 1923 Paramount/93A The Navigator © 1924 Metro-Goldwyn Pictures/93B Sherlock Jr. © 1924 Metro-Goldwyn Pictures/96A Safety Last © 1923 Hal Roach Studios/102 Bonnie Scotland © 1935 Hal Roach Studios/103A, 103B, 104 Big Business © 1929 Hal Roach/MGM/103C, 105 Two Tars © 1928 Hal Roach/MGM/106 The Finishing Touch © 1928   /108, 109 The Jazz Singer © 1927 Warner Bros./113 Godzilla © 1956 Toho/114 Gone With the Wind © 1939 MGM David O. Selznick/115 Three Little Pigs © 1933 Disney/117 Baby Doll © 1956 Warner Bros./119A Adam's Rib © 1949 MGM/119B Destry Rides Again © 1939 Universal/119C Somewhere I'll Find You © 1942 MGM/120A, 137 I Am a Fugitive From a Chain Gang © 1932 Warner Bros./120B, 140, 141 The Life of Emile Zola © 1937 Warner Bros./120C The Barefoot Contessa © 1954 United Artists/121A, 201 The African Queen © 1951 United Artists/121B The Wagons Roll at Night © 1941 Warner Bros./122 The Wizard of Oz © 1939 MGM/128A, 131A, 131B Public Enemy © 1931 Warner Bros./128B Little Caesar © 1930 Warner Bros./129 Big House © 1930 MGM/130 The Asphalt Jungle © 1950 MGM/136 The Grapes of Wrath © 1940 20th Century-Fox/139, 167 Fury © 1936 MGM/146 Never Give a Sucker An Even Break © 1941 Universal/147 Tillie and Gus © 1934 Paramount/148 My Little Chickadee © 1940 Universal/150A, 152B, 152C The Big Store © 1941 MGM/150B, 152A Go West © 1940 MGM/151A, 151B A Night At the Opera © 1935 MGM/152D At the Circus © 1939 MGM/154, 155 It Happened One Night © 1934 Columbia/156A Mr. Deeds Goes To Town © 1936 Columbia/156B Meet John Doe © 1941 Warner Bros./157A Mr. Smith Goes To Washington © 1939 Columbia/157B Lost Horizon © 1937 Columbia/158A, 158B, 159 Nanook Of the North © 1922 Paramount/160A Moana © 1926 Paramount/160B Man Of Aran © 1934 Gainsborough/Gaumont/160C The Land © 1942 U. S. Department of Agriculture/161B Louisiana Story © 1946/48 Robert J. Flaherty Productions/162, 163 Andy Hardy Is a Good Kid Andy Hardy Comes Home Life Begins For Andy Hardy Out West With the Hardys Love Finds Andy Hardy Andy Hardy's Private Secretary © MGM/164 The Blue Angel © 1929 UFA-Paramount/166A Metropolis © 1926 UFA/166B M © 1931 Nero Film A-G-Ver. Star Film GMBH/168 The Big Heat © 1953 Columbia/171 The Informer © 1935 RKO/172A, 172B Stagecoach © 1939 United Artists/173A My Darling Clementine © 1946 20th Century-Fox/173B She Wore a Yellow Ribbon © 1949 RKO/173C The Man Who Shot Liberty Valance © 1962 Paramount/173D How Green Was My Valley © 1941 20th Century-Fox/176 Pinocchio © 1940 Disney/178 Snow White and the Seven Dwarfs © 1938 Disney/179 Dumbo © 1941 Disney/182A Foreign Correspondent © 1940 United Artists/182B Mrs. Miniver © 1942 MGM/183 Casablanca © 1942 Warner Bros./184 Meet Me In St. Louis © 1944 MGM/187 Warrendale © 1966 Allan King/188, 198, 199 Citizen Kane © 1941 RKO/191 The Best Years Of Our Lives © 1946 MGM/192, 193 Tarzan Finds a Son © 1939 MGM Tarzan the Ape Man © 1918 National Film MGM Tarzan's Peril © 1951 MGM Tarzan and the Valley of Gold © 1966 MGM/194A, 194B, 195 Sunset Boulevard © 1950 Paramount/196 An American In Paris © 1951 MGM/197A High Noon © 1952 United Artists/197B Giant © 1956 Warner Bros./200 Macbeth © 1948 Republic/202 The Treasure of the Sierra Madre © 1948 Warner Bros./203 Beat the Devil © 1953 United Artists/204 Ace In the Hole © 1951 Paramount/205A Some Like It Hot © 1959 United Artists/205B The Lost Weekend © 1945 Paramount/206A A Streetcar Named Desire © 1951 Warner Bros./206B East of Eden © 1955 Warner Bros./207A, 207B, 207C, 207D On the Waterfront © 1954 Columbia/208 Bringing Up Baby © 1938 MGM/209A Gentlemen Prefer Blondes © 1953 20th Century-Fox/209B I Was a Male War Bride © 1949 20th Century-Fox/210A Rio Bravo © 1959 Warner Bros./210B Red River © 1948 United Artists/210C, 210D, 211 Monkey Business © 1952 20th Century-Fox/212 The Man Who Knew Too Much © 1934 Gaumont British/214A The Birds © 1963 Universal/214B Vertigo © 1958 Paramount Alfred Hitchcock/215 North by Northwest © 1959 MGM Alfred Hitchcock/216 Strangers on a Train © 1951 Warner Bros. Alfred Hitchcock/218 Sound of Music © 1965 20th Century-Fox/219A Hello, Dolly! © 1970 Chenault Productions-Fox/219B Cleopatra © 1963 20th Century-Fox/220A, 232, 233 Bonnie and Clyde © 1967 Warner Bros./220B The Graduate © 1967 Embassy Pictures/221 Butch Cassidy and the Sundance Kid © 1969 20th Century-Fox/224 Help! © 1965 Walter Shenson Suba Films/225 The Knack © 1965 United Artists/226 Spartacus © 1959 Universal Stanley Kubrick/227A Dr. Strangelove or: How I Learned To Stop Worrying and Love the Bomb © 1963 Columbia/228, 229, 242 2001: A Space Odyssey © 1968 MGM Stanley Kubrick/230A The Left-Handed Gun © 1958 Warner Bros./230B Mickey One © 1964 Columbia/231 The Miracle Worker © 1962 United Artists/234 Ballad of Cable Hogue © 1969 Warner Bros./235 Ride the High Country © 1961 MGM/236 The Wild Bunch © 1969 Warner Bros./240, 241 M*A*S*H © 1969 20th Century-Fox.

Acknowledgments

More than a few people helped in the preparation of *Movies in America.* I would like to thank particularly:

Linda Beath and Jana Vosikovska of the Canadian Film Institute: Linda for suggestions and unstinting help in locating and checking source material and Jana for her tireless and enthusiastic work in locating stills;

Joseph Dispenza of the American Film Institute, for his ideas and assistance in finding information and stills;

Alan Oddie, who encouraged me to write the book and who helped delineate the approach;

Allen Green and particularly Estelle Redd of Films, Incorporated, both of whom were extremely helpful in arranging screenings;

Marlene Shebu of Pflaum/Standard and Bob Kraske, who were much more than editors;

Donald Wigal, Richard Koszarski, and Gene Andrewski for invaluable help in locating special stills;

Brother Alexis Gonzales, who reviewed and criticized the manuscript;

John Carr, Ron Weinberg, Paul McGuff, Shirley Drevich, Billie Andersson, Tommy Causey, and Robin Weinberg for their inestimable help on the teacher's guide;

and the many teachers and students who have been the largest part of my own education in film . . .

Permission to quote from the following works is gratefully acknowledged:

The Film Till Now by Paul Rotha and Richard Griffith, 1967 Edition, © 1967 by Paul Rotha. Reproduced by permission of The Hamlyn Publishing Group Limited, Feltham, Middlesex, England.

The Immediate Experience by Robert Warshow, Doubleday & Company, New York, New York. Quotations used with the kind permission of Paul Warshow.

Arthur Penn by Robin Wood, by permission of Praeger Publishers, Inc. © 1969 by Movie Magazine Ltd.

Theory of the Film by Bela Balazs. Dover Publications, Inc., New York. Reprinted through permission of the publisher.

The Stars by Richard Schickel. Quotation used with permission of the publisher, The Dial Press, New York, New York.

Agee on Film-Vol. 1 by James Agee. Copyright 1949, 1950 © 1958 by The James Agee Trust. Published by Grosset & Dunlap, Inc.

W. K.

PREFACE

Recently I saw a delightfully funny film that says it all. The film is called *The Projectionist* and it stars Chuck McCann as the little man who sits in a projection booth and runs old movie after old movie after old movie in a revival house. The more he watches, the more he becomes what he watches, until one day he begins fantasizing that he is part of all those old Flash Gordon serials and those John Wayne westerns. Donning a cape, he steps into the screen as Captain Flash, a particularly inept hero, to chase after Godzilla and to mix in with the likes of Humphrey Bogart and Sidney Greenstreet. What I liked most about *The Projectionist* was the delight of recognizing myself—someone who is trapped forever in all those miles and miles of winding celluloid, someone whose imagination has been forged by the flickering light of the movie screen.

We are all children of the movies—whether of the Saturday matinees with their endless serials or of the late late show. True, movies are coming to be recognized as *the* art of our century: the one form of artistic effort which is accessible to everyone, about which we all have some knowledge, some feelings, some opinions. But more than this, movies—particularly old movies—are also a living embodiment of our recent past, a means of knowing what it was like to live in 1942 (*Casablanca, Mrs. Miniver*) or 1927 (*Underworld, Sunrise, The Crowd*) or 1956 (*Invasion of the Body Snatchers, Giant*). An old movie is something like a time machine, transporting us into an audience of another era, letting us feel what people felt then, helping us to relive their struggles and emotions and loyalties. One night recently I watched as a friend, a staunch pacifist, cheered John Wayne on as the Duke slaughtered platoons of Japanese in *Sands of Iwo Jima.* A contradiction? I don't think so; more of a concession to nostalgia—how many of us *weren't* there at one time or other, cheering Wayne on in the final big battle?

But here we do have to face a question about the old movies, one that will keep cropping up through this book: to what extent have the movies shaped the audiences who saw them, and shaped, over time, the cultural history of the twentieth century? It's a knotty question. To some extent the products of Hollywood have always reflected their times. It is no coincidence that the bright optimistic twenties were the heyday of silent comedy, the richest period of screen hilarity. And the Depression had more than a little to do with the rise of the somber gangster films and a fresh attempt by Hollywood to tangle with social evils. Perhaps more than any other medium of the century, the movies have acted like a mirror, reflecting our anxieties and discomforts, our fantasies and hopes—and in doing so, possibly intensifying and further confirming those feelings and attitudes.

In writing *Movies in America,* I have tried to follow two main threads of development: the sophistication and broadening of the movies as an art form, and the complex interrelationships between a period and the movies of that period. This book is not a year-by-year history of the American film as such, but it uses film history as its format and design, its "plot," simply because it is helpful to know where an idea or technique started and how it developed.

Throughout the book you will find a good deal of time being spent on directors. One could as easily have emphasized studios or genres—western, comedy, musical. I have concentrated on major directors, partly because they have created their own styles and have explored the possibilities of film more consciously than anyone else involved in the production of movies, and partly because they offer a counterpoint to the emphasis on placing a film in its time period. The work of John Ford, for example, stretches from 1917 to 1966—almost 50 years. And whether you are seeing *The Informer* (1935) or *The Man Who Shot Liberty Valance* (1962), you know immediately that you are watching a Ford film: the clean composition, the exacting use of camera, the gentle insinuation of feeling. Despite the years, Ford's genius has not lessened. It is important to know how styles and themes and ideas have undergone transition through the years. But it is also important to recognize how a style or idea has remained consistent: history is not all change.

There are a number of "interruptions" running through the text, dealing with topics like the movie columnists, newsreels, and the serials. These "cameos" are footnotes of a sort, an attempt to focus on some aspect of American movies often neglected in a book of this kind.

Obviously, it will not be possible for anyone to see all the films discussed or alluded to in the text. But every year the films become more accessible. Universities usually run some type of film program and often these include the older and rarely seen silent films. Revival movie houses are appearing in many of the major cities. And television, despite the interruptions and the diminution of the screen, is still a rich source of vintage movies.

A book like this cannot begin to encompass all the movies. The movie stream is far too rich and broad and complex. But you can think of *Movies in America* as a guide, a way of learning, at the very least, which way to flick the TV dial when you're not totally sure. For ultimately, the movies are not there for us to study; they are a heritage and a vision of history, a source of unending discovery and feeling.

WILLIAM KUHNS

CONTENTS

CAMEOS

**Chapter One
The Earliest Years**

ELECTRIC THEATRE
WHERE YOU SEE ALL THE LATEST LIFE SIZE
MORAL AND REFINED PLEASING TO LADIES,

FOR ONLY A NICKEL

It began as a toy, a novelty, a showman's gimmick. Between the invention of the Kinetoscope by an assistant of Thomas Edison in 1887 to the emergence of that Olympian director, D. W. Griffith, about 1910, the motion picture progressed sporadically from the sneeze (the first movie ever made) to two-reel melodramas. It was a lively and energetic infancy, in some ways the most critical period in the development of the movies.

Most historians pinpoint the beginning of the movie with the Kinetograph and the Kinetoscope, the respective forerunners of the present motion picture camera and projector. W. K. L. Dickson, an English assistant of Edison, developed the Kinetoscope with Edison through the 1880s. (Indeed, even until 1910 and later Edison would consider the invention of only novelty interest, a simple sideshow entertainment.)

Because of conflicting patent claims and the complex "borrowings" of those making and refining cameras and projectors in this period—both in America and abroad—it is difficult to sort out exactly what came first and who deserves credit for what. The Kinetoscope seems to be the first invention—involving a single lens, moving reels and a shutter which would flash open at each frame on a long single loop of film. It was followed shortly by Thomas Armat's Vitascope, developed in 1895-96. The Vitascope provided a more consistent form of movement than had been possible on the Kinetoscope, and contributed several technical features to what would become the standard cameras and projectors after the next 10 years or so.

Both Edison's Kinetoscope, and the Vitascope were used as peephole novelties. That is, images were not projected on a screen, but the viewer looked into a peephole and watched the film as it ran past a light source. By 1896, Edison had established his "Black Maria" studio—the first American film production studio—in which his assistant Dickson supervised the production of hundreds of brief action films, most of them single shots. For pennies a viewer could watch a man walking down the street, see a dog do tricks, or watch a horse-drawn carriage arrive and depart. The Kinetoscope peepboxes flourished at penny arcades, carnivals, and sideshows. At one time, when Edison brought the Kinetoscope to a major exhibition in New York, he was surprised to hear that a number of people wanted him to make something larger, something that would project the images on a screen so that bigger audiences could view the film, Edison considered the idea economically foolish. Edison thought films did best, and would do best, within a peepshow setup like the Kinetoscope.

But the notion of creating larger, life-size images was quite popular in the mid-nineties. Already, in France, Louis and Auguste Lumière had successfully refashioned the Vitascope into a projector and had staged a public showing in December of 1895. Less than four months later, on April 23, 1896, the movies had their first American premiere at Koster and Bial's Music Hall in New York. The films—all made by the Lumière brothers—included two girls dancing, surf break-

3

ing on a pier, a comic boxing match, and a skirt dance. W. K. L. Dickson called it "an object of magical wonder—the crown and flower of nineteenth century magic."

The enthusiasm created by the Koster and Bial premiere led other vaudeville halls throughout the country to buy these new projectors—called Vitascopes. Movies were rarely longer than two minutes and usually featured single actions shot from one perspective—horses jumping over fences, girls dancing, parades, boats, acrobats. But they were popular and became, at least in the large cities, a standard feature of most vaudeville shows. A measure of their popularity can be seen when, in the fall of 1900, the vaudevillian actors went on strike. Some theaters, rather than close, announced that the program would consist totally of moving pictures. To the genuine astonishment of the managers, these programs were well attended.

Between the years 1900 and 1903, movies spread beyond the large cities and were shown at social gatherings of all kinds. Movies became immediately popular with all audiences, convincing showmen that this new kind of entertainment could and would make money. The art of the motion picture would yet require major steps beyond the primitive techniques being used in the early movies. But during those critical early years a number of young, eager showmen saw in the movies the possibilities of profit; an industry was born.

Kinetoscope Parlor 1895

On the production side, three companies managed to monopolize the field: Edison, Biograph, and Vitagraph. By refusing to sell cameras to anyone else, these companies dominated all moviemaking in the early years. On streets, boardwalks, beaches—virtually anywhere—they shot films running between 50 and 500 feet. They sent out catalogues describing the films, then sold the films outright to vaudeville theaters, social organizations—anyone with a projector.

As the market grew, a new kind of theater burgeoned for showing these new films: the nickelodeon. The first one appeared in Pittsburgh in 1905. Using colorful surroundings, comfortable seats, and a show bill dedicated totally to movies, these theaters were the first version of what we know today as the motion picture theater. As the Pittsburgh venture succeeded, penny arcades and empty stores were reconditioned and named nickelodeons. By 1908, there were about 9,000 nickelodeons operating throughout the country, an indication of the incredibly rapid growth of this new entertainment—moving pictures.

FORERUNNERS OF TECHNIQUE: GEORGES MELIES AND EDWIN S. PORTER

It may seem difficult to believe today, but the show that in 1896 astounded and delighted almost a thousand New York socialites at Koster and Bial's consisted entirely of separate films that were in themselves single shots. A camera would be placed in a room and in front of it an acrobat would twist and turn in the air, careful to stay within the frame. In effect, the early movies consisted of movement totally within the frame: the cameras rarely moved, and no one even gave a thought to the editing principle—joining two separate pieces of film to create new relationships within the film.

In the attempt to create a narrative form—and by 1899 a number of filmmakers were attempting this—films would be built around several scenes. To accomplish this, they used different camera setups. In *Love and War,* made in 1896 by James H. White of the Edison studios, four separate scenes were used. The camera took up a different position for each scene. It was a simple film, barely 70 feet, which told the story of a young man who departs for battle, is injured in battle, taken to a military hospital, and finally returned to health and his family. All the shots were taken about 10 feet from the

Edison's Record of a Sneeze

actors. Not until the time of the innovative filmmaker D. W. Griffith would the close-up become an integral part of film art.

The film was indicative of a number of problems faced by the filmmakers at that time. In the hospital scene, the top part of the frame showed the hospital wall as a stage set and not a real hospital wall. Audiences didn't seem to mind these little discrepancies, though. Once tantalized by these magical moving images, they came back again and again.

Clearly, though, the potential of the film went further than using a camera simply as a recorder of what took place in front of it. During those very early years, two men took enormous—and entirely different—strides in determining the technique of the motion picture: Georges Méliès in Paris and Edwin S. Porter in America.

It has been said that Méliès opened the way to the use of film as illusion and Porter to the use of film for narrative. Certainly Méliès and Porter took distinct approaches to the films they made. Méliès made fantasies— stories of man flying to the moon, new versions of fairy tales like *Red Riding Hood* and *Cinderella*. Porter told stories. His best-known film, *The Great Train Robbery,* used new techniques (such as different camera placement) less for their own sake than to make the narrative more exciting.

Méliès's background was the theater: he had acted, staged, produced, and done magic. Indeed, it was with the twin interests of the theater and magic that Méliès approached the movie camera. He saw it as an instrument that could perform wonderful magical tricks that could never be achieved on a stage.

Méliès's discovery of the movies' magic was abrupt and accidental. On one of the first days he had a camera and was wandering the streets of Paris, shooting everything he could with it, the aperture gate jammed. He fumbled to get the film moving again and resumed shooting. Later, looking at the devel-

5

oped film, he was astounded to see a bus suddenly turning into a hearse. The simplest of editing combinations, known as the jump cut, appeared to him—and henceforth to audiences that numbered in the thousands—as magic.

Before the turn of the century, Méliès had explored various techniques in trick photography which could be used in innumerable films after him: disappearances and sudden appearances, walking through walls, people being cut in half, people flying through the air, superimposition, character transformations, backward movement. The titles of his films suggest his preoccupation with the magical and the mysterious: *The Haunted Castle, The Laboratory of Mephistopheles, Cagliostro's Mirror, The Bewitched Inn.*

In 1900, Méliès made his most—and to that time *the* most—ambitious film: *Cinderella.* The film was carefully scripted (Méliès called it "artificially arranged scenes") and contained 20 separate scenes. Admittedly, the camera stayed at a fixed position within each scene—before Porter introduced camera movement, Méliès never considered it—but the complexity and duration of the story far outstripped that of most other films being produced. Moreover, Méliès used elaborate, glittering sets: the ballroom, for example, was probably the most opulent set yet to appear on a movie screen. Dissolves involving ballets and marches were used, anticipating the dissolve montage of the twenties and thirties.

Wallace Beery, Dreamy Sweedy 1914

Cinderella was eminently successful, not only in Europe, but in America as well, where a number of theater owners copied the print and put their own names on it. Like two important films to follow it—*The Great Train Robbery* and *The Birth of a Nation*—*Cinderella* helped the early film gain respectability and recognition as a new art form, an art of its own.

The success of *Cinderella* plunged Méliès more energetically into film production, and two years later he made what is considered his most typical and, perhaps, most important film: *A Trip To The Moon*. Even today, after the real thing has happened, Méliès' film looks—for all its theatrics and limitations—strikingly impressive. A rocket ship takes off and flies through space to the moon—making something of a crash landing.

Yet Méliès's techniques reveal the limitations of his craft. For example, to show the moon approaching as the rocket flies through space, Méliès devised a papier-maché moon on a ramp and had the moon roll down the ramp toward the camera. As critic Arthur Knight comments, "It was as if the camera were the sole spectator at an elaborate pageant or play, occupying the choicest seat in the house but never budging from that seat." Méliès's films were, above all, theatrical productions—not movies as we know them now. Yet, in searching for increasingly elaborate theatrical effects, Méliès lit on a variety of techniques which would significantly influence future film production.

The most important techniques to give momentum to the narrative film did not come from France, however—nor immediately from America. Between the years 1900 and 1902, the English led in establishing the key innovations: the close-up and the principles of editing within the scene and intercutting between scenes.

Close-ups had been used before in films. Indeed, the first film made, Fred Ott's sneeze, was a close-up of sorts. But the idea of inter-cutting a close-up with medium or long shots of characters did not appear until 1900, in the films of the Englishman G. A. Smith. Smith recognized the importance and potential of close-ups, but he also felt obligated to give the close-ups some obvious justification. In *Grandma's Reading Glasses,* he has a boy looking at objects—such as a newspaper, a watch, and a canary—through reading glasses. In one film, *The Little Doctor*, there is a single close-up of a kitten. Smith called the shot a "short telescopic view."

The English also made several technical advances in editing between 1900 and 1902. *Attack on a China Mission,* made early in 1901, is a story taking place during the Boxer Rebellion. The filmmaker, James Williamson, introduced some of the basic ideas of continuity editing. The early part of the film shows people in a compound, then the Chinese breaking in the gates. Then—a totally new concept for film at this time—a sudden shot of armed sailors outside, approaching the

compound. In *Mary Jane's Mishap* (1901 or 1902), G. A. Smith uses close-ups within a scene of a maid trying to clean boots with kerosene and light a fire at the same time.

For all the innovations of the English, it was an American, Edwin S. Porter, who capitalized on these innovations by drawing them together and using them for narrative force. Porter's film, *The Great Train Robbery,* is his most celebrated, but historically perhaps less important than *The Life of an American Fireman* (1902), which is the first of his films to combine the techniques developed by G. A. Smith and James Williamson. Drawn partly from the British film, *Plucked From the Burning* (1898), *The Life of an American Fireman* opens with a fire chief sleeping, dreaming assumedly of his loved ones—a woman and child whose faces are in the corner of the frame. The film cuts to a close-up of a fire-alarm box with a hand pulling the lever, then to the dormitory of the firefighters who awaken, quickly dress, and slide down the pole. Next, to the interior of the engine house: horses are being chased from their stalls and hitched to the fire rigs. In the next shot, we see the exterior of the engine house: the large doors swinging open, the horses rushing forward, the men clambering aboard and the whole ensemble moving swiftly past the camera. Following is a shot depicting the rigs racing down the street at top speed. Smoke is billowing out of the engine stacks, and the horses seem to be moving with every sinew of muscle. Cut to the fire. A house is

GRANDADDY OF THE MONSTER MOVIES

He stood 50 feet tall, a god, and a captive behind high barred fences, but nonetheless terrifying natives on the uncharted island of Kong. Of all the thousands of monster movies made since **King Kong,** few have dealt with their monsters with such complexity, even sympathy; and few have created such intricate and believable special effects.

□ Over 25 models of Kong were built for the movie although the most frequently used model stood barely 18 inches high and was animated, painstakingly, by moving its limbs in consecutive brief motions and shooting at single frame. The largest model of Kong was eight times the size of a real gorilla; inside its chest span of 30 ft., six men operated the 85 motors that controlled its movement. This model of Kong was used only once in the film—for a sequence in which Kong holds Fay Wray and examines her. It took 23 hours to shoot this sequence which provided 23 seconds of screen time in the film.

□ **King Kong** was the brainchild of Merian C. Cooper and Ernest B. Schoedsack, who worked from a story by mystery writer Edgar Wallace. Cooper and Schoedsack hired Willis O'Brien—perhaps the most famous name in the history of special effects—to produce the special effects. O'Brien was one of the most imaginative and technically knowledgeable special effects experts in Hollywood at the time. Cooper and Schoedsack prepared a sample reel of **King Kong** footage (Kong toppling the log on which the sailors were scurrying away from a Styracosaurus) and showed it to RKO stockholders. Given full freedom to make the film, they worked a year on the project and spent the nearly unheard-of sum of $650,000. O'Brien designed and executed the complex techniques that enabled Kong to move not only his body but also, in subtle convincing ways, the lines of his face. In some sequences, O'Brien used seven or eight different techniques to give convincing characterization to Kong and his island world. No monster film since has used special effects so well.

□ **King Kong** may have fathered a thousand monster films, but of itself it hardly belongs to the monster category. Children who see the film tend to identify not with the crew or Ann Darrow (Fay Wray), but with the poor giant gorilla, torn from his island world and set up as a monstrous exhibition in Manhattan. The destruction Kong wreaks on Manhattan has a certain appealing fascination, and audiences felt an uncanny satisfaction as Kong mounted the Empire State Building and swatted at the attacking military airplanes as though they were buzzing flies.

□ Ultimately, **King Kong** is a romantic tale: a brilliant, sometimes horrific, sometimes exotic, but always ingenious exposition of the basic "old Arabian proverb" that opens the film: *And the Beast looked upon the face of Beauty and lo! his hand was stayed from killing and from that day forward he was as one dead.*

□ Kong is less a monster than a victim; we fear him less than we admire and pity him. A grotesque bestiary of oversized monsters would be pouring out of Hollywood over the decades to come but none would ever— or could ever—match Kong. Kong was the finest, the greatest, and, finally, the least monstrous of them all.

burning furiously as the fire engines arrive. We see the firemen pull out the hoses, the ladders, and move frantically around. Then the shot dissolves to a room in the house in which a woman paces the floor energetically, eager to escape, and even flings open the window and signals desperately to the crowd below. Suddenly the door is smashed open by an ax. The fireman smashes the window, orders the ladder, and lifts the woman to carry her down. The scene shifts back to the exterior, where we watch him coming down the ladder with the woman in his arms. Once released, she pleads for her child—still in the building. Volunteers are requested. The same firefighter reappears, is given permission, and climbs the ladder. A long wait, while smoke pours out of the cavity in the wall. Finally, he appears with the child, whom he returns to the mother. Fade-out.

In two scenes particularly, the viewer can see that Porter was struggling for a new structure for the motion picture, some way of creating a narrative out of smaller juxtaposed parts rather than simply letting the camera record a staged story. Scene two, the hand pulling the signal on the alarm box, is the first dramatic use of a close-up in a film. Not until seven years later, with Griffith, would the close-up become so critical, or so dramatically effective.

Even more important, perhaps, was the last scene. Within this scene, Porter used three separate shots: the firemen arriving at the burning house; the woman in the room being rescued by the heroic fireman; and the return of the fireman to the house to save the child.

Wherever it was shown, *The Life of an American Fireman* excited audiences. It was a film they could not simply watch—it involved them, made them feel with the fireman, made them catch their breath as the fire engines raced toward the fire. The film affected audiences with its drama and pace, but it made almost no impact on other films. In a sense, it arrived too early.

A year later, in 1903, Porter made the film which would exert an almost inestimable influence upon filmmaking. Porter had wanted to make *The Great Train Robbery* ever since the success of *The Life of an American Fireman.* He saw in such a film the opportunity to carry some of the ideas of close-ups and editing into an even longer, more forceful narrative.

The Life of an American Fireman comprised seven scenes and nine shots. In *The Great Train Robbery,* Porter used 14 scenes and as many shots, but the movie has about it an incredible use of action and movement. Briefly, the film depicts four robbers who force a train to stop for water, get on board, take over the train, stop it, and rob the passengers. Meanwhile the operator sends a message and a posse forms. The robbers are pursued and eventually killed in a violent battle. The closing shot (often used as the opening shot) depicts one of the bandits taking aim and firing at the audience.

The Great Train Robbery did little to advance filmmaking technically. Every scene used only one shot, and virtually all shots were long shots. Yet the excitement that the film generated through its skillful handling of cross-editing made it possibly the most important film of the decade. An audience that had thrilled to *The Great Train Robbery* could not be satisfied anymore with simplistic three-scene morality stories. As historian Lewis Jacobs commented, this film alone "initiated an American film style of vigor, movement and melodrama."

Porter advanced his editing technique in later films, but only incidentally. In *The Ex-Convict* (1904), Porter turned to contrast editing to depict the difference between an ex-convict and a wealthy manufacturer. The differences between the affluent home of the manufacturer and the poverty-stricken home of the ex-convict help bring across not only the plight of the ex-con but also Porter's

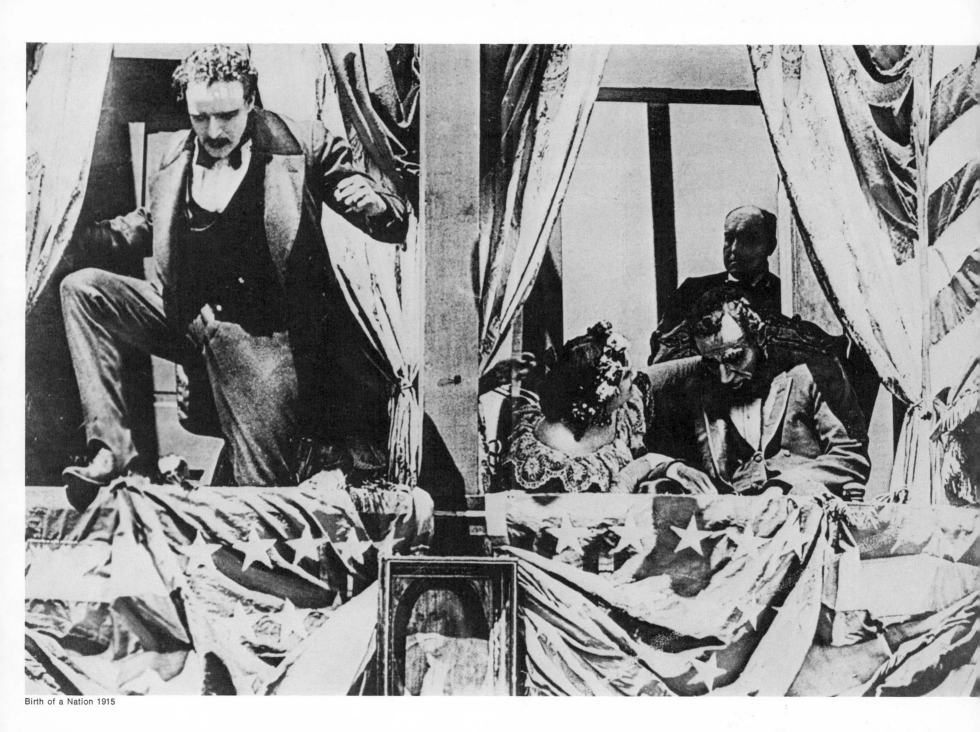

Birth of a Nation 1915

THE EARLY HEROINES

We all remember Greta Garbo, Marlene Dietrich, Katherine Hepburn, Bette Davis, Judy Garland, and Joan Crawford; they have become stars of the late-night movie circuit on television. But who remembers Lillian Gish at her best, in *The Scarlet Letter,* or Mary Pickford in *Pollyanna,* or *A Poor Little Rich Girl*—playing "The World's Sweetheart," a creature caught somewhere between the mustache-twirling episodes of Victorian melodrama and her unique role as the biggest star of an industry suddenly grown star-conscious?

The early great female stars—and one can almost count them on his fingers: Mary Pickford, Lillian Gish, Gloria Swanson, Pola Negri, Clara Bow, and Theda Bara—were as much responsible for creating the "star system" as the market-conscious producers who goaded the nation to accept the system. These were not awe-stricken drugstore salesgirls who, mag-ically chosen by a direc-tor, were suddenly vaulted to fame. Gloria Swanson is reputed to have said, "I have gone through a long appren-ticeship. I have gone through enough of being nobody. I have decided that when I am a star I will be every inch and every moment the star. Everyone from the studio gateman to the highest executive will know it." The women worked hard for their money and their recognition—and largely it was they who pressed that recognition to its extreme limits in the twenties, to the status of goddesses living in palatial temples. The women were the first real "stars."

Theda Bara was the first, but her appeal was mostly manufactured by William Fox, who draped her in exotic jewelry amid Egyptian or Arabian settings, and told the press that she had been born in the shadow of the Sphinx, the daughter of a French artist and an Arabian princess, weaned on serpents' blood and was "a crystal-gazing seeress of profoundly occult powers." Theda Bara was the original "vamp"—the woman so aptly described in Rudyard Kipling's poem "The Vampire," in the line "We called her the woman who did not care."

Lillian Gish   Mary Pickford

But Theda Bara only helped initiate the spate of silent star-heroines. She could not compete with a rising actress of far greater strength, like Lillian Gish, or one of much broader appeal, like Mary Pickford, or the later, more continental and aristocratic stars, like Pola Negri and Gloria Swanson. Lillian Gish was perhaps the best actress of all. David Shipman writes in *The Great Movie Stars:* ☐ *Given the strong Victorian sentiment which inspired D. W. Griffith and some others among her directors, she reacted with a spirituality and a charm which not only harmonized with it, but sometimes infected it with a sense of urgency; and while her frail body cowed under the blows inflicted on it in the cause of melodrama, the camera recorded a peculiar and very personal intensity.*

But it was Mary Pickford who made the movies a star's medium. She alone, more than any of the ladies and more than the men—including Chaplin—dominated the studio life of the mid-to-late silent era. For 14 years pollsters es-tablished that she was the most popular wo-man in the world. And Benjamin B. Hampton in his book *A History of the Movies,* has said of her: *Woman's place in bus-iness has grown enor-mously in importance in the last three decades, but Mary Pickford is the only member of her sex who ever became the focal point of an entire industry. Her position is unique; probably no man or woman will ever again win so extensive a following.* Her acting was another thing—adequate for her roles, but more striking for her vitality and charm than for subtlety or acuteness.

The twenties were dominated by a fresh group of female stars: most notably Pola Negri, the alluring Polish actress who exuded a kind of regal sexuality; Gloria Swanson, with her dour face and the ability to capitalize on her rising popularity; and Clara Bow, Hollywood's favorite flapper of the twenties. It was the first and the freshest era of stardom; and the women who rose to their heights in that era helped incalculably to give resonance and meaning to that word "star."

growing social concern.

In *The Kleptomaniac,* Porter advanced the use of contrast editing even further to show the difference between a poor woman and a rich woman. Both women steal, but only one is jailed.

Porter's social concern could be seen particularly in the closing sequence of this latter film. He depicts a draped, blindfolded figure of justice holding the scales. Balanced on the scales are a loaf of bread and a bag of gold. The scales tip toward the gold. The blindfold is taken off, which reveals that the figure has only one eye—gazing at the gold.

Porter's last important film was more characteristic of his French predecessor Méliès than of the action-adventure Porter. *The Dream of a Rarebit Fiend* shows the dreams of a man who has eaten a little too much Welsh rarebit and drunk a little too much ale. After he falls asleep, the man's shoes walk out of the room. A table and a chair bounce away. A steaming dish appears from the man's head. His bed comes alive and sails out of the room, over the city, finally getting caught on a church steeple. The concept and the execution are both superior to anything done by Méliès. Indeed, Edison's Vitagraph Company advertised the film, quite rightly, with the statement: "Some of the photographic stunts have never been seen or attempted before, and few experts will be able to understand how they were done."

Porter did nothing of any great significance after 1906. He left the Edison studios in 1911 and directed a film with Adolph Zukor's Special Players Company, *The Count of Monte Cristo.* It was never released, however, and his next feature, *The Prisoner of Zenda,* while a competent piece of craftsmanship, had neither the artistic nor the technical significance of his earlier work. Porter continued to direct features until 1915, when he retired.

Of all the early figures in the development of film technique, Porter stands alone beside Griffith. Between the two men, the technique of editing was born and was raised to an art. Moreover, Porter endowed his early films with a sense of social significance which no other filmmaker at the time was attempting. Porter depicted a society in which injustices ran rife, and, by making films like *The Kleptomaniac* and *The Ex-Convict,* suggested implicitly that filmmakers had a responsibility to do more than simply present melodramas and comedy.

THE EMERGENCE OF AN INDUSTRY

It was not until the appearance and the proliferation of the nickelodeons—about 1909—that it became obvious that films were more than a novelty: they were a means of making good financial returns, sometimes spectacular returns, on small investments. Between the years 1905 and 1909, fresh talent and fresh money entered the movie business. To the older production studios (or "factories" as they were then called) of Edison, Vitagraph, and Biograph were added new ones, such as Lubin, Selig, Kalem, and Essanay.

One thorny problem that plagued the whole industry in those early years—and it remained a problem into the second decade of the century—was the question of patent rights. Edison had invented and patented the Kinetoscope, the basic mechanism of most movie cameras and projectors. But he failed to register the patent outside of the U.S. This gave film exhibitors and filmmakers in foreign countries the freedom to use it without paying royalties—which they did, quite frequently. In America, virtually every production company was working with cameras and projectors that, if not made by Edison, had been copied from Edison's models—though, in many cases, enough modifications had

Thomas A. Edison

been made to enable those using them to secure a patent.

Edison considered the motion picture camera and projector to be solely his inventions. He pursued dozens of lawsuits against anyone using equipment based on his designs. Most of the lawsuits were futile and led only to an extension of the quandary. Finally, in 1908, nine manufacturers of equipment (who were also among the major producers of movies) organized a trust. They called it The Motion Picture Patents Company. By pooling their patents—and paying a small royalty to Edison for their films—these companies avoided lawsuits among themselves. More important, they began the first of many concessions and agreements which would help define their corporate venture as an industry and lead to the establishment of a single moviemaking capital—Hollywood.

There have always been three basic aspects to the film industry: production, distribution, and exhibition. One of the tensions running through the history of the motion picture industry is the relationship (and often the conflicts) among these three aspects.

From the first use of Kinetoscopes, the basic method of merchandising films was

15

that the studios, or movie companies, would produce them and sell them outright to the exhibitors. This method began to reveal its weaknesses as nickelodeons and production companies alike grew in numbers. There were simply too many films. For the nickelodeons, the exhibitors, the cost of purchasing all of them—even granting numerous reshowings—was prohibitive.

In 1903, an enterprising man named Harry J. Miles began the Film Exchange. His company acted as a clearing house between the producers and the exhibitors. The idea caught on quickly and, by 1907, over a hundred different film exchanges were operating within the 35 largest cities in America. Rental rather than purchase became the rule. Exhibitors were encouraged to continue showing the same film as long as it could draw an audience. Until this time, the film program usually was changed every day.

Going to a movie theater in the first decade of this century was an experience considerably different from what it is today. Most of the nickelodeon theaters were relatively small, rarely seating over two hundred. Often they were little more than reconditioned stores. They had no sloping aisles, sometimes no permanent seats. In the larger cities, the theater front was alive with electric lights, using such names as "Bijou Dream," "Pictorium," "Dreamland." The audiences were usually the poorer, working-class people for whom the images on the screen had a special appeal, an unending fascination.

A typical bill might include a narrative film, a comedy, and some sort of novelty short—perhaps a travelogue or a recreated event, such as a famous fight. Sometimes a lecturer would explain what was going on in the film, but more often the theaters would rely on a balladeer who sang along with the movie. Confections were sold by children walking up and down the aisles announcing, "Peanuts, popcorn, candy!" Intermittently, slides would appear on the screen with such messages as "Ladies and Gentlemen, Please Remove Your Hats," "No Smoking or Spitting Allowed—Order Board of Health," "Positively No Whistling, Stamping or Loud Talking Allowed in This Theater."

A fast turnover in audiences was the only way in which the nickelodeons could make money. This put enormous pressure on the studios to produce more films faster and faster. By 1908, production had been standardized. Every director working for a major production company was expected to produce at least two one-reel movies a week. While this schedule severely hampered creative possibilities, it forced producers to generate new ideas, develop new story sources, attempt new methods—often shortcut ways to tell stories. The motion picture did not languish during the latter part of the first decade, but it did not progress very radically either.

In these years, there were really no "studios" as we know them now: sprawling tracts of land, barn-like buildings large enough to house several immense sets at once. The early studios were small, cluttered affairs, with sets rarely larger than an average living room. And only the larger, richer companies like Biograph and Edison could afford such studios. Smaller production companies did most of their shooting on the street or in natural settings. The cost difference was considerable. A one-reel film shot in a studio might cost $500, whereas a non-studio film of the same length could be made for about $200.

In 1906, the mercury vapor lamp appeared. Previously, studios had glass roofs, like greenhouses; shooting could only be done in daytime. With mercury vapor lamps and the possibility of bright, controlled light, the studios painted over the glass and moved in the lights.

By 1908, production had become so regular and the output so large that the major companies had distinct filmmaking categories and a separation of the crafts involved in making a movie. Actors, cameramen, lighting men, set designers, costume designers, and writers became separate functions, even though a great deal of overlapping remained.

(One chronic complaint, heard particularly from actors accustomed to theater acting, was that they were being forced to sew and paint and sometimes do dangerous stunts.)

Anyone who looks at the films from that period is struck by the frequently jerky, hasty movements of the actors. People walking seem to be running; arm and leg movements appear overly speeded up. There is a reason for this. The only cameras available at that time had to be hand-cranked. Not only did some cameramen crank slower than they should (curiously, they were rarely faster), but frequently they would crank even more slowly to make sure an entire scene got onto the reel of film in the camera. When these scenes are projected at modern projection speeds, the result is the familiar "speeded-up" look.

The movies of that period were bound by a procedural code of sorts; somewhat primitive, but influenced enough by Méliès and Porter to include the very basics of film editing. One of the standard practices of the code was that all shots include all the people in the scene. Partly a carry-over from the theater, this rule was stringently observed by most filmmakers and held back the use of the medium shot and close-up until Griffith.

Film historian Lewis Jacobs has noted other practices in this unwritten code. Each scene must open with an entrance and close with an exit, as on stage. Each actor must face the camera at all times. Any background action must happen slowly and be exaggerated to guarantee that the audience would spot it. All gestures and facial expressions must be exaggerated and extended longer than usual to make sure they were observed. These rules, of course, made for something closer to theatrical melodramas than to what we know today as movies.

Generally, the movies in the first decade served less to establish aesthetics or techniques of film as much as an industry in which aesthetics and techniques would have room to burgeon. It was only under the pressure of a hungry, growing audience that filmmakers with imagination and foresight would emerge —as, in the next decade, they did.

TEARS, TORMENT, TRAGEDY

Movies are the most democratic of the arts. They require of viewers no educational or social background; their cost is not exorbitant. There are no exclusive seats in movie theaters, and no way of defining the poor and the rich, the powerless and the mighty, in a darkened movie theater.

It is appropriate, then, that in their first years movies were shunned by the elite, the upper classes, and the critics. Until Griffith's *Birth of a Nation* in 1915, the cultured and the rich looked upon nickelodeons and their fare as a crude novelty that would soon run its course.

Meanwhile movies were being made and being seen by hundreds of thousands every week. And the content of those movies clearly reflected the desires and interests of the audience. Despite the techniques opened up by Méliès and Porter, the majority of films were not fantasies or classic romances. They were stories of the streets, of thieves and robbers, of factory workers and policemen and firemen. The filmmakers had not yet gone to novels for source material for their movies, and as a result their films had a vitality and an immediacy that they never could have possessed, were they somehow the province of the "cultured."

It was Porter, more than anyone else, who established the dominant twin themes in the motion picture: action and an implicit social concern. The success of *The Great Train Robbery* made the action melodrama the most usual type of film over the next 10 years; chases and gunfights became common; the lives of criminals became a favorite motif among early, as well as later, filmmakers. These films, e.g., *Burglar Bill, The Jail Bird, The Bandit King,* and *Raffles,* would either depict the criminal as a victim of circumstances and environment or sympathize outright with him. The common man may be

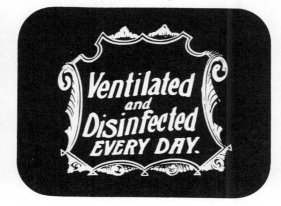

"Around this town the only reason friends pat you on the back is to find a soft spot where to break it."
Joan Blondell, *Bullets or Ballots*, 1936

"The soup sounds good."
W. C. Fields, *The Old-Fashioned Way*, 1934

IMMORTAL LINES FROM THE MOVIES

The introduction of sound meant that actors would be *able* to talk; it didn't guarantee them anything significant to say. Half the delight of sitting through a thirties gangster movie, or a creaking horror flick, is in catching the rich lines—some that deserve to be immortalized and some that, since the films are around, are getting immortalized anyway. Here are a few such lines—both kinds:

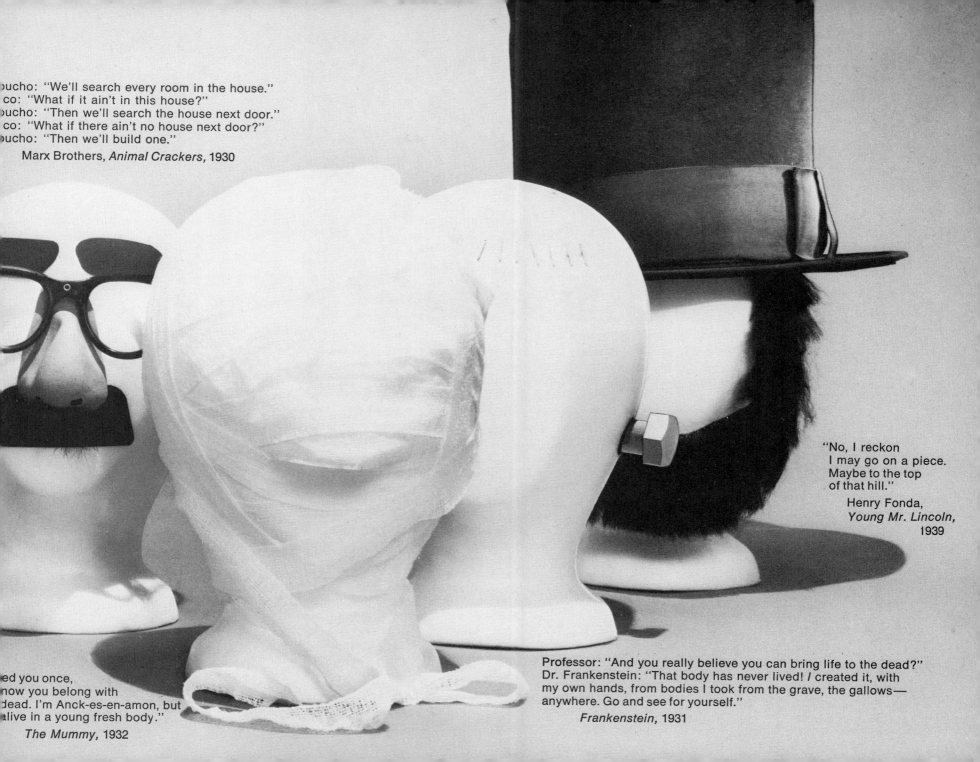

ucho: "We'll search every room in the house."
co: "What if it ain't in this house?"
ucho: "Then we'll search the house next door."
co: "What if there ain't no house next door?"
ucho: "Then we'll build one."

Marx Brothers, *Animal Crackers,* 1930

"No, I reckon
I may go on a piece.
Maybe to the top
of that hill."

Henry Fonda,
Young Mr. Lincoln,
1939

ed you once,
now you belong with
dead. I'm Anck-es-en-amon, but
alive in a young fresh body."

The Mummy, 1932

Professor: "And you really believe you can bring life to the dead?"
Dr. Frankenstein: "That body has never lived! *I* created it, with
my own hands, from bodies I took from the grave, the gallows—
anywhere. Go and see for yourself."

Frankenstein, 1931

The Exploits of Elaine 1914/15

obligated to certain social norms, the movies seemed to be saying, but he also needed sympathy and understanding when he ran into grievous trouble.

A favorite theme of many early films was the life of the poor. Their vulnerability, their hopelessness, their desperation were excellent stuff for the melodramatics of film and sure-fire appeals to audiences who had no difficulty in identifying with such characters. The theme of the helpless victim resounds through many of these early films. An ad for an Essanay film made in 1907, for example, reads:

An honest Italian attending to his peanut stand is bothered by a bully. The Italian resents this and a fight results during which the bully falls and strikes his head, which kills him. The Italian is arrested, convicted of murder and sentenced to die. Wife makes a plea to the governor, who turns a deaf ear. She comes home overcome with grief. Her children are stirred to action. They go to the governor, and beg for the life of their dad . . . At last the governor's human nature is touched and he hands a pardon to the two tots. They lose no time in delivering it and reach jail as the father is led out to meet his fate. The pardon is delivered at the eleventh hour. Happy reunion.

Other themes found in early films reflect some of the dominant concerns and tensions of the decade: new freedoms for women, the put-down of the rich and aristocratic—particularly bankers, the evils of drink, and the need for prohibition. Generally, though, filmmakers were not conscious of dealing with "topics" or treating "themes:" they intended to entertain audiences who came back, week after week, some of them night after night, to see the latest film.

To look at those old films today, a viewer is struck by their stilted and overdone acting, their simplistic and repetitious stories, their thick and sentimental emotions. Yet one must recall that these were the first films. Audiences had never seen anything else. Somehow the films satisfied the audiences' expectations and stimulated their desire for more.

20

Chapter Two
Two Giants: Griffith and Chaplin

By the end of the first decade of the twentieth century, movies had established themselves as a new king of entertainment, a
pleasant way to spend an evening or an
afternoon. But most movies were still relatively crude, unimaginative things immensely dependent on the stage conventions
that they had unwittingly inherited. Scenes
were depicted in long, single shots from a
single perspective; stories were simple and
either mawkish in their sentimentality or obvious in their contrivances, or both. The
movies were popular, but they were still
only a faint glimmer of what they might
one day be.

Between 1910 and 1920, two men did
more to reshape the medium than anyone
else ever would. One gave it a grammar and
a syntax: a range of techniques which lifted
the use of the camera out of theatrics into
film art. The other, the first and greatest
star of them all, made the screen come alive
with a poetry and a pathos never before
known and never since recaptured. Between
these two men, the movies took on a new
stature and significance. A novelty became
an art.

22

D. W. Griffith

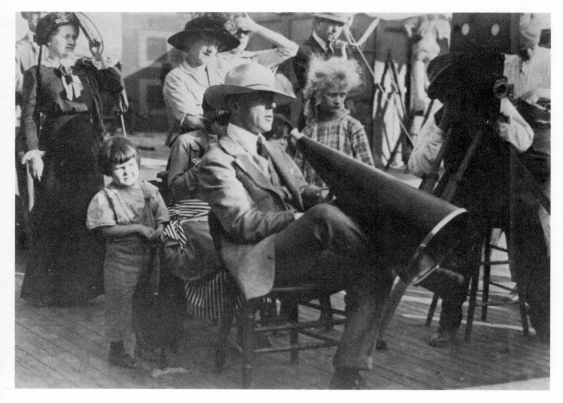

DAVID WARK GRIFFITH

In 1924, Griffith wrote the following lines (*Colliers*, May 3, 1924):

The motion picture is a child that has been given life in our generation. As it grows older it will develop marvelously. We poor souls can scarcely visualize or dream of its possibilities. We ought to be kind with it in its youth, so that in its maturity it may look back upon its childhood without regrets.

Read today, the lines ring with a fine irony. Because of Griffith, the movies rose far beyond what anyone in the first decade could have believed possible. Moreover, he —more than any director of the period— made it possible to look back upon the childhood of the movies "without regrets"— and better, with wonder and awe.

The curious thing about this greatest of all directors and innovators of the American film is that he never really wanted to get too involved in movies. As a part-time actor and would-be writer, the young Griffith looked upon movies much as other stage actors and writers did at the time: as a crass novelty, without a future, without either substance or the possibility of substance, Indeed, Griffith used the name Lawrence Griffith throughout his early movie career. He was convinced that one day he would step out of films and make a great name for himself as a writer. Only then would he begin to use his real name.

Griffith was the fifth child of an impoverished Kentucky family. He grew up amid an aging but still powerful Victorian system of beliefs—Southern romanticism and a haughtiness that would affect all of his work, often marring the best of it.

The young Griffith worked as a sales clerk, a newspaper reporter, and, most assiduously, as an aspiring writer. He published an occasional story or play, but was not very successful. He also dabbled in acting. In New York City in 1907, an actor friend suggested that he work temporarily for Biograph. Griffith applied and attempted to sell a story to Edwin Porter. Porter turned down the story but offered Griffith the lead role in his next picture. Griffith took it, and, unwittingly, began one of the greatest careers in the industry.

When Griffith was first offered an opportunity to direct a movie, he was reluctant. Should he fail at that, he thought, he would be out of an acting job. But, after a few pictures, it became apparent that Griffith's métier in the movies was not acting, or even writing, but directing.

Griffith improvised, invented, polished, and experimented endlessly. Between 1908 and 1912, he fashioned, single-handed, a new range of expression for the movies. He transformed editing from the stage-dominated succession of scenes to a visual dynamic that shuttled time and space to achieve dramatic impact. He made the close-up a standard technique of movie making. He developed editing principles that made it possible to jump back and forth between scenes at a quickening pace, thereby achieving a dramatic momentum never known before in the movies. He experi-

Douglas Fairbanks

mented with lighting, to achieve tonal qualities and mood. He lured good actors from the stage and—something hardly known in movies at the time—made them rehearse before shooting a scene, thus creating a fresh realism.

We have become so familiar with film as Griffith shaped it that it is difficult to appreciate the impact and range of his innovations. Essentially, what Griffith did was extricate film from the conventions and established techniques of the stage. During the early years, movies were little more than flickering replicas of short, melodramatic stage plays. Each scene was shot from a single camera position; the area that the camera caught became the "stage." Because of this stage convention, all the actors required for the various scenes would have to be present during the scene. Most scenes opened with someone entering the scene, and closed with someone leaving. The time within the scene was real time, and no attempt was made (except by very few filmmakers) to manipulate it.

In virtually all of his innovations, Griffith showed that the key unit of the film is not the scene, but the shot. Film can present so much to the eye—so much detail, so much in a human face and in an object—that to force film to work within the constraints of the stage play was to severely impair its power. Griffith discovered that by using the shot as the basic unit and juxtaposing that shot with other shots, the audience could come far closer to what was happening on the screen, feel more involved, be caught up in the action.

During the years Griffith was at Biograph, from 1908 to 1912, he expanded and developed his techniques, even though he was turning out films at the frantic pace of two per week. In *For Love of Gold*, he changed the camera's position mid-scene. In *Enoch Arden*, he used the close-up and combined it with an even more dexterous

Mary Pickford (right)

manipulation of camera positions in the scene. In *The Drunkard's Reformation*, he discarded the flat lighting used in most films and introduced a specialized lighting that gave the effect of a fireside. In *The Lonely Villa*, made at the end of his first year at Biograph, he introduced the to-the-rescue cross-cutting which Porter had attempted, but which had never been used on quite such a scale before.

Other studio workers protested each innovation. Audiences wouldn't be able to follow something that jerky and broken up, they claimed. Griffith has been credited with the classic comeback, "Doesn't Dickens write that way?" Griffith recognized in the film the potential for the purest kind of storytelling.

During his years at Biograph, Griffith sought out new material. The first source he went after was the classics. Most of the films in the first decade were strikingly obvious melodramas, e.g., chase movies, villains persecuting poor widows. Not surprisingly, such fare helped to give a certain image to the movies—not only among the American public, but in Europe where only a few American films were considered good enough to show. Griffith, tantalized with the audience potential for this new medium, was eager to deal with more expansive themes, more subtle forms of story development, more complex characters, and more sophisticated plots. He adapted from Poe, O. Henry, Shakespeare, and Browning. Again, despite the reluctance of the Biograph owners to produce them, the films were enormously successful. More filmmakers came to recognize that the public appetite for movies was more than just a voracious demand for more film stories.

In 1909, Griffith noted that a number of independent movie makers had gone to California. The natural scenery, the sunshine, the year-around fair weather all seemed far more hospitable to the produc-

Charles Chaplin

tion of movies than were conditions in the New York City area.

In the winter of 1909-1910, Griffith convinced Biograph to let him move his own company to the outskirts of Los Angeles. This did more than help establish Hollywood as *the* film production capital of America; it also gave Griffith an added authority over his own company, and a freedom from the Biograph executives that he hadn't enjoyed in New York.

Over the years that Griffith had been at Biograph, the one-reel film was standard. Such films rarely lasted longer than 16 minutes, and Griffith was discouraged by the limitations this put upon his storytelling. In 1911, he made a two-reeler, *Enoch Arden,* Biograph argued that theater owners would not buy a two-reel film for twice the cost of the ordinary feature. They insisted on selling it in two parts. Most theater owners bought both parts and the film proved highly successful. Moreover, it did a great deal to establish the two-reeler as the standard.

Up until 1911, Griffith had been chiefly interested in experimenting, attempting new techniques, developing fresh ways to tell a story through film. The success of his two-reeler *Enoch Arden,* however, combined with the success of historical recreations like *Custer's Last Stand,* led to a stirring sense of ambition: the desire to make the world

aware that he was its greatest movie director. The American competition was not particularly stiff, but the European competition was. British dramas with a famous stage name like Sarah Bernhardt, French historical romances, and particularly the Italian spectacular, *Quo Vadis,* led Griffith to a project which he knew Biograph would never approve, yet which would establish his name at the top of world cinema.

He made the film with his own company, shooting north of Los Angeles, telling no one (not even those in his troupe) what it was all about. Single settings were designed at great cost and with meticulous care. The actors rehearsed for hours. Most people thought he was making several films at once. In 1913, when the picture was completed, he gave the four reels to Biograph. Company officials were astonished, angered, and refused to release it. Only a year later was *Judith of Bethulia* released: a massive spectacle of crowds, battle scenes, and romantic episodes. The film, while far superior to *Quo Vadis,* seemed to do little more in terms of Griffith's work than to sum up his technical advances. It did not take his art into any new dimensions, nor did it mark a turning point in any sense for films or for audiences. Only in two years, with *The Birth of a Nation,* would Griffith achieve that—and more.

THE BIRTH OF A NATION

In reprimand for his secretive making of *Judith of Bethulia,* Biograph took Griffith off directing and gave him a job supervising other productions. Griffith balked, checked out some other film companies, then quit He joined a younger outfit, Mutual (Majestic-Reliance). The work there was unexciting, but the money ($1,000 per week) was necessary for what Griffith saw as his major picture. During 1913 and early 1914, he began organizing the project. It would be based, somewhat loosely, around Thomas Dixon's novel *The Clansman.* It would be long, longer than any previous film ever made. It would be an epic, a romance, a historical drama of sweeping scale and momentum.

Griffith took many of his original Biograph company with him. He began active production in 1914. His cast and technicians were astounded that he used no shooting script. War shortages made production difficult—Griffith had a hard time getting the horses he needed for some of the battle scenes—but eventually he completed production. The film came in at a cost of about $100,000, an unheard-of figure for making a movie. More staggering was the length of the film: 12 reels. Distributors refused to handle a movie of such awkward size, and Griffith was forced to establish his own distribution outlets.

In February, 1915, *The Birth of a Nation*

27

Birth of a Nation

was released. Although the admission was a seemingly outrageous two dollars, crowds gathered to see the movie that critics and newspapers were hailing throughout the country as the greatest movie ever made. President Woodrow Wilson saw the film and described it as "like writing history in lightning." The skeptical movie industry watched aghast as Griffith's monumental film not only made a fortune, but made history.

In technique and in narrative, *The Birth of a Nation* was advanced far beyond anything yet to appear on the screens of movie theaters. The story centered around two families, the Stonemans from Pennsylvania and the Camerons from South Carolina. The boys from the families all enlist to fight in the Civil War, and several are killed. Captain Phil Stoneman, of the Union Army, takes over the Cameron estate and holds Ben Cameron prisoner. Meanwhile, Captain Stoneman's father, Austin, an influential Congressman, fights for punishment of the South. After Lincoln's assassination, Congressman Stoneman comes South with his mulatto protégé, Silas Lynch, a man whom he has ordained a leader in South Carolina. The Camerons are astounded and horrified, and through their activities we see the birth of the Ku Klux Klan.

The story leads to a climax in which the Klansmen come in the nick of time to save the Cameron family from Negro militiamen.

The Birth of a Nation was a double-edged sword. On one hand, its technique, its narrative drive, its epic sweep, it brilliant use of the film medium, clearly made it one of the greatest of all films. At the same time, Griffith had made a film which presented the black man as little more than a stupid savage, which depicted the Civil War as the North's vendetta against the South, and which justified—even extolled—the Ku Klux Klan.

The controversy aroused by the film was no doubt partly responsible for its incredible

29

30

Birth of a Nation

commercial success. In many ways, the film made an appeal, and a passionate one, for recognition of the inferiority of the black man and his total segregation from white society. In a number of Northern cities, important figures denounced the film, and it became a major issue in a number of political clashes. Generally the attacks were made on Griffith, and Griffith responded. He published articles and pamphlets upholding the right to "freedom of the screen."

Despite the undercurrent of prejudice in *The Birth of a Nation*, the film remains an exemplary and brilliant example of the art of the medium. There is about it not even a lingering remnant of that sense of the filmed stage play which dominated filmmaking to this time. The shots and editing coexist in a fluid relationship, and the film—for all its length—moves with a pulsating rhythm that rarely flags. Griffith seemed to be experimenting with temporal-spatial relationships in a way he never had before. During the Civil War battle scenes, for example, he opens one scene with a long shot of a field strewn with bodies. For a moment, he holds the camera, suggesting a geography of horror that only a long shot could create. Then he closes in on single figures: a man draped over a cannon, a boy whose empty eyes face the sun. Very long shots often are juxtaposed to very tight close-ups: suggesting the awful relationship between the macrocosm of war and the microcosm of the soldier.

The editing is unquestionably superior to anything that went before it, and to much of what would come after it. In the scene depicting the assassination of Lincoln, for example, Griffith builds the tension by a complex crosscutting from Lincoln, to the stage, to the assassin planning his entry into Lincoln's box. The pace increases, and everything seems to build to that moment of which no one is aware except the assassin.

The use of cinematography reached new artistic heights with *The Birth of a Nation*. In depicting General Sherman's march to the sea, Griffith opens with a small iris shot of a woman weeping beside her children. The iris expands; the camera reveals a long line of soldiers marching through a land of burning and gutted houses. A long, extended panning shot shows the length of that army, and a group of medium shots depict the pillage of specific houses, and the suffering of distinct people. Finally, the entire sequence closes with the woman and her child again, suggesting that this—and this alone—is what Sherman's march was all about.

Perhaps the most extraordinary section of the film is the climax of the Reconstruction episode, when Lynch (the mulatto) wants to marry Elsie Stoneman (Lillian Gish), while the Ku Klux Klan is organizing and preparing its ride. Griffith builds the suspense here with incredible skill, depicting the fierce mulatto in the room with Elsie while showing the Klan members gathering far away. As the tension among Lynch, Elsie, and Elsie's father rises, so do the numbers of the Klan riders who are preparing to attack the town. The events are complex, and yet not difficult to follow. More important, the way in which Griffith handles them shows to what extent careful and ingenious editing can give a motion picture momentum and emotional force.

The Birth of a Nation is rich in fine moments that use fresh modes of expression. The acting is generally restrained and

Birth of a Nation

Birth of a Nation

INTOLERANCE,
BROKEN BLOSSOMS, LATER YEARS

effective; even to this day, much of it appears excellent. Often Griffith conveys feelings not through a specific facial expression but via some symbol. In one scene, Elsie Stoneman grasps a bedpost in ectasy: all we see are her hands on the fine mahogany. Lynch kicks a dog: a brief, but clear reflection of his character.

It cannot be said, finally, that *The Birth of a Nation* is an unflawed film. Even excepting the passionate Southern and segregationist viewpoint, the film exposes Griffith's key weaknesses: his sentimentality, his Victorian simplification of moral problems, his eagerness to cast villains as demons and heroes as gods. Throughout the film, the printed titles reflect a filmmaker's injection of feeling into the statements of characters. Congressman Stoneman, for example, is credited with saying: "We shall crush the white South under the heel of the black South." And when Lynch wants to marry Elsie: "The black's mad proposal of Elsie." The close of the film, with the Ku Klux Klan members riding through town, is entitled, "The Parade of the Liberators."

Nonetheless, *The Birth of a Nation* is one of the greatest films ever made, and perhaps historically the most important. Porter's advances had led to a general improvement in the technique of film; Griffith's movie gave other filmmakers something to strive to match, something to work against, and work toward. It was a major achievement for the film as an art, just as it was a critical turning point for the movies as an industry.

The success of *The Birth of a Nation* hardly stemmed Griffith's desire to make more movies, even larger in scope and conception than what was already acclaimed as his masterpiece. At 39, he felt his future as a filmmaker was before him. He had changed his name (shortly after leaving Biograph) to D. W. Griffith and accepted film as his chosen career. In preparing his next project—a multi-episodic movie based on the theme of intolerance—he said, "If I approach what I am trying to do in my coming picture, I expect a persecution even greater than that which met *The Birth of a Nation*."

Intolerance was a daring film. Its structure was unique, its conception original, its cost extravagant. The film was to include four separate stories: "The Mother and the Law," based on the then-prominent Stielow case; the fall of Babylon; the story of Christ; and the massacre of the Huguenots on the Eve of St. Bartholomew. Each story was to be separate, but interlinked in theme (and editing) with the others. As Griffith explained, the stories "will begin like four currents looked at from a hilltop. At first the four currents will flow apart, slowly and quietly. But as they flow, they grow nearer and nearer together, faster and faster, until in the end, in the last act, they mingle in one mightly river of exposed emotion."

Production of *Intolerance* was so expensive that it forced Griffith to go heavily into debt. At $2,000,000, it was clearly one of the most expensive films of the silent era and, at 13 reels, one of the longest.

The film opens with a statement of the theme and the image (which recurs throughout it) of a mother cradling her child—for Griffith, the symbol of people victimized by intolerance. Each story is told only in part, then abruptly followed by the proportionate aspect of another story. Through this technique, Griffith intended to use editing to show the thematic similarities between the stories—how intolerance is the same in every age. His technique is superlative: the film is full of startling juxtapositions that bring out the comparisons he wanted. As Jesus weaves his way to Calvary, the film cuts to a girl rushing to forewarn Balthazar that the priests have betrayed him. As the Huguenot battles through the streets to rescue his lover, the wife of a condemned convict rushes to the prison with a pardon. Griffith uses tension and suspense in the film as they were never used before: to propel the action to ever spiraling heights, holding the audience captive with the images rushing across the screen.

The production was opulent. The gates of Babylon stood hundreds of feet high while thousands milled below. In the banquet scene of the Balthazar story, Griffith spent a reputed $25,000 for the lavish effects. The cast was enormous, the sets magnificent. And as ever, Griffith's cameras recorded not only the scope but the minor details that gave even greater credibility and meaning to the scene: the faces, the costumes, the finely-honed spear points.

Griffith used a number of techniques which had been anticipated in earlier films. Now, he gave them greater scope and development than ever before. He experimented throughout with various framing devices: irises to concentrate on a face or an action, wipes that moved across the screen in specific relationship to some object on the screen (one, for example, began at the monstrous Babylonian gate and moved outward, parallel to the gate). He used tracking shots often; one traveled for several hundred feet, from a distant shot of the entire Babylonian set to a medium shot of one scene.

Nonetheless, *Intolerance* was an uneven film: in some ways, the greatest of Griffith's movies, in other ways the most faulted. The enormous sets, particularly in the Babylonian sequence, tended to distract from the story. As a reviewer for *Photoplay* remarked, "The fatal error of *Intolerance* was that in the great Babylonian scenes you didn't care which side won. It was just a great show."

Moreover, of the four stories that Griffith promised, he only delivered two—the contemporary story (the best developed) and the Babylonian story—more of an epic spectacle, really, than a story. The narrative in the Christ and Huguenot episodes was weak, and audiences tended to wait out those episodes to find out what was really happening in the exciting stories.

Finally, Griffith's own sentimental bias hurt the film. He used names such as "Little Dear One" and "Brown Eyes" for characters—something that had generally vanished from filmmaking before Griffith left Biograph. Some of the violence—such as cutting off a head—was downright gory and gratuitous.

Nonetheless, one can't help but feel that, with *Intolerance*, there was more at stake: that Griffith was reaching for further degrees of experimentation, struggling to find some new unifying principle to advance the art of film, much as he had in *Birth of a Nation*. If Griffith did fail, it was perhaps partly because of the enormous distance between what the audiences could cope with and the limits to which Griffith wanted to test the manipulation of form.

The failure that crippled Griffith most brutally, though, was not the film's artistic failure, but the fact that it flopped so badly in the commercial market. It would take him years of work on movies without total creative independence to repay the debts incurred by *Intolerance*. With the loss of his creative freedom, Griffith lost much of his enthusiasm for endless experimentation. Eventually, despite glimmers and sometimes brilliant moments of creative achievement, Griffith's work sank to the level of cheap potboilers. By the mid-twenties, he was turning out cheaply produced, barely cared-for movies that suggested only dimly the creative talent of the man who had made them.

The decline of Griffith is a sad epoch in film history, but one that reveals something about the precarious relationship between art and industry in filmmaking. The Griffith of the Biograph years, of *Judith of Bethulia*, of *The Birth of a Nation*, of *Intolerance*, was a creative, experimental spirit searching for the best ways to use the medium to communicate powerfully to audiences. The later Griffith was far more concerned with fame and wealth and recognition; he seemed to care less about what he did with a film than how boldly his name was printed on it, and with the money a film would make.

There were other reasons behind Griffith's decline. His Victorian sentimentality, which had marred earlier films, now seemed even more pronounced—and more obviously out of step with the changing tastes of audiences. His interest in film itself declined; he spent more time writing on various themes like

Hearts of the World 1917

the future of movies, planning extravagant projects that never materialized and speaking on various subjects to whomever would listen.

Griffith made two features during World War I: *Hearts of the World* and *The Great Love*, both of which were thin reflections of his talents and barely shaded forms of propaganda. After the war, he returned to the type of films he had been doing: soft, melodramatic romances, which of course had lost virtually all their appeal for postwar audiences.

The industry at large was foundering, searching out new subjects for film; Griffith, too, foundered. For a time, he wandered between production companies. Then, in 1919, he became part of the organization that formed—with Charles Chaplin, Mary Pickford, and Douglas Fairbanks—United Artists Corporation. The prominent names that formed United Artists guaranteed it financial backing. But it also forced the company to aim its products straight at the box office, a quality tacitly present in the films of the other three, but dangerous for Griffith.

Griffith's first movie for United Artists was *Broken Blossoms* (1919). It was also his last major movie. *Broken Blossoms* is a film that vacillates between a genuine poignancy and a number of novel effects and gimmicks that Griffith included largely to guarantee its commercial success. The story of a Chinaman's affection for a badly treated girl, *Broken Blossoms* uses sets in a quiet, natural way both to achieve a sense of realism and to evoke mood. Lillian Gish, playing the girl, acts with a gracious naturalness and believability. The editing in some of the sequences—such as the brutal beating of Gish—belongs among the best of Griffith's work.

Broken Blossoms was received well. The *New York Times* called it "a masterpiece" and the *New York Evening Telegram* de-scribed it with the statement: "It is as if Dickens had spoken by means of the camera." The film's success, both critical and commercial, did a great deal to improve Griffith's sagging reputation. But it also convinced Griffith that he was everything the critics and public said he was: "Our Greatest Poet," the "Shakespeare of the movies." He began announcing even greater things: a film 72 reels long; a chain of theaters bearing his name. Griffith the filmmaker had become Griffith the publicist— and a self-publicist at that. The films he made seemed to lack his imagination, and were gradually either delegated to others or made with peremptory speed and with as little imagination and innovation as possible.

Yet Griffith had made film history. He had taught the movies to move, to expand beyond the limits imposed upon them by the stage, and to speak with an eloquence and a power never known before. For that Griffith cannot be forgotten.

Broken Blossoms 1919

THE REEL THING

The earliest newsreel, so the historians say, goes back to 1896 in the filming of the British Derby. From that point on the newsreel was thoroughly ensconced as a part of what people saw "at the movies."

Early silent studios—Pathé, Universal, and Paramount—ran newsreels in theaters before World War I. Newsreels recorded everything: disasters like the explosion of the zeppelin "Hindenburg;" the beginnings or conclusions of great events—such as Charles Lindbergh speaking a few words before getting into The Spirit of St. Louis on his flight across the Atlantic; the appearances and speeches of prominent world figures—Wilson, Mussolini, Roosevelt, Churchill, Hitler; the collapse of "Galloping Gertie," a famous bridge in Washington state wrecked by a storm.

The introduction of a soundtrack gave new impetus to the newsreel and new studios entered the act. Soon, along with Pathé, Universal News, and Hearst's Metronome, there were the Fox Movietone ("The Eyes and Ears of the World") and The March of Time. With sound, the newsreels became longer and slicker; sound effects and swelling music were added—in a word, newsreels became productions. The announcer would introduce events in a heavy, authoritative tone and amid the pomp of the music and elaborate optical effects (like iris wipes), audiences would watch world leaders strut to their verandas, or long distance runners panting into the stretch of an Olympic race. Often, newsreels would close with some little tidbit of "general interest"—such as a dog with two tails, or the latest record-breaking stint in goldfish swallowing.

The announcers supplied at least half of the newsreel's impact. Westbrook van Vooris intoned "The March . . . of Time" with an accentuation and heaviness that made you feel acutely aware that you were about to witness terrible events. Ed Thorgerson used to announce the "sports roundups" with a vitality that transformed a pallid tennis match into the one-in-a-century Wimbledon. Lowell Thomas, narrating one story of a flyer who wanted to go back to battle after being rescued from the sea, said, "That kind of spirit will win this war. And if you don't think so, you're as crazy as Hitler!"

In an essay "The Eyes and Ears of the World," John Tebbel describes the all-newsreel theaters that appeared in the thirties. "People went to the newsreel theaters for a variety of reasons. Sometimes the audiences contained sociologists, politicians, commentators, and other people-watchers who carefully noted audience reaction to the images of politicians on the screen. The reactions often were uninhibited, as *The New Yorker* noted in a famous cartoon depicting a Union League Club-type saying enthusiastically to his friends, "Let's all go down to the newsreels and hiss Roosevelt.' "

Of course it was television that killed the newsreels, but in *more* than one sense the newsreels had been the real precursors of television news.— particularly in creating a brief format for major world events on film. However, TV has toned down its presentation of the news; we no longer have the fast cuts, the vivid montages, the rumbling chords of an orchestra, or the narrative emphasis that used to be part of the drama of the theater newsreels.

THE

THE

THE

THE

THE

THE

THE
MARCH
of TIME

Modern Times 1936

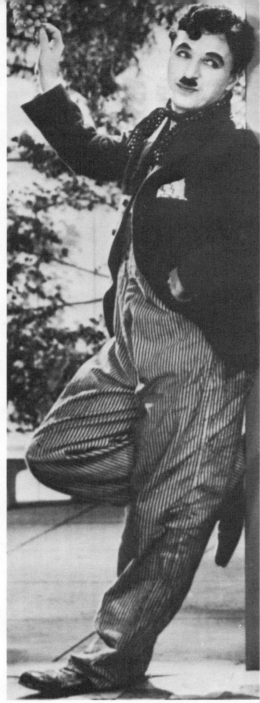

Modern Times 1936

Modern Times 1936

38

The Kid 1920

CHARLES CHAPLIN

If Griffith gave the film its syntax, then Chaplin gave it the first glimmerings of human magic that somehow went beyond the melodramas and slapstick comedies of the period. In more than just his comedy, Chaplin elevated the silent screen, capturing in pantomime some of its largest possibilities. Through his character of the tramp, Chaplin endeared audiences to himself and to movies. He was at once the greatest performer and certainly one of the greatest of comedy directors.

Charles Chaplin was English, the son of impoverished vaudevillians in London. As early as the age of six, he played stage roles in his parents' troupe. Eventually he began to work for another troupe—Karno's Number 2 Company—which provided him with a rich background of experiences on which he would later base his pantomimes.

In 1910, at the age of 21, Chaplin came with the Karno Troupe to America. During one of the performances, he was spotted by a friend of Mack Sennett, the major comedy director of Keystone Studio, who encouraged Chaplin to go into movies. Sennett offered him a year's contract at considerable more than he was making with Karno. Chaplin was wary—stage people still felt that cinema was a step down—but he took it.

Chaplin's career grew quickly. Yet, after almost a year, he felt unsure that he wanted to stay in film; his dreams had always been of the stage. Indeed, he saw himself as a serious actor in the theater, not as a comedian. But encouraged by his minor successes at Keystone, he stayed on, and his talents ripened.

There was an almost inevitable friction between Chaplin and Keystone, particularly in the first few months. Mack Sennett's Keystone style was fast, violent, a whirlwind of tricks and gags jammed into a tight, two-reel framework. The pace rarely flagged in Sennett's films, and Chaplin, who felt more comfortable doing his comedy touches at a slower pace (though he was certainly capable of the Keystone speed), was constantly arguing with directors about how a shot or scene should be handled. More often than not, the directors gave up and let Chaplin try out his own stunt simply out of exhaustion. Besides, the audiences had begun to notice Chaplin; he was considered one of the rising stars in Sennett's entourage.

Chaplin devised various means to guarantee that they kept his own comedy bits in the films. As he wrote in his autobiography:

I made about five pictures and in some of them I had managed to put over one or two bits of comedy business of my own, in spite of the butchers in the cutting room. Familiar with their method of cutting films, I would contrive business and gags just for entering and exiting from a scene, knowing that they would have difficulty in cutting them out.

Sennett came close to firing Chaplin. It was only the growing demand of the distributors for Chaplin films that convinced Sennett to keep Chaplin on. Using this leverage, Chaplin insisted that he be allowed to co-direct his films. Sennett, torn between a proved film formula and a talent who

seemed able to do comedy best outside that formula, reluctantly gave in.

Chaplin learned quickly. He discovered the importance of camera placement, the subtle effects possible through lighting, and —a kind of heresy at Keystone—that a breakneck pace of gag piled on gag isn't always as funny as a human situation which gradually gets out of control.

Chaplin knew that his timing and Sennett's were at odds, and he did everything in his pictures to force the directors to slow down the scenes and emphasize the characters over the ludicrous situations. After directing his first comedy, *Caught In the Rain*, Chaplin was given the director's role in all his movies. It was something he would keep throughout his life, permitting a rare freedom denied most screen comedians.

Toward the end of his first year at Keystone, Chaplin began to consider moving elsewhere. It wasn't only the discrepancy in style; Chaplin wanted $1,000 a week, and Sennett adamantly refused. At the age of 25, Chaplin signed with G. M. Anderson, known as "Bronco Billy," to make films for a year at Essanay.

He didn't like Essanay, even though his year there accounted for the most dramatic rise in his popularity. The executives seemed like bankers, the whole setup was organized too vaguely with none of the electricity and enthusiasm which had been so notable at Sennett's studio. Chaplin moved from studios in San Francisco to Chicago, then to Niles, and finally settled in a rented studio in Los Angeles. He made some fine films during that year, but by mid-1915 his contract expired and again he began looking elsewhere. At this point Chaplin was the most popular comedy star among audiences throughout the country. He could—and with the Mutual Film Company did—command his own price: $67,000 for 12 two-reelers.

Working out of a rented studio in Hollywood, Chaplin entered his most successful period of filmmaking. He acted in two-reelers like *Easy Street*, *The Immigrant*, and *The Adventurer*. The Tramp had now become a basic fixture of Chaplin films—that bowlegged, bewildered little man with the cane, bowler hat, and oversized pants.

Chaplin wrote his movies, selected his casts, directed and starred. His directing talents were hardly those of a Griffith: editing and the use of cinematic effects are minimal in Chaplin's films. Mostly the camera is there to record what could be successfully staged as pantomime. Yet Chaplin's genius for a warm, particularly human form of comedy and his incredible inventive talents kept his films from ever slackening. Audiences were almost never disappointed by his films—even though they often had to pay twice as much to see one.

Chaplin described the period he spent doing the 12 Mutual films as the happiest in his life. It was also the richest period in his filmmaking career. The films are full of brilliantly witty and inventive moments. In *The Pawnshop*, for example, the Tramp has just been fired and pleads with the boss to keep him. He has 11 children: each one a little taller—until the fourth is taller than himself. The boss relents, and the Tramp jumps on the man in gratitude, entwining his legs around him.

By the end of the Mutual contract, Chaplin had established himself as the world's greatest screen comedian. He had been making movies for only three years, was just 28 years old, but his name was the most magical and attractive in the movie industry. His newest contract, with First National Pictures, permitted him to do anything he wanted. He could take more time with his pictures, had more production money backing them, and was no longer limited to two-reelers.

In *A Dog's Life* (1918) he gave an added

The Pilgrim 1922

dimension to the Tramp—playing him somewhere between a kindly philosopher and a wandering bumpkin. In *Shoulder Arms* (1918) he compromised the Tramp's inexorable love for freedom by donning a soldier's uniform. *Shoulder Arms*, though released after the Armistice, was Chaplin's most successful film to date.

His postwar films—*Sunnyside, A Day's Pleasure, The Kid*—all display typical Chaplinesque themes. By now his technique was polished, and Chaplin could deal with his favorite character in his favorite way: the Tramp who wanders through the modern world dreaming of a happier life, but never quite getting there. The Tramp lives at the edge of society, is the instinctive enemy of policemen and aristocrats. The Tramp doesn't live by normal conventions, and indeed, enjoys scoffing at them. Such putdowns were among the most frequent, and enjoyable, of Chaplin's comic gags.

In 1920, Chaplin went abroad for several months. He returned with a desire to expand his range of filmmaking. His next three films—*The Idle Class* (1921), *Pay Day* (1922) and *The Pilgrim* (1923)— were all Tramp features, but the indictment of society was more emphatic, more direct, and more scathing than it had been in his earlier films. None of these was a major effort, nor was his next—*A Woman of Paris* —neither was it a comedy. The story, of a French girl who runs away from home and becomes the mistress of a wealthy Parisian, was Chaplin's first venture into dramatic filmmaking as a director. The film was successful, but has not worn so well with time as Chaplin's comedies or his dramatic efforts of the forties, such as *Monsieur Verdoux* (1947).

Chaplin's *The Gold Rush*, made in 1925, was one of the funniest and finest of his feature films: a tale of the Tramp living in Alaska, beset by the cold, the other prospectors, and the woman he loves. The film reflects and wryly comments on the frenzied money madness of the twenties while at the same time reinstating the Tramp in his familiar role at the periphery of organized society.

The Circus (1928) was Chaplin's last film of the silent period. It is perhaps the most self-contained portrait of the Tramp that Chaplin has made. The closing scene, in which Chaplin is left behind in the empty tent looking down at the clown's star, has about it all the pathos that Chaplin was capable of rendering. The Tramp gives a look of terrible loneliness, then turns and goes his way.

The end of the silent period meant an end to virtually all the silent comedians— and in one way, to Chaplin. His films of the thirties and forties are enough, in their own right, to support his reputation as a master director of American films. But they are in a different key, and reflect a different, more matured talent. *City Lights* (1931) and *Modern Times* (1936) both resuscitate the Tramp. He continues to be silent, even though the characters and things around him are thoroughly audible.

In *City Lights*, Chaplin moves around in the Depression world, cheering a down-and-out broker, helping, in his own pathetic way, a blind girl. *Modern Times* is a vicious indictment of the world of machines and assembly lines. After working all day on an assembly line, Charlie walks home, his body jerking with the day's work rhythms, his arms pumping like pistons. As in so many of his other films, *Modern Times* reflects the helplessness, the terrifying ambiguity of the man caught in a world he cannot understand. In some ways, it is Chaplin's most depressing film because the character cannot help but capitulate to larger forces.

Chaplin's career did not end with *Modern Times*, though it took different directions after that. *The Great Dictator* (1940) was a pointed, if uneven, satire on Hitler. *Mon-*

City Lights 1931

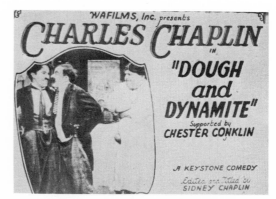

sieur Verdoux was a dramatic masterpiece. In a business in which all too many artists are left behind by the times, Chaplin has proved, at the very least, that he is larger than his times, and that what he can do on film reaches beyond any period's sophisticated technique.

It was the French critic Elie Faure who pointed out that, of all the movie stars of the silent screen, Chaplin was the only one who never moved his lips as if seeming to speak, which is another way of saying that no one brought to the silent screen the natural genius of pantomime that Chaplin did. In a Chaplin movie, sounds, or even the visual suggestion of sound, mattered hardly at all. The effect was visually immediate, and often extraordinarily complex. Through his deft movements, his poignant facial expressions, and his unceasing inventiveness, Chaplin could take a situation and gradually build it into something that was at once hilariously funny and poignantly human.

For beneath the comedy—or more ac-

43

Modern Times 1936

The Great Dictator 1940

curately, at the center of it — Chaplin revealed a profound human understanding: an almost instinctive sense of that slippery edge of human fraility which so easily summons both laughter and tears. As his art progressed, Chaplin took his audiences closer and closer to that edge, creating effects which were more complex, more emotionally involving, than anything else in movie comedy. In *The Gold Rush,* Charlie the prospector invites three girls—one of whom he wants to marry—to join him for dinner on New Year's Eve. Destitute, he shovels snow to buy the food. When the evening arrives, we see Charlie pacing his cabin, dressed in evening clothes, nervously adjusting everything: checking the roast, putting out favors, touching up the table settings. He daydreams, imagining the girls enjoying the party with him. Part of the dream is a little dance of two rolls on forks which he plays deftly on the table while he smiles above them. The moment is not really comic so much as poignant; it is filled with a warmth that radiates from all of Chaplin's films.

The central character in all of Chaplin's comedies after his Keystone days was Charlie. Known to audiences by his stiff, rolling walk, his baggy pants, his rattan walking-stick, his flat, rectangular mustache, and the inevitable bowler, the character of Charlie came to take on an identity that was once personal and universal. Charlie resented authority and pomp; he clung desperately to his own freedom, even if that meant only the freedom to make mistakes. He was a dreamer, a sad little man who could feel good simply because a promise awaited him on the horizon. He was humble, but he could be stubborn. He was gentle and obliging, but he could be firm and demanding. Though he lived at the edge of society, he did give in halfway; he knew he had to acquiesce to some conventions, some standards. In one film, Charlie arrives late to the theater and apologetically and sensitively steps over everyone's toes to get to his seat. When he discovers he is in the wrong row, his face reflects the pain of being caught in the humiliation of having to go through all that again.

A major motif in the American film, and particularly in comedy film is the put-down of authority and aristocracy. Chaplin's stance toward authority derives partly from his experience at Keystone: no chase in a Mack Sennett film was ever quite complete without the bumbling cops. But Chaplin has added another element, giving the put-down more personal dimension. For Charlie, despite and because of all his oddities, is a kind of everyman: a free spirit wandering in the modern world, largely at odds with it, but willing to struggle. So much of his appeal and charm derive from the secret desires of audiences to put down authority the way Charlie can. So much of the pathos of Charlie's episodes is created by our recognition that it is always the little man who suffers most.

Chaplin's films are clearly the product of one of the great comic geniuses of the century. Chaplin was not a gag comic, though he had learned much from Mack Sennett. Indeed, the Sennett influence is notable throughout all his films. Though Chaplin slowed down the pace of his work from the frenetic romps of the Keystone two-reelers, many of the gimmicks and ideas he used are pure Sennett. The cabin perched so precariously over the ledge in *The Gold Rush*, the fight with the other employees in *The Pawnshop*—these are clearly products of that important apprentice year with Sennett.

But ultimately Chaplin's humor was not built around gags—no matter how funny—but rather on the subtle facial expressions, the inflections and reactions to what was happening around him. In *The Gold Rush*, he eats a boot: the situation is funny enough, but Chaplin's face tells us that he is acting as if this were a steak at the Waldorf. His face is also telling us that it isn't.

Possibly no one in silent comedy used inanimate objects quite so effectively as Chaplin. Chaplin was always having difficulties with brooms, ropes, and buckets. They seemed to rebel, to do exactly what he didn't want them to do, and often a bout with a rope or a bucket would lead to acrobatics and disaster. This whole theme is summed up best in *Modern Times*, in which the Tramp spends the factory day getting increasingly enmeshed in the feeding machine, which pelts him with food, soup, nuts, and bolts.

Chaplin's art is inexhaustible. His fertile imagination, his sensitive, deft, often brilliant touches, and his comic genius have provided us with movies that have not grown old over the years. As film critic James Agee said in his famed essay on silent comedy:

The finest pantomime, the deepest emotion, the richest and most poignant poetry were in Chaplin's work. He could probably pantomime Bryce's The American Commonwealth *without ever blurring a syllable and make it paralyzingly funny into the bargain. At the end of* City Lights *the blind girl who has regained her sight, thanks to the Tramp, sees him for the first time. She has imagined and anticipated him as princely, to say the least; and it has never seriously occurred to him that he is inadequate. She recognizes who he must be by his shy, confident, shining joy as he comes silently toward her. And he recognizes himself, for the first time, through the terrible changes in her face. The camera just exchanges a few quiet close-ups of the emotions which shift and intensify in each face. It is enough to shrivel the heart to see, and it is the greatest piece of acting and the highest moment in movies.*

47

In a sense the animated cartoon came before the movie. The zoetrope, for example, invented by William Horner in 1834, used a band of pictures—somewhat like a comic strip— which revolved inside a moving drum. When you twirled the drum and looked through slits along the side, the drawn images inside appeared as a consistent moving image—a major forerunner—or "fore-sight" —of the motion picture.

Probably the earliest American cartoon film was Gertie the Dinosaur (1909), made by Windsor McKay, the cartoonist who drew the daily strip "Little Nemo." McKay used simple line drawings, the basic techniques of the comic strip; later, as animation techniques were refined, that technique was to disappear until the more experimental approaches of animation filmmakers in the '50s and '60s returned it to use.

The advantage of the cartoon is total freedom—the animator can draw anything he wants; he can transform any figure into whatever he wants it to become. Thus the history of the cartoon is rich in characters like a talking Duck, a wisecracking Bunny, a rollicking Mouse. For the years that the major studios like MGM and Warner Brothers and UPA and Disney produced the bulk of animated cartoons, this was indeed the main development: to use the cartoon to create a story built around animals that behaved like people, or for a time (mostly the thirties) trees and flowers and machines that sang and danced.

The great years of big studio animated shorts— roughly from 1935 to 1955—saw the development of numerous familiar comic characters: Tom and Jerry, Road-runner, Heckle and Jeckle, Tweety Bird and Sylvester, Woody Woodpecker, Bugs Bunny, Chip n Dale, Mr. Magoo—generally repeating the formula in cartoon after cartoon: coyote plotting extravagant traps for Roadrunner, for example, that invariably backfire, leaving the coyote broken or squashed or maimed till his next attempt.

It appears that the theatrical cartoon short, like the movie serial, is another casualty of television. Most of the major studio animation departments have closed down in recent years. In many ways this is not altogether a loss. The best recent work in cartoons, both short and feature, has come from independents such as John and Faith Hubley, with their charming, pastiche-like figures and rich uses of sound; Teru Murakami, whose cartoons have a clean, understated wit; and others, such as Charles Eames, Ernest Pintoff, or Saul Bass.

A magnificent example of this experimental trend in recent animation can be seen in the feature Yellow Submarine, where both characters and story are developed in unusual, wildly graphic ways. Figures like the Dreadful Flying Glove and the Vacuum Man come closer to dream images than to the standard cute animal figures of the earlier studio cartoons. Indeed, Yellow Submarine suggests that the major direction of animation is a kind of experimentation: with color, with shapes and forms, with wildly inventive narrative techniques that use the drawing board as their world and move on from there.

Zoetrope

Donald's Dream Voice 1948

THE CARTOONS

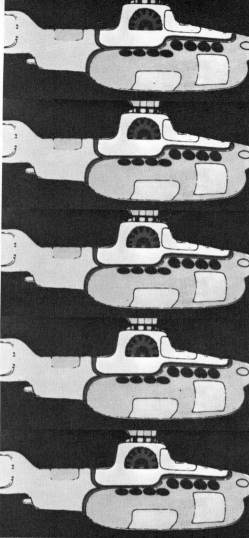

Yellow Submarine 1968 © King Features

49

Chapter Three
Golden Era of the Silent Film: 1917-1928

(IMP) Independent Motion Pictures Company (later Universal) studio group

WAR AND ITS AFTERMATH

For all its incredible growth and the fortunes it was making for many stars and producers, the movie industry was economically precarious for everyone involved. Nothing for the movies pointed that out so much as the experience of World War I and its traumatic aftermath.

Costs had already been mounting in 1913 and early 1914. The concept of the two-reeler had spread, and more and more film projects were becoming ambitious—with enormous sets, costly stars, and generally mounting production budgets.

Despite the rising costs, however, the filmmakers were optimistic—and never so optimistic as when war broke out. For one thing, the disruption of film production from the key European countries (Germany, France, Italy) due to the war meant that the United States would have a virtual monopoly in the world-wide film market. For another, the impressive successes of a number of the young studios brought hordes of businessmen, showmen, and get-rich-quick schemers to that new mecca of the American Dream, Hollywood.

Hollywood was a geographical reflection of the high hopes and the extravagant expectations of the industry. Land was being grabbed and sold at spiraling costs. Studios were building larger and larger buildings. The economic boom that would hit America after the war and rise until it shattered on

the Depression had already hit Hollywood.

But in 1914 Hollywood was more of a hope and a promise than the capital of American glamour and decadence. Its attractions had less to do with its being the established center of moviemaking than with its year-round sun, its varied, wild landscape, its proximity to the Mexican border (an advantage for many of the smaller independents who raced there hours ahead of their creditors). In the critical years between 1914 and 1920, Hollywood would establish itself as the movie capital not only of America but of the world.

World War I broke out in Europe in the summer of 1914. The first response of the American film industry was the newsreel. Already a staple in theaters, it became an important means of communicating the events of the war to the American people. Old newsreels, imported German and French films, and eventually fresh newsreels appeared in the theaters. The pleasant fantasies and comedies of the prewar period quickly gave way to a type of production whose purpose was more propagandistic than escapist.

At first the movie industry pleaded for neutrality. Movies like *Civilization* and *Or He Who Returned* by Thomas Ince, and *War Brides* by Herbert Brenon, depicted war as a horrid, futile venture and praised those who remained neutral and pacifist

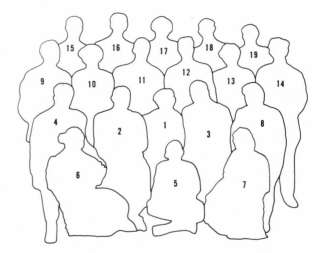

1 Mary Pickford
2 Owen Moore
3 King Baggott
4 Thomas Ince
5 Jack Pickford
6 Isabel Rae
7 Lottie Pickford
8 Joe Smiley
9 William Shay
10 Mrs. David Miles
11 Joe MacDonald
12 Hayward Mack
13 Mrs. Joe MacDonald
14 John Harvey
15 George Loane Tucker
16 David Miles
17 Mrs. Pickford
18 Robert Daley
19 Tony Gaudio

D·W·GRIFFITH'S
SUPREME TRIUMPH
HEARTS OF THE WORLD
A LOVE STORY OF THE GREAT WAR
18 MONTHS IN THE MAKING
BATTLE SCENES ON THE BATTLEFIELDS OF FRANCE
MANAGEMENT WILLIAM ELLIOTT·F·RAY COMSTOCK & MORRIS GEST
J.H TOOKER LITHO.CO.N.Y.

throughout it. Part of this sentiment stemmed no doubt from the idealistic and pacifist beliefs of the filmmakers. But part was a response to the isolationist and neutral mood of a large part of the country.

The mood, however, disappeared rapidly. As Germany made greater advances and as the war stretched out longer than many had believed was possible, the murmurs of war involvement grew louder. D. W. Griffith's *Intolerance*, a powerful indictment against the forces that give rise to war, appeared early in 1915. Much pro-war antagonism was directed at this movie. The feeling was so fierce that it severely hurt the film's reception at the boxoffice and—typical of Hollywood's way of changing—forced the film producers to change their approach to the war in films.

The first wave of pro-war films was made by J. Stuart Blackton, a strong advocate of involvement. In movies like *Wake Up America!*, *The Glory of the Nation*, and *The Battle Cry of Peace*, he blatantly set out to stir movieviewers to impassioned feelings of anti-German hostility. In *Battle Cry of Peace*, for instance, he depicts the Germans as bloodthirsty barbarians—wild-eyed men who desired only to rape and plunder. It was the first in a long history of Hollywood propagandistic stereotypes that culminated in the grinning "Jap" and the civilized, sadistic German officer of World War II.

Comedies, adventure films, espionage stories, and battle sagas came in the wake of the Blackton movies. All of them unhesitatingly cried for intercession in the war, for American responsibility to join in what they depicted as a grand test of manhood and an adventure lover's paradise. Such

films almost never showed the grisly consequences of war: the homeless, the maimed, the orphaned, the soldiers whose faces would forever wear a mask of horrified shock.

It probably can never be ascertained to what extent the pro-war films drove the American public to the brink of war. Movies tend to reflect public moods as well as to shape them. This first example of Hollywood as a propaganda machine suggests that most producers (apart from the quite conscious Blackton) were not interested in propaganda so much as they were in box office successes. Nonetheless, the very emphasis on the glory and adventure of war—at the cost of minimizing the darker side of war—made Hollywood an ally of the pro-war propagandists. It also pointed out the enormous propagandistic potential of Hollywood—though only a few commentators said anything about this at the time.

The United States declared war on April 6, 1917. The rising pro-war mood had by this time assumed a cloak of patriotism, so that anyone who appeared pacifist or even neutralist was vigorously attacked as a kind of traitor. The onrush of nationalism and patriotism overcame any Hollywood resistance and the movies, as well as their stars and celebrities, moved to the forefront of the war effort.

The films of the war period were, of course, largely battle movies: sagas of men in action, inevitably bold and handsome Americans defending freedom against the barbarous, Hun-like Germans. The titles alone suggest the vehemence with which these movies viewed the Germans: *The Kaiser, Beast of Berlin*; *To Hell With the Kaiser*; *The German Curse In Russia*. Other films, using domestic or historic settings, emphasized loyalty, patriotism, courage: *The Spirit of '17; Over There; Daughter of Destiny.* Even Chaplin's *Shoulder Arms,* a comedy released only after the war had ended, aimed not a little vitriol at Germans and their leader.

The measure to which the moviemakers sought to infuse the war effort with larger and larger meanings can be seen in the use of religious and social themes to further the patriotic ideals supposedly behind American involvement in the war. In films such as *Safe For Democracy* and *The Battle Cry of Liberty,* the winning of the war was equated with the winning of a classless society and a new rebirth of the human spirit. The earlier social themes of a Porter or a Griffith were stripped of their conscience and tacked on to any number of war movies, strictly to make the pitch of the battle cry a little more strident.

The signing of the Armistice in November, 1918, ended not only the war but a phase of American moviemaking. At the time, the signs were hardly auspicious. Most studios had only war stories with patriotic themes. Within days, it became apparent that audiences were not interested in them. The studios, which had slipped largely into formula movies over the past several years, were threatened by the lack of demand for their backlog of war films. Only the producers that could move quickly were able to catch the splintering postwar movie market. Those who hesitated lost out. As in earlier transitions in Hollywood—the switch to two-reelers, the recognition of the importance of the star system—some producers disappeared along the way.

The basic motifs in movies after the war

were adventure and romance: Westerns, Foreign Legion stories, historical romances. The movies became, as never quite before, the glittering dreams of society. Costs spiraled. The movies ran longer—by the early twenties a standard feature lasted six or seven reels—and the sets and costumes became more elaborate, the stars more costly, the entire productions far more extravagant. But the American people could and did pay to see these movies. Economically, things had never been better. War-shattered Europe was buying from America, and the world market depended on the country for everything from automobiles to wheat. Stocks were rising. It was a period of great economic optimism. The movie industry rode this crest eagerly, pouring out feature after feature, solidifying a popular amusement into a major industry.

Merry-Go-Round 1923

55

THE DIRECTORS

One of the basic differences between the studios before and after World War I lay in the approach taken to production. The earlier method was usually to give a director a project, often without full script, and let him do everything. Not only was the director free to develop a project in whatever way he saw fit, but he did not have to route every idea, every fresh departure through a "front office."

As the industry solidified in the postwar period, however, this creative control gradually ebbed away from the director. The studios were increasingly streamlined for production. Producer-supervisors took over the functions that once had belonged to directors: the location and development of an idea, the script, casting, even set design. These producer-supervisors tended to be less and less movie craftsmen than businessmen. As a result their decisions and choices in making movies were dominated far more by economic criteria than by a passion for craftsmanship or good filmmaking. It was far more important, for example, to have a big name star than to use an original or interesting story; far more important to spend enormous sums on expensive sets and crowd scenes than to make sure the camera was used inventively or that the acting was authentic. Movies were commodities to be sold. In the best tradition of the American marketplace, the new generation of producer-supervisors knew that a commodity was as good as the lures it held out to the customer.

Out of this came a one-dimensional approach to movies: a box office success was all that mattered, be it a good or a bad movie. It was true that the public did tend to prefer better films, and some directors—generally the more competent (and sometimes more inventive) ones—were more successful at the box office than others. But the emerging system was designed for the sole purpose of making every production investment as certain as possible, and the qualifications of a director did not usually fit into the category of certainty that big-name stars, huge production budgets, and a reputed novel or play so often did.

It would seem that, under this system, movies were hindered from progress, and in many ways they were. No new D. W. Griffith emerged in the twenties, no American equivalent to a Russian film genius like Sergei M. Eisenstein or a consummate film artist like Carl Dreyer. Yet the twenties did mark one of the high periods for the American director. Native directors like Thomas Ince, Cecil B. DeMille, Henry King, Rex Ingram and James Cruze kept American movies moving—however slowly—toward a cinematic realism and a more sophisticated use of the medium. Even more important, though, were the great immigrant directors brought to Hollywood from the filmmaking capitals of Europe, most notably Germany: F. W. Murnau, Erich von Stroheim, Ernst Lubitsch, Josef von Sternberg, and Victor Seastrom. All in all, the twenties were, for American moviemaking, a rich, fertile period—but thanks far more to the directors than to the producers.

THOMAS H. INCE

Ince really belongs to the second decade rather than to the twenties. It was before the war that he made most of his films and in 1916 that he reached the peak of production and recognition in the industry. Only two other directors could rival him at the time: D. W. Griffith for his trenchant storytelling and bold use of new techniques, and Mack Sennett, established at this time as the greatest of comedy directors.

Ince almost anticipated, in some ways, the coming role of the producer-supervisor. When his studio, Triangle Corporation, was in its best years, Ince would spread a number of movie projects out among various directors and specify on the shooting script exactly how each shot was to be made. Then he would edit every film and take credit as director. Surprisingly, most movies made this way came out rather well, and Ince rarely felt that he had lost any real creative control. Mack Sennett used the same technique with an equal degree of success. Others, like D. W. Griffith, never found the technique very helpful.

Ince developed a style of movie storytelling notable for its visual vitality, its engrossing manner, and its tough, clean economy. His films were planned carefully and elaborately beforehand. Each shot was structured into the shooting script (which Ince was the first to follow consistently). In the editing room, Ince would chop off any footage that he considered unimportant to the progress of the story.

His movies never quite reached the heights that Griffith achieved, but Ince's

successes were far more consistent. Dramas like *The Battle of Gettysburg, The Iron Strain, The Gangster and the Girl, The Italian, The Clodhopper, Viva La France!* and *The Wrath of the Gods* broke away from the melodramatic tendencies of the time and struggled with a more realistic and tightly controlled form of narrative.

Ince was one of the early moviemakers to mold the Western into a major mode of the Hollywood production. Attracting a Broadway actor of impressive skills to Hollywood in 1914, Ince featured William S. Hart in dozens of Westerns which stood clearly above the standard Western fare of the period. Ince's passion for large, impressive exteriors, unflagging action, and tough, realistic narrative come across powerfully in the William S. Hart Westerns.

Don't Change Your Husband 1919

CECIL B. DeMILLE

The name of DeMille has come to be associated with super-spectacular movies: movies with elaborate historical sets, fantastic crowd sequences, expensive costuming. But DeMille was always more of an extravaganza showman. Repeatedly, throughout most of the history of the Hollywood film (his movies range from 1913 to 1956), he anticipated a change in public taste and beat a score of other filmmakers to a new idea. When Mary Pickford was about to leave Paramount—and leave them bereft of a leading lady—he convinced the studio head that he could make movies without name stars. Indeed, his movies would *create* the new stars—something no one had been able to do except Griffith. In the twenties, he made the bath the most enticing and opulent interior setting known till then. As Richard Griffith and Arthur Mayer said of DeMille in *The Movies*:

He had and has a form of extrasensory perception that makes him aware of an approaching tidal wave of public taste long before anyone else, least of all the public itself, has detected the faintest ripple—or perhaps he just knows how to take a ripple and magnify it into a tidal wave.

Stories were never all that important to DeMille. Titles, sets, styles, the familiar ceremonies of disrobing and bathing and sleeping and attending opulent balls—these fixed DeMille's name in the popular imagination and assured enormous numbers of moviegoers that his newest epic would not disappoint the expectations created by his last. DeMille was always fascinated by moral failure and the power of temptation. Indeed, his film *The Cheat*, made in 1916, anticipated the movies of the twenties by moving beyond the absolutely good hero and absolutely rotten villain toward the tension experienced by people who were neither thoroughly good nor thoroughly bad.

DeMille loved to parade decadence and rife immorality before the screen while insisting in the titles that all of this was garish and evil and sinful. Audiences would watch a ridiculously opulent ball degenerate into an orgy and all the time be reminded, via titles, that such immorality should be deplored by any right-thinking man. It was DeMille's way of appealing to what he perceptively saw as the breakdown of Puritanism, while at the same time placating it by timely little messages.

Curiously, for a man whose devotion lay almost totally in the appeal of a motion picture, DeMille made impressively well-wrought movies. He had a sense of timing, an awareness of structure, and a visual appetite that keep even his earlier films interesting to this day. Movies like *Don't Change Your Husband* (1919), *Male and Female* (1919), *Adam's Rib* (1923), and *The King of Kings* (1927) retain a certain splendor and directness, even after all these years.

Detail, Loew's King's Theatre, Brooklyn

Even today the most durable of them survive in New York and Chicago and dozens of cities throughout the midwest. They were built less as places in which to watch movies than as places in which to worship the gods. Vaulted ceilings rose hundreds of feet. Statuary, curtained vestibules and intricate rococo flourishes cluttered the walls. Some, like the Grauman's Chinese Theatre in Hollywood, hardly even looked like theaters. No, these elaborate, baroque movie houses were more than theaters and more than palaces—they were temples, fit places for the American movie audiences to encounter their stars.

The biggest of them all was the Roxy in New York. It cost $10 million to construct, sat over 6,200 people, contained six box offices and unbelievable ornamentation. The promotional literature called it "The Cathedral of the Motion Picture" —and it was not far wrong. What the European cathedrals of the twelfth and thirteenth centuries were to the Age of Faith, the great movie palaces were to the great age of movies.

The Great, Gilded Movie Palaces

The designers of these palaces spared nothing. Writes Ben M. Hall in *The Best Remaining Seats:* □ "The architecture of the movie palace was a triumph of suppressed desire and its practitioners ranged in style from the purely classic to a wildly abandoned eclectic that could only have come from men who, like the Khan himself, 'on honeydew had fed, and drunk the milk of Paradise'."

The theater designers pursued incredible effects. It was not enough to build walls studded with the most baroque, jewel-like fixtures. Soon the theaters took on a fresh attempt: what John Eberson, the initial designer, called "atmospheric." In an atmospheric theater, there were more than statues and balconies and embroidery; various techniques were used to give the moviegoers the sense of being next to a star-studded lagoon or underneath a moonlit sky. Eberson has said of Holblitzelle's Majestic Theatre in Houston, Texas, that it was "a magnificent amphitheater under a glorious moonlit sky . . . an Italian garden, a Persian court, a Spanish patio, or a mystic Egyptian temple-yard . . . where friendly stars twinkled and wisps of cloud drifted." Friendly stars twinkling? Wisps of clouds drifting? While the movie was showing? Exactly. In these cathedrals of illusion, one had only to add another projector to cast another illusion. Projectors, such as the Brenograph, were used to depict clouds and stars on the naked ceilings.

Loew's King's Theatre *left wall from stage*

Loew's King's Theatre *proscenium arch from balcony*

Neither Byzantium at its height nor Persia in its most glorious era had ever known quite the extravagance which the designers and theater chain owners lavished on these grand palaces in the twenties. Many of them are gone now, victims of urban blight, urban renewal, or simply a changing attitude toward movies. Indeed, from the beginning of the Depression, even though Hollywood thrived, the movie palaces were already out of step with the mood of the country. Yet a few remain, dotting the inner core of large cities, reminders of a time when people believed in movies with a fervor of almost religious intensity.

Loew's King's Theatre *foyer from mezzanine looking toward lobby*

FRED W. MURNAU

The rise of the German film in the early twenties gave Hollywood not only a jolt of competition from an unexpected quarter—defeated Germany—but also made audiences a little more conscious than ever before of the artistic possibilities of the motion picture. The natural response of the American studios was to import German directors. Fred W. Murnau's German films (most notably *The Last Laugh*, *Tartuffe*, and *Dracula*) had shown a new understanding of the potential of the movie camera. In *The Last Laugh* (1924), he handled many lengthy shots with a totally fluid, mobile camera. The camera would wander through a scene, not simply zipping across straight tracks, but ambling in and out of corridors and other places, becoming an observer rather than simply a recorder of the action.

Murnau's first, and by far his most important, American film was *Sunrise* (1927). Brought over by the Fox Film Corporation in 1924, Murnau was given a totally free hand at making whatever movie he wanted. The Fox people watched, astounded, as Murnau had a set for a city constructed—hardly a realistic city, more an abstract, semi-dream city with cavernous halls and splendid entrance ways.

The film was developed in two parts. The first part took place on a farm. It told briefly the story of a simple man and his wife, splintered by a woman from the city who had won the husband's affections and who encouraged him to drown his wife and claim her death as an accident. Part two follows the man and his wife through the

city. Here the mood, and even the style, changes. It is as though Murnau had sought out two camera styles to depict a pastoral world and the cosmopolitan urban world.

Sunrise is a film rich in texture and stylization, and more notable for its gentle shifts in mood than its narrative. Murnau used the techniques popular among German filmmakers of the twenties: soft-focus, mists, double exposures, soft lighting, obviously artificial sets to achieve a kind of stylization previously foreign to the American screen.

Murnau's style is so totally visual and evocative as to require almost no titles. Every scene is rich in imagery, much of it solely to evoke a mood or articulate visually an impression. In the scene on the lake, where the husband anticipates murdering his wife, the trees hang low and despondent, and mists cling to the water. The entire world at that moment becomes a reflection of the young man's dark and seething mind.

Murnau made two more films in Hollywood: *The Four Devils* (1928) and *Our Daily Bread* (1931). Like many other silent film directors, he felt that the art of the motion picture lay in its silence, and that the sound picture could never truly evolve as an art. The question of what Murnau would have done in an era totally dominated by the sound film has never been answered, however. After filming *Tabu* with Robert Flaherty in the South Seas, Murnau returned to Hollywood and died shortly after.

"Real art is simple," Murnau said in *Theatre Magazine*, January 1928, "but simplicity requires the greatest art. The camera is the director's sketching pencil. It should be as mobile as possible to catch every passing mood, and it is important that the mechanics of the cinema should not be interposed between the spectator and the picture. . . . The film director must divorce himself from every tradition, theatrical or literary, to make the best possible use of his new medium."

Sunrise 1927

ERNST LUBITSCH

Of all the directors brought over from Europe in the twenties, none reached the top of the Hollywood establishment so quickly, or in such a grand manner, as Ernst Lubitsch. The very name Lubitsch came to mean, in the late twenties and early thirties, that lucky (if not lofty) combination of artistic quality and box office success that Hollywood so admired. Movies like *The Marriage Circle* (1924), *Kiss Me Again*, *Lady Windemere's Fan* (1925) and *So This Is Paris* (1926) were successful with the critics and the public.

Lubitsch's movies are a kind of genre unto themselves: movies of manners, almost, in which, as film critic Andrew Sarris stated so well, "grace transcends purpose." As a director whose spirit remained in many ways with the order and decorum of pre-war Europe, he made films in which the slightest failures in human behavior—from bad table manners to an abrupt apology—became the focal points of a film, the keys to its moral structure.

Yet Lubitsch adjusted himself to America in ways that few other émigré directors ever have. He became, like DeMille, a barometer of public taste, gradually slipping more and more into his films—and becoming very shrewd about what he would leave out. Lubitsch followed sexual involvements and breakdowns between couples with a touch of innuendo so exact that it always let the audience in on what was happening, but never even began to faze the censors. His talent for getting his characters into one another's boudoir—without quite getting into bed on screen—came to be known as the Lubitsch touch: a cool style for handling the hottest of movie subjects.

The arrival of sound did not threaten Lubitsch nearly so much as did most of the prominent directors of the twenties. Typically, Lubitsch played it cool. He waited several years to let the primitive thrust of the sound film—sound for sound's sake—work itself out. He watched a number of movies very carefully, and by the time he moved into production on a sound film—*The Love Parade* in 1930—he knew, far better than most directors of the time, exactly what he was doing. Just as *Forbidden Paradise* had been a model for sophisticated comedies in the twenties, The *Love Parade*, a sprightly, witty musical, became the model for dozens of musicals in the early thirties. In *The Love Parade*, verbal banter rarely distracts from the visual flow. The cutting between scenes is smooth, and often incisive in its juxtapositions. The camera doesn't hold still for long, unflagging scenes, but moves deftly around the characters, within the scenes, retaining the fluidity it had in the mid-twenties.

Lubitsch went on to broaden his form. He experimented with musicals, a more earthly type of comedy, and a fresh type of historical romance. Yet his sympathies remained with subjects and sensibilities that were in many ways closer to audiences of the twenties that audiences of the thirties. While he never stopped being inventive and never lost any of the deft competence that made him the grand master of the movie of manners, Lubitsch gradually lost touch with drastically changing times. After the mid-thirties, audiences gradually found his comedy too sophisticated and chose the more familiar devices of a Frank Capra or a Preston Sturges.

64

ERICH VON STROHEIM

Murnau was a poet of lyrical grace who struggled with the Hollywood establishment. Lubitsch made comedies that were successful enough to enable him to conquer Hollywood. In no émigré director, however, was the relationship with the Hollywood establishment so stormy, so uneven, ultimately so catastrophic, as that of Erich von Stroheim. Here was a man who excited the imagination of the moviemaking world at the beginning of the twenties in a way no one had done quite since Griffith—yet a man who would, within half a decade, be outlawed by that very industry.

The dominant tradition in the silent film was the one which can be traced back to the Lumières at the turn of the century: illusion as the basis for man's fascination with movies. Whether a melodrama, a horse opera, or a Chaplin comedy, most movies presumed a somewhat different world on the screen, and they appealed largely because of that presumption. Erich von Stroheim created movies that seemed to work outside of that tradition. They were imbued with a startling realism, a sense of actual life, and real people. What the novels of Frank Norris and Theodore Dreiser were to the romantic popular fiction of the time, von

Stroheim's movies were to the whole industry: the tough, stern stuff of the natural world.

Unlike most of the other émigré directors, von Stroheim came to America in his youth, not after he had made several movies abroad. He began in the industry working with D. W. Griffith, Douglas Fairbanks, and Thomas Ince. Out of a job after the war, he went to the home of Carl Laemmle, the head of Universal Pictures, and asked to make movies. Laemmle enabled him to make *Blind Husbands* (1918). It began a career that spanned only 14 years, but which changed the industry.

In all his films, von Stroheim was obsessed with the most devastating human vices: greed, lust, debauchery. His early films—*Blind Husbands, The Devil's Passkey* (1919), *Foolish Wives* and *Merry-Go-Round* (1922)—all treated this theme in a realistic, effective way, avoiding most of the melodramatic conventions and tendencies of other films of the time. However, it was *Greed* (1925) that made von Stroheim's genius as a filmmaker fully apparent.

Based on Frank Norris' novel *McTeague*, *Greed* is a wrenching, grisly tale of the power that lust for gold can have to break

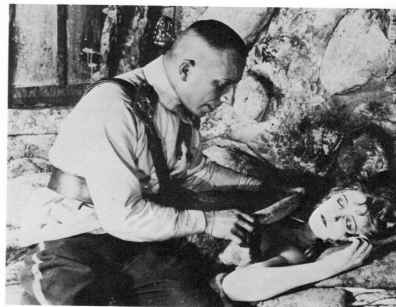

Foolish Wives 1922

Greed 1923/24

down human relationships and disintegrate
a personality. The film begins with the court-
ship and marriage of Mac and Trina, both
from a mining community. Von Stroheim
concentrates on particular details to suggest
not only their relationship but their larger
relationship to the world around them. In
one shot, for instance, at the train station,
Mac embraces Trina just as a train roars
by—the train suggesting the pent-up feelings
in Mac. Close-ups—of Mac picking at his
nose or moving his fingers across his leg
nervously—catch his character brilliantly.
Somewhat in the manner of Lubitsch, von
Stroheim uses inflection as a major form
of character development.

Greed is filled with brief sardonic moments and juxtapositions for which von
Stroheim was famous. During the wedding
ceremony between Mac and Trina, we
glimpse a funeral procession through the
window of the house. When Mac murders
Trina for the money she has so scrupulously
saved, the Christmas decorations add grim,
mordant commentary.

Von Stroheim spares the audience nothing. Where so often he could use sentimentality or leave an emotional impact clear
and unclouded, he goes on and gives us
more, stealing from us an easy identification
or the satisfaction of having the heavy mood
dissipated. In one scene, for example, Mac
comes into the house, starving, and begs for
food. He argues that he has not eaten in
days, and that even a dog deserves to be
fed. No audience could be ready for what
happens at that point. Trina raises her finger

—the one that Mac had earlier bit partly off—and says bluntly, "Not a dog that bites you."

Von Stroheim's original version of *Greed* filled 70 reels: almost 20 hours were required to view it. The studios had to cut it down, and—despite von Stroheim's sharp denunciation of studio butchery—managed to avoid wrecking it completely. Yet the breaks in narrative flow needed to be filled with titles, and *Greed*, for all its visual power, is inextricably tied to far more titles than it deserves—and perhaps far more than it requires.

There were other faults: von Stroheim established a mood and never let up, which made for a kind of sustained monotony and unrelieved heaviness. Structurally, the story was weak with much that was vague or inexplicable. Yet *Greed* was a major accomplishment of the American film, a movie perhaps as honest and relentless in its pursuit of human beings as any ever made.

Not surprisingly, *Greed* was a box-office flop. The times were too bright to sustain interest in a movie as grim and pessimistic as this. Von Stroheim, not yet accustomed to the idea of becoming a martyr for art in Hollywood, bounced back into favor with the producers by making *The Merry Widow*. A brusque, sexual comedy much in the manner of Lubitsch, *The Merry Widow* had an undertone of sarcasm, sometimes even of cynicism, as von Stroheim deftly cut below his laughing, abandoned characters to show the ultimate emptiness of their lives.

Even though *The Merry Widow* grossed over four million dollars—an enormous return on a movie for that period—von Stroheim had alienated the producers by heaping up enormous expenses in production. He was a realist not only in the effects he wanted to achieve on film, but in the organization of minor props. For one sequence involving a Prussian army, for example, von Stroheim ordered genuine Prussian underwear for all extras. Such fidelity to minute detail, studios found of no help in producing motion pictures. Von Stroheim found himself increasingly out of favor with them, and though he was able to make several more movies, only one, *The Wedding March* (1928), was released in a condition hardly resembling the form in which he had prepared it.

By the early 1930s, von Stroheim was blacklisted by the film industry. Yet the prophet was not without honor in his own country. The tough naturalism that he had fought to achieve influenced a number of younger directors, such as King Vidor, William K. Howard, Mervyn LeRoy, and Josef von Sternberg.

The Merry Widow 1925

The Wedding March 1926/27

THE SERIALS

Ming, the emperor of the planet Mongo, speaks, his long mustache curled down almost to the collar of his robe: "Radioactivity will make me Emperor of the Universe, of the Planets, of all Creation!" Dale Arden, Flash Gordon's girl, stands trapped by two of Ming's grisly henchmen awaiting that terrible moment when the gong sounds and she becomes wed to him forever, inextricably. Meanwhile,

Flash has been trapped in a sealed vault with spiked walls, that even now are closing in on him like a slow-moving vice. The walls grow closer and closer, and the sharp spikes begin to touch Flash's clothes, and. . . . THE END! Continued next week.

Up until the advent of television, the serials were as much a part of the movies as popcorn. In the silent years, the serials took the normally melodramatic tendencies of the silent film to even more uncanny proportions: not only once would the heroine be tied to a railway track, but two, or even three times! And, whenever a reel would end without a train coming, there would always be a handy sawmill or cliff to threaten our heroine. Such serials as *Bound and Gagged* (1919), *The Adventures and Emotions of Edgar Pomeroy*

(1920-21), *Go Get 'Em Hutch* (1922), *Perils of Pauline* (two versions—1914 and 1933), *The Lightning Raider* (1918-19), and *The Veiled Mystery* (1920) drew audiences back week after week (or in some cases night after night) to see what had become of the heroes and heroines they had left dangling at the edge of destruction in the end of the previous episode.

The sound film brought to the serial the enormous possibilities of a musical track (always loud and ferocious music) and more elaborate sets, but little in the way of added sophistication. The serials were much like the comic strips from which many of them were drawn (Batman, Superman, Little Orphan Annie, Dick Tracy, Flash Gordon, Buck Rogers, Red Ryder, Captain America, The Phantom): very little plot, very little character development, but unflagging action and impossible situations. RKO, Columbia, Universal, and particularly Republic Studio churned out dozens of serials each year to meet audience demand. Saturday afternoon matinees were nothing without at least one ongoing serial. And some theaters booked two or three in lieu of a double feature.

(By the way, Flash makes it out of the squeezing walls all right, just in time to stop the gong; but he winds up smashing into an active volcano at the end of the next reel . . .)

Flash Gordon 1936

The Wind 1928

VICTOR SEASTROM

Murnau, Lubitsch and von Stroheim had come to America from Germany; Seastrom was from Sweden. He was closest in technique and spirit to Murnau, a lyricist of the camera who believe in capturing the raging struggle between man and his environment —whether the raging forces of nature or the social world. But Seastrom chose to emphasize selected detail within the shot—much as von Stroheim—rather than move the camera. Whereas other German-American directors like Murnau, Lubitsch, and von Stroheim were fascinated with peculiar angle shots and long, complex camera dollies, Seastrom used the camera merely to record the images he felt most valuable for the film.

Most of Seastrom's efforts are representative of the better silent films: *He Who Gets Slapped* (1924), *The Tower of Lies* (1924) and *The Scarlet Letter* (1926) are particularly fine films. Seastrom's great film, however, is *The Wind* (1928), a movie which unfortunately was all but totally missed by the public because it appeared at the time of the first deluge of sound films.

The Wind is a kind of master allegory about man and his relationship to the elements. Structurally it uses a tragic love story (and a melodramatic one) as the framework upon which to build a study of the impact that the wind makes upon two people, and the ways in which the wind reflects their passions, fears, and loneliness. Throughout the film, the wind appears, its mood proportionate to the mood of the characters. The wind is responsible for the meeting between the Eastern girl and the cowhand, and it whips through a desolate world as he violates her. As the film progresses, the girl (Lillian Gish in perhaps her best-acted role) is driven to obsession by the wind, which seems to have stripped her of all refinements of the East and exposed her to a naked, destitute world. The windstorm reaches a climax when the girl's madness finally pushes her to murder.

In *Cinema*, C. A. Lejeune wrote:

With the Scandinavians, as with no other people in the world, we get a vivid sense of inborn life in every stick and stone; the craftsman merely gives utterance to a mute energy, develops a power already lying dormant. The old personification of the elements has never quite left the Scandinavian mind, and wind, wood, water, are still alive; light and darkness are still elementals.

While Seastrom, like other European directors, modified his craft within the American studio system, his American films—particularly *The Wind*—retained something of that Swedish fascination with the elements.

The Wind 1928

The Scarlet Letter 1926

He Who Gets Slapped 1924

The Scarlet Empress 1934

THE FACE OF THE POSTWAR FILM

World War I had changed American life more drastically than anyone at the time recognized. Until 1914 many aspects of American society had remained fundamentally consistent with the way they had been 20, or 30, or 40 years earlier. It was as though the war, a shattering blow to so many of the comfortable illusions cherished by the Victorian era, had epitomized the entire transformation going on within Western society. The movies reflected this change, and the differences in films before and after the war were acute.

One fundamental change within movies lay in audiences. Before the war, movie audiences tended to be lower-class workingmen and their families, and most movies were made specifically for that audience. But as the nation grew wealthier in the twenties, many of the people who had been considered lower-class moved into new houses, bought refrigerators and radios, and became the new middle class. Movies after the war were made to appeal to the middle class; they dealt more with man at leisure than man at work. They didn't usually assume economic hardship, but assumed a certain basic wealth—man's ability to spend a dollar on the spur of the moment if he wished.

Most drastically, films of the twenties reflected a basic change in the moral climate of the country. The Victorian ethic of duty —duty to one's family, to one's country, to one's religion, to one's job—had permeated films up to and during the war. In a pre-war film, the classic hero would be torn between his duty to his wife and the hot lips of the vamp. He might fall before temptation, but

before the film was over he would repent
to his wife. Clearly, he had sinned. In 1919,
Cecil B. DeMille's *Male and Female* broke
through this neat curtain of duty and fidelity.
The film depicted a butler (Thomas Mei-
ghan) and a genteel lady (Gloria Swanson)
cast adrift on a desert island. The point of
the film was that, though the lady was married (and not to the butler), duty didn't
matter. Class barriers and a whole range of
Victorian principles were dismantled in that
film, to the utter delight of postwar audiences.

The new permissiveness appeared in films
of the twenties in a myriad of ways. Largely
due to DeMille, bedrooms and bathrooms
became key locales, and enormous, expensive sets were designed to catch the aura
of magnificence and glitter that marked so
much of Hollywood's style in that period.
The old standard distinctions between good
guys and bad guys, between vamps and vir-
gins, between sin and sanctity, broke down
as Hollywood probed more complex motives
and a changing moral climate. It was not
that stereotypes had disappeared, rather
that old stereotypes were replaced with new
ones. The vamp disappeared, to be replaced
by the flapper or the good-bad girl. The
churlish villain with waxed mustache left
the screen, only to be replaced by a dozen
less obvious (but no less crafty or spiteful)
variants.

Part of this fresh approach to screen material in the twenties can be seen in the elab-
oration of different types of films, from the
relatively new bedroom romp to the older,
but now more sexually pointed exotic adventure.

The Devil Is a Woman 1935

Underworld 1927

BEDROOM ROMPS

Whether handled with a Continental brilliance and all the pomp of pre-war aristocracy by a Lubitsch or strictly played for laughs in the familiar American way, the bedroom romp or the sexual-triangle movie tended to be quite popular through the twenties. Elinor Glyn, whose books on a rich but decadent aristocracy had been bestsellers before 1914, was hired by MGM to write scripts. What she did was to oversee productions like *Three Weeks* (1924), *His Hour* (1924), and *Love's Blindness* (1926). These films, all about the indiscretions and failings of royalty, were popular enough to generate many more stories like them.

The popularity of aristocracy, royalty, and the rich-but-decadent people during the twenties—a time when America as never before turned middle class—offers some suggestions on the real appeal of movies and how that appeal intersects with a cultural mood.

The spirit of the twenties was wild and extravagant. It was the age of jazz, raccoon coats, flivvers and flappers, a nation reeling beneath the loose clamps of prohibition. Decadence and sexual license were prime movie subjects, but best presented within some context, however remote. With aristocrats and royalty, audiences could share vicariously the fun of sexual innuendo and frolic while at the same time silently clucking their tongues at the obvious moral decadence they saw portrayed. Besides, with the very rich, everything was so splendid, so opulent. Decadence could at least have its proper setting.

THE EXOTIC ADVENTURE

One of the most successful movies of the entire era of the silent film was *The Sheik*, starring the greatest of the Latin lovers, Rudolph Valentino. Intended originally as a minor film starring a little-known ex-dishwasher, the film swept the country. Valentino's sheik was a kind of Arabian prince who had little more to do than lure women into his tent. The women protested, but never too vigorously. Commenting on Valentino's acting, producer Adolph Zukor said that it "was largely confined to protruding his large, almost occult, eyes until the vast areas of white were visible, drawing back the lips of his wide, sensuous mouth to bare his gleaming teeth and flaring his nostrils."

Perhaps more of a movie phenomenon than Valentino and his imitators was the plethora of exotic adventures: desert sagas, swashbuckler epics, historical romances of all kinds. Movies like *The Mark of Zorro*, *Son of the Sheik*, *The Black Pirate*, *Don Juan*, and *Beau Geste* gave the twenties much of their flair and romantic vitality. Stars like John Barrymore, Francis X. Bushman, Douglas Fairbanks, and Ramon Navarro fired the public imagination of the time by their masculine, always active performances.

The Sheik 1921

THE WESTERN

Westerns are as old as the movies themselves. Some films in the Library of Congress catalogue for 1895-1903 are obviously about the West, men and horses, men and guns. The relationship is not surprising. The "formula" Western contains, after all, the key ingredients for a successful use of the motion picture. There is always plenty of action, movement, and scenery in the chase, the showdown, and the gunfight.

The first Western hero was an unlikely one. Bronco Billy, or Gilbert M. Anderson, was an unsuccessful vaudeville performer who turned to one-reeler Westerns in 1907. For over 10 years he turned them out, rarely varying from a basic sheriff-bad guy-posse-capture formula. Yet, for the period, they were enormously popular with movie audiences, popular enough to stimulate larger efforts.

William S. Hart began his career as a Western actor just about the time that Bronco Billy's was peaking. Previously a Broadway actor, Hart presented a convincing figure on the screen: lithe, with a tough facial expression (as opposed to Bronco Billy's rather bulkier figure). He brought not only excellent acting to the Western but a new concept of the genre—as a framework for fairly complex dramas, in which good and bad were not always totally separate. He came to be known as "the good bad man," an outlaw who could, in instances, side with the law. His films reflect the real West in a way that few films for the next few decades would: a rugged and violent place that could only be tamed by rugged and violent men.

William S. Hart

Since he was an outlaw, the Hart character often had to meet a tragic end—unthinkable in later Westerns, but basic to the kind of dramas that Hart developed. In 1923, the French critic Louis Delluc wrote of Hart, known to the French as Rio Jim (*The Movies*, Griffith and Mayer):

I think that Rio Jim is the first real figure established by the cinema . . . and his life the first really cinematic theme, already a classic—the adventures of an adventurer in search of fortune in Nevada or the Rocky Mountains, who holds up the mail coach, robs the mails, burns the rancher's house, and marries the sheriff's daughter.

After 1920, Hart's films, though still forthcoming from the Ince studios, lost their popularity. Hart complained—and rightly—that the studios did not want to do anything that interfered with their own (and the public's) concept of the Old West. For Hart, who had grown up amid the Sioux Indians, a Western required some authenticity. He constantly lamented "errors that would make a Western man refuse to speak to his own brother." But the studios were out to establish a myth, not capture a real past, and Hart, despite the quality of his films, was a casualty of the trend toward the Hollywood Western.

It was the next major figure of the Hollywood Western, Tom Mix, who created the model on which Western stars have since been cast. Like Hart, Mix's background contained real experiences in the West: he had been a sheriff in Kansas, a deputy marshal in Oklahoma, and a Texas Ranger. Nonetheless, Tom Mix avoided the authentic Western developed by Hart in favor of the romantic West through which a lone man rode and conquered all oppressions— a kind of sagebrush Robin Hood.

As the twenties wore on, Mix's movies often came to resemble DeMille's epics rather than simple adventure stories. The sets became cluttered and garish, and the costuming far more glittering and ostentatious than anything known in the real West. But this fazed neither Tom Mix nor his fans. By the end of the twenties, Tom Mix had established himself as one of the major characters in Hollywood's own fanciful movie of itself.

Tom Mix

Bronco Billy, William S. Hart, and Tom Mix formed the major thrust in the development of the Western during the silent period. But there was another trend, strictly during the twenties, which would be more important in terms of later films—the Western epic. The most famous of these, *The Covered Wagon*, was made in 1923. Although filled with the kind of unreal details that William S. Hart so often derided (no wagon train would camp for the night in a box canyon), the movie was an enormous box-office success, and spawned others of its kind, such as *The Pony Express* (1925) and *The Pioneer Scout* (1928). Only later, however, at the hands of masters like John Ford and Anthony Mann, would the Western find its true expression in great moviemaking.

The Covered Wagon 1923

King Vidor

SOCIAL REALISM

The twenties was not a rich period for
films of bold social commentary and criticism—not, at least, in the way that the
thirties would be. Some movies stand out,
however, as major accomplishments of social analysis and almost documentary realism. Among these perhaps the greatest was
King Vidor's *The Crowd*.

Made in 1928, *The Crowd* anticipated
the thirties in attempting a new kind of
storytelling. Rather than focusing on larger-
than-life figures, it treats the relatively normal lives of two people who meet in a
crowd. What makes the movie such a drastic
contrast to most of the Hollywood products
of the time is its total avoidance of the standard situations and characters. It is a film
without a hero, without a heroine, without
a star, without virtually any romantic theme
or ending.

The Crowd is a chilling and convincing
movie. The opening shot uses a roving camera to suggest the sweep and majesty of the
modern city, then selects one skyscraper,
tilts upward, catching the windows and the
men who look alike and sit behind identical
desks. The camera keeps moving, probing,

82

until finally it selects one man out of this crowd—and follows that man into other crowds. Throughout the film, King Vidor startles the audience with further and further indications of the tragic isolation of this man in the midst of the modern urban masses. When the baby is dying, for example, the father, feeling that his child's death is being hastened by the noises from the street, rushes down and tries—in a bold yet vain attempt—to stop the traffic.

Vidor's use of space is fascinating in this movie. In few other motion pictures is the long shot used consistently so well. Visually, the motif is a mass movement or a standardized repetition of forms against which one man moves with increasing boldness, and in utter desolation and failure. The film anticipates the novels of Franz Kafka and the films of Michelangelo Antonioni in showing the individual as helpless and alienated in the unfeeling mass of modern society.

Needless to say, *The Crowd* was not financially successful. It would take the Depression and years of real hardships to turn the American audiences and Hollywood toward social realism.

Not the least of Hollywood's accomplishments in the twenties was to become the world center of a new, shimmering aristocracy: the movie stars. As the twenties became more crazed, more raucous, it became apparent that nowhere were the extravagances of the country better reflected than in that capital of the new American mythology—Hollywood.

One of the poignant threads in the history of our society's relationship to the movies has been our adulation of the star. Of course the star system can be explained as the invention of some clever producers about 1912, men who, with the aid of well-paid publicity departments, were able to create public sensations of a handful of actors and actresses, on screen and off. But the star system worked only because it struck a chord, met some kind of need—and not one totally fabricated by the studios.

A major theme running through all societies, the anthropologists tell us, is the need for mythical heroes: men (and sometimes women) whose lives reach higher proportions, achieve greater stature than ours, and to whom we can look as models for our behavior and our customs. In a world bereft of the old Christian certainties—and heroes—the movie stars became our new secular saints. They were well fitted for it. They were beautiful people, and when we saw them, they were always larger than life on a shimmering screen and surrounded by a more exotic, less precarious and less dull world.

It was, of course, part of the allure of Hollywood that the stars soon began to imitate their movies. In this new land of Oz, the line between the reel world and the real world became more and more ill-defined. Stars built themselves enormous mansions with unbelievably expensive furnishings and fixtures often inspired by sets for films they had completed. A studio publicity department eagerly and vividly described to the world Marion Davies' 14-carat gold ceiling. The stars, after all, were another kind of citizenry: by all rights they should inhabit a loftier and more extravagant world.

It was in the twenties that the myth of Hollywood, tangled with the economic and entertainment fact of Hollywood, became a fixture in the American imagination. Hollywood has never attained the splendor, the haughtiness, or the calculated decadence of those years: the diamond-studded robes, the manipulated marriages and divorces and re-marriages, the publicity departments' enormous parties. The Depression would force stars to become more like earthly mortals. The sound film would steal a little of their immortality by making them more like us—giving them a voice. Besides, another trend had already begun early in the twenties which would hasten tighter studio controls on the Hollywood extravagances—the Will Hays Office.

Hollywood, of course, thrived on scandals. But in the early twenties they reached a tempo that brought violent public indignation to the studio door. In 1922, the murder of the director William Deane Taylor (William D. Tanner), brought out a strange triangle between him and his two leading ladies: Mabel Normand and Mary Miles Minter. Months earlier another Hollywood actress, Virginia Rappé, who appeared in numerous two reelers, was found dead after a party given by Roscoe "Fatty" Arbuckle (one of Mack Sennett's comedians). Fatty Arbuckle was accused of manslaughter and, though freed legally, was blacklisted by the studios. Finally, the death of Wallace Reid at 30 revealed him as a drug addict and led to a pressman's holiday on the excesses of movie people.

Public pressure grew. Studio executives, dismayed by what they recognized as an interior threat to a system they had struggled hard to build, decided they needed a moral watchdog. Following the example of baseball, they chose someone reputed for his unimpeachable moral rectitude: Will Hays, Postmaster-General under the Harding administration.

Hays was given the powers of a czar. He could fire actors, have scenes deleted from scripts of finished movies, or even keep a movie from being distributed. He actually went further, tempering the language of publicity departments in their press releases. Finally, he turned to movie production itself to fight the evils by means of the system. With director James Cruze he made *Hollywood*, the story of a girl who comes to Hollywood and does *not* become a star. (One particular evil of Hollywood at the time was the number of young girls who came to Hollywood lusting after stardom and winding up as prostitutes.) Another Hays-inspired effort, *Human Wreckage*, starred Wallace Reid's widow in a vehement attack on narcotics. (For more information on the influence of the Hays Office, see ". . . Enter the Hays Office . . . Cut!" page 116.

Of course, even Will Hays could not reform a city that existed more in the public imagination than in reality. Hollywood mattered less for what happened there—or even for what the press releases claimed happened there—than for the imprint it made upon American culture, the new mythical Olympus it had become. Hollywood, as the anthropologist Hortense Powdermaker put it so well, had become the dream factory of American society. But no dream was put over quite so well as Hollywood itself in the roaring twenties.

**Chapter Four
From Boffo to Belly Laugh:
The Silent Comedians**

Mack Sennett

Of all the arts developed in movies of the silent period, none plunged downhill so swiftly or so completely as comedy. Though few were fully aware of it at the time, the addition of sound was to mean for the screen the loss of that rollicking, side-wrenching humor so familiar to the silent screen.

There were any number of things that made silent comedy as lively as it was: the soundless screen's affinity for wild chases, violent fights and all the stuff of slapstick; the genius of men like Mack Sennett and Buster Keaton, who were able to seize upon the potential of a form which was new enough to make every fresh excursion a new discovery; audiences who held no assumptions about what they would be shown, but only wanted to be amused and led into gales of laughter.

Most of the great names we associate with silent comedy were the performers: Charles Chaplin, Buster Keaton, Harold Lloyd, Harry Langdon, Stan Laurel and Oliver Hardy. But in terms of creating an entire style of movie comedy—the style which dominated the period and profoundly influenced every performer including Chaplin and Keaton—the most important figure was Mack Sennett, head of the Keystone Company. Though not a performer himself, he was one of America's great all-time comic geniuses.

MACK SENNETT

He began as an actor with D. W. Griffith at Biograph, and he learned from Griffith what makes a movie exciting and valuable for an audience—that it has to move, that tempo and flamboyance can be more important than structure or narrative tidiness. By the time he began his Keystone Company in 1912, he had definite ideas on the best tricks of movie comedy. His ideas turned out to be sure-fire; by 1916, Mack Sennett was established as one of three great directors of the time, alongside Griffith and Ince.

Sennett made two kinds of movies: parodies and slapstick. The parodies would pounce upon some popular movie or social event and, through the spiraling, dizzying circumlocutions of inane events, utterly deflate whatever had been there to begin with.

Slapstick was Sennett's favorite technique. For Sennett, slapstick meant that things should move faster than in normal life, happen more often, more drastically, and involve more people. If it was funny for one cop to get splattered with an egg, Sennett would have a dozen cops rounding a corner where a frightened girl would be heaving eggs—and every one a bull's-eye. If it was funny for a chase scene to turn into a fight, Sennett would turn it into a riot, involving a dozen "innocents" off the sidewalk who had no real idea what was going on, but who loved to brawl nonetheless.

Sennett used plots in his movies, but paid little attention to them. It's fairly normal in a Keystone movie to lose track of characters, indeed lose track of a whole line of development. Often, in production, a story would reach a certain point and somebody would suggest a wild excursion, like, "Let's have everybody fall into the swimming pool." Suddenly the story shifted drastically, and the earlier action was lost while everyone was busy falling or getting pushed into the swimming pool. In a sense, the movies were only a reflection of the madcap insanity that ran rampant at Keystone.

Sennett used old gags, new gags, improvised gags, totally abysmal flop gags. He seemed less concerned that a joke would work than it would keep the action going. Among his favorite gags were the constant threats that hot stoves, electric fans, or bulldogs could pose to clothing; the ability of a fence slat or a Ford seat to propel people hundreds of feet into the air; the chase scene in which the poor hero would be pursued by dozens of frenetic cops, many of them often reduced to wearing only underwear.

Objects themselves became funny in Sennett's films. Characters always had some prop with which to heighten the violence, but often these props didn't act as they were supposed to.

Sennett used the camera to highlight the action. While his comedy did not depend on the camera tricks of a Méliès to create a sense of the absurd, he often used speeded motion and jump-cuts for disappearances, but always solely within the structure of a story in which the action of the characters was the main focus of attention.

The Keystone Company was an informal place to work. While he oversaw all productions and often directed the movies himself, Sennett was aware that far more ideas were needed for a good running gag movie than he could provide. He was eager to draw ideas from anyone—actors, prop men, and cameramen. The spirit of the studio reflected that openness. In his brilliant essay, "Comedy's Greatest Era," James Agee described the story conferences:

Sennett used to hire a 'wild man' to sit in on his gag conferences, whose only job would be to think up 'wildies.' Usually he was an all but brainless, speechless man, scarcely able to communicate his idea; but he had a totally uninhibited imagination. He might say nothing for an hour; then he'd mutter 'You take . . .' and all the relatively rational others would shut up and wait. 'You take this cloud . . .' he would get out, sketching vague shapes in the air. Often he could get no further; but thanks to some

1 Hank Mann
2 Chester Conklin
3 Mabel Normand
4 Ford Sterling
5 Juanita Hansen
6 Ben Turpin
7 —
8 —
9 —
10 Mark Swain
11 —
12 —
13 —
14 —
15 —
16 Charlie Chase

kind of thought-transference, saner men would take this cloud and make something of it. The wild man seems in fact to have functioned as the group's unconscious mind, the source of all creative energy.

Sennett's films had at once the touch of the preposterous and the logic of real situations. Characters in Keystone films, for example, were very fat or very skinny, wore clothes that were either super-straight or downright ludicrous. Rooms inevitably were papered in the most garish, obvious kind of wallpaper imaginable, heavy polka-dot, for instance. Pies were always custard, and somehow never seemed to get eaten.

Yet, within this ridiculous world, the situations had a certain ring of honesty and authenticity. A married couple goes to bed in a bungalow on the beach and the next morning, when they awaken, gradually discover that they have been taken out on the tide. Two men fight over a girl who is really interested in neither of them. As the fight grows larger, it engages everyone within pie-throwing distance.

Sennett was a genius at calculating the ways in which a fairly everyday situation could escalate into a major fracas. And while all of them were wild, loaded with gags and preposterous kinds of violence, the basic truth of that escalation was always there. Slapstick never meant for Sennett—as it came to mean for future and lesser comics—a license to do anything inane or ridiculous. No matter how out-of-control a Sennett two-reeler looked, it never escaped the control of its producer.

It may be impossible to estimate the full impact that Sennett's work made upon movie comedy in the silent era. Almost every major movie comedian of that period—Keaton, Lloyd, Langdon, Chaplin—spent some time under Sennett's tutelage working at the Keystone studios. (Laurel and Hardy, whose career barely began in the silent period, worked for Sennett's rival, Hal Roach. But their best director, Leo McCarey, had trained at Keystone.) Sennett's influence on the movies can be seen in the stars and directors who—usually at the very beginning of their careers—trained with him: Gloria Swanson, Wallace Berry, Marie Dressler, Carole Lombard, Frank Capra, and George Stevens.

In the twenties, Sennett tried to modify his comedy. Though his popularity didn't decline, the speed and vitality of his movies did. But until the introduction of sound, Sennett remained the undisputed King of Comedy, and no one—except for the stars he himself had fashioned—could come near him in slapstick or parody.

Sennett's Keystone Lineup

"He-Men *Without* Women," by Ben Maddox. Hollywood Husbands on Holiday! Read this exclusive account of the unique vacation of Douglas Fairbanks, Jr., Robert Montgomery, and Laurence Olivier.

"*Why* Joan Crawford 'Gets' You," by William E. Benton. From Riches to *Rain!* How can the sensitive Crawford play hard-boiled Sadie Thompson? You'll want to read this intimate analysis of the girl whose character and career spell D-R-A-M-A.

"Why the Perfect Wife's Marriage Failed"
"Shirley Temple's Last Letter to Santa"
"Clark Gable Talks About Triangles"

They had titles like *Hollywood, Screenland, Photoplay, Modern Screen, Motion Picture*, and *Screen Book.* Some of the survivors, and plenty of their descendants, can be found on the magazine stand in the corner drugstore. But as Martin Levin points out in *Hollywood and the Great Fan Magazines,* the movie magazines were never quite the same after the thirties.

"The fan literature of the 30s," writes Levin, *"creates the Hollywood style and character. How else would you know that William Powell is a recluse who shuns publicity unless you read about it in four lavishly illustrated stories in four movie magazines during the same month? How else would you learn that Joan Bennett is hot tempered, favors blue and white in her beach house, and took Gene Markey from Ina Claire who married John Gilbert, who later married Virginia Bruce, who then married director J. Walter Rueben?"*

THE FAN MAGAZINES

WIN BING CROSBY'S PERSONAL RADIO!

5¢ a copy

Hollywood

April
NSC

5¢
SAME PRICE IN U.S.
AND CANADA

HOLLYWOOD

Natural Color Study of
GLORIA STUART
in "Shark Island"

I Guard SHIRLEY TEMPLE

The fan magazines told you all you needed to know about the stars and more. How Jean Harlow has overcome her personal tragedies. How Clark Gable overcame a threat to his marriage. How James Cagney grew up on the lower East Side of New York and how the movie gangster had almost become a real gangster. How Joan Crawford suffered because of her fame. You could read it all, including grief-stricken letters of fans who had lost faith in their stars, and the stars' advice on such homey things as preserving peaches or their oracular statements on momentous problems, such as **"Getting Him To Say I Do."**

The fan magazines offered a precious intermediary between the stars and the fans, indeed, almost a two-way form of communication. True, when a star was quoted as having "said" that she was the most happily married woman in Hollywood, in all likelihood the words belonged to her overworked press agent—but no matter; in the land of fan magazines, people believed their stars, and believed in what they said. In most of the magazines, and certainly in the best-selling of them, the emphasis lay in showing the star to be human and considerate, despite all the fame and money. Scandal stories or vicious bits of gossip rarely appeared. The magazines were not out to destroy stars or even, entirely, to exploit them; rather they existed to cement the bonds between moviemakers and their audiences—and this they did superbly in their heyday.

BUSTER KEATON

His face was a constant dead-pan, yet it was a rich, fascinating face, almost sweet, almost pathetic, almost tough, a face that became the constant counterpoint and expression of some of the funniest comedy ever to appear on the silent screen.

Buster Keaton started at a very early age in vaudeville, doing tumble acts with his parents. After a stint with Sennett, he eventually developed his own style. By the early twenties, he was directing his own films—some of them the most popular and successful comedies ever made.

Buster Keaton's films were in some ways the most unusual and original of the four great movie comics. To a large extent, Keaton sought a mode of comedy which was more cinematic, more classical, more metaphysical than that of Lloyd, Langdon, or Chaplin. Keaton was funnier fighting the elements than he was outracing cops or his girl's father (though he could be enormously funny then, too). There was always something abstract about Keaton's character: his dead-pan expression, his naked exposure to a world he didn't understand, his symbolic, recurrent gesture of staring at the far-off horizon, his hand to his forehead in the cliché Indian pose.

Throughout his films, the Keaton character remained somewhat the same. It didn't have the easy charm and warmth of Chaplin's tramp. Nonetheless, it encouraged audiences to identify, and to feel some peril and fear in the escapades in which he quickly became enmeshed. If Chaplin's films—particularly his early ones—often hovered on a sentimental brink, Keaton's movies frequently touched the edge of melodrama.

Keaton flirted with physical danger more often than Chaplin's tramp flirted with women. At times, he seemed a human automaton, at odds with all the products of technology in the modern world. He ran afoul of locomotives, automobiles, steamships, balloons, prefabricated houses. Keaton himself never used a stuntman, and some of his stunts were the most dangerous ever performed in movies. In one film, an entire wall of a house fell down on him, with Keaton escaping injury by just barely fitting through an open window frame. In another, he jumped onto a rope dangling from a branch jammed into rocks, over a 30-foot waterfall.

There is probably a greater abundance of cinematic tricks in Keaton's films than in the films of any of the other major comedians of the period. For one reason, Keaton was curious about the dual possibilities of the camera recording what happened in front of it and its ability to create illusions about what was happening. In *Balloonatics* (1923), the Keaton character stumbled into the basket of a runaway balloon. It deposited him with a lovely girl who's camping alone on a hillside. At first, the girl wants him to go away, but after he clubs a bear (somewhat unwittingly), she falls in love with him. The two take a canoe down the river, and are kissing oblivious of what the camera shows ahead—a monstrous waterfall. They go on kissing as the canoe drifts closer to the brink. When it finally reaches the waterfall, it doesn't go over but continues drifting on —through air. Only when the camera pulls back do we see that the canoe has somehow been hooked to the forgotten balloon.

The theme that recurs in Keaton's films, as his biographer Rudi Blesh observed, is

that of fantasy staying the hand of fate. It is as though Keaton were saying, "It's only a movie, and this is what movies are all about."

One of the most famous sequences in Keaton's films deals with the nature of movies. Besides being hilariously funny, it constitutes one of the most striking uses of film editing in the history of Hollywood film. In the opening scene of *Sherlock, Jr.* (1924), Keaton is lying asleep at the projector of a movie theater. A second, semi-transparent self rises from his body and goes down next to the screen. The film on the screen shows the front of a mansion. Buster walks into the picture and immediately becomes part of it. A character comes out of the door, walks around, goes back inside. Buster knocks on the door, but nothing happens. As he walks down the steps, the scene changes. Keaton finds himself stepping down onto a bench in a garden. He tumbles over, shakes himself, and begins to sit down when the scene shifts—Keaton sitting down on a busy street filled with heavy traffic. The scenes keep shifting: from the street, to a mountain precipice, to an African jungle, to a vast desert, to a rock in the middle of an ocean, to a snowbank. What makes this sequence so incredibly funny is not the constant switching of scenes, but Keaton's elaborate gymnastics which run through these scenes, so consistent and convincing that we are caught in the double world that has imprisoned him: the same body, but drastically changing locales.

Throughout all these events, Keaton seems unperturbed: his calm, granite face endures, despite the vengeance that an inconsiderate fate wreaks on him. As James

Agee said of that great Keaton face:

No other comedian could do so much with the dead pan. He used this great, sad, motionless face to suggest various related things: a one-track mind near the track's end of pure insanity; mulish imperturbability under the wildest of circumstances; how dead a human being can get and still be alive; an awe-inspiring sort of patience and power to endure, proper in granite but uncanny in flesh and blood.

The things that had made Keaton's comedy so great—the visual antics, the overlapping catastrophes, the rising crescendo of physical feats—were totally silent in their nature and appeal. They could not survive the sound film. Keaton attempted some movies after sound, but his voice, though it had the same dry, flaky quality of his body, ruined the simplicity and pure effect of his great silent creations.

Sherlock Jr. 1924

Harold Lloyd

HAROLD LLOYD

He looked a little out of place among the
other major comedians: the touch of sadness in Chaplin, the vague, distant gaze of
Keaton, the wide-eyed pathos of Langdon.
In contrast, Harold Lloyd was the all-American boy, perhaps a shade Ivy League—
wide-open smile, large impressive forehead,
horn-rimmed glasses. He was the kid down
the street who tried to sell you a magazine
subscription or a book of raffle chances.

Oddly enough, Lloyd began slavishly imitating Chaplin, then—aware of that extreme
—slavishly *not* imitating him. For the duration of his early years in Hollywood (1915-
1921), he swung from Chaplin imitations
(using a character called "Lonesome Luke")
to a series of breathless, stunt comedies
which also weren't his form. Only in 1922,
with *Grandma's Boy*, did Lloyd begin to
show himself as a major comedian in his
own right, someone who could draw laughs
without imitating older styles and without
using a repertoire of worn gags.

Grandma's Boy is not a particularly funny
or important comedy, but it does show the
beginning of Lloyd's true talent and appeal.
Structured like many films of genteel humor,
it told of a young man who was transformed
overnight by a story told by his grandmother—of how his grandfather had out-
witted some Union officers during the Civil

War. Lloyd drew on slapstick to portray this episode, but it is tempered slapstick, without the zaniness and anything-for-a-laugh antics of earlier slapstick. When one of the officers slaps Gramps on the back, for example, Gramps returns the gesture (in a beautiful economy of movement) by smashing a pistol butt over the man's head. The action is at once friendly and aggressive, reciprocal and original. We laugh, but the laugh has a new ring to it. It is that slightly off-key ring of laughter that Lloyd nurtured and developed in his best comedies.

There are a number of similarities between Chaplin's Tramp and Lloyd's childlike young man, but they tend to be surface similarities. At close inspection, they reveal significant differences. Both Chaplin and Lloyd strike the viewer as romantic souls wandering through a complex world, relating to it with a simplicity and innocence both touching and endearing. But Chaplin's way of dealing with the world tends to be aggressive, active, the result of initiative. Lloyd is different. He goes through the world doing the things he thinks he is supposed to do, and in that he is beset by improbability and by heightening complications. Chaplin, a little warier and wiser than Lloyd, can clobber a cop and smile—but that smile is not all innocence. When Gramps clobbers the

Union soldier, his smile *is* innocence. Lloyd not only maintains the illusion of his boyishness on the screen; he makes that the essence of the character's predicaments and humor.

No doubt the most famous sequence in Lloyd films—and perhaps the funniest—is the building-climbing episode in *Safety Last*. Here Lloyd plays a clerk who feels that, to win the love of his girl, he must succeed at something. As far as his job goes, he will be forever, inescapably, a clerk. So he decides to climb a six-story building, creating the reputation of a great human fly. Here we have one of the great sequences of silent comedy and one that points out its ultimate genius: the ability to make laughs rise on a rhythm that reaches ever higher and higher peaks.

The young man, of course, meets obstacles on his way up the buildings: six to be exact. The first is a flock of pigeons, who think of Harold as some misplaced statue, but for which they are nonetheless grateful. Escaping them, Harold barely makes it to the next ledge when someone in a sporting supply store drops a tennis net out the window. Harold struggles with the net, flailing out, exaggerating his motions until he is doing a precarious dance on the ledge. He seems unmindful of the distance

below, only frustrated at the clumsy net that appears to get more and more entangled. At one point, an onlooker comments, "Why don't you take the net off? It's in your way!"

Throughout the climb, Harold tries to greet each obstacle with a certain nonchalance—after all, the crowd below is watching, and his success as a human fly depends on this achievement. But the smile gradually erodes from his face as each obstacle becomes more menacing.

The classic obstacle is the clock—an enormous clock on the corner of the building for which Harold desperately grabs. As he pulls on the second hand, however, it springs downward and out. Desperately he grabs for a rope—just slightly out of reach —that a friend on top of the building has thrown him. What the audience knows— and Harold doesn't—is that the rope isn't attached to anything. Only at the second that Harold grabs the rope does his friend fasten it.

Once atop the roof, we want to sigh with relief. But Lloyd won't let us. Atop the ledge, he bumps into a wind gauge and wanders dizzily at the edge of the roof, swaying out toward the open crevass of the street below. Then—as if to reach even further pinnacles of the fantastic—he steps

Safety Last 1923

into a coiled flag rope and swings out, over the pole. Only after a few swings does he finally return to the building roof and into the arms of his girl.

The running theme in *Safety Last* is typical Lloyd: that man is caught in the web of his own manipulations. There is no enemy, no squadron of cops, no clique of aristocrats, who are so threatening to Lloyd as he is to himself. A certain dark current runs through his movies, an inescapable sense of the futility, pain, and embarrassment of trying to survive one's own efforts to improve one's place in the world.

In *The Freshman* (1925), Lloyd further amplifies some of his comic ideas and develops new ones. Of all his films, *The Freshman* has worn best over the years. As Donald McCaffrey comments in his study of silent comedians, it is no doubt the greatest comedy film ever made about university life.

What makes *The Freshman* successful is perhaps the ultimate alliance between Lloyd himself and the character he plays. The buoyant optimism of Lloyd, so pronounced in earlier films, had never had such an appropriate setting or story. There seemed no strain whatever, no discrepancy between that bright happy face and the character it played.

Lloyd, as Harold Lamb, the college freshman, desires social acceptance and will pay any price for it. He goes out for football and is made the tackling dummy. In one of the funniest scenes in the film, he is spilled over by a beefy tackler, and winds up kneeling down with the severed leg of a dummy twisted up in front of his own left leg, which is hidden from the sight of both Harold and the audience. The comic discovery of the false leg is crowned when he grabs the leg and pulls it free.

Harold Lamb brings out something that is present in all of Lloyd's characters, but muted elsewhere: the shining enthusiasm of

Harold Lloyd and Bebe Daniels

the zealous young. Lloyd never really tempers what he does. He jumps into every situation brightly confident of its outcome. As complications loom greater and greater, he never becomes concerned about the possibility of failure. Somehow that image, that undiminished confidence, that wholehearted enthusiasm, belong strictly to the twenties in a way that neither Chaplin nor Keaton comedies ever did. (Film critic Andrew Sarris suggested that the reason Lloyd was so unsuccessful in the sound film was not that his art was so profoundly silent, but because his buoyancy and enthusiasm never diminished, his face never seemed to age. His optimism could not survive the changed audiences of the Depression.)

Lloyd was less a creator of great films than of great film moments. While not of the stature of Chaplin or Keaton, he was clearly one of the major comics of the period and, at moments, one of the funniest.

Black Man

Too often we permit the glories and triumphs of Hollywood to obscure its deepest failures, and one of the greatest of these failures is its treatment—both on the screen and in the studios—of the Black man. From Edwin Porter's 1903 version of *Uncle Tom's Cabin,* through the downright racist viewpoint in Griffith's *Birth of a Nation,* and deep into the films of the Thirties and Forties, Negroes have been depicted in the most demeaning stereotypes and caricatures. What do we see of the Black man in Hollywood films before World War II? Bojangles and the black-faced troupe of singers; Hattie McDaniel's Mammy; Butterfly McQueen's shrill, manic Prissy in *Gone With The Wind;* and an unending succession of handymen, doormen, cooks, manservants, shoeshine boys and railroad porters.

Hollywood has too often consigned Blacks to roles and stock portrayals that lack dignity, intelligence, and character. Nervous about controversy and audience rejection, the studios tended most often to employ Blacks either to create a kind of nostalgic, Uncle Remus charm (as in *Hearts in Dixie* or Disney's *Song of the South)* or in displays of "Negro talent"— meaning song-and-dance offerings like *The Jazz Singer* and *Cabin in the Sky.*

Hollywood has made some striking attempts to present Blacks in a more honest, penetrating way. *Imitation of Life* (1934,

and a 1959 remake) dealt with the terrors of a black servant with a half-White daughter. *Intruder in the Dust* (1949), based on the Faulkner novel, depicts a Negro— played by Juano Hernandez—brought almost to a lynching; yet Hernandez's character is the most noble and dignified in the film. Elia Kazan's *Pinky* (1949) treats a light-skinned girl who can pass for White and her tense reception when she returns home to the South. *One Potato, Two Potato* (1964) deals openly with the pressures, external and internal, created by an interracial marriage. And *Nothing But a Man* (1964)—significantly an independent, non-studio production—takes the decisive step forward of dealing with Blacks not as exemplars of a Social Problem, but as people, so that by midway through the film we are no longer aware of color, but only of characters and their very human dilemma.

In recognition of the growing Black audience, Hollywood has tried to shape a number of Black "stars"—Jim Brown, Diahann Carroll, Godfrey Cambridge; but none has approached superstar status with anything near the success of Sidney Poitier. Poitier is an intriguing actor, less for his talents (which are considerable) than for his style, which tends, in fact, to limit the full use of his talents. In most of his roles Poitier is all style: he moves with

the deliberation, intensity, and precision of a man totally controlled from within and impeccably exact without. His toughness has little or nothing to do with sexuality or rage; it comes entirely from the fact that he has mastered the White man's culture and can outsmart or outmaneuver just about any White man in it. Poitier's best roles *(A Raisin in the Sun, Lilies of the Field, In the Heat of the Night)* have dealt with the subtle tensions between his cool, tough character and a White world's blanket reaction to his color: Where these tensions have been played too obviously, as in *Guess Who's Coming to Dinner,* Poitier has been reduced to a spoof of himself.

Poitier helped open new paths for Black actors and directors and technicians in Hollywood, as can be seen from films like *Cotton Comes to Harlem* (1970), a cop-genre film directed with unique flair by Ossie Davis. But perhaps more significant —and foreshadowing a fresh Black cinema of the Seventies—is Melvin van Peebles' sassy and insolent *Sweet Sweetback's Badasssss Song* (1971). Independently produced on a small budget, *Sweet Sweetback* is a brilliant reflection of the vitality and fantasies and rage of the ghettoes: at one moment wildly satirical, at the next moment hopelessly self-indulgent, the film succeeds in capturing the flavor and the tempo of urban Black culture as perhaps no previous film ever quite did.

The success of these films triggered a mild explosion of Black movies, many of

them mindlessly violent, few of them touching the full range of the Black experience. Calculated to exploit the large Black urban audience, these movies recalled, if only in quantity, an earlier era of film history.

In 1937, the *Motion Picture Review Digest,* in its review of the all-Black *Harlem on the Prairie,* estimated that there were about 800 inner city theaters, most of which specialized in totally Black productions. Most of the theaters have disappeared and with them many of the films they showed. What was once a thriving film industry in America—the production of all-Black feature films—has been almost forgotten.

Few people have heard of films like *Scar of Shame, Bronze Buckaroo, Broken Strings, Murder on Lennox Avenue, Moon Over Harlem,* or *Bargain With Bullets*—a few of the hundreds of Black productions made in America between 1914 and 1950. As Norman Kagen comments in his article "Black American Cinema: A Primer:" "The history of American Black filmmakers is almost a national secret." Few of the films are available in archives or among distributors; even less is known about the production companies and filmmakers who created them. Yet for over 30 years independent companies such as Gate City Film Corporation in Kansas City and individual like the energetic Oscar Micheaux in Harlem were producing features that were being seen throughout the country.

Hattie McDaniel

Sidney Poitier
Diahann Carroll

The early development of the American
[bl]ack film—from 1914 into the late twen-
[tie]s—was impelled by a "black-lash"—
[ag]ainst the racism of films like *Birth of a*
[Na]tion and the eagerness of entrepreneurs
[—]both Black and White—to draw upon
[th]e large potential audiences represented
[by] Blacks throughout the U.S. Companies
[lik]e Ebony Films, Gate City Film Corpora-
[tio]n, and Famous Artists emerged to pro-
[du]ce one-reelers, two-reelers, and features
[in] which Blacks were the main and some-
[tim]es the only actors. Precious little is
[kn]own of the producers and writers and
[dir]ectors of these films. Supposedly many
[we]re produced and made by Whites, using
[Bl]ack casts.
[I]n 1927 the Colored Players Films Cor-
[po]ration in Philadelphia produced *Scar of*
[Sh]ame, a movie seldom seen or men-
[tio]ned, yet one of the classics of the silent
[Am]erican cinema, a film as unsparing in
[its] characterizations as von Stroheim's
[Gr]eed. Scar of Shame deals in a taut,
[str]aightforward way with the class struc-
[tur]e among Blacks. The story tells of a
[co]ncert pianist who befriends and marries
[a g]irl of a lower class, and how, through a
[ser]ies of painful circumstances, their lives
[are] thwarted and disrupted by the conflict
[of c]lasses. When finally the girl takes her
[life] in despair—she will never, she feels,
[be] good enough for this more talented,
[bet]ter educated, lighter-skinned man—the
[pia]nist is permitted to marry a girl of a

better class. The film is poignant and disturbing, reflecting a rigid discrimination
among Blacks even as it makes some attempts to probe and condemn that
discrimination.
   The single most prodigious Black filmmaker is clearly Oscar Micheaux, who
wrote, produced, directed and distributed
over 20 films between 1918 and 1940.
Micheaux was something of a Cecil B.
DeMille of the Black film. He controlled
and directed every operation connected
with his films, and made certain—sometimes by gimmicks as simple as inserting
footage of dancing girls almost gratuitous-
ly into a story—that audiences wouldn't
lose interest in the movies. Like DeMille he
assumed, quite correctly, that rural audiences wanted to see the sins of the big
city. But Micheaux tried as well to deal
explicitly with the tensions and struggles
of Blacks in a world which made them feel
a kind of contempt for themselves as a
result of their color. His best films, such
as *God's Step Children, Body and Soul,*
and *Ten Minutes to Live* depict Black people torn by feelings and confusions which
they finally cannot comprehend or sur-

mount. As Norman Kagen comments about
God's Step Children and *Scar of Shame:*
"Valuable and complex as art, their
'stories' are the products of minds which
live in a racist nightmare. The wife in *Scar
of Shame* and Naomi in *God's Step Children* are attractive, energetic characters
who are punished and destroyed for aspiring to a loving equality with others."
   Beyond *Scar of Shame* and the work of
Oscar Micheaux, most of the Black films
that we know about today are essentially
"B" genre movies, reflecting little about
Black culture beyond the dark faces of the
actors and the accents present in the spoken lines. Westerns like *Bronze Buckaroo,
Two Gun Man From Harlem,* or *Harlem on
the Prairie* and crime stories like *Moon
Over Harlem* and *Murder on Lennox Avenue* and a score of musicals or musical-
gangster films came to dominate Black
productions, movies that were cheap,
quick, and not an alternative to Hollywood
but an attempt to imitate the successes of
Hollywood. Often these films have an en-
gaging way of developing a character or
story: touches of ghetto slang and actions
and gestures that would not be found in
the major studio productions.

   The Black production companies gradually dwindled away through the Forties and
early Fifties, casualties of the economic
downswing of the post-War recession and
television. Only recently have scholars and
film archivists turned their attention to locating and preserving these films—a rich
lode of American filmmaking too long
ignored.
   It is too early to suggest the importance
of the Black films in the development of the
American cinema. Certainly their influence
on the mainstream of Hollywood films was
slight. Though they provided the stepping-
stones for a few actors of note (Paul Robe-
son went from the Micheaux film *Body and
Soul* to his role in the 1934 film *The
Emperor Jones),* most of the Black independent films were rarely seen or acknowledged beyond the large city ghettoes.
Perhaps the best assessment of their value
is that made by the historian Thomas R.
Cripps, who commented that these films
were the first—and for a long time the
only—films to depict Black folk as people
rather than social problems.

the Spy

Scar of Shame

Spyin' the Spy

HARRY LANGDON

When his face tightened into the sad mask he used so often, it became a clown's face, a face of loneliness and sadness, one that evoked pity and a strange, unique sympathy. And Harry Langdon used it well.

Of the four major comedians of the silent period, Langdon is perhaps the least remembered. None of his works was major in the sense of Chaplin's *The Gold Rush,* Keaton's *The Navigator,* or Lloyd's *Safety Last.* Moreover, Langdon didn't just languish after the coming of sound; he quietly disappeared (and died earlier than the others, in 1944). Compared to Chaplin's unbroken fame, Keaton's decade at the top, and Lloyd's half-decade, Langdon reached the peak of his profession for only a brief span—two, possibly three years.

Yet Langdon made comedies that bore the unmistakable touch of comic genius. He could, as James Agee said, "do more with less than any other comedian." He was a mime and a clown in the tradition of Chaplin, and most of the early critics approved of him in terms of his similarities to Chaplin. Yet Langdon was unique. He created laughs with an edge to them that Chaplin never approached. There is a frailty, a simplicity, and a downright stupidity in the Langdon character which Chaplin's Tramp—made of stouter stuff—never revealed. The Langdon character wanders the world gazing with dumb fascination at everything he encounters, barely understanding it, being pulled into its complications in a totally witless fashion.

Like Lloyd, Langdon matured relatively late as a comic. Although he had been making one- and two-reelers for some years, it was only in 1925, when Frank Capra and Arthur Ripley wrote *Lucky Star* for him, that his talents began to blossom. (Frank Capra wrote or directed all of Lloyd's better films.) The character took on a form and a solidity that shot Langdon to almost overnight fame.

Lloyd's touches of humor depended largely upon facial mime—an art which, until that point, only Chaplin had really mastered. The difficulty of facial mime is to suggest, without being too obvious, what thoughts or half-formed impressions are running through one's mind in any particular situation and to do it in a way that strikes the audience as humorous. In *Remember When?* (1925) Langdon meets a bearded lady and pauses, trying to decide what to do. Should he shake hands? Should he take off his hat? Perhaps—the moment has a gleam of inspiration about it—he should give her his cigar. No, he discards that idea and finally reaches out to stroke her beard and then touches his own cheek. Langdon strikes the audience in a strange, sad-funny way in such moments, the true mark of a great mime.

Langdon's first full-length feature, *Tramp, Tramp, Tramp* (1925), dealt with a soldier whose war-winning escapades, like those of Chaplin in *Shoulder Arms*, turn out to be a dream. Yet the film was successful and made critics and the public aware of Langdon's unique talents. It would be *The Strong Man* (1926) that brought out the best of Langdon. In this film one of the major comic situations lies in Langdon trying to court a girl who is, unknown to him, a gunman's moll. At one point, she slips a roll of money into his coat pocket. Later, her efforts to get it back without Harry finding out create some of the funniest moments in the film. In a cab, Harry is happily munching popcorn while she, sitting next to him, cautiously feels for the money. She discovers it has slipped through a hole in his pocket and is now in the back of his coat. We see Harry's face as he takes the popcorn, kernel by kernel, and chews it, oblivious of what we know is going on inside his coat behind him. Suddenly his eyes pop open, he spills popcorn, and jumps forward in his seat. He stares horrified at her, and pops another kernel into his mouth. Finally, he slides over to the corner of the seat and eyes her suspiciously.

Langdon used "thrill" material in some of his films—the death-defying but hilarious situations, so frequent with Keaton and Lloyd—but it was usually reserved for climaxes. Langdon clearly could do his best work without it. In *The Strong Man*, he takes on an entire barful of big, brusque truck-driver types, one at a time, with a growing sense of desperation, but finally successfully.

Langdon's last major feature, *Long Pants* (1927), is not so consistently funny as *The Strong Man*. It does, however, have many fine moments and the plot is tighter than in other Langdon movies—or in most other comedy movies of the period. In one sequence, he is trying to attract the attention of a cop—only it is a stage dummy. Each gesture he makes becomes a little more desperate, a little more forceful until finally Harry is choking and feigning a paralytic stroke on the street. Of course, in the good old tradition of slapstick, by the time he gets fed up with himself and grabs a brick to hurl at the cop, the stage dummy has been replaced by the real thing.

After *Long Pants*, Langdon very swiftly dropped from public popularity. Two things particularly hastened his departure: the coming of sound films in 1927, and Langdon's grievous mistake of firing his director, Frank Capra.

Ultimately, Langdon deserves attention not so much as a major silent comic, but as an actor who was able to do remarkable things with extremely limited material. His character—dumb, childish, naive—presented too few opportunities for the rich and complex reactions that can be found in Chaplin or sometimes in Lloyd. The utter lack of aggressiveness, of imagination, and of initiative in Langdon's character kept a sharp curb on the comic situations he could get into. He could be very funny, but there was always a point at which audiences knew that the comedy wouldn't get any funnier—and that, finally, spelled the end.

LAUREL AND HARDY

Stan Laurel and Oliver Hardy, perhaps the most famous comedy team ever to make their way through Hollywood, stand apart from the great silent comedians in a number of ways. For one thing, though they had been making silent two-reelers and features for some years during the silent era, they were able to bridge the transition to sound comfortably—and no other comedian did. (W. C. Fields also bridged the two forms, but his voice brought out comic dimensions which clearly gave him a greater range in the sound era than he could have earned in silent movies. This was not true of Laurel and Hardy: sound seemed to make little difference, one way or the other.)

Chaplin, Keaton, Lloyd, and Langdon were all masters of slapstick who, in one way or another, managed to transcend slapstick—to explore comic ideas that were larger in scope than slapstick. Laurel and Hardy never really transcended slapstick, but they made so much of it, and were so funny using it, that one almost doesn't want

them to go beyond it. Along with Mack Sennett (whom they never worked for, but whose influence on their comedy was profound), Laurel and Hardy were the silent and sound screen's finest tribute to the art of slapstick.

Laurel and Hardy made most of their films with Hal Roach, Sennett's most important competitor in comedy during the twenties. Between 1927 and 1929, they made dozens of two-reeler silent films, among which can be found some of their

Big Business 1929

Big Business 1929

Two Tars 1928

best work. When Roach discovered that
these two characters could talk as well as
pantomime, he put them into sound shorts
immediately, and, after 1931, into features.
Popular in a dependable kind of way, Laurel
and Hardy ground out hundreds of films
under dozens of different directors and writers. More craftsmen than comedy artists,
their films fluctuate from brilliantly funny
to downright awful. Yet when they were
funny—and they were funny often enough
to risk a bad film now and then—they could
be as funny as anyone else making films in
Hollywood.

Consider *Big Business*, one of their more
hilarious films and easily one of the best
two-reeler comedies ever made. It begins
quietly and simply enough: Laurel and Hardy
have gone into business, and try to sell a
man—played by James Finlayson—a Christmas tree. Finlayson isn't interested. They
try a new tactic which begins a small campaign that gradually rises into a war. Laurel
and Hardy go from ripping up Finlayson's
fence to smashing his windows, breaking his
furniture, and hacking down his tree. A
puzzled cop, sitting in his car in the front
yard, jots down each fresh transgression in
a notebook. He doesn't consider interven-
ing; he seems more interested in trying to
figure out what is happening. Meanwhile, the
war rages. Finlayson angrily attacks Laurel
and Hardy's car, stripping it and smashing it
systematically until there isn't much left.
Finally, with neighbors lined up watching

the war, Finlayson goes to the cop and pleads his side of the story; Laurel and Hardy tell theirs. As they explain, they burst into tears and soon they, the cop, Finlayson, and the neighbors are all crying vigorously.

Pure slapstick, true, but slapstick handled with a deftness, verve, and psychological impact rare even in those golden days of comedy. The rise of the war—unbelievably unreal and yet so believable—is handled with a calculated rhythm that makes each laugh rise a little louder and higher than the last.

Most comedy teams have a standard relationship: the smart guy and the fall guy, the one who is worldly wise and the other who is dumb and naive. Oliver Hardy, the heavy, tends to be a little more self-confident and adroit; he is the planner, the leader, the saner of the two. On screen, his most distinctive trait is his impatience. Stan Laurel is dumb. He tends a little toward the oafish, the inept, the fool. But Laurel is no dunce and Hardy no sharpie; the two characters are far more alike than different. Consequently, their richest and funniest humor doesn't take place when they engage each other, but when they face some common threat or challenge in the world around them.

There is a certain pathos in the characters that Laurel and Hardy portray: a constant failure to make what they want out of their intentions. They are constant planners, organizing new projects and ideas, and almost

inevitably suffering as their best-laid plans backfire mercilessly. In *The Finishing Touch* (1928), they are subcontractors hired to put the finishing touches on a house. When the customer appears, the inevitable fracas ensues, and soon they are throwing stones at one another. Laurel and Hardy reach for a large stone and for a moment fight between themselves, forgetting that it holds the lorry in place. When they do lift it, the lorry slips down and flattens the house.

While their career spanned two decades (together they made films between 1927 and the end of World War II), most of the best Laurel and Hardy films came at the end of the silent era, in the year 1928 and 1929. Such two-reelers as *From Soup to Nuts*, *You're Darn Tootin'*, *Early to Bed*, *Two Tars* (all 1928), *Liberty*, *Wrong Again*, *That's My Wife*, *Big Business*, *The Perfect Day*, and *The Hoosegow* (all 1929) really mark the pinnacle of their career. These films, most of them silent but with music, brought out the best of the two comics—their easily aroused anger, their snowballing conflicts, their clumsy efforts to right a wrong by aggravating it. In the history of slapstick, there were perhaps two great creative periods: Mack Sennett's Keystone productions between 1914 and 1916, and the Laurel and Hardy two-reelers of 1928 and 1929.

As in the character portrayed by Harry Langdon, though with significant differences, it was the stupidity of the Laurel and Hardy

Two Tars 1928

Even though Laurel and Hardy made the transition into sound without losing their audience, their films weakened noticeably. It became obvious, by the early thirties, that comedy for the sound film would never be what it had been for the silent film. The loss was a profound one. It not only meant the loss of that contagious, rising laughter which audiences of the silent film knew so well, it meant the loss of a kind of humaneness, warmth, and fun in the movies—a loss which has never been recaptured.

characters which ultimately limited their comedy. With two people so dumb that they kept fighting even though they lost the war (and even though the initial reason for fighting was so minor as to seem ridiculous once the battle began), the comic alternatives were rather limited. It amounted to a question of whether one will use a custard pie or an axe or a firehose as the weapon of assault. Within these constraints, Laurel and Hardy created some fine and utterly hilarious comedy. But one muses whether these two burlesque performers might have been capable of something larger, something in which their control, sense of slapstick, and timing might have played a large role, but not the only role.

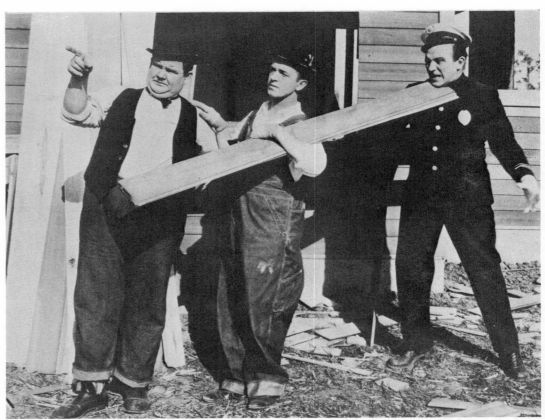

The Finishing Touch 1928

106

**Chapter Five
The Thirties**

THE INVASION OF SOUND

Looking back, after some forty years of talking movies, it is hard to comprehend the resistance of critics, studios, and producers to the innovation of sound. The silent film was hampered by the absence of sound. Except for the rousing chords of the pit organ, silent movies had to communicate on a totally visual basis. When the twigs of a tree clicked against a window-pane, the audiences could only imagine the sound, or hear a distant approximation of it from the organ. If speech were absolutely necessary (and how many stories can be told entirely without speech?), the visual rhythm of the movies was interrupted for a subtitle. In effect, movies, which promised a means of showing the world in a fresh way, were restricted totally to a visual means of reflecting the world. And despite the sophistication that movies had achieved by the late twenties, this simply wasn't enough.

Attempts at sound, like attempts at color, could be traced back beyond the turn of the century. In 1889, Edison had tried to synchronize his Kinetoscope to his phonograph. Some brief French films from the 1890s—rarely over a minute long—recorded the voices of actors delivering great lines. But most attempts at a theatrically successful sound system foundered, not because there were no means of guaranteeing synchronization (several systems had been patented for that), but because of the problem of amplifying the sound so the entire audience could hear it.

It was Dr. Lee de Forest, inventor of the selenium tube amplifier, who eventually gave the movies both amplification and the most sensible system of synchronization. Earlier

methods of synchronization generally involved two separate sources: the film itself and a phonograph record. De Forest saw that this entailed serious complications. If a few inches of film were spliced, they could throw the rest of the reel out of synchronization. Besides that, there was no way to guarantee that projector and phonograph would run at exactly the same speed.

By 1923, de Forest had devised a method which involved photographing sound. Using the beam of a light against a photoelectric cell, he showed how thin jagged lines could break the light, causing patterns of vibrations which, when amplified, produced sound. The optical system of sound was ideal for film. It guaranteed synchronization, since film and sound were together on the film throughout the reel. Moreover, it made the printing of sound films relatively inexpensive, since the film and the sound could be photographed and duplicated simultaneously.

Despite his lively promotion of the optical system, de Forest was surprised to discover that studios were not interested. Warner Brothers, the only studio looking toward sound (and this only from the desperation of near-bankruptcy), had already bought the Vitaphone—a phonograph developed by Bell Telephone which was large enough to accommodate a record as long as a reel of film.

It was Twentieth Century-Fox's success with a series of novelty sound shorts which forced Warner Brothers to look beyond the Vitaphone. Warners purchased de Forest's optical sound system and, in 1927, released the first sound feature, *The Jazz Singer*. The era of sound had begun.

Even in the wake of the incredible success of Al Jolson's *The Jazz Singer*, industry leaders were more than hesitant to adopt sound. They considered it a novelty, a passing fad. Audiences would soon tire of sound and return to the movies—meaning silents. But audiences didn't. Instead they lined up in front of the few theaters designed for sound, to see Mack Sennett's *The Family Picnic*, or "the first all-talking picture" *The Lights of New York*, or "the first *all* all-talking picture" *The Terror*, or "the first all-talking, all singing, all-dancing, 100% all-color movie" *On With the Show*. By the end of the twenties, it was evident to the industry that sound had become as much a part of movies as the long shot, the medium shot, and the close-up. Hollywood was in pursuit of sound. And the place it went to get sound was Broadway.

It amounted to an invasion. Broadway writers, Broadway stars, Broadway directors, Broadway technicians: never before (and never since) had Hollywood been so overwhelmed by the migration from another medium. Some studios tried to adapt their stars, writers, and directors to sound. But actors who appeared so handsome and exciting on the silent screen turned out to have small, scratchy voices. Most of the studios attempted major overhauls, replacing their actors, directors, and crews with Broadway people. Producers assumed that, since the public wanted sound, movies had to be no more than filmed stage plays. And, in the late 1920s, that meant drawing-room comedies.

The failure of the Broadway invasion was partly a result of the inability of Broadway people to create movies. It stemmed largely, however, from a vast gap in the different audiences that the Broadway theater and the movies attracted.

Movies in the 1920s were not yet an art. Their appeal was strictly on the basis of fun, excitement, relaxation, entertainment. The

Marlene Dietrich

audiences were largely lower class and lower middle class people from small towns. These audiences could relate to the farcical events of a Mack Sennett comedy; they could feel the emotional surges of a Valentino or a Pola Negri melodrama. But the drawing-room comedy prevalent in New York in the late 1920s was alien and pointless to them. A movie in which Lady Diana Delatour traded gently barbed quips with her husband provided no movement, no vitality, no emotion. As author Richard Griffith commented:

In greater America in the year 1930, a woman might dislike her husband or she might love him, but she was seldom in doubt about it. The fact that Lady Diana's indecision was expressed through dialogue made her more than ever irritating to the majority, to whom it seemed that 'teacup drama' got nowhere. It left its characters where it found them, and the interim of polite badinage had no more connection with fundamental emotions than a game of Ping-Pong.

There is no question but that the Broadway invasion of the late twenties and early thirties marked a regression in movies. Movies became stage plays, filmed with less vitality, less editing, less visual excitement than movies made 15 years earlier. But the regression was perhaps a necessary step toward the successful sound film. The studios, after all, were faced with a number of imponderables. How *do* you tell a story using sound? More critical and immediate, how do you overcome the opposition created between microphone and camera?

The technical problems that the microphone introduced were nearly insurmountable. The "mikes" in those days were large, clumsy affairs, which would pick up any stray sound. The noisy, whirring cameras had to be placed in special soundproof booths, curtailing camera movement and making fresh set-ups a much greater chore than simply "moving the camera." A new form of technician emerged, the sound technician, and immediately it became evident that his decisions would override those of directors, stars, producers. The sound technician dictated not only camera position, but the frequency of cuts and the uses of camera shots as well. He would place microphones inside flowers, telephones, upholstery, permitting shots that included a large area (like Broadway stages) but which made local movement for the actors impossible. Accordingly, the movies not only sounded like stage plays, they looked like stage plays. And for the most part they were.

Audiences, critics, and studios alike soon came to recognize that "talkies" weren't necessarily movies—at least not the kind of movies that audiences were accustomed to seeing. Through the experiments of directors like Ernst Lubitsch, King Vidor, Lewis Milestone, and Rouben Mamoulian, the studios came to recognize that sound didn't *always* need to be synchronous, and—possibly more important—that the mike should follow the camera, not vice versa.

Rouben Mamoulian's *Applause*, made in 1930, was among the first sound films to give control back to the camera. Mamoulian used several overhead mikes at one time to enable both greater movement of characters and greater camera movement. Movies during the next two years, such as King Vidor's *Hallelujah* (1930), Lewis Milestone's *The Front Page* (1931), and Ernst Lubitsch's *Monte Carlo* (1930) began to reflect the new possibilities of the wedding between sound and movies.

In *The Front Page*, for example, Milestone speeded up dialogue and constructed the story around swiftly paced scenes, freeing the film from the long scenes that dialogue had imposed. King Vidor explored the emotional power of natural sounds in *Hallelujah*. In a chase through a swamp, all we hear is the man's labored breath, the thrashing of feet through grass, the swishing of brush, sounds of birds and frogs.

When sound arrived in 1927, it imposed on the movies a tyranny of verbal and aural criteria for filmmaking. The older scenario —which described the action, the visuals— was replaced by the script, the modified screenplay. Sound was used as the major expressive element. The information that the audience received was in the words, not the images. Throughout the early thirties, the best directors began to explore the meaning of sound *within* the movie. They discovered that sound didn't always need to be synchronous with the action, that sound could counterpoint the visuals, help create mood and suspense, draw the attention of the audience into the screen by the combination of sounds and silence.

By the late 1930s, sound had been integrated into film through the innovations of directors and the development of new technical equipment: the sound mixer, the directional microphone, new methods of moving microphones and cameras. The prophetic words of film critic Bela Belazs, written over 10 years before the first sound feature, had begun, by the end of the first decade of sound, to achieve reality:

Only when the sound film will have resolved noise into its elements, segregated individual, intimate voices and made them speak to us separately in vocal, acoustic closeups; when these isolated detail-sounds will be collated again in purposeful order by sound-montage, will the sound film have become a new art. When the director will be able to lead our ear as he could once already lead our eye in the silent film and by means of such guidance along a series of close-ups will be able to emphasize, separate and bring into relation with each other the sounds of life as he has done with its sights, then the rattle and clatter of life will no longer overwhelm us in a lifeless chaos of sound. The sound camera will intervene in this chaos of sound, form it and interpret it and then it will again be man himself who speaks to us from the sound screen.

SCIENCE FICTION MOVIES IN THE FIFTIES

"An intellectual carrot? The mind boggles!" The journalist in *The Thing* was at once skeptical and exhilarated by the discovery of this eight-foot creature encased in ice where some saucer-shaped metallic object had landed.

The year was 1951, the year that Earth was smashed by a renegade planet *(When Worlds Collide)*, the world became victimized by *The Man from Planet X*, when men first flew to Mars *(Flight to Mars)*, and when the Earth ceased to rotate *(The Day the Earth Stood Still)*.

In the fifties—a decade plagued by the knowledge of overhanging nuclear disaster—monster and horror movies and all those infinite remakes of Frankenstein and King Kong, were not enough to threaten audiences. Almost necessarily, the threats had to become cosmic, and increasingly they came not from a mad scientist's laboratory but from the depths of outer space. Yet the films that sprouted in that fertile period of 1950 to 1959 were not science fiction in the tradition of the great sci-fi writers like Robert Heinlein, Arthur C. Clarke and Isaac Asimov, but were standard "scare" movies, this time with the threat carrying all the contagion and superlative knowledge of alien intelligences.

Virtually all of the films were predictable in the extreme. Some strange sound and light in the night: the saucer's landing; a rising terror amid people in the countryside; the alien's first victims; the skepticism of law officials ("Creatures that walk on three legs and have only one eye? Luke, haven't I told you to go easy on the bottle?"); the intrusion of the aliens into the town and the beginning of really sizable destruction; the calling out of the Air Force and the Marines (but to no avail—"Bombs won't stop 'em"); finally, the young scientist's *plan,* and the risking of his life (and his girlfriend's!) to stop the alien. Science fiction movies, showing at drive-ins in double or triple features, were as much a fixture of the fifties as Eisenhower or The Communist Peril.

There *were* a few really fine science fiction pictures to emerge from this period, movies that not only used the science fiction framework to probe interesting themes, but which gave their characters at least some basic *feeling* of existence in real time, and used special effects subtly and well. The existence of the foreign invaders is palpable and vividly felt in *War of the Worlds* (1953) and *Them!* (1954); the horrors of a misguided scientific experiment take on a nameless shock at certain moments in *The Fly* (1958) and *The Incredible Shrinking Man* (1957)—both films ending on a dark, eerie note; and, the science fiction "standard" of humans being transformed into aliens is used as a metaphor of vacant lives in Don Siegel's scathing *Invasion of the Body-Snatchers* (1956).

Yet most science fiction movies were endless repetitions on the same theme: aliens who invade us and are immune to our paltry weapons, but whom we are finally able to conquer. The titles suggest just how wretched some of these movies were: *Attack of the Fifty-foot Women; I Was a Teenage Werewolf; The Crawling Eye; The Astro-Zombies; The Brain Eaters* and *The Green Slime.* Yet, somehow these movies (now shown on TV) are entertaining simply *because* they are so poorly made, and since the cliché dialogue and grisly acting somehow defuse whatever fear there might have been in viewing them.

Gone With the Wind 1939

BOOMING IN THE DEPRESSION

The stock market crash of 1929 left its indelible mark upon every American institution—including the movies. Only it affected the movies in ways unique to that unique industry. Whereas most other businesses were suffering acutely in 1930 and 1931, films were drawing crowds as hardily as ever; an estimated 50 million people were going to the movies every week. In the hardest of times, the "escapist entertainment" that the movies offered became a necessity. People were discovering that, not only did they like movies, they needed them.

Nonetheless, the studios were in trouble. The costs of using sound and of expanding theater chains were beginning to spiral, and only through consolidation were the studios able to keep up with mounting expenses. Studios began merging with other studios. Many merged with electronic companies to put their talkies in the theaters. The greatest merger was between Radio Corporation of America, American Pathé Pictures and Keith-Albee (one of the largest of the theater circuits), forming the Radio-Keith-Orpheum Corporation—RKO Pictures.

Wall Street had never shown much interest in the studios. Moviemaking was an exorbitant business, with uneven returns and a notorious waste of money. But by the early thirties it became apparent to the most conservative of investors that, whereas solid businesses were faltering, the movie industry was making money as never before. The new

influx of investment money helped keep Hollywood vital through the early years of the Depression. It also began the gradual movement of studio ownership from the West Coast to New York.

It was, ironically, both the growing Wall Street ownership of studios and the Depression which had triggered that ownership, which led in 1933 to a minor depression within the industry.

If the Depression had any single economic effect on the process of making films, it was toward the big-budget movie over the small-budget film. By the mid-thirties, studios were discovering that formulas didn't work so well as they had in an earlier, simpler time. The star system, also, seemed shaky. *Variety* reported in 1933 that there were at most 10 stars who could make movies that were absolute guarantees of success. The studios' response was to spend more money on each film. From an investment viewpoint, a million dollars spent in a lavish production was safer than a million dollars spent in two or three tightly budgeted movies. By the late 1930s, with the exception of a few studios (such as Warners, with its B-gangster movies), most films were considered "major productions."

There were enough innovations to spend the money on. Besides sound, the major technical innovation of the period was color. Attempts in color filmmaking can be traced to efforts by French filmmakers, in the early

114

part of the century, to have the colors painted onto film, frame by frame. Tinted films were used with little success during the 1920s. By 1932, however, Technicolor Corporation had developed a successful three-color process (red, blue, yellow) which was used first by Walt Disney in *Three Little Pigs*. But the use of color in features came slowly—owing partly to the technical weaknesses of color film, partly to the artistic challenge that color represented, and partly to the considerably higher costs of color.

By 1939, however, the use of color for stunning artistic and dramatic effect was shown in David O. Selznick's *Gone With The Wind*, with its dynamic use of high-contrast colors, especially reds, and in John Ford's *Drums Along The Mohawk*, a movie rich in pastels and muted tones of color. But it was not until the 1950s that color films became commonplace, nor until the mid-sixties, with the economic pressure from television, that it became virtually obligatory.

In retrospect, the Depression was more important for Hollywood in terms of the themes it introduced and of the new audience that it forced studio moguls to recognize than for any economic strictures thrust upon the studios. Which is to say that, in the thirties—possibly the greatest decade in the history of the motion picture—movies were changing more on the inside than on the outside.

Three Little Pigs 1933

115

Will H. Hays

ENTER THE HAYS OFFICE . . . CUT!

The cries and criticisms had been mounting for years. Local PTAs in small towns, women's guilds, and church societies pressured studios for reform, control, and censorship. How much of the movies' audience —or indeed of the populace—this pressure represented is questionable. Most likely the effect on the industry was greatly disproportionate to the number of people (mostly women) who had exerted the pressure. But the studios, always great believers in heavy promotion and the power of the press release, interpreted the pressure as the firm stand of a powerful minority which could lead—if studios did not respond—to some unpleasant talk in Washington about government action.

The response of the studios was the Hays Office, which took its name from its first director, Will Hays. Hays had been hired in 1921 as a figurehead to avert public suspicion from the recurrent scandals then plaguing Hollywood. Hays was perfect for the figurehead job, though possibly a little too energetic for the second. A native of Indiana, he was starchy, old-fashioned, and thoroughly respectable.

The function of the Hays Office was strictly internal to the industry, and totally of a censorial nature: to keep blatant immorality out of films. The Production Code that it helped create and spent over 30 years maintaining was quite explicit. A camera could not show the inside of a woman's thigh; double beds were prohibited; a man could touch a woman only on the arms, shoulder, or head.

It was the very explicitness of the Code which enabled some filmmakers to slip past it. The double entendre, that classic ruse of slipping the risque into a throwaway line of dialogue, became a standard technique in the sophisticated comedies of Mae West, William Powell, and others. For example, *The Thin Man*, made a year after the Code came into force, had William Powell and Myrna Loy bantering about newspaper reports of his wounding by a gangster. "You got shot five times in the tabloids," she observes. "That's not true," counters Powell, "he never got near my tabloids."

The Code was designed to keep the industry "clean" from within. Every producer, director, and editor became a censor— though the Hays Office made its own censors available as well. The standard procedure was for a film to be made with the help of Code censors; then the film was sent to the Hays Office itself for the seal. There was no law on paper that a film required a seal. But until the studios lost their theater chains in the early fifties, it was economic suicide to release a film without a seal.

The Hays Office kept the pressure on Hollywood from within; the Legion of Decency applied pressure from without. Formed by the Catholic bishops in 1934, the Legion of Decency was an attempt by the Catholic hierarchy to force Hollywood to mend its ways and to keep Catholic audiences from patronizing immoral and indecent films. Catholics were required to take an annual pledge to the Legion. Films were rated as acceptable, objectionable in part, and "condemned." Many bishops, such as Francis Cardinal Spellman of New York, in-

Baby Doll 1956

sisted that viewing a condemned movie was
at least a venial sin, and easily a mortal sin.

One of the objects of the Legion of Decency was to engender mass boycotts of
condemned films. To this purpose, the bishops asked leaders of other congregations to
help them. In the mid- and late- thirties,
Protestants were leery of doing anything
with Rome, but eventually a number of
Protestant churches agreed to support the
Legion of Decency. In large cities, widely
publicized campaigns were mounted against
condemned films. In terms of box office re-
ceipts, these campaigns sometimes caused
a little drop, but often the adverse publicity
abetted the success of a condemned film.

It is hard to see how the censorship of
the Hays Office or the mounting pressure of
the Legion of Decency did anything other
than hurt the movies. A film involving social protest, such as Elia Kazan's *Baby Doll*
(1956), became a definite risk for the studios. Better to stick to the kind of movie
that audiences and censors both approved—
the Westerns, the swashbuckling romances,
the fluffy bedroom comedy with inviolate
virginity and ironclad morality—which is
precisely the direction Hollywood took. So
many of the themes which endeared movies
to audiences in the twenties—the love affairs
of goddesses, the humiliation of high authority, the clash among gangsters, the success
of the little man—gradually disappeared
over the late thirties and early forties. The
entrance of the Hays Office and the Legion
of Decency had given a new meaning to the
oldest word in the film production lexicon:
"Cut!"

117

Marlene Dietrich

THE NEW SUPERSTAR

Inevitably, the coming of sound meant the arrival of new stars: men and women closer to the audiences than to the gods. A few, like Garbo, made the transition without losing their place in the heavens. But for too many silent screen stars, the microphone was a deadly enemy, and eventually caused their downfall. Stars who had mastered the nuances of facial and body movement were at a loss when it came to the nuances of speech and inflection. The old pantheon crumbled. Gloria Swanson, Pola Negri, Clara Bow, Wallace Reid—the great stars of the twenties became anachronisms in the thirties.

One of the causes for the demise of many stars was the audience itself, and their economic troubles. It was appropriate, in the extravagant twenties, that Gloria Swanson should bathe in a solid gold bathtub. But what did this mean to hungry audiences in the Depression-stricken thirties? Movie stars had to be closer to real life, had to exemplify the attitudes of audiences toward a world which had suddenly turned stony hard and unyielding. Film critic Richard Schickel commented:

A new kind of star came to the screen. The age of the American hero, tough, cynical, wise-cracking, frequently unchivalrous toward women, was upon us. Gone were the Latin lovers; gone, for the most part, were the vamps, the sloe-eyed sensualists who had tempted many a good American boy to his doom on the silent screen. Even the virginal staple underwent a transformation. She did not lose her virtue, but she did tend to be a good deal more knowledgeable about the world and its ways than the Gish sisters or Mary Pickford had been. More than one commentator has noted that when James Cagney pushed the grapefruit into Mae Clark's face in Public Enemy, *screen love, and for that matter, screen manners changed forever. Certainly the moment is one of those bench marks in social history that cannot be ignored.*

Even today the names evoke images of the hard modern facades of cities and the clipped, cynical outlook of the loner: Humphrey Bogart, James Cagney, Edward G. Robinson, Gary Cooper, Spencer Tracy, James Stewart, Clark Gable. And the females were no longer the vamp-or-virgin stereotypes, but richly developed personalities who almost invariably suggested a morally ambivalent attitude toward sex: Greta Garbo, Mae West, Marlene Dietrich, Bette Davis, Jean Harlow, Katherine Hepburn, Carole Lombard. These stars were capable of harsh, vehement lines and behavior. We identified with them because they suggested our most fertile fantasies, our ultimate responses to a world turned against us.

Adam's Rib 1949   Destry Rides Again 1939   Somewhere I'll Find You 1942

I Am a Fugitive From a Chain Gang 1932

The Life of Emile Zola 1937

The relationship between being a star and being a great screen actor is usually an adverse one. Critics generally agree that Paul Muni was a more gifted, versatile, and brilliant actor than Humphrey Bogart. Paul Muni played drastically different parts, infusing them with wholly distinct identities. There is hardly a wisp of a relationship between Muni as the stodgy Emile Zola in *The Life of Emile Zola* and the young, desperate man in *I Am a Fugitive From a Chain Gang*. Bogart almost always played Bogart—whether as a private eye in *The Maltese Falcon*, a drifter in *The Petrified Forest,* a nightclub owner in *Casablanca,* or as an amateur prospector in *The Treasure of the Sierra Madre*. He was always Bogart, the loner who was at once tough and pathetic, the man surviving at the edge of society by sheer will and style.

Bogart typifies, better than any other star of the thirties and forties, a growing popular ambivalence toward society, formality, and authority. Bogart's presence, at once incon-

120

The Barefoot Contessa 1954

The African Queen 1951

spicuous and magnetic, gave every scene he entered a new emotional undercurrent. Raymond Chandler, who created Bogart's character, Philip Marlow, in *The Big Sleep;* said in R. Schickel's *The Stars*: "Bogart can be tough without a gun. Also, he has a sense of humor that contains that grating undertone of suspense. Ladd is hard, bitter and occasionally charming, but he is after all a small boy's idea of a tough guy. Bogart is the genuine article. Like Edward G. Robinson, all he has to do to dominate a scene is to enter it."

Bogart's first important film role was in *The Petrified Forest*, a 1936 film built on the Robert Sherwood play. The film was stagy and slow, but a better than standard production of a Broadway play on film. What makes the film unforgettable is Bogart —not his performance, but simply Bogart. Playing the gangster Duke Mantee, who holds a group hostage, Bogart suggested a muted ruthlessness, a cynicism that masked deeper anxieties, a mood ranging from a

glowering darkness to private fear.

The role lasted. Bogart became the American film's quintessential tough guy, never far from the sardonic self-mockery that was, at root, less a reflection of the society than of inner forces within Bogart. Indeed, Bogart was one of the few actors associated with the gangster genre of the thirties who survived its dissolution at the beginning of the war. Bogart's great roles— in *Casablanca*, *The Big Sleep*, *The Treasure of the Sierra Madre* and *The African Queen* —took place in an era in which other stars of the thirties experienced their decline.

Better, perhaps, than any other star then or since, Bogart suggested the infinite power of the star to mesh with the mood of his audience. For Bogart the difference between a smile and a sneer was minuscule. The narrowness of that difference was precisely what made Bogart appealing and *important* to movie audiences over two decades.

Bogart's screen magic lay almost entirely in his presence; with Spencer Tracy it was

almost the reverse. When you think Bogart you think: tough, hardbitten, the worldly-wise drifter with that look of irony in his eyes. But when you think of Spencer Tracy you think of specific performances: Tracy as an unscrupulous entrepreneur in *Dante's Inferno*; as an oil wildcatter in *Boom Town*; fitting the role as no one else ever has in *Dr. Jekyll and Mr. Hyde*; as the stump-armed loner in *Bad Day at Black Rock*, as the glowering judge in *Judgment at Nuremberg*—or in dozens of other roles, all of which Tracy played with a tough, resilient polish.

Bogart said of Spencer Tracy that he was the best actor Hollywood had produced: "You don't see the mechanism working, the wheels turning. He covers up. He never overacts or is hammy. He makes you believe he is what he is playing." And Tracy was that rarity among Hollywood stars—there was no typical Tracy role, no typical Spencer Tracy movie. What gave Tracy his breadth of life on the screen was largely his ability

121

The Wizard of Oz 1939

to get into a part and control it totally from within. Particularly in his later films, Tracy brought to his acting the nuances of inner tensions, hinted at only sporadically, by a flicker in his face, or a barely discernible knotting of muscles. Spencer Tracy was a star, but not because he imposed his personality on his roles. Quite the opposite. He gave the screen moments of rare acting genius, an almost uncanny precision of role.

Screen stars cannot be discussed without mention of Clark Gable. Gable played every role with the same undaunted confidence and near bravado; he was Hollywood's image of the thoroughly forthright, thoroughly self-confident male. From his first major role on (*A Free Soul*, 1930), Gable was often cast opposite the rich, haughty society girl whom he alone could—and did —tame. No woman could hold out forever against Gable's rough, hard-fisted (if he couldn't woo them, he often tried to slap sense into them) advances. In the typical Gable role he played a footloose adventurer, bound less by social responsibility or family ties than his own hearty lust for women, stiff whiskey, and a tough manly brawl. Movies such as *It Happened One Night, The Dancing Lady, Boom Town, The Hucksters*, and, of course, *Gone With the Wind*, seem almost tailored for Gable. No one else could play the leading roles in these movies with the same elan, the same certainty, or the same husky vitality that Gable brought to them. Over the years—Gable acted from 1930 until the late fifties—Gable aged, but

his appeal never diminished in the slightest. He was always Clark Gable, King, a man's man and—no question about this— a woman's man.

James Stewart is almost the direct opposite of Gable. In the thirties, Stewart invariably played a bumbling, midwestern young man who, out of stubborn pluck and something like moral outrage, was able to overcome the larger forces into which he had been plunged. He was the only major star at the time who didn't suggest the absolute cool of a Bogart, a Cagney, a Gable or a Tracy. Indeed, it was largely Stewart's nervousness, his unsure, sometimes bumbling manner, his high-pitched tripping voice that at once insured his star status and locked him into the popular image of "Jimmy" Stewart—the all-American boy thrust into the spotlight too early. Such a tightly-locked image has destroyed lesser actors, and it is a measure of Stewart's talent and persistence that after the war he sought out a far wider range of roles— from a cynical reporter in *Call Northside 777* to the decadent lawman in John Ford's *Two Rode Together*. The mature Stewart has demonstrated far better than the Stewart of the thirties the real range of his talent and its absolute rightness for the movie screen. The stumbling speech and the long, gawky face remain, but Stewart has made them work for an effect of highly believable screen naturalism. Stewart is perhaps the most believable of the major stars to emerge from the thirties.

BUSBY BERKELEY AND THE 30's MUSICAL

A Busby Berkeley musical number can fool you. It will open modestly, perhaps with two people like Dick Powell and Ruby Keeler singing together on a stage. Then gradually the frame seems to expand, introducing one chorus line, then another, and then—by some geometrical magic of the camera—the screen is engulfed with hundreds of dancing girls, moving in semi-formal patterns, creating rhythmic flowing designs. In one number ("By a Waterfall," *Footlight Parade),* the girls, who are grouped in concentric circles, move their bodies and legs to create a lavish effect of flowers opening out and closing in. In another film, *Golddiggers of 1935,* the "Lullaby of Broadway" sequence begins with a long shot, a woman's face spotlighted in the surrounding darkness. She starts to sing "Lullaby of Broadway" in a thick, enticing voice. As she sings, the camera moves gradually closer until her face fills the screen; then, she turns profile and the figure of her profile becomes a skyline of the city, and an extensive montage of a dancer's daily life in the city begins.

Never was Berkeley's penchant for making his production numbers bigger and bigger so evident as in his use of steps—sets that begin with modest risers that suddenly grow and grow until the dancers are mounting (or coming down) vast panoramas of steps, veritable Himalayas of steps, steps that suggest nothing so much as the notion that this is no longer a stage or the earth—this is heaven, this is the infinite. It was largely this constant reach beyond proportions, the attempt to stretch a few dancers into thousands and a small stage into a galaxy, that made Berkeley's production numbers so astonishing in the feelings they aroused—and so distinctly his own.

Busby Berkeley used props as never before, or since, in the history of the musical. In "The Shadow Waltz" of *Golddiggers of 1933,* he used 100 lighted violins. In yet another number, "The Words Are In My Heart" *(Golddiggers of 1935),* Berkeley outfitted 100 girls in grand pianos, pianos that moved in formation as formal and decorous as the best of his other production numbers.

Berkeley was fascinated with the effects created by silhouette, circular motion (a predominant camera angle was directly atop the action below), long telescoped spaces, and of course, the ever-burgeoning scale of a musical number that would not stop—that simply mushroomed into larger and larger proportions. The music in his numbers may be dated, but the numbers themselves are as fascinating and ingenious as they were in the thirties when he made them.

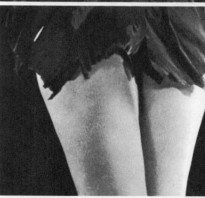
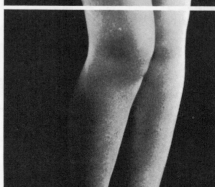

Greta Garbo

Then there is Garbo.

"Garbo," said John Barrymore, "has only to flash on the screen to seize our attention. Her brilliance dispels our dullness. She takes us out of ourselves by the mere accident of her presence. It isn't acting; it is something which holds us in its spell—a kind of magic." Greta Garbo, a Swedish actress brought to Hollywood by Louis B. Mayer, was to become the criterion against which a female star is compared. Her movies were mostly vehicles: flimsy romantic contraptions with little to hold them together beyond Garbo's galvanizing presence. But nothing has matched that presence, before or since. Garbo's slightest gesture, her subtlest shift in mood, became the focus of whatever film she appeared in. Strangely, her acceptance as a star in America was not nearly so overwhelming as her acceptance throughout Europe. Only rarely was she able to make the movies she wanted to make as in her greatest successes, *Queen Christina* (1933), and *Ninotchka* (1939). And until the late thirties, all her roles depicted her with a somber, almost leaden seriousness. Yet Garbo has survived, as very few female stars have: the woman eternal, the mystifying, intoxicating presence of what is most alluring and unattainable in the female.

Chapter Six
Society Good and Bad

With the Depression, a dark mood settled over the country, a spirit that swung between crushed hopes and deep bitterness. For the first time since their origin, films began to appease more than the audience's need for entertainment. The success of the gangster film, the rise of a number of movies of excoriating social comment, the emergence of the tough, cynical hero and the equally tough heroine—these films began to reflect a different dream, a dream closer to the spirit and mood of the times. People still went to theaters for escape. But they also went, albeit unconsciously, to share in a vision of life: to identify with stars like Cagney, Bogart, and Gable who could kick dust back at society, men who would not let their environment dictate *all* the terms. It is hard to imagine, seeing it over television today, the impact that a film like *The Public Enemy* made on audiences in 1931. James Cagney's swagger, his cocksure stance, his knife-'em-in-the-back morality were perceived not as the trademarks of the gangster-villain, but as the flaws in an ultimately tragic hero. The audience followed Cagney through boyhood and early adulthood, from poolhalls to barrooms, from picking pockets to petty thievery to major thefts to organized crime. But never was Cagney himself indicted for his crimes; society had failed him more grievously than he had failed society. Audiences felt a surge of excitement when Cagney shoved a grapefruit into Mae Clarke's face. And the final comment, with Cagney's body being dumped on his mother's doorstep as perfunctorily as a meat delivery, brought home to audiences not their fear of the gangster, but the depth of evil in a society which so easily maligns and cripples its own.

This chapter will probe the films of the thirties and forties which reflected an ambivalent attitude toward society: the gangster films, the emerging genre of social realism, the rise of censorship and the comedies. Throughout these films, society is portrayed in a variety of ways: as the creator and arbiter of fate, as the world from which the hero hopes to escape, as a vicious, bitter, hopeless—but never neutral —entity. Society could be good, society could be bad; it was an era when movie audiences cared which way it went.

Little Caesar 1930

'GET EDDIE'

Two words in a film script, naked, empty of inflection and context. But when Little Caesar (played by Edward G. Robinson in the 1930 film of that name) learns that Eddie is planning to rat and has just gone into a church, his words take on chilling significance. We know as soon as we have heard those words that Eddie's fate has been sealed as surely as though a jury had just returned a death verdict. The gangster world is as simple as that: a curt command, the squeal of automobile tires swerving around a curb, and the staccato burst of a machine gun. And, at the heart of the gangster film is the dark sense of anonymity that hallmarks the gangster: his environment, his movement, his life, and finally his death are—no matter how much we know about him—ultimately anonymous.

Early gangster movies, such as Josef von Sternberg's *Underworld* (1927) and Lewis Milestone's *The Racket* (1928), had to foreshadow a movie genre in which the audience's sympathy lay not with the arbiters of law and order—the police—but with the characters of the underworld. Sound gave the gangster film much of its unique impact: the raucous explosions of a machine gun, the squeal of tires and brakes, the cry of a trapped gangster echoing against the brick walls of a back alley. The gangster movie gave the screen in the early thirties a new synthesis of image and sound. It enabled directors to use strong effects in lighting, camera angles, and editing while at the same time taking advantage of the innovations of sound. Some of the best naturalistic dialogue of the period appeared

Big House 1930

in gangster movies. Phrases like Edward G. Robinson's, "So you can dish it out but you can't take it" gave the films a flair, and a new touch with the realities of life beyond Hollywood.

The major cycle of gangster films lasted only briefly, between 1930 and 1933. Some, such as *The Big House* (1930), *The Secret Six* (1931), and *Quick Millions* (1931) were essentially melodramas, opposing gangsters to law enforcers. But the best of the genre—*Little Caesar* (1930), *The Public Enemy* (1931), and *Scarface* (1932)— were written as "documentary mosaics"— a term used by Richard Griffith to describe crime stories taking place within convincing

settings and suggesting the peril of living at the perimeter of an unstable society.

The themes that emerged in the gangster movies of the early thirties might have appeared subversive to Depression-stricken audiences. In *Smart Money* (1931) and *Quick Millions* (1931), the heroes argued that a man could make far more money in the business of crime than in legitimate industry. Of course, these movies ended with the hero dying by the very violence that had enabled him to rise. Even before the Hays Office Code, satisfactory endings were a Hollywood obligation, if not all too often an obvious appeasement to ladies' organizations and church groups.

The introduction of the Hays Office marked the decline of the gangster film. The wanton violence, the fundamental law of reprisal in the gangster world, were too clearly offensive to what the Office called "the accepted canons of American morality." Warners continued to churn out B-gangster movies until World War II, at the rate of about four a year. But these had the tinny, lifeless quality of sluggish imitations. After the war, a new genre emerged, bearing the stamp but not the fire of the early gangster originals. Some of the police and gangbuster movies, such as John Huston's *The Asphalt Jungle* (1950), returned to the criminals, and probed their personalities and lifestyles with a far more discerning eye than was turned on the lawmen.

In *The Asphalt Jungle*, Huston uses the documentary style, the pervasive enclosures of the city, the faces of men at the edge of society. Best of all, however, he juxtaposes the criminals—for whom the audience can feel sympathy, admiration, and sometimes respect—with the police, who ultimately lack that saving grace of the gangsters, the ability to understand another human being. The police commissioner, for example, speaks of Dix (Sterling Hayden—possibly in his best role) in terms that are at once hard and uncompromising: "In some ways he's the most dangerous of them all, a hardened killer, a hooligan, a man without human feeling or mercy." Huston cuts to Hayden making his desperate getaway from the city, eager to return to a Kentucky horse farm of his boyhood. The closing shot depicts the dying Dix stumbling across a Kentucky pasture, finally lying still, his face nuzzled gently by a horse.

In some ways, *The Asphalt Jungle* represented the end of a rich tradition that began with *Little Caesar*. Not even *Bonnie and Clyde*, that lyrical and perceptive tribute to gangsters (and gangster movies) of the thirties, would again disclose to audiences the confining, rectangular environment of the city, or use the vocabulary ("You boned me!" "Ditch him." "On the lam." "The heat is on.") which gave the gangster's world its independent "nationality" and its own cultural boundaries.

Ultimately, the gangster genre is probably more important for its mythology—which is to say, the reason for its popularity with audiences—than for any lasting contributions it made to the history of movies. In his provocative essay, "The Gangster as Tragic Hero," the critic Robert Warshow suggests that the gangster film represents a totally American mode of tragedy. Fundamentally, the gangster movie is a success story: the rise—and fall—of a gangster, whether Little Caesar, *The Public Enemy*'s Jimmy, or *Scarface*'s Big Louie. But in the gangster world, success has been stripped of its respectable trappings. We see success in its most naked form: as a man climbing, quite literally, to success over the bodies of those he has destroyed. The gangster film is, finally, not simply another version of the Horatio Alger story, but a moral indictment of the Horatio Alger myth: the price of success is one's soul, and, as the gangster movies never neglected to emphasize, one's life.

"At bottom," writes Warshow, "the gangster is doomed because he is under the obligation to succeed, not because the means he employs are unlawful. In the deeper layers of the modern consciousness, *all* means are unlawful, every attempt to succeed is an act of aggression, leaving one alone and guilty and defenseless among enemies: one is *punished* for success. This is our intolerable dilemma: that failure is a kind of death and success is evil and dangerous, is—ultimately—impossible. The effect of the gangster film is to embody this dilemma in the person of the gangster and resolve it by his death."

Little commentary is needed to see the attraction that the gangster film must have had for audiences in the thirties. It was not simply that people like to "side with the underdog." Nor was it the fascination of crime and violence. Whereas most other films depicted society within the framework of the American mythology of success, hard work, and material goods, the gangster film challenged this mythology by charging the city, the gangster, and the relationships between gangsters with a fresh but basically recognizable meaning. Audiences not only felt close to James Cagney and Edward G. Robinson, they drew from their characters a valuable antidote to their own beliefs and environment. The gangster films may have hardened audiences a bit, may have given them a more callous and cynical outlook toward established order. But perhaps they also made life in the midst of failure a little more salvageable—and did it without being dishonest.

Public Enemy 1931

CHARLES BRONSON

RICHARD WIDMARK

ROD STEIGER

JACK PALANCE

GEORGE KENNEDY

JAMES MASON

STERLING HAYDEN

RICHARD BOONE

HAROLD SAHARA

KARL MALDEN

VINCENT PRICE

FRANK SILVERA

Why is it that the stars—almost always good guys—
get so much attention, and the heavies so little?
The heavies work as hard; sometimes harder.
And they have to bear the guilt of doing most of the killing,
kidnapping, and assorted mayhem that we expect of them.
Yet, some of the heavies have emerged over the years
as superb actors in their own right.

Can you match the names to the faces?

WHEN THE POPCORN TASTED BAD

There were a few films made during the thirties and the forties—not a great many—in which very few people got up to buy more popcorn. Looking back at some of these movies—*I Am a Fugitive From a Chain Gang, Fury, The Life of Emile Zola, They Won't Forget, The Grapes of Wrath, Meet John Doe*—it seems surprising that people could eat popcorn at all. With only a few exceptions, like von Stroheim's *Greed* (1923), Hollywood films had never before attacked social injustice with such fervor or emotional intensity. To see the furtive face of Paul Muni in the closing shot of *I Am a Fugitive From a Chain Gang*, innocent but forever pursued by the law, or to watch the almost ritual burning of the prison in *Fury*, or to follow the Joad family from starvation in Oklahoma to desperation in California in *Grapes of Wrath*—audiences glimpsed as never before the face of society as a cruel and sometimes vengeful arbiter of human fate.

The forces of law and justice could themselves be corrupt and indifferent (*The Life of Emile Zola, The Prisoner of Shark Island*), the political order a vast con game played on the public (*Mr. Smith Goes To Washington, Meet John Doe*). In these films, little men such as Spencer Tracy's character in *Fury*, Muni's character in *I Am a Fugitive*, the Joads in *The Grapes of Wrath*, or Dreyfus in *The Life of Emile Zola* were totally at the mercy of their

society, and their society was hostile or worse, indifferent. On one level, such films reflected the audience's experience of and bitterness at the Depression years. But on another level, the best of them proved forever the incalculable power of movies to make audiences feel so strongly that their consciences were stung.

Admittedly, there were only a few great films of social protest, and a great many "topical" films that dawdled between standard Hollywood storytelling and the emotional impact of grievous injustice. In 1930, Warner Brothers announced that, as much as possible, movies from the Warners' studio would be based on spot news. This was less a statement of the studio's obligation to pursue meaningful themes than a concession to the popularity of the gangster genre at the time. But it permitted the writers to strike out in new areas, and lent a new tone of realism, sometimes almost documentary force, to movies by Warners and other studios. Films like *The Dark Horse* (1932) and *The Phantom President* (1932) unveiled the hypocrisy so rife at the core of American politics. Major receptacles of public respect were exposed one after another: judges (*Night Court*, 1932), lawyers (*The Mouthpiece*, 1932), newsmen (*The Front Page*, 1931; *Blessed Event*, 1932), sports heroes (*The All-American*, 1932), even the most venerated of institutions, banking (*American Madness*, 1932).

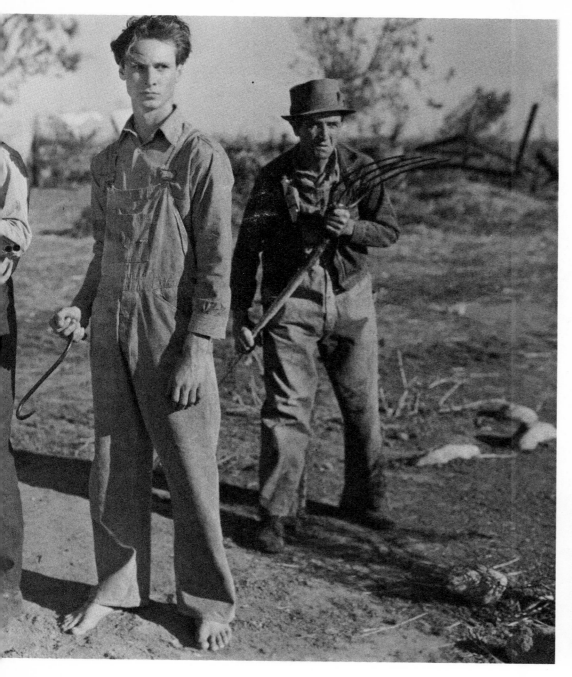

Of the early cycle of social realism films, the most important, and the most lasting, was *I Am a Fugitive From a Chain Gang* (1932). Paul Muni starred as a war hero—a Congressional Medal of Honor winner—who is sentenced for another man's crime on scant circumstantial evidence. Once he has joined a chain gang, the horror mounts. His pleas go unheard, his desperation drives him to the edge of insanity. Escape is followed by recapture, and each outbreak leads to a new, more dangerous threshold.

The film is rich in great moments: Muni trying to pawn his Medal of Honor, and returning to his wife for only a few moments, a shadow among shadows. The close of the film must rank as one of the most unforgettable in the history of movies. Muni is asked by an old friend, "How do you do it? How do you live?" He answers in the

I Am a Fugitive From a Chain Gang 1932

muted tone of the condemned: "I steal . . ." The camera closes on a face that has accepted the horror, then the face disappears in the shadows.

After 1933, Hollywood softened its indictment of society. The forces of new ownership, the Hays Office, an audience growing more hopeful that the new President —Franklin Roosevelt—could lead them out of the crisis all led away from stern realism toward more pleasant films, and movies that were more romantic than reproachful. Many socially critical films were being made, of course, particularly at the Warners' studio: *Wild Boys of the Road* (1933), *Massacre* (1933), and *Black Fury* (1935) to name a few. Gradually, however, such films became less and less typical of Hollywood's total output. By the late thirties, the most caustic comments on society would be coming not from the hard realistic films inspired by yesterday's headlines but from biographies (*The Life of Emile, Zola, The Prisoner of Shark Island, Life of Louis Pasteur*) and sophisticated comedies (particularly those of Frank Capra and Leo McCarey) that probed the effects of the Depression on the rich and would-be rich.

One of the last great films of the thirties based on a newspaper account is Fritz Lang's *Fury* (1936), a unique masterpiece, largely neglected since its release. Fritz Lang was one of the last of the European directors to come to Hollywood on the basis of a well-deserved reputation. At least two of his German films, *Metropolis* (1926) and *M* (1931), had shown Lang to be a brilliant if sometimes obsessive director. Few directors then could match Lang's visual impact on the screen. *Fury* proved that, despite Lang's difficulties with the American idiom, verbally and visually, he could make a film in Hollywood that resonated with the force and suspense of his best earlier works.

Fury begins with a service-station owner, Joe Wilson (played by Spencer Tracy) engaged to a girl named Katherine (Sylvia Sidney). On his way to meet her for the wedding, he is stopped by a sheriff's deputy in a small town on suspicion of being a kidnapper. Two shreds of evidence—peanuts in his pocket and a dollar bill that was originally part of the ransom money— are enough to spread the rumor through town, "The sheriff's got him." The tension builds, the gossipers become a crowd and the crowd becomes a raging mob. Soon they have overtaken the sheriff and his deputies and set the jail on fire. Joe, however, escapes. Lang approaches this sequence—a mighty example of camera virtuosity and visual effect—with neither documentary realism nor the cynical eye of a director like Billy Wilder (there is a similar sequence in Wilder's movie *The Big Carnival*). The action rather—a woman flinging a torch into the jailhouse, men rushing the door with a battering ram—seems stylized to a point of objectivity. The mob's attack is interpreted by the camera not as a grievous, bestial assault but as a kind of absurd choreography, a dance of death. Lang heightens the terror by exaggerating the shots: each new angle seems to reflect a more grotesque and distorted scene. The sequence is at once a powerful climax of the drama and a stunning visual metaphor of the demonic forces unleashed by intolerance.

Fury has been termed an "anti-lynching movie" by its director. But the film pursues more themes than that, and each of them— as in Lang's other major films—leads finally to the question: at what point and at what cost can man master his own fate? Disregarding the soapy ending (Joe and Katherine kissing in the courtroom—an ending which Lang found appalling and fought unsuccessfully), the film raises questions about retribution and perhaps the ultimate impossibility of justice. For example, by sending his ring anonymously to the judge, Joe Wilson is able to make the court a co-conspirator in his revenge. The film is not simply a powerful indictment of lynching—as the first viewing might suggest—but a complex and devious parable about the basic instability of society, rooted in the basic instability of every man—including the film's Everyman, Joe Wilson.

Fury 1936

The year after *Fury* was released saw the appearance of another socially incisive film, *The Life of Emile Zola*. While not so successful at the box office as either *I Am a Fugitive From a Chain Gang* or *Fury*, *Zola* has proved over the years to be one of the most politically potent movies made in America. *I Am a Fugitive From a Chain Gang* and *Fury* could depict justice failing and condemning an innocent man, but they did it through the venality of people in power and the coincidence of matching evidence. *Zola*, a film based largely on the infamous Dreyfus trial in nineteenth century France, portrays the mechanisms of justice (in this case military justice) being manipulated consciously to condemn an innocent man and to keep him condemned.

The Life of Emile Zola 1937

The Life of Emile Zola spends the first two reels following the development of France's great naturalistic novelist—from his garret days in the 1860s to his position of fame and eminence toward the turn of the century. The director, William Dieterle, infused the rather trite story with an exceptional visual technique. For example, Zola (Paul Muni) is discussing with friends the failure of the French army in the Prussian wars of the late 1860s. He says emphatically, "I will show what led France to its downfall." The scene cuts immediately to the cover of a book, *The Downfall*, by Emile Zola. The camera backs away and we see that the book is being held by a general, outraged at what he is reading. The relationship between Zola and his responsibilities as a writer are never so evident as in the face of that brazen, imperious general.

Paul Muni gives Zola a character with whom we can identify at once and whom we do not question, just as he does not question, regarding the comforts and insulations he has created around himself. When his old friend, Paul Cézanne, tells him that he has lost his passion and courage, the audience makes little of it. It is only through the rebirth of passion—Zola's appeal for Dreyfus—that Zola, or the audience, can look back to those fat, compromising days to see how empty and deadly they really were.

"Military justice is to justice as military music is to music," Georges Clemenceau once quipped about the Dreyfus trial. The

story of the original trial is told honestly, explicitly, and quickly in the film. Essentially what happened was this. Alfred Dreyfus, a Jewish lieutenant in the Ministry of War, came under suspicion as the author of a letter containing state secrets—a letter destined for the German embassy. Since someone must be prosecuted for such a dire crime against the state, the military selected Dreyfus, almost at random. Despite the absence of any convincing evidence, Dreyfus was hailed as a traitor and sent to Devil's Island for life imprisonment. This was 1894, a time of passionate nationalistic feelings. Few people in France doubted that a man whom the military high tribunal had condemned could possibly be innocent.

Fresh evidence appeared three years later. Major C. F. Esterhazy, formerly of the Ministry of War, was clearly engaged in espionage, and his handwriting matched that of the letter which had condemned Dreyfus. The man who amassed the evidence, Lieutenant Colonel Georges Picquart, was quietly sent to a distant outpost. Meantime, dissent was growing; both nationalistic fervor and a wave of anti-Semitic feeling gave the whole affair a sense of precipitous alarm.

When his wife showed Zola the evidence and asked him to fight for Dreyfus' release, Zola was initially indignant. Who was he to question it? But a lingering doubt led him to read over the evidence, then to write his famous letter to a newspaper, "J'accuse!"—accusing the military of falsely

Zola

trying one man and of suppressing evidence that could convict another.

Zola's trial is portrayed in the movie as a wild, unbridled circus. False and undisclosed evidence is given better leverage by the judge than the careful documentation of Esterhazy's conspiracies. Ironies and jarring juxtapositions abound. Zola's lawyer to the Court: "I'll say what I have to say if this trial lasts six months!" The judge: "Court is adjourned." Above the furor of the courtroom, a surprisingly large crucifix hangs on the wall. And throughout all the murmur, all the raucous controversy, all the obvious manipulations of law by the military, people go on saying, "Impossible! French justice today just doesn't make mistakes."

Visually, the film, and particularly the trial episode, is rich. One memorable scene depicts hundreds of umbrellas under a rainy sky outside the courtroom. The public was waiting, and it knew what it wanted to hear.

At the close of the film, Zola's death is signaled by his pen scratching to a halt.

The Life of Emile Zola was all the more forceful because of its careful documentation of a real event. Admittedly, the movie ignored aspects of the original event: it downplayed the rampant anti-Semitic feelings of the time; it suggested that Zola's motives were pure; it simplified the controversy somewhat. But few American movies have carried the sting that *Zola* contains. In 1952, it was singled out by a Congressional subcommittee as a "subversive and Communist-inspired" film— the only film to receive such a strong attack for its political content.

The "social conscience" movies of the thirties didn't always reflect an acute conscience. One of the bitterest sources of rage and conflict in the thirties was the growth of organized labor. Much of the political turmoil of the period—the popularity of Communism, the growing suspicions that Big Business had somehow usurped democracy—stemmed from the difficulties of organized labor to succeed in obtaining wage increases, better working conditions, and other ameliorations from industry.

The movies reflected this social turmoil, but often their depiction was rather pallid. Quite a number of these films sympathized ultimately with the men who controlled the system. In *Red Dust* (1932), *Riffraff* (1935), and *Black Fury* (1935), the whole controversy was made explicable on the level of personal jealousy or the venality of in-

considerate workers. The strikers were "Reds" or troublemaking foreigners, their leaders gangsters and racketeers. The question of a justifiable strike was waylaid by identifying the employer as good guy and the strikers as threat. In *Black Fury*, the strike among the mine workers is presented with almost no relationship to the workers themselves, their deprivations and demands. Outside agitators had caused the strike, and audiences found it difficult throughout the movie to assume any identification with the strikers.

The outbreak of World War II brought an end to the distinctive films that lanced at American society throughout the thirties. The passionate loyalties and patriotism of the war forced Hollywood films to take a totally new orientation, as a following chapter will show. The caustic social criticism of the best movies of the thirties could not survive the war. And when, after the war, directors like Billy Wilder and Elia Kazan turned to films of social criticism, it was with a new eye, in a style totally distinct from their forebears of the thirties.

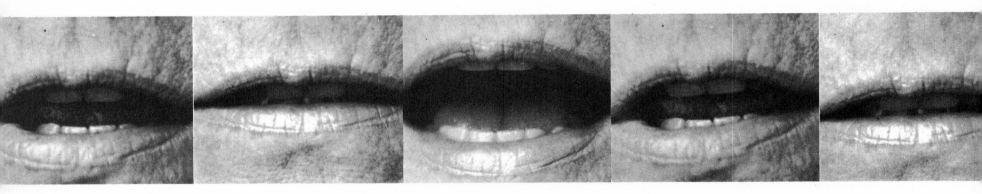

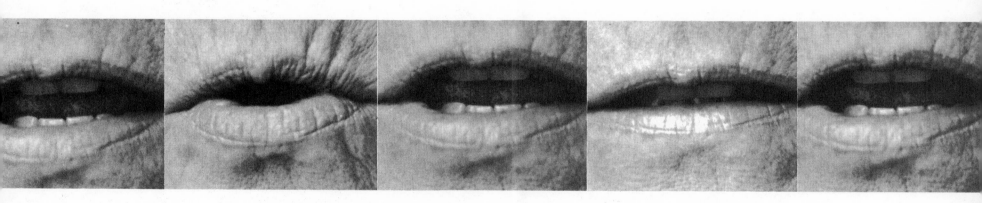

They sniped. They bit. They stung. Given a whiff of sin, they
hinted at the unspeakable. They engineered more marriages and
divorces than the most industrious Japanese marriage broker.
When aroused, they could attack the biggest of stars and leave a
shroud of suspicion hanging over his personal life. Their power to
spread innuendos in a world teetering on the brink of its own
fantasies was incredible. When Hedda Hopper died in 1966, her
column at that time was running in 400 newspapers with a total
circulation of over 32 million. In the heyday of Hollywood, the
thirties and forties, possibly no one's power was more consistently
felt throughout the movie world than that of Hedda Hopper, Sheilah
Graham, Louella O. Parsons and Walter Winchell. They were more
                    than columnists. They were fearsome institutions.
Hedda Hopper has said of her beginnings in the column-writing
business in 1936: "Louella O. Parsons had the town in her hand
when I came on the scene, so I had to be aggressive and sometimes
brutal. Actors, producers, and directors are all like children. They
may scream and holler but they love to be spanked. They want to
                    be noticed—just like kids."
And, just like columnists. If there was any secret to a columnist's
success, it was that ability to be at the right place at the right time
and overhear that precisely right piece of chitchat—and of
course, to blow it into a full-scale revelation or attack. The columnists attacked the stars, but never with the vehemence with which
they attacked one another. For almost two decades Louella
Parsons and Hedda Hopper, the two major Hollywood columnists,
carried on an acerbic feud in which one would become angry and
resentful at a star if some tidbit of information were given to
                    the other first.
The major columnists, particularly Louella Parsons, had an almost
phobic need to be "the first to know"—and if one did not inform
a major columnist of some decision or event, it could result in
a seething antagonism which might go on indefinitely. In *The
Fifty-Year Decline and Fall of Hollywood,* Ezra Goodman writes:
"Some years ago, when Parsons had the field pretty much to herself,
it was considered standard procedure to notify her before getting
married or divorced. Hollywood legend had it that a glamour boy
and girl, ready to elope, forgot Parsons' phone number and had
                    to call the whole thing off."
The reign of the columnists did not end with the gradual collapse
of Hollywood—which only goes to confirm their tightly held power.
Eddie Cantor once commented frankly at a "testimonial dinner"
to Parsons: "I am here for the same reason everyone else is: they
were afraid not to come." The columnists—for all the color and
and noise they might add to Hollywood—have always represented
one of the more preposterous aspects of Hollywood's strange
topsy-turvy world: the power that comes of a kept press.

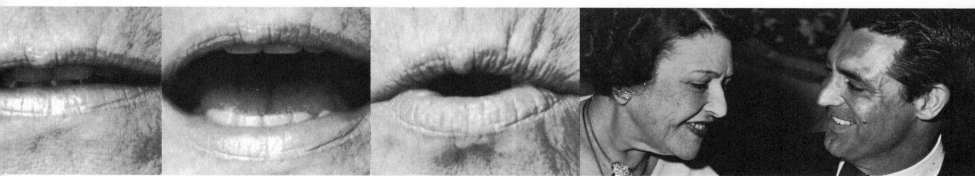

Louella Parsons and Cary Grant

145

'A THING WORTH HAVING IS WORTH CHEATING FOR!'

The onset of sound upset no film genre more than comedy, for the simple reason that comedy had progressed far beyond any other kind of film in its use of the silent screen. The gradual buildup of a major laugh from a small gag to unimaginable atrocities was a tactic of the silent screen. In Laurel and Hardy's *Big Business* (1929), for example, a minor scuffle between the two Christmas tree salesmen (Laurel and Hardy) and a prospective customer gradually escalates into demolition: Laurel and Hardy chopping, breaking, ripping up the house and its furniture while the infuriated home owner makes a rubbish pile out of their car. Such a sequence would not have been hurt (or, for that matter, totally helped) by sound effects, but dialogue would have been pointless.

It was not so much sound but dialogue—both the public's expectation of it and the studios' avowal to satisfy that expectation—which hurt movie comedy. There is a great difference between a visually funny moment and a verbally funny moment. The visual gag is immediately and objectively funny. A man walks out of an ice cream parlor with four ice cream cones and an enemy trips him; the ice cream lands all over his face. What we see is funny: directly, simply, immediately funny. Contrarily, verbal comedy is indirect. Words are spoken, and it is our perception of the meanings of those words—a much less immediate route—which can make them funny. Then, too, the words themselves are not so simple or objective as a visual image. Who is saying the words? With what inflection? To whom and in what context?

This is not to deny the impossibility of great screen comedy with dialogue. Some of the funniest moments in movie history have been lines spoken by actors like that chronic hater of dogs and children, W. C. Fields: "I recall once seeing a dog chew on a little kid, which is not in itself a bad idea . . . but it does show a dog's intentions." Groucho Marx to Chico Marx: "I wish you were in your other suit. It's being pressed—no, mangled."

But the sound screen didn't attract, engage, and develop many great comedians as the silent screen had. Throughout the thirties, the only significant comedians were W. C. Fields, Mae West, and the Marx Brothers. By the late forties, even they were gone.

In her article in *Photoplay* magazine, September, 1942, "If I Were Queen of Hollywood," Dorothy Kilgallen commented on W. C. Fields: "I fail to see anything even slightly amusing in any of his pictures . . . I find him such a bore."

Yet Fields' ability to carry off brilliant and incisive comedy was the very thing that alienated him from Dorothy Kilgallen, and from many females and traditional moralists in general. Some people *do* find it hard to identify with a man who cheats at poker, hates dogs, abominates children, and sings the praises of the bottle. Fields' marriage was an armed truce; his relationship with his mother-in-law a pitched battle. Fields was a grumpy, griping old salt, a veteran misanthrope.

"I didn't squawk about the steak," Fields once told a waitress in a diner, "I merely said I didn't see that old horse you used to have tethered out back." The best of

Fields' humor was always barbed with venom, the retorts of the man who has been suckered and pulled under by the world. He suspected everyone. Even a conversation with Edgar Bergan's dummy Charlie McCarthy in *You Can't Cheat an Honest Man* (1939), led to premonitions of violence: "Ah, my diminutive little chum, how would you like to go out and ride piggy-back on a buzz-saw?"

Fields had good reason not to trust people. Society, in its hypocritical fashion, had no place for a man who preferred the simpler pleasures to hard work, someone who was not afraid to be forthright about the joys of the bottle. Fields sensed no particular obligations to other people as a result. In *The Bank Dick* (1940), he is passing a car where a man is working on the engine diligently. With typical bravura, Fields offers his assistance. The man isn't sure, the audience isn't sure, but after Fields tinkers for a moment inside the engine it falls out. Fields walks off as if he had completed the job. Later he is passing by, with the man engaged in the now larger job. Fields comments to him: "Still at it, I see."

A quintessential Fields sequence takes place in *Man On the Flying Trapeze*. On his way to a boxing match, Fields is signaled by a cop to pull over to the curb. The cop gives him a ticket and a lecture, and no sooner has he disappeared than another cop appears to give him a ticket for parking in a no-parking zone. Fields accepts the ticket with minimal protest—what is protest in a world that will get you anyway?—when a chauffeur-driven car stops directly behind him. Then a truck driver deposits an enor-

Tillie and Gus 1934

147

mous box just in front of him. Fields backs into the car and incurs the wrath of its chauffeur. (The rich, it appears, can park in a no-parking zone; only Fields cannot.) He waits for the car to leave. The cop appears again and gives him another ticket. The geometric progression of assault was a standard device in silent comedy, but rarely was it used with the psychological cutting edge that Fields could give to it. As television announcer Ed McMahon commented on Fields' quips: "The world crushes him and he crushes the world and sometimes it's all happening at once, or it's difficult at least, to tell just who is crushing whom."

"The wise and intelligent," Fields once stated, " are coming belatedly to realize that alcohol, and not the dog, is man's best friend. Rover is taking a beating—and he should." Fields' famed love for booze and hatred of dogs and children was more than his personal variant of the eternal need to have someone to pick on; Fields *genuinely* hated children and dogs. "A dog will run up and lick your hand. No bottle will do that . . . If the whiskey ever starts licking your hand, I would advise you lay off it for awhile, say five or ten minutes." Fields knew he could take out his vengeance on society through dogs and children.

But Fields never quite won his running battle with society. He was, after all, outnumbered—as well as outsmarted, outmaneuvered, and outfoxed. But he kept the battle warm, which was enough to keep audiences coming back for more. Society was not simply bad for Fields, it was dangerous, and threatened him at every turn. Audiences may have recognized that in any of his roles —as The Great McGonigle, as Ambrose

Mae West

Mae West

Wolfinger, as Professor Eustace McGargle, or as Larson E. Whipsnade—Fields would have been impossible to live with, or even live near. But on the screen, ah!—he was one of the funniest men alive.

Mae West never had quite the comic stature of W. C. Fields. Her roles provided neither the basis for Fields' vindictiveness nor the bite of Fields' humor. But Mae West did something that even the Marx Brothers in their most brilliant moments never quite managed to do: turn sex into an explosively funny joke.

Mae West appeared at a critical time for Hollywood. The Hays Office and the new pressures on the front office to keep movies "clean and decent" forced movies to downplay sexual accessibility. The old female stereotypes—the vamp and the virgin—had already disappeared. But the old themes had not. The problem was: how to give those themes a sense of urgency and passion when the relationships between men and women were straight-jacketed by Code rulings?

Mae West flouted the Code, just as she flouted every rule of female decorum and modesty in Western culture. She got away with it partly because she acted largely in comedy vehicles, partly because she kept her clothes on all the while, but perhaps mostly because she was Mae West. There was *so* much oozing seductiveness in her voice ("Come up 'n see me sometime"), so much suggestion in those well-displayed contours, so much of the vamp's confidence in her appeals to men that audiences just *knew* this couldn't be for real. Mae West took the movies' own technique of showcase sexuality to its extreme.

But her comedy was built on more than simple exaggeration. In *My Little Chickadee*, the famed movie in which she co-starred with W. C. Fields, there is a marvelous sequence on their honeymoon night. Fields is already in bed, waiting for his new wife to join him, when she recruits the services of a goat. The comedy builds as Fields first hears the goat and comments on how lovely she sounds. When Mae West slips the goat into bed with him, Fields adds comment to comment; it is a long time before he discovers that his little chickadee isn't a chickadee.

The sequence shows the real thrust of Mae West's comic style. By blinding men with infatuation for her, she possessed the final controls in any relationship with them. Legally she might be married to a philanderer like Fields, but she owed him nothing, and she knew it. Most important, she could get away with it.

Mae West was the earthiest of sex goddesses. She exuded sex, it was almost a natural perfume, an aura, surrounding her body. The theme of lost innocence, frequent enough among Lloyd, Keaton, and Langdon, was taken to new extremes by Mae West, who not only relinquished her innocence but who seemed to celebrate its departure.

If the loss of innocence was the hallmark of Mae West, then the demeanor and chaotic consequences of innocence were the hallmarks of the Marx Brothers. These men were not motivated by greed, ambition, or lechery. Their zaniness sprang from pure hearts: hearts so clean, in fact, so undefiled by the world, that the Marxes were totally free to do what they wanted. And they did. Clipping ties off stuffed shirts at a banquet, setting an orchestra adrift on a large raft, confounding everyone with Groucho's cloudy logic—the Marx Brothers scampered through their films like a horde of impetuous children. The strictures of society and the unwritten law to behave by conforming had no meaning for the Marx Brothers except as targets. The Marxes enjoyed nothing more than pricking aristocratic bubbles.

The combination of characters was a unique one. First, consider Groucho. The closest of the Marxes to the rest of us, he is the only one who will dress in suits (even if they are three sizes large) and talk something like the rest of us, even if most of what he says is dense and confusing. (Speaking to an angry staff who want higher wages, he uses his impenetrable logic: "Wages? You want to be wage slaves?" "No!" "No, of course not! Well, what makes wage slaves? Wages! I want you to be free. Remember, there's nothing like liberty except *Colliers'* and the *Saturday Evening Post*. Be free, my friends, one for all and all for me and me for you and three for five and six for a quarter.") Like his brothers, Groucho is exuberant, but unlike them he is capable of at least some kind of conversation with society.

Harpo is simpler than Groucho, and his needs are better defined. He is speechless, but that hardly restricts him. His facial expressions tell us what he is thinking—or more usually, what he is feeling. For Harpo is always feeling something: joy or delight or anger or sullenness. He chases women, though once he has them he isn't interested in sex at all, but only in playful games. Indeed, life is a series of games for Harpo; everything he does seems to make more sense as a game than as a legitimate activity. For example, he steals. He doesn't plot; the stealing is impetuous and usually pointless. Throughout the Marx Brothers films, Harpo seems constantly to be shaking knives and spoons out of his sleeves. The most pronounced feature of Harpo, however, is his appetite. In *The Cocoanuts*, he nibbles on flowers, buttons, and tries taking on a telephone. Harpo is a child, more innocent than his brothers, and consequently even more impulsive.

150

A Night at the Opera 1935

Chico seems characterized mostly by stupidity. Half of Chico's activity seems directed toward baffling Groucho. In *At the Circus*, Chico foils Groucho's efforts to stall the villain by smoking his cigars at such a furious rate that the villain's excuse for staying soon vanishes. No situation, however out of control or threatening, seems to make the slightest inroad on Chico's dim brain. He bumbles through the conventional social world with no desire to adhere to its norms— or, for that matter, to consciously rebel. Chico's behavior seems dictated finally by a kind of positive stupidity; what Allen Eyles calls "stupidity exalted." Chico glories in his goof-offs; he thrives on confounding anyone with a pretension to reason. As the child who insists that the universe must become as chaotic as his own wild soul, Chico is in a sense the quintessential Marx Brother, the most crazed of these crazies.

Go West 1940

The Big Store 1941

At the Circus 1939

The fourth brother, Zeppo, appears only in a few of the Marx Brothers films. Not nearly so funny or interesting as the others, he is closest to Groucho, though straighter and more predictable.

The funniest of the Marx Brothers films— *Monkey Business* (1931), *Duck Soup* (1933), *A Night at the Opera* (1935), and *A Day at the Races* (1937)—do not oppose the Marx Brothers and society so much as they show the inevitable disaster of any clinches between the two. The Marx Brothers are not "out to get" society as W. C. Fields was. Their inanities spring more from their basic playfulness, their unremitting sense of fun. Even hostilities are part of the game. When Groucho mutters to Chico, "I'll bet your father spent the first few years of your life throwing stones at the stork," he is not simply chiding Chico; he is indulging in the fun of mockery.

Yet society is a target for the Marx Brothers simply because it is there. And the more pretentions the Marx Brothers find, the more devastating their conquest. Rich old ladies who "harumph!" and carry handkerchiefs, wealthy men in topcoats and formal hats, authority of any species—nothing can bring the high so low as the antics of Groucho, Harpo, and Chico. Indeed, it leads one to believe that their inanities were more than a child's recklessness; they were inspired. "The liberation of the human mind," columnist H. L. Mencken observed, "has never been furthered by dunderheads; it has been furthered by gay fellows who heaved dead cats into sanctuaries and then went roistering down the highways of the world, proving to all men that doubt, after all, was safe . . . One horse-laugh is worth ten thousand syllogisms. It is not only more effective, it is also vastly more intelligent."

**Chapter Seven
Directors of the Thirties**

It Happened One Night 1934 (Claudette Colbert)

The arrival of sound was a critical turning point in the development of many major Hollywood directors. Some—like John Ford, Rouben Mamoulian, Howard Hawks, George Cukor, and Frank Capra—found their distinctive style and mode of making movies only with sound. Others, such as Erich von Stroheim, Buster Keaton, F. W. Murnau, and Mack Sennett, were defeated by sound; their movies—mighty works of art during the silent era—were built on a purely visual aesthetic. Finally, several directors bridged the introduction of sound gracefully; it seemed to have little ill effect on their movie styles: King Vidor, Ernst Lubitsch, Fritz Lang, and Alfred Hitchcock are four examples.

This chapter will concentrate on six major directors of the thirties, men whose talents burgeoned in those years: Frank Capra, Robert Flaherty, Josef von Sternberg, Fritz Lang, John Ford, and Walt Disney.

FRANK CAPRA

Capra had learned to direct comedies in Mack Sennett's studio during the late twenties. By that time, Keystone had lost much of its original punch-and-pummel audacity, and directors were freer to pursue their own styles. Capra's early comedies, particularly those with Harry Langdon, showed him to be competent at swift characterization, complex gags, and a steady, fluid rhythm. But it was not until sound in the thirties that Capra evolved a distinct style which was to make him the most successful director of the sophisticated romantic comedy.

Frank Capra began directing movies in 1926. His early films, such as *Tramp, Tramp, Tramp* (1926), *The Certain Thing* (1928), *Rain or Shine* and *Ladies of Leisure* (1930) showed Capra to be a competent director. His first major hit, *It Happened One Night* (1934), won him the Academy Award for the year's best director. Ironically, the film marked a turning point—

Mr. Deeds Goes to Town 1936

Meet John Doe 1941

156

it was at once a summation of Capra's earlier films and style, but it also suggested themes and tone that would dominate his later, best work.

It Happened One Night involves Clark Gable as a feisty newsman with a rapid-fire tongue and Claudette Colbert as a rich heiress running away from high society. The movie was a standard early-thirties comedy with Colbert outfoxing people pursuing both her and Gable. But the independence of Colbert and Gable, and the use of America as a backdrop for people who did not share in its major aspirations—these were themes typical of Capra.

Two years later *Mr. Deeds Goes to Town* appeared. Though perhaps not his best work, this is Capra's best-known and most typical film. Longfellow Deeds, a rural hick, inherits an incredible fortune and moves to New York. He is at once attacked by characters who might seem right off the pages of Damon Runyon. The vultures make the mistake of appealing to Deeds' ambition and greed. Seemingly, he has none. The money is used to help poor farmers and laborers, and eventually Deeds, bewildered but unimpressed with the big city, goes home. The vultures, good men at heart, realize that Deeds is a finer man than they. The movie is slick, cliché-ridden, and reekingly sentimental. But it was one of the great successes of the thirties.

More important, it showed the unique relationship between Capra and his audiences. If a good man is strong enough and follows his convictions, he can win—even in the

welter and traps of New York City. As historian Richard Griffith observed:

The thesis of the sentimental comedy was welcomed by huge sections of the American public. What need for the social reorganization proposed by the New Deal if prosperity and peace could be recovered by the redemption of the individual? This idea, absolving the middle-classes from realistic thinking about the forces which governed their lives, has proved perennially popular.

Later films by Capra continued in this vein: *You Can't Take It With You* (1938), *Mr. Smith Goes to Washington* (1939), *Meet John Doe* (1941), and *It's a Wonderful Life* (1947). Each of these films dealt with an unsophisticated young man—a modern variant of the classic bumpkin of good will in literature—who somehow finds himself in a seething cauldron of greed, larceny, and the protection of selfish interests. Of course, he is immediately conquered by powers-that-be, but his integrity is unscorched. Through an appeal to the "little people," he masses the strength required for battle, and succeeds.

In *Mr. Smith Goes to Washington*, for instance, the young Mr. Smith (James Stewart) tries to introduce a bill making some public land into a Boy Scout preserve. Older, worldly wise politicians have vested interest in the land and are bemused at Smith's efforts to save it. As the battle mounts, Mr. Smith faces rejection from the Senate. As a holding action, Smith monopolizes the floor,

Mr. Smith Goes to Washington 1939

reading such documents as the Declaration of Independence and the Bill of Rights. His defeat seems inevitable. The senators oppose him and, even in his home state, the boss whom Smith has attacked makes sure no word of Smith's heroic attempt reaches the ears of the home-state people. But Smith's boys, hundreds of them, get to work on pamphlets which they attempt to distribute until the boss's henchmen scoop up the pamphlets and wreck their press. All looks glum until another senator—part of the plot to get the land—undergoes an eleventh hour conversion and breaks down on the Senate floor. Suddenly all is right with politics, and our belief in the smooth functioning of democracy is reinforced.

Such a film has about as much relationship to the real workings of the American legislature as does Walt Disney's *Bambi*.

But Capra used a striking cinematic realism and obtained convincing performances from his actors to give the drama an acute touch of reality. As Richard Griffith commented on the movie:

Its significance, it seems to me, lies not in its truth or falsity but in its persistence as an idea and its popularity with audiences. Individual idealism is no solution for any practical problem, but it is the totem people worship when every other way cuts across their thinking habits. A film which embodies this phenomenon enjoys, to my mind, an importance beyond itself. It is to be evaluated less as a mirror of life than as a document of human psychology, an index to the temper of the popular mind.

Frank Capra is one of those special filmmakers—Cecil B. DeMille is another—whose ultimate importance lies not in advancing the art of the film significantly, but in making visible the relationship between a movie and its audience. The fact that all of Capra's films (with the exception, partially, of the glaringly romantic *Lost Horizon*) have dated badly suggests how perfectly *right* his films were for their own time, their own audiences. Capra did not make movies for all time, but for the people of the Depression-worn thirties. There is no better guide to the mentality of that era than a viewing of Capra's films.

No other single director maintained quite the relationship to the times which can be found in Capra's films. Some directors, viewed at the time as the best of the era,

have become in retrospect merely very good technicians who were able to bridge the gap between the silent film and the static microphone. Men like Rouben Mamoulian, King Vidor, Mervyn LeRoy, and Lewis Milestone did make very good films for that period. But only a handful—such as LeRoy's *Little Caesar* and *I Am a Fugitive From a Chain Gang*, Milestone's *The Front Page*—have really lasted beyond World War II.

Lost Horizon 1937

157

Nanook of the North 1920

Nanook 1920

Nanook 1920

ROBERT FLAHERTY

The documentary film has always been a weak stepsister of the feature film in America. Until recent years, with the ripening of new documentary artists like Frederick Wiseman and the Maysles brothers (Alfred and David), the only single major name associated with an American documentary genre was Robert Flaherty.

Flaherty was never completely successful in Hollywood. Like von Stroheim, Murnau (with whom he collaborated unhappily on one movie) and, later Welles, Flaherty was denied the opportunity to make movies within the system and was forced to seek his own financing on most of his films. His failure with Hollywood was hardly surprising: though Flaherty did film his documentaries in distant and sometimes exotic locations, they were tough films that probed the ways in which other peoples survived a world that could be hard and unyielding. (These themes reflected Flaherty's original interest and occupation—that of an explorer.) Whatever Flaherty's films were, they bore only a distant similarity to the standard producer's concept of movie entertainment. That itself was enough to bar Flaherty from the studios.

Flaherty began his first documentary before the word had entered the film vocabulary. In 1914, the 28-year-old explorer took along a movie camera to record what he saw in the Leaf Bay area of Hudson Bay, Canada. He met and became friendly with several Eskimos. So impressed was he that he shot thousands of feet of film—only to have the film accidentally burned to ashes in the editing room back in the states. But Flaherty, as tough in his way as the people he followed with his camera, returned to Canada and shot a longer, more sustained film—a movie that would become the first and possibly the greatest major documentary: *Nanook of the North*.

Though shot in 1919 and released in 1920, *Nanook of the North* still conveys the awesome starkness of the Northern terrain and the warm, charming intimacy of Nanook and his family. The film, which follows a loose narrative structure about surviving the rugged arctic year, is rich in dramatic moments that were wholly new to the 1920 screen: Nanook grinning at the camera—a grin that belied the presence of the camera —the great seal hunt (which Flaherty later

admitted had to be staged because of the slow seal season), Nanook's delight and wonder at hearing a phonograph for the first time. Such moments suggest and even justify the whole meaning of the documentary: the movie as a means of capturing real life, rather than a technique for creating illusions about it.

Nanook of the North, which had a surprising success in American theaters, changed the young Flaherty from an itinerant explorer to a serious documentary filmmaker. It is doubtful whether, in any of those early years, however, Flaherty thought of himself as a "documentary" filmmaker— or as the "father" of the documentary film. He was less interested in "pure" documentary—a type of film in which the camera did no more than record events, something similar to newsreel footage—than in a collaboration between himself and the people whom he was filming. Their lives, he knew, were as interesting for audiences as anything that the major Hollywood screen stars might say or do. But the problem was somehow to give structure and meaning to that life and capture it alive on film.

159

Flaherty's next three films—*Moana* (1926, with director W. S. Van Dyke), *White Shadows of the South Seas* (1927), and *Tabu* (1931, in collaboration with F. W. Murnau)—were shot in the South Seas. The tenuous struggle for existence in *Nanook* here gives way to a people whose wants are easily satisfied, and whose lives revolve around not survival but ritual and play. The films, particularly *Moana*, are fine and typically rich, but they lack the inherent dramatic power that Flaherty had caught so precisely in *Nanook*.

It was Flaherty's next project—the filming of a group of fishermen on an island off the west coast of Ireland—which revealed, perhaps better than any other film, the extraordinary power of the documentary form and Flaherty's unique sensitivity as a documentary filmmaker. Flaherty had long had in mind a project which he called "Man Against the Sea," but previously he had thought of making it in Samoa. When he heard of the Aran islanders, and particularly once he had visited them, he came to realize that nowhere else could he find a struggle for survival waged in such fundamental terms. The Aran islanders carried seaweed up rocky cliffs to supplement the thin soil atop the island for potato growing. They fished in waters that at best would boil and foam, and at worst threatened to smash their

wooden boats against craggy rocks with every wave.

In *Man of Aran* (1934) Flaherty caught it all: from the woman silhouetted against a stark landscape and a grim, darkening sky to the deadly waves that rush over the returning fishermen and engulf them in foam, even as they try to pull the boat on shore. The film moves with double force: an epic sweep of land, sky, and sea, combined with the menial and unending demands on the fishermen and their families. It is a potent, gripping film, virtually untouched by the sly sentimentality that had crept into earlier Flaherty narratives. It marks at once the high point of Flaherty's career and—in some ways—the low point of public recognition of his genius.

Both in America, and particularly in England, the Depression years gave birth to a number of would-be documentary filmmakers: young men who saw in the documentary form a vehicle for social change. They viewed the documentary less as a means of recording the real world than as a form of implicit propaganda. At first, many acknowledged Flaherty as the pioneer who had shown the potential of the documentary camera. But gradually, as Flaherty continued his theme of man against nature in a world that was becoming increasingly industrialized, these young men saw Flaherty pur-

suing a romanticism that was irrelevant to what they considered the point of the documentary. At a time when Flaherty should have been attracting disciples, he was castigated by his most promising candidates. (Of course, looking back at the documentaries that emerged from the thirties, there is nothing by any of Flaherty's detractors that can come near *Man of Aran*; next to this film, most of the urban documentaries are tired, lifeless, and very boring.)

Flaherty's next two projects—like so many of his efforts—eventually bogged down in questions of control and ownership, and Flaherty had to relinquish creative control. The first, *Elephant Boy* (1937), was a considerable disaster—standard Hollywood devices thrown over some exquisite Flaherty sequences shot in India. *The Land* (1942) was a film made just before the war, and released only in a brief version for nontheatrical showings. Flaherty captured the plight of the rural unemployed with a grim, disturbing honesty. The U.S. Film Service, which had commissioned the film, overlaid a grotesque sound track which all but ruined Flaherty's sensitive camera work.

Flaherty's last major venture was one of the most successful in his career. Standard Oil, recognizing the public relations potential in a Flaherty documentary, offered to foot the cost of a Flaherty film on oil drill-

Robert Flaherty

ing. At the same time, the company required absolutely no control over the film: in fact, the negative would belong to Flaherty, and distribution rights belonged to him entirely. The arrangement worked well. Flaherty made *Louisiana Story* (1948), a lyrical, if uneven story of a boy in the Louisiana bayous who watches an oil drilling operation begin near his home. The old educational film device of seeing some marvel of technology through a child's eyes had already, by the time of Flaherty's film, been worn thin, but Flaherty brought to it a rich and convincing portrayal. The film was flawed —its narrative seemed awkward and at times nonexistent—but the photography easily ranked with the best of Flaherty's work. Some of the episodes, the first oil drilling sequence, and the alligator episode in the swamps, catch Flaherty—the documentary dramatist—at his best.

Robert Flaherty not only pioneered the documentary, he provided a model which documentary filmmakers could well look up to. His films, despite their romantic preoccupation with man versus the land, are controlled by a craftsman who had disciplined the camera to an awesome extent.

Here was a man who could spend three years making a 70-minute film; who could be ruthless in discarding almost-perfect footage, only vaguely confident that he

Louisiana Story 1946/48

would be able to get better shots; a man who fought against his own expectations of what a movie should become, letting it—through long, patient shooting and waiting—unfold before him, letting sequences and events move at their own pace, not his. Flaherty's style, like his art, was the antithesis of the fabricated Hollywood movie: he sought reality and fought till he got it.

Critic John Goldman wrote of Flaherty in a retrospective account of the editing of *Man of Aran* (quoted in *The Innocent Eye* by A. Calder-Marshall):

There are two kinds of creative people. Those who create by inspiration and those who create by revelation. Flaherty did not work by inspiration but by revelation. And the way is long, laborious and frustrating, requiring fantastic patience and a degree of sustaining perception that is exceedingly rare. Flaherty possessed these qualities in excelsis.

Once upon a time—before drugs and sex and X- and R-rated movies—MGM made a series of films that showed what it was like to be young in America. Mickey Rooney, then one of the biggest marquee stars alive, starred as the irrepressible Andy Hardy, producer Louis B. Mayer's image of the all-American boy-next-door. Andy Hardy didn't go in for all these "things" that were to vex the parents of later generations. It was strictly cars and girls and stammering moments before his father, the stern Judge Hardy.

Eight Andy Hardy films were made, all but one of them between 1937 and 1944. The series began with *A Family Affair* in 1937, with Lionel Barrymore as Judge Hardy. The film was not particularly successful, but exhibitors and various women's groups applauded the movie for its clean, decent portrayal of an American youngster. Louis Mayer, in his firm belief that America needed more solid wholesome movies (especially if they were good box office), immediately arranged for a sequel and with *You're Only Young Once* (1938), the Andy Hardy series took on the surfaces that would be so familiar to it over the years: the town of Carvel, with its soda fountains and Carvel High; Lewis Stone now in the role of the serious father who now and then flashes a brief smile of understanding; and Fay Holden as the mother who gives in all too quickly and all too often to Andy's rash appeals ("Gosh Mom, you're . . . swell!").

Predictably, Andy Hardy's life is not cluttered with problems of being a little runt or being in danger of becoming drafted. Two anxieties beset Andy Hardy and only two: girls and cars—Andy has too much of one and not enough of the other. The girls (these being MGM "productions") are really little worth complaining about: Judy Garland, Lana Turner, Esther Williams, Kathryn Grayson, Donna Reed, and—the one eternally faithful to Andy even as he keeps ignoring her—Ann Rutherford. Cars are another thing altogether. Andy's own painted-up junker always seems to be at the edge of catalepsy, and Judge Hardy never has to face lawyers as persistent as Andy is when he needs the family car for a dance.

And on it goes. The Andy Hardy movies were a reflection, of a sort, of the small-town concerns and dreams of the late thirties and early forties. But ultimately they were a refraction of what the producers—Louis Mayer in particular—thought the public wanted to see. Most of the Andy Hardy movies were made during World War II, while the young men of America fought and died in Europe, North Africa, and the Pacific. And the Andy Hardy movies heightened the belief that there was something at home worth dying for: not exactly freedom, but the small-town, high school student's version of The American Way of Life—Mom and Pop and the girl down the block, and a sputtering clunker that gives up the ghost every block and a half. Andy Hardy was pure Americana: sentimental, trite, small-minded, but just the thing to make you feel, "Gosh, ain't it just wonderful?"

andy hardy is a good kid

JOSEF von STERNBERG

He was one of those rare, uneven talents that fit only clumsily into the studio system. Indeed, in his later films, he seemed more of a painter than a movie director, a man obsessed with sensuous lighting, soft-focus close-ups, exotic sets and unbroken dissolves. No one, not even Jean Renoir, has explored the camera as an instrument for capturing shades and tints of light quite so much as von Sternberg.

His first film was made in 1925: *The Salvation Hunters*. A potent melodrama obviously influenced by von Stroheim's *Greed*, *The Salvation Hunters* captured, with an eerie fidelity, the milieu of the derelict and the down-and-out. Von Sternberg used various effects which would later appear again and again in his work: for example, shadows of river barges keep appearing with the characters, visibly pursuing them. The movie was rich in the slow, stylized movement and continual richness of detail which would become von Sternberg's hallmark.

Chaplin, enormously impressed with *The Salvation Hunters*, commissioned von Sternberg's next film: *The Sea Gull*. The film, said to be "a lovely collection of photographs," was never released. Von Sternberg's next film, *Escape*, was made for MGM and began to give people in the industry the impression that von Sternberg was hardly an apt talent to direct successful movies. Then von Sternberg astounded them all with

Marlene Dietrich

the movie which would be far more successful than his others: *Underworld* (1927),
the first of the Chicago gangland pictures.

Written by von Sternberg in collaboration
with Ben Hecht and starring Clive Brook
and Evelyn Brent, *Underworld* told the story
of Feathers McCoy, a Chicago gunman.
Done with a tight control of characterization
and plot movement, *Underworld* caught the
criminal world in that half-light so characteristic of von Sternberg's films. But here the
manipulation of light, the striking close-ups,
the continuing use of symbolic settings
worked. It was as though von Sternberg's
technique were more suited to the grim,
morbid underworld than to the exotica of
Shanghai or Cairo.

Three underworld movies followed: *The
Dragnet, Docks of New York*, and *The Last
Command* (all 1928). None was as compact
or as dramatically effective as *Underworld*.
Each one progressed toward the total visual
fascination of von Sternberg's camera. In
his next film, *The Case of Lena Smith*
(1929), von Sternberg kept the camera
moving tirelessly throughout the film. It was
as though he were trying to create a new
kind of canvas out of the moving camera
and the strange, sensuous lighting.

The Blue Angel (1930) was von Sternberg's first sound film and, in the opinion of
many critics, his finest film. Curiously, it was
his only film made outside Hollywood.

Based on a novel by Heinrich Mann and
made in Germany, the film depicted an aging, unpopular professor who is duped and
run dizzily aground by a sluttish cabaret
singer. The movie progresses with a momentum and a rhythm that seem uncharac-
teristic of von Sternberg's slow, dwelling
habit. The ironies run deep, and end on a
bitter note: the betrayed professor, on a
cabaret stage, dressed as a clown, crowing
like a rooster.

The Blue Angel blends von Sternberg's
cherished art of "painting with movement"
with his unquestioned (but often suppressed)
dramatic talents and adds something new—
rich, three-dimensional characterizations,
particularly of the cabaret singer. Von Sternberg had chosen a virtually unknown German actress, Marlene Dietrich, for the part.
She was vivid and electric in it. He brought
her to Hollywood, and she was to star in
most of his later movies. Dwight MacDonald called Dietrich von Sternberg's *femme
fatale*; and so, very likely, she was. Her face
conveyed such an elegance, a rush of moods,
a primitive feminine power that von Sternberg, the portrait photographer, could hardly
resist catching it in all its tones, under all
sorts of lighting, within any possible exotic
setting. In a sense, the rest of von Sternberg's
career would be dedicated to moving por-
traits of his new star. He had found a subject worthy of his talents.

It is difficult to assess whether the rest
of von Sternberg's movies really represent
the downfall of an artist or the rise of a
strange, unusual perfectionist. Movies like
Morocco (1930), *Shanghai Express* (1932),
The Scarlet Empress (1934), and *The Devil
Is a Woman* (1935) carry his absorption
with lighting, with camera movement, and
with unique kinds of composition into a
totally new sphere. Plot and characterization become increasingly less important in
these movies, and von Sternberg seems to
glorify the raising of a coffee cup, the entrance of a character into a room, the supple
play of light through branches or vines on
a barely moving face.

The film critic Andrew Sarris has called
von Sternberg "a lyricist of light and
shadow." Von Sternberg's later works leave
little doubt that this is true. But does a
thorough absorption with tonal quality,
lighting effects, carefully fabricated opulent
sets, and close-up after close-up after
close-up—to the neglect of story, momentum, character, conflict, and theme—constitute a movie or a museum piece?

165

Metropolis 1926

M 1931

FRITZ LANG

Von Sternberg built his reputation totally within the American studios; Fritz Lang came to America, his reputation as a major German filmmaker preceding him. Two of Lang's movies in particular, *Metropolis* and *M*, had realized critical and financial success in America. *Metropolis* (1926) presented a stylized and brutalized world in which men were enslaved and confined to an underground nether world, among the machines that propelled the world above the surface. The film was one of the great achievements of the German expressionist movement.

M (1932), one of Lang's first sound films, was an entirely different kind of movie: a psychological study of a sadist and child molester who generated incredible fear within a community. It was in *M* that Lang revealed his real talents: tight, dramatic structuring, the ability to reveal a character through action, and one of the best touches in movie history for generating intense suspense.

Lang's first two movies in America were perhaps his best: *Fury* (1936) and *You Only Live Once* (1937). *Fury* has been described at length in the previous chapter. In it, Lang not only created a potent drama centering on a serious social problem, but he also captured local America in a way that few American filmmakers had previously. Lang's touches—his faces, his group shots, his small town sets—give *Fury*, despite its violence and melodramatic crescendo, a profound believability. Lang was able to create a sense of place, time, and people that seemed real and at the same time had the quality of an everyman, everywhere, everytime.

You Only Live Once dealt like *Fury* with grievous social injustice, and again like *Fury*, was centered around falsifying evidence and the horrors into which it plunged an innocent man. Eddie Taylor (Henry Fonda), a small-time criminal who—after his third conviction and a lengthy prison sentence—has decided to go straight, finds himself unable to get a job. He is blamed for a murder—a hat with his initials is found near the scene—tried, and convicted. Like *I Am a Fugitive From a Chain Gang*, the nightmare grows: Eddie becomes more desperate and lawlessness becomes his only means of survival.

Lang's ability to create taut, poignant drama came across well in *You Only Live Once*. The film is rich in moments characteristic of Lang. In the death cell, we see Eddie waiting amid the stark shadows thrown out by a bright, naked bulb. When he makes his escape across the prison yard, the entire scene is shrouded in dense fog—much as Eddie's whole world has become fogged. As the film progresses, we see Eddie increasingly confined to places that throw shadows over him, keeping him apart from society.

Both *Fury* and *You Only Live Once* dealt with the growth of paranoia within good men, as well as with the social pressures that created that paranoia. Lang's next important movie (after a thin, social drama and two Westerns) showed the growth of near-paranoia that resulted from a single man's messianic fervor to destroy the German Fuehrer, Adolf Hitler. *Man Hunt* (1941) was at once a classic of the chase melodrama (alongside Hitchcock's *The Thirty-nine*

Fury 1936

Steps and *North by Northwest*) as well as a brilliant character portrayal. It was one of Lang's best.

Based on the novel *Rogue Male* by Geoffrey Household, *Man Hunt* depicts a wealthy British sportsman, Captain Thorndike (Walter Pidgeon) who, for what he claims is the "sport" of it, slips into Germany and gets within firing range of Hitler at his mountain resort. He shoots—click, no shell. He loads the gun, lines up to fire, and pauses. Then he is caught. He meets his antagonist, played by George Sanders, a major and a Hitler aide who is also a sportsman. Sanders is familiar with Thorndike's reputation and eager to defeat him at his own game. Thorndike argues he had never intended to shoot: it was all the sport. The Major arranges for Thorndike to be killed in a "hunting accident." And here the chase begins. Across Germany, over the English Channel and through England, Thorndike is gradually transformed from the bored sportsman to a hunted, haunted man who sees in his predicament an image of the condition of Britain in the face of a monstrous Germany. It is a kind of paranoia that we see, but paranoia with a difference: Thorndike's fear becomes rage and his rage becomes resolve. After the tense climax and his gradual recuperation—a period punctuated on film by the surge of German invasions—Thorndike takes with him a high-powered rifle and a knapsack and parachutes from a plane onto "the rooftops of Germany." The propagandistic side of the film reaches a feverish pitch here, and, as the narrator says, "this time he knows his purpose and unflinchingly faces his destiny."

167

The character of Thorndike, so painstakingly revealed throughout the film, is all at once transformed into a cardboard caricature.

Man Hunt drew upon Lang's most familiar talents: his finely attuned sense of locale, his rich dramatic development, his ability to place characters under enormous stress and bring out fresh, convincing aspects of their personalities. As the story progresses, for example, we become convinced that, at least subconsciously, Thorndike *had* wanted to pull the trigger. The entire chase serves only to make him consciously aware of that earlier, repressed resolve. His relationship to the young streetwalker (Joan Bennett) also brings out a change in Thorndike: he treats her with patronizing fondness that bespeaks his aristocratic upbringing. But when he learns what the Nazis have done to her, his face—already stricken and angry—takes on a new hostility, a primal vengeance that we have never before seen. Thorndike's progression through the film strips him of just about all the accretions of civilization, reducing him to the barest instincts, the most brutal of forces.

Man Hunt was made early in 1941 and released in the fall of that year, the most critical year before America's entrance into the war. The propagandistic intentions of the film are as obvious as those of a John Wayne-U.S. Marines epic. Propaganda appears within the film, however, in an entirely different way. Our identification with Thorndike, and our immersion in his dilemma, leads us to his rage at the Germans, his awareness that on that fatal day he *should* have pulled the trigger. As Paul Jensen remarked in *The Cinema of Fritz Lang*, the struggle that forces us to hate Germany is an internal rather than an external struggle—and by virtue of that, all the more forceful, all the more effective.

The years 1941 to 1945 saw a host of propagandistic movies urging the American people to fear, hate, and fight Germany: few are so intrinsically persuasive as *Man Hunt*.

Lang's next several movies were all made with his dramatic edge intact, and represent the latter part of his richest period: *Hangmen Also Die* (1943), *Ministry of Fear*, *The Woman In the Window*, and *Scarlet Street* (1945). Throughout each, Lang forced imminent dilemmas on his characters, pushing them to extremes, and with them, the audience. Like Hitchcock, Lang liked to take reasonably normal people and plunge them into nightmares that forced them to draw upon instincts and resources long repressed by modern society. It is a tricky way to handle a movie, for it requires a balance of audience manipulation and a gingerly handling of theme, while at the same time keeping the world from turning obtuse and awkward on the screen.

After 1945, Lang continued making movies, somewhat irregularly, until 1961. With few exceptions (*Rancho Notorious*, 1952, and *The Big Heat*, 1953), his later movies lacked the tight dramatic control and the gradual, fine characterization that typified his earlier works. There were still touches of the careful, intense Lang craftsmanship in the sets and acting of his later movies. But it looked as if the studio system—with which Lang had never been totally at home—had finally gotten to him, and had eroded the inner substance of his films. Nonetheless, Lang's best work, of both the German period (*Dr. Mabuse, Metropolis, M*) and the American period (*Fury, You Only Live Once, Man Hunt, The Woman In the Window*) remain a striking testimonial to one of the great dramatists and darker spirits of screen history.

The Big Heat 1953

JOHN FORD

The career of that quintessential American director, John Ford, spanned so many decades—from 1917 to 1966—that it seems almost foolhardy to place him within the context of any single decade. Yet in many ways he belongs to the thirties as he does not to the forties or the fifties. Not that his art did not progress. It did. There is a deepening and a broadening with every decade. But the thirties seemed to contain more of Ford's major works than any other decade: *The Informer* (1935), *The Prisoner of Shark Island* (1936), *Stagecoach*, *Young Mr. Lincoln* (1939), and *The Grapes of Wrath* (1940). Moreover, the thirties was Ford's most experimental period—he dealt with characterization, lighting, and confined sets (*The Informer*), historical drama on a fresh scale (*The Prisoner of Shark Island*, *Young Mr. Lincoln*, *Drums Along the Mohawk*), and singlehandedly revitalized the ailing Western (*Stagecoach*).

169

Orson Welles was once asked which American directors impressed him most. He answered, ". . . the old masters. By which I mean John Ford, John Ford, and John Ford. . . . With Ford at his best, you feel that the movie has lived and breathed in a real world."

There is no easy distinctive feature about Ford's work, as there is, say, to Capra or von Sternberg. Yet a John Ford movie is immediately identifiable on the screen: the organized composition, the sense of pictorial space that Ford created on the other side of the camera, the unobtrusive but always smooth and beautiful camera work. Ford is not the type of director who leaves the arrangement of the camera or the composition to his cameraman. A craftsman of the highest rank, he wants to know exactly what is being shot. His camera angles, camera distance, and all the uses of the camera tend to be clean, sensitive, and dominated by a man of acute visual awareness.

Ford began in the silent era making two-reelers, then features. He was an acknowledged craftsman, a director who could bring a film in under budget and often in advance of the deadline. But his films of the silent period revealed only a glimpse of the strong director who emerged in the thirties. The silent era was Ford's apprenticeship. And, judging merely by the visual quality of much of his later work, it served him well.

Ford's talents blossomed slowly, even after he began to work in the sound film. *The Lost Patrol*, made in 1934, was a strong but uneven work. An adventure story about a World War I army patrol stranded in the Sahara, it shows Ford's ability to use the narrative framework to probe various characters. By and large the characterizations are tight and effective, but the film's rhythm is slow and uneven. It also lacks the sustained dramatic rise of later films.

The Informer, made in 1935, was Ford's earliest major movie. It was a project that Ford had wanted to do for some years and only in the wake of the success of *The Lost Patrol* was he able to. Based on the novel by Liam Flaherty, *The Informer* tells of a cheap, mean-spirited man named Gypo Nolan who turns informer on a leader of the Irish revolt. The story is not all that much: it takes place in an evening, and most of what we see is Gypo's all-night spree in which he spends the money he got from turning in Frankie McPhillip. But Ford handles the story with consummate skill in creating atmosphere and in depicting his characters visually. For example, early in the film Gypo sees the poster announcing a reward for Frankie's whereabouts. As he walks away—obviously affected by what he has seen, and the awareness of what he is about to do—the poster blows away and flaps up against his legs: a brief and totally cinematic image of Gypo's tormented conscience.

The tempo is slow, the mood dark and ominous. Exteriors are foggy, and the film takes place almost entirely in the evening. Ford uses lighting to get closer to the mind of Gypo. Throughout the evening, as the fog settles more densely over the streets, so does Gypo's own fog seem to grow—the liquor he consumes seems only to make it heavier. For instance, just after turning in Frankie, he sees a blind man, whom he feels is looking at him accusingly. He grabs the man only to realize he is blind. It is a potent image of Gypo's struggle with his own conscience, struggling to reach the surface of his mind.

Stagecoach 1939

The year after *The Informer*, Ford made two of the historical dramas which would, like his Westerns, become a standard part of his over-all work. One of these, *The Prisoner of Shark Island*, reflected Ford's growing dramatic control as well as his fascination for Americana. Basically the story of Doctor Mudd, the Southerner who put splints on John Wilkes Booth's broken leg, the film follows Mudd through his horrendous trial and into the grim confinement of Shark Island. As often happens in Hollywood biographies, history is a bit muddled, but Ford is careful where he takes his liberties. For example, the whole episode of the typhoid epidemic serves not only to give Mudd a potential release from Shark Island, but it brings several characters to a dramatic point of ultimate conflict.

In 1939, Ford made two of what would later be considered his best movies: *Young Mr. Lincoln* and *Stagecoach*. *Young Mr. Lincoln* depicts the Illinois lawyer as a stoop-shouldered, gentle Henry Fonda, a man who, riding into town, glances wistfully at a play poster of Hamlet, regretful that he doesn't have the money to see it. The film is heavy with that aromatic Americana so familiar with Ford: a subtle, enhancing blend of the schoolboy's Lincoln and Hollywood's affectation of diffidence and naïveté via the "Aw, shucks" Fonda style. Yet the movie is finely made, with rigorously controlled composition, excellent acting, and a firmer sense of reality than is found in most historical romances. Indeed, it is difficult to judge whether Ford merely built on the schoolboy's Lincoln or has himself given it a new dimension.

Stagecoach was one of those epochal movies that became the measure by which others in its genre are judged. A simple and familiar enough story—an assorted group of passengers on a stagecoach traveling through Apache territory—but Ford handled it with consummate dramatic and cinematographic skill. Each character takes on sharp focus early in the movie, and the action rises with fine, dramatic intensity.

Stagecoach was the first film in which Ford used his favorite setting, Monument Valley, a stretch of the Navaho Indian reservation straddling the Arizona-Utah border. Monument Valley typified the clean, grandiose exteriors that Ford liked best in his movies: huge mesas rising suddenly out of the flat desert soil. Ford's West was less a country of trees and grazing cattle and sagebrush than of the stirring horizons of a Monument Valley.

Like the thirties, the forties were success-studded years for Ford: highly acclaimed "major" films such as *The Grapes of Wrath* (1940) and *They Were Expendable* (1945), and more of the extraordinary Westerns that only Ford could make: *My Darling Clementine* (1946), *She Wore a Yellow Ribbon* (1949). Throughout the forties, those little touches which have become so typical of Ford, so "Fordian," became apparent in the movies: the almost obligatory community scene, the exquisite, classical composition, the themes of loyalty, courage, reparation.

Of Ford's Westerns—and Ford has dominated the Western genre much as Hitchcock has dominated the suspense genre—one stands as equal alongside *Stagecoach* for its dramatic power, its sweep, and its evocative brilliance. *Wagonmaster*, made in 1950, was based on an original story by Ford. The movie tells of two young cattlehands who are recruited, partially against their wishes, to guide a Mormon wagon train through the desert and mountains. Yet the power of *Wagonmaster* lies less in the story than in the way Ford tells it; less in the characters than in the odds that Ford depicts them as overcoming.

Tensions lie loosely in the film. First,

there are the Mormons, an unwanted people seeking a land they can make their own. Ostracized from a town, they are forced to move even before they have a guide to help them. Ford depicts the Mormons as a rugged, fiercely resilient bunch. They are not a band of religious outcasts but a clan who can survive only by their loyalty and ministrations to one another. In that sense, they become the Okies of *The Grapes of Wrath,* the Welsh of *How Green Was My Valley,* the Irish of *The Informer.* In one of the film's best sequences, Ford suggests just how much these people have going for them by intercutting a Mormon campfire dance as bandits approach. Many of the images are no more than shadows on wagon tarps, yet it becomes apparent that these are people that Ford admires, people he wants us to admire.

The framing, the lighting, the composition of *Wagonmaster* give the film a beauty rare even for Ford. It is a slow, reflective movie, one in which the camera lingers, and in which mesas and sunrises become more important than simply settings against which the action takes place. *Wagonmaster* is not only about a people crossing and overcoming the land; it is about people discovering the land. In the concluding sequence, the wagons must cross a dangerous rocky hillside to enter the valley that the settlers have sought. Ford places a camera in one of the wagons, and its precipitous journey down the hill becomes ours. But its reward —that rich fertile valley so evocative to Ford and to us—becomes our reward as well.

Wagonmaster gives the viewer a sense of Ford at his best. It is a stirring movie, and a deeply beautiful one. Even Ford's usual sentimentality is tempered here by the harshness of the circumstances and by the absence of characters who are neither more nor less than we believe they might be.

My Darling Clementine 1946

She Wore a Yellow Ribbon 1949

The Man Who Shot Liberty Valance 1962

How Green Was My Valley 1941

173

THE POSTERS

"TORTURED BY A NATION FOR HIS ACT OF MERCY! THE TRUE STORY OF A NATION'S HIDDEN SHAME. Tricked by fate into helping an assassin, an innocent man is torn from the woman he loves . . . shackled . . . condemned to a living death on a fever island where brutes are masters and sharks are guards! THE STARK DRAMA of "I am a Fugitive from a Chain Gang." THE MIGHTY POWER of "Les Miserables." *The Prisoner of Shark Island* starring Warner Baxter."

Movie posters and movie advertisements have never been content merely to announce a movie; they have depended on a type of sales pitch all their own, one in which phrases like "high drama," "explosive power," and "romantic saga" appear again and again. Graphically, they tend to be active and eye-catching, a brief suggestion of what incredible moments await you in the theater.

Of course, if a future historian were to try to interpret past American movies solely from the posters and ads, he would quickly come to the conclusion that movies contained nothing more than raw violence and varied flirtations with sex. Rarely do the posters suggest anything more. But no matter. The posters, like the movie, need not justify their appeal; seeing them is satisfaction enough.

WALT DISNEY

Walt Disney falls somewhere between the innovative directors and the greatest of the movie moguls—and even then in a separate, special classification. For Disney's genius, like that of DeMille, had less to do with artistic genius than with anticipating and meeting shifting audiences.

In the thirties fame came with Mickey Mouse, and millions of moviegoers often sat through long, uncomfortable features just to see the 10-minute short starring that mouse. In the forties Disney moved his focus to full-length animated features and nature films. When television appeared, threatening and gradually eroding the financial independence of the studios, Disney was Hollywood's only mogul to take over television on its own ground—and make another fortune there. Then there is Disneyland, and now Disney World in Florida. Disney never stopped. He seemed infatuated with the possibility of making his fantasies a permanent fixture of the American consciousness, and to an incredible extent he succeeded.

Walter Elias Disney, a young man from Kansas City, had moved restlessly in and out of art studios and advertising companies. By his mid-twenties, he had decided upon the near-impossible: setting out for Hollywood to establish his own animation studio. It was an ambitious, almost reckless move. The young Disney was guided far more by his desire to make a fortune and build an empire than by his interest in making movies. Yet, as Richard Schickel pointed out in *The Disney Version*, young Walt did have an advantage—indeed, a supreme advantage—over the moguls, writers, and directors who made up Hollywood in the mid-twenties. He had an instinctive touch with the American Midwest, with the heartland's tastes, appetites, and sensibilities. He did not have to go out and struggle to discover American culture; he had it in his bones. On that premise, he founded the industry's most enduring empire. And he began with a mouse.

Mickey Mouse was hardly Disney's first animated short, but it was his first cartoon hit. Earlier shorts, such as the *Alice in Cartoonland* series, enabled Disney to begin his own modest studio, but not much more. But Mickey Mouse (originally named Mortimer) somehow broke through his fantasy presence on the animated screen to become the first genuine cartoon star—and a star who could easily vie with Chaplin, Keaton, or other Hollywood figures. The first two Mickey Mouse shorts were silents with music added: *Plane Crazy* and *Gallopin' Gaucho*. In the third, *Steamboat Willie*, Mickey spoke, and at that point established himself as a major attraction to audiences throughout the country. Soon the tiny Disney studio was able to grow, develop new techniques, and add new characters to the cartoon pantheon: Minnie Mouse, Pluto, and Donald Duck.

The novelist E. M. Forster said of Mickey that he was "energetic without being elevated. . . . No one has ever been softened after seeing Mickey or has wanted to give away an extra glass of water to the poor." Indeed, Mickey was a thin, rough-edged, sometimes nasty little creature—hardly the "lovable mouse" that later, in future cartoons and comics, he would become. The addition of a larger galaxy of cartoon figures did not soften Mickey so much as expand the cartoons from their raucous,

177

intense atmosphere to a cooler, more relaxed mode.

Disney's studio, while thriving with business, was kept in a tight economic pinch, largely because Disney insisted on improving each cartoon, on adding more dimension, giving the characters more rhythmic motion, indeed, experimenting on virtually every level with the problems and possibilities of animation. If Disney deserves any niche in the art of motion picture innovation and technique, it is that, throughout the early thirties, he and his staff virtually created the art of the animated cartoon. Animated films of the twenties had been jerky comic strips, with movement barely convincing enough to resemble real life. Disney did not introduce the idea of anthropomorphizing animals and inanimate objects, but he did perfect it. He could make a mouse scream convincingly in rage, a table walk away in disgust, a flower beam happily. Moreover, throughout the thirties, Disney struggled to add depth to his cartoons. He wanted to avoid a flat, two-dimensional effect. He did so by using specially designed animation tables with cels (the transparent cellulose sheet on which drawings are made) numbering up to a dozen.

Disney did not draw many of his cartoons, even in the very early years. His talents as an animator *per se* were probably negligible. It always bothered him that he himself could not draw the mouse—not even scratch one out on a note pad—which had made him famous. But what Disney could do was recognize an idea that appealed to the public, and see it through to execution and promotion. He was a mogul of sorts, presiding over productions that he controlled from beginning to end. Rarely were the ideas his, rarely was any of the animation work his, rarely were the innovations his; but by recognizing and developing them, he could take credit—and did.

As the studio grew, Disney's ambitions expanded. Shorts were fine—he knew they

Snow White and the Seven Dwarfs 1938

would continue to provide the basic income for his studio—but he was eyeing wistfully the first animated feature, with his name over it. By 1934, he had begun organizing production on *Snow White and the Seven Dwarfs*. The production problems this film encountered far surpassed anything Disney had expected. For one thing, he insisted that it be slick and stylized—far more so than the shorts. He believed audiences would not sit still for the crude, jittery style of the Mickey Mouse shorts if extended to feature length. Problems of movement, rhythm, and giving people and animals shapes that were natural and yet capable of smooth movement on the two-dimensional animation board forced Disney's production staff to a new level of sophistication. Morover, it became clear that there were problems in making most of the human characters "people." Animals were far easier to animate than people; when they reacted, their whole bodies came into play. "But how," said Disney, "does a human being react to stimulus? . . . . He is the victim of a civilization whose ideal is the unbotherable, poker-faced man and the attractive, unruffled woman. Even the gestures get to be calculated." It's no mystery why the animation of animals dominated the cartoon field.

Snow White was three years in production. When finally released, it suggested the future of the Disney studios—more animated features. The technical advances that Disney's staff had made in putting the film together, and the development of the multiplane camera enabling up to a dozen cels to be used in a shot, encouraged Disney to invest in further animated features. Production began on *Pinocchio* and a pet Disney project, *Fantasia*—a feature which would integrate animation and classical music.

Fantasia was an oddity for Disney, who had long sworn that the sole purpose of his films was to entertain. Yet, throughout

Dumbo 1942

the thirties, particularly the late thirties, he was receiving awards and accolades from intellectuals and critics. He apparently felt some responsibility to match the expectations of his enthusiastic supporters. It is typical of Disney, however, that his approach to animation as a kind of popular high art would not be to attempt radical new animation techniques or ideas—for which a number of the young animators on his staff were thoroughly capable. Rather, Disney's approach in *Fantasia* was to use the music of admitted masters—notably Stokowski, Tchaikovsky, Beethoven, Bach and Moussorgsky—as "background" for a variety of usually standard animated sequences. There *were* fresh ideas in the film's animation, admittedly: *The Sorcerer's Apprentice* sequence has a fine rhythmic flow, perhaps one of the most skillful uses of rhythm within a cartoon. The grotesque scene in the *Bald Mountain* sequence has a stirring, vibrating power unusual to animation. Yet the film attempted to interlock drastic opposites. It tried for a style that was both

Walt Disney

classical and modern American. Its failure was a double failure, of conception and of taste. For example, in *The Night on Bald Mountain*, the hideous creatures of the night —bats and gargoyles and grotesque limbs of trees—all vanish on the coming of dawn and of the baroque *Ave Maria*. *Fantasia* at its very best showed the power and intensity inherent in animated features; at its very worst, it suggested that Disney's artistic competence was best delivered at the level of the fairy tale or the Mickey Mouse cartoon.

The compound problems involved in making *Pinocchio* and *Fantasia* just about ruined the Disney studio. It took most of the forties for the company to recoup. Disney continued shorts and features through the forties, but the features, such as *Dumbo*, *Bambi*, and *Cinderella*, lacked the sustained rhythm, the constant inventiveness, and the raw excitement of his earlier features. It was partly an ossification process: Disney's studio had always been a one-man operation, and as it expanded, it came to discourage both the interchange of ideas possible earlier, as well as the type of animator who was likely to have a number of good ideas. Moreover, Disney himself tended to approach new projects without the old stirrings of enthusiasm.

It is ironic but telling that, in the fifties, when studios and Hollywood in general had fallen into a period of discouraged moviemaking, Disney should come again to the fore. There were a number of things that sparked Disney's rebirth: the nature series —animals and nature depicted with amazing camerawork; the production of two of his better features—*Alice In Wonderland* and *Peter Pan*; and television, which Disney saw and conquered. Not least of all, there was Disney's newest, though in some respects his oldest, dream: a fantasy-land of previously untouched dimensions, a world that would mirror in its geography and its pave-

ments the world he had so long created on the screen. The fifties was the last decade that Disney saw out while he was yet alive, but during that period his studio reached the stature of a major Hollywood company. And Disney amalgamated all his previous work to establish himself clearly as the master of a particular genre of American entertainment.

Disney's career began in the Midwest and, in terms of the fantasies and images he nurtured, it ended there. His movies are filled with a sense of wholesomeness, of a boy growing up in clean and simple times with a wide-eyed wonder at an expanding (but not *too* expanding) world, of problems that are neither moral nor social but simple and simply resolved, of humor that lacks bite, of pleasant cartoon characters who are all charming, yet totally without obligation or failure. While Disney's impact on the filmmaking world was not particularly significant, his impact on the millions who saw his films was indeed incalculable. Disney was our modern Aesop, with a grim difference: the moral was always shaped from sentiment, thus making it oh! so easy to take.

WORLD WAR II

The call of war in late 1941 caught Hollywood, much as it caught the rest of the nation, only half prepared. Already the movies had been depicting the seething forces in Europe as a new cauldron of war. Producers had been careful not to promote American involvement *too* obviously—the isolationist, non-war feelings ran high in the country, particularly in the Midwest—millions of Americans had already seen grinning "Japs" and mean, sardonic Germans on the screen. *Four Sons* (1940) depicted a Czech family in the midst of the Nazis' rise to power; *Mortal Storm* (1940) showed a similar family, in Germany, split apart by Hitler's regime. Suspense movies such as *Man Hunt* (1941), *Escape* (1940) and *Foreign Correspondent* (1940) took place against the panoply of German victories in Europe. Such films suggested the dimensions of the rising spectre of war. In *Foreign Correspondent*, Joel McCrea spoke across the Atlantic through a mike from bomb-blasted London: "The lights are going out in Europe! Ring yourself around with steel, America!" Words to chill audiences and curdle the isolationists.

What followed, of course, was war, and war movies. One of the first and best was *Sergeant York* (1941), Howard Hawks' film of a pacifist who, when seeing the destruction of World War I, became a hero. The story was told realistically and sympathetically: war was a grim reality, not the playground for mock heroics that so

Foreign Correspondent 1940

Mrs. Miniver 1942 (Greer Garson)

182

many later war films would suggest. Once America had entered the war, movies about war became dominant billboard fare. A few were reasonably honest about war and the horrible catastrophe it was: *Action In the North Atlantic* (1943), *Thirty Seconds Over Tokyo* (1944), *To Have and Have Not* (1944), *They Were Expendable* (1944), *The Story of G.I. Joe* (1945) were a few. By and large though, the battle epics were little more than backlot slaughter stories, with tough, wisecracking GIs demolishing entire battalions of Nazis or "Japs."

Not surprisingly, the best movies of World War II were not battle stories, but rather stories that took place against the background of war. Two of the finest movies of this type were *Mrs. Miniver* and *Casablanca* (both 1942). *Mrs. Miniver* was William Wyler's strong, emotional story of a London family caught in the Nazi blitz. Rather than concentrate on war as a spectrum of battle-fields and bodies, *Mrs. Miniver* showed war as it was experienced by a family that Americans everywhere could identify with. It was one of the most successful movies of the war.

Casablanca has become the film with which its star, Humphrey Bogart, is best identified. And deservedly so. The role was perfect for Bogart, much as Bogart was ideal for the role of Rick Blaine, a free-wheeling American who has smuggled arms to Ethiopia and joined the Loyalists in the Spanish war but who, even in the midst of

Casablanca 1942

Europe's greatest war, cannot choose sides. *Casablanca* depicts Rick's indecision and what little grip he has on himself—his nostalgic love for Ingrid Bergman ("Play it again, Sam")—against the realities of conflict and betrayal that eventually force Rick to choose. The battlefield in *Casablanca* is a man's soul, and most of it is played out in Rick's cafe. But the movie was perfect for its time. It took the tough, swaggering, independent hero of the thirties and cast him adrift in the midst of a conflict that was larger than his ability to deal with it *solely* on the basis of his independent style. It was the Bogart of *The Maltese Falcon* who became embroiled in the subtle subterfuges of *Casablanca*. His old habits of playing every hand for himself, of staying a step ahead of the opposition, no longer worked. *Casablanca* gave Americans a realization that it was time for the tough individual of the thirties to commit himself to something larger than his own games and stratagems.

Not all the wartime movies, of course, were war movies. One of the most successful genres through the war—and in terms of the number made, perhaps the most successful—was the musical. In 1943 and 1944, fully 40 percent of the films released by major studios were musicals. The enormous success of the musical during wartime was hardly limited to movies: Broadway was loaded with musicals, and one of the

most successful Broadway musicals of all times, *Oklahoma*, premiered in New York in 1943—at the lowest ebb of the war. Part of the reason for the success of musicals, of course, lay in their escapist appeal: nothing could be further from war, further from conflict and human misery, than a delightful song-and-dance show.

But musicals were important in another way. If war did anything to Hollywood, it made the producers, writers, and directors conscious of something that is happening all the time in movies, but is rarely recognized by those who make them—the subtle propaganda inherent in films. All American films promote, consciously or not, an "American style of life." And musicals, because they are organized to do nothing more than entertain audiences, tend to promote a kind of pleasant Americana even more so. True enough, the values in these movies are not at all near the surface; yet they are present. What made wartime musicals different from those before and after them was the degree to which their creators were aware of those values and the impact they would have on the moviegoing public.

Musicals such as *Alexander's Ragtime Band* (1938), *The Wizard of Oz* (1939), *Babes In Arms* (1939), *Strike Up the Band* (1940), *Babes On Broadway* (1941), *Stage Door Canteen* (1943), and *Meet Me In St. Louis* (1944) were more than song-and-dance shows; they were a summons to American loyalties. The themes of "We can do it together," "The show must go on," "How great we've got it in America," became all-important. Often the stories outdistanced the production numbers in their fascination for audiences.

There were "war musicals" as well, most of them better forgotten than remembered. But two particularly stand out: *Yankee Doodle Dandy* (1942), a nostalgic biography of George M. Cohan which gave musical tribute to the American Way of Life much as the stage musical *Oklahoma* sang praise of the spirit and tradition of rural America, and *This Is the Army* (1943), an all-stops-pulled musical with unending marching scenes, flag-waving scenes, and no less than 17 Irving Berlin songs. It seemed as though Hollywood were out to win the war using musicals as its heaviest artillery.

If the war marked anything for Hollywood, it was the end of an era—not only an era in American history, that long economic struggle of the thirties, but of an era when the industry could take its place in America for granted. The war made producers and directors a little more cognizant of their role in shaping the consciousness of the American people—and, by that fact, a little more careful (or, in some cases, more careless) as to what went on film. Moreover, the end of the war signaled the beginning of what would become for the industry its greatest threat: television.

NEW DIRECTIONS

Within five years following the end of World War II, three shifting elements within the movie industry and in American society made it obvious that movies would never again be the same—nor, most emphatically, would the industry.

The first of these was, in some ways, the last to be detected by the major studios: a fresh influx of foreign feature films and a growing audience which reached out for them, particularly the Italian neo-realism films, such as *Open City, Shoeshine*, and *The Bicycle Thief*—movies almost documentary in their approach, casting non-actors to play the parts, taking place not in studios but in the ruined villages and cities of Italy.

These movies were alien to the familiar studio products. People would struggle through an hour and a half of hardship and conflict only to glimpse, at the end, a dim ray of hope—a far, far cry from the glittering rainbows at the end of American features. Admittedly these films did not make a great inroad on the majority of the American audience, but the newer generation of directors, such as Billy Wilder, Elia Kazan, Jules Dassin, and Carol Reed, were obviously influenced by this trend. Elia Kazan's *Boomerang* (1947), for example, is handled in a style closer to that of a sustained newsreel than to the standard Hollywood production. In the late forties, directors began to move out of studios and

185

The French called it *cinéma vérité*—genuine cinema, the camera as unblinking observer catching small moments of truth in the lives of the people before it. "Cinema," said one of the French New Wave's liveliest proponents, Jean-Luc Godard, "is reality at 24 times a second." To some extent, the French filmmakers used scripts and professional actors, but the difference was telling on the screen; in movies like Godard's *Breathless* and François Truffaut's *Jules and Jim,* the characters seem to suggest a life of their own, a life beyond the movie, a life with rhythms and pulses and moments of expressive immediacy barely ever caught in Hollywood. The viewer felt that this life preceded the camera's visit, and would continue after the camera turned away.

The impact of *cinéma vérité* on America came not in the Hollywood studio feature film, but in the return to an old, little-developed film genre: the independent documentary. Except for the documentaries of an individualistic filmmaker such as Robert Flaherty, the form had previously been a tool of social reform and social analysis verging on propaganda. It had been used more emphatically to reveal a social situation rather than to explore the nuances or subtleties of that situation. But in the mid-sixties, with films like Frederick Wiseman's *The Titicut Follies,* the Maysles Brothers' *Salesman,* and Allan King's *Warrendale,* the documentary took on a fresh vitality and a score of new directions. For example, *The Titicut Follies* graphically caught the inner life of a Massachusetts mental hospital—it was like a Dantean venture into the bowels of hell: old men stripped and hosed down as a form of "shock therapy;" doctors and assistants acting with more cruelty and grotesque hatred than the most emotionally crippled of the inmates. *Salesman* (1969) focused on the world of door-to-door Bible salesmen. This is an amazing piece of purest Americana, a study of a species, men who work desperately to sell fifty-dollar Bibles to people who can neither afford to buy them nor resist the salesmen's rousing appeal to faith and family solidarity.

Only a few recent documentaries have been box-office successes—Michael Wadleigh's *Woodstock* and the Maysles Brothers' *Gimme Shelter,* both documenting rock concerts—but a fresh audience for documentaries has emerged, and the documentary filmmaker no longer works plagued by his inability to find an audience. Indeed, an audience is emerging that finds the documentary more convincing, more believable, and more involving than the scripted feature. The documentary lives.

THE NEW DOCUMENTARY

Warrendale 1966

187

Citizen Kane 1941

into the streets—not in any great numbers, but enough to offer a small group of films which clearly ran against the current of standard productions.

The second major event was the United States government's action against the major studios for violating antitrust laws—owning both production facilities and outlets; that is, for making movies and owning the theaters in which they were shown. The suit, begun in 1945 and protracted through the late forties, and court rulings destroyed forever the absolute authority of the studios. Until then, major film companies—MGM, Paramount, Universal, Columbia, Fox, Warners—held a virtual monopoly on the distribution market. (One incident that points out the dangers of such a monopoly: when the Hearst publishing empire tried to stop Orson Welles' *Citizen Kane* from being shown in the theaters in 1941, it influenced the major studios to turn down producer RKO's request to show it in their theaters; only later did Warner Brothers relent and permit bookings in its theaters.) The single most important effect of the antitrust action was new competition for the major studios, in the form of independent producers and independent productions.

There had, of course, been independent productions before, any number of them in the heyday of the independent, roughly between 1908 and 1919 and after those years. (Robert Flaherty and Orson Welles, among others, made most of their films independently.) But because of the studios' control of the theatrical outlets, the independents were unable to get decent bookings in theaters or proper promotion—in effect, a valid footing for competition with the majors. Now, with the studios required to sell their theaters and to relinquish control of distribution outlets, the independent producers had at least a chance—which they eagerly took.

Perhaps the most important early development after the antitrust suit was the emergence of United Artists as a motion picture company without studios, a company whose function was strictly to bankroll and distribute the productions of independents. Reorganized from the long-failing United Artists (begun in 1919 by Charles Chaplin, Mary Pickford, and Douglas Fairbanks) by two lawyers in 1951, United Artists astonished the industry by purchasing foreign films and by bankrolling low- and high-budget features. The company made enormous sums of money while the big studios didn't.

Throughout the fifties, one of the major trends among studios would be to function as bankrollers of independent productions rather than to act as total overseers and producers of assembly-line movies. This trend, begun in the early fifties, would become increasingly significant in the sixties, when studios like MGM and Warner Brothers sold off their backlots and much of their film inventories, doing little work in the studios other than television.

In all, the antitrust action against the major studios was a heavy blow, but a healthy one. It ensured a finer quality of production and it provided a way of breaking through one of Hollywood's most grievous nemeses: the standardization of production. Movies began to carry the signatures of men who had made them—not the obvious imprint of the machine that had stamped them out.

The third, and certainly the most important, innovation of the post-war years was television, the first real competitor movies had ever known. Of course, when commercial radio became popular in the early twenties there had been a brief flutter of concern. Would people stay home to listen to radio in the evenings rather than go out and see a movie? But radio was no serious competition for movies, and besides, by the thirties, when the movies

took on a voice, they became quite adept at snapping up the most popular radio stars: Bing Crosby, Bob Hope, and Jack Benny.

Television was something else. Television was so much *like* movies: it had visual movement, sound, and—what threatened the studios most of all—it was free, sitting there in one's own living room. Between 1947 and 1950, television grew from an infant toy to a major American pastime. By the early fifties, studios recognized that they had to face the challenger.

They leaped at the obvious: ways of making the movie screen and the movie experience as unlike television as possible—more colorful, more involving. Much of the energy of the studios in the early and mid-fifties went into technical innovations that would hopefully stem the threat of television. Enormous sums were spent on fresh color processing, to make musicals and comedies almost blinding in their bright reds and yellows. New wider screen processes were developed: Cinemascope (which was to become almost standard in major productions) and, at the very edge of the spectrum, Cinerama, a screen which surrounded and virtually enfolded the audience, filling the visible spectrum and totally engulfing the audience in the action. Using three projectors, the Cinerama movie took the audience out of the normal viewer-to-story relationship and introduced a new relationship, one more in the nature of an actual participant in what happens on the screen. The problem here is that subject matter becomes very limited indeed. What can one do on a Cinerama screen beyond sending the audience on roller coaster rides or on skis somewhere in the Swiss Alps? It was all very exciting, very breathtaking, but it signaled no major advance in movies. By the early sixties, Cinerama was considered a dead end and was dropped.

So-called "three-dimensional" movies had

3-D Movie Audience

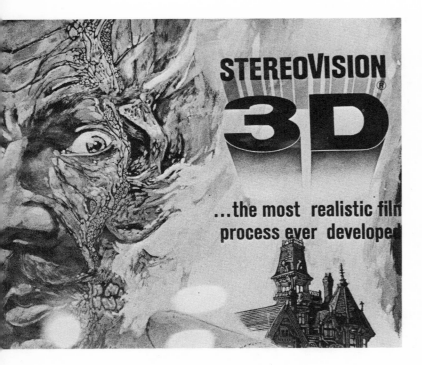

STEREOVISION® 3D

...the most realistic film process ever developed

an even shorter life span. As long ago as the turn of the century, French film-makers such as Lumière and Abel Gance had complained of the two-dimensional limitations of the movie screen. It could connote depth, just as a good photograph can connote depth. But ultimately everything is flat, and the audience is forced to "fill in" psychologically for the lack of depth—in other words, to pretend to believe that the movement we see on the screen is more than two-dimensional. The three-dimensional process ("3-D") used two projectors simultaneously, with slightly overlapping images. By wearing polarized glasses with two separately colored filters, audiences were able to see a double screen as a single screen, and sense an illusion of depth at those rare moments when an object or arm or torso would jump out from the screen. It was a short-lived phenomenon and produced no films of any significance. Perhaps most important of all, it discouraged the studios from seeking out more technical improvements as the most satisfactory response to television.

The movie studios never tried *too* hard to combat television—for the simple reason that they were in an excellent position to grab a big chunk of TV's economic pie. Stations and networks were clamoring for old movies that brought increasing revenues to studios that had long discarded the idea of making any money out of their enormous backlogs in the vaults. Moreover, the de-

mands of television production turned increasingly to adventure and action series that were better made on film than in TV studios—and better made on the Hollywood backlots than anywhere else. By the late fifties, movie studios were producing the dominant number of series on prime time television, and this relationship would—for the producers and studio heads, if not for the exhibitors—assuage the harm that television was doing to the theaters. Only late into the sixties, when it became apparent that the only dependable productions many studios could control themselves were for television, and when movie attendance dropped even more critically, would the studios be caught in between the pressures of television and the exhibitors.

It is difficult at this point to assess what the final outcome of the present dilemma of the studios will be. The trend now is toward the studios acting mostly as financial, promotion, and distributing agents for independent producers. Clearly the age of the great movie moguls like Jack Warner, Samuel Goldwyn, and Darryl F. Zanuck is over. The major studios continue to churn out enormous numbers of productions, but largely they are for television. Movies are contracted and assembled elsewhere, under considerably less control by the front office. Yet Hollywood is a myth, a symbol, and a system that will not easily die—even though the forces it now confronts threaten to make that nightmare come true.

TRENDS IN THE POSTWAR FILM

World War II helped—if only in a minor way—to expose to Hollywood the emptiness of its own tired themes, its own sentimental tendencies, its failure to deal honestly with human conflict. One does not so easily step out of mankind's greatest debacle and return to making cheery bedroom farces. Throughout the late forties and well into the fifties, a small but intense group of directors and producers worked at making movies that were serious in theme, honest in their approach, and concluding with something other than the classic "happy ending."

The first, and among the best, of these was *The Best Years of Our Lives* (1946). Produced by Samuel Goldwyn, directed by William Wyler, it told the stories of three airmen returning after the war, caught between the weariness of the war-years they had just lost, and the economic uncertainties of the new world they faced. *The Best Years of Our Lives* was *the* preeminent postwar picture, a movie that in many ways would suggest the directions and caliber for others to follow.

Somehow, the reality of war had penetrated Hollywood's unwillingness to deal with so-called "controversial" subjects and themes. Films of the late forties took on a new and deeper interest in psychological and social problems. *The Lost Weekend* (1945) depicted the traumas of an alcoholic on a weekend bender. Though handled a little clumsily at spots, the movie made audiences

The Best Years of Our Lives 1946

HOLLYWOOD—THE LAND OF A THOUSAND REMAKES

Successful movie formulas don't die; they live on, and on, and on . . .

A case in point is *Tarzan of the Apes*. The book, by Edgar Rice Burroughs, was first published in 1914. Hollywood showed interest shortly afterward—and hasn't stopped since. There have been silent Tarzan films, sound Tarzan films, Tarzan serials, an Andy Warhol Tarzan film, and with television, a Tarzan series and a Tarzan cartoon series. Here, in chronological order, are some of the Tarzan titles with the stars who featured as the Ape Man:

1918	*Tarzan of the Apes*	Elmo Lincoln		1948	*Tarzan and the Mermaids*	Johnny Weismuller
1918	*Romance of Tarzan*	Elmo Lincoln		1948	*Tarzan's Magic Fountain*	Lex Barker
1920	*Son of Tarzan*	P. Dempsey Tabler (serial)		1949	*Tarzan and the Slave Girl*	Lex Barker
1921	*Adventures of Tarzan*	Elmo Lincoln (serial)		1951	*Tarzan's Peril*	Lex Barker
1921	*Return of Tarzan*	Gene Polar		1951	*Tarzan and the Jungle Queen*	Lex Barker
1927	*Tarzan and the Golden Lion*	James Pierce		1951	*Tarzan's Savage Fury*	Lex Barker
1928	*Tarzan the Mighty*	Frank Merill (serial)		1952	*Tarzan and the She-Devil*	Lex Barker
1930	*Tarzan the Tiger*	Frank Merill (serial)		1955	*Tarzan's Hidden Jungle*	Gordon Scott
1932	*Tarzan the Ape Man*	Johnny Weismuller		1957	*Tarzan and the Lost Safari*	Gordon Scott
1933	*Tarzan the Fearless*	Buster Crabbe (serial)		1958	*Tarzan's Fight for Life*	Gordon Scott
1934	*Tarzan and His Mate*	Johnny Weismuller		1959	*Tarzan's Greatest Adventure*	Gordon Scott
1935	*New Adventures of Tarzan*	Gordon Brix		1959	*Tarzan the Ape Man*	Denny Miller
1936	*Tarzan Escapes*	Johnny Weismuller		1960	*Tarzan the Magnificent*	Gordon Scott
1937	*Tarzan and the Green Goddess*	Herman Brix		1962	*Tarzan Goes to India*	Jock Mahoney
1939	*Tarzan Finds a Son*	Johnny Weismuller		1963	*Tarzan's Three Challenges*	Jock Mahoney
1941	*Tarzan's Secret Treasure*	Johnny Weismuller		1964	*Tarzan and Jane Regained Sort Of*	Taylor Mead
1942	*Tarzan's New York Adventure*	Johnny Weismuller		1966	*Tarzan and the Valley of Gold*	Mike Henry
1943	*Tarzan's Desert*	Johnny Weismuller		1966-7	*Tarzan (TV series)*	Ron Ely
1943	*Tarzan Triumphs*	Johnny Weismuller		1967	*Tarzan and the Great River*	Mike Henry
1944	*Tarzan's Desert Mystery*	Johnny Weismuller		1968	*Tarzan's Jungle Rebellion*	Ron Ely
1945	*Tarzan and the Amazons*	Johnny Weismuller		1968-9	*Tarzan and the Jungle Boy*	Mike Henry
1946	*Tarzan and the Leopard Woman*	Johnny Weismuller		1970	*Tarzan's Deadly Silence*	Ron Ely
1947	*Tarzan and the Huntress*	Johnny Weismuller				

intimately aware of that gripping edge of desperation that an alcoholic faces. *The Snake Pit* (1948) depicted Olivia de Havilland in a mental institution: it was at once a searching look at mental illness and at the crime that society perpetrates against those who it deems unfit for its ranks. The problems of the black man in America—exposed to blacks and whites alike during the war—suddenly became visible on the screen in *Home of the Brave, Pinky,* and *Intruder In the Dust* (all 1949). Elia Kazan's film *Gentleman's Agreement* (1948) probed anti-Semitism.

Throughout the war, a good proportion of the films seen by the American public (and the armed forces as well) were documentaries: battle documentaries, war-effort documentaries, documentaries on any subject that would intensify the public's urge to win the war. The style appeared in a number of feature films of the late forties and early fifties. It was apparent that directors like Elia Kazan and Jules Dassin were forging a new, semi-documentary cinematic style. The first of such movies was *The House On 92nd Street* (1945), a story of an enemy spy ring in New York City. Using exteriors (and many interiors) shot on location, and taking techniques from the old *March of Time* newsreel series and war documentaries, director Henry Hathaway built the film around seemingly real events—not what looked to be an acted screenplay. The ideas in the film seemed all the more striking and forceful because of their semi-documentary presentation.

Two years later Elia Kazan made *Boomerang*, a tale of political corruption in a small town and the inability of outraged citizens to end it. Beginning with the assassination of a priest—filmed as though a hand-held newsreel camera were doing the shooting—the movie followed not the ordinary plot sequence, but a pieced-together organization that one would expect from a long, complex documentary. But not only was Kazan able to give the film a documentary structure. For one of the first times in America movies, he hired mostly non-actors to play roles of townspeople. A number of lines in the movie were not actually scripted. The result was a movie that not only resembled documentary, but that somehow engaged the audience in the reality of documentary.

Jules Dassin's *Naked City* (1948) further opened the technique of the semi-documentary to the studio moviemaking apparatus. Whereas *The House On 92nd Street* and *Boomerang* had both dealt with serious themes and were directly gauged to cause a disturbed pause among their audiences, *Naked City* was a cop story—part of a genre that was more oriented toward melodrama than truth. Shot almost entirely in New York City, on its streets and bridges and in its buildings, and presenting daily New York as a jungle inhabited mostly by high-society women and heroin addicts, *Naked City* brought realism back to the cop movie.

While the semi-documentary technique did not really survive the fifties, it would re-appear again in the sixties, less in specific movies than in adaptation of its techniques—the hand-held camera, the newsreel-type organization, the dependence on actual locations for the flavor and orientation of the films.

Hollywood took on other themes, other styles. One thing it took a searching look at was itself. In that fairyland world of studios and stars, what relationship actually existed between myth and reality? *Sunset Boulevard*, a powerful movie and Billy Wilder's most incisive, dissected Hollywood as if with an unerring scalpel. It told the story of Joe Gillis, a hack writer who becomes a paid escort and companion to a shriveling Hollywood silent film star, Norma Desmond (played brilliantly by Gloria Swanson). Time becomes

Sunset Boulevard 1950

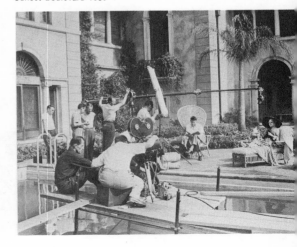

194

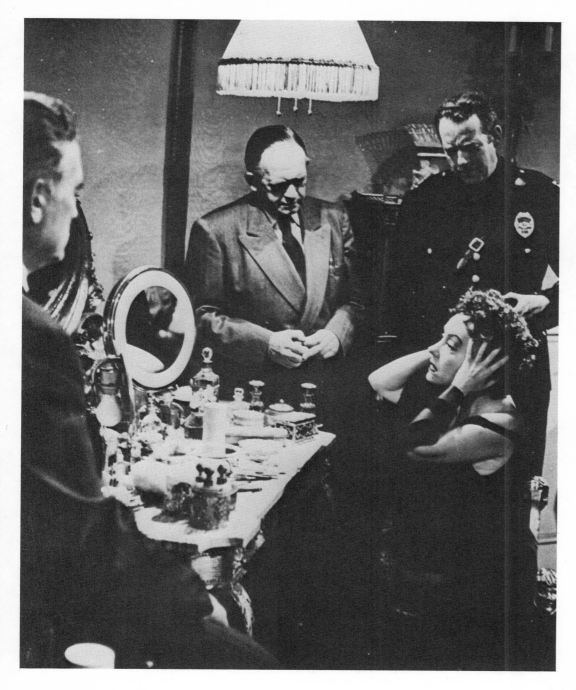

the wedge that Wilder levers under the whole idiocy of Hollywood, that American Babylon. As the movie progresses and horrors rise to the surface, we begin to recognize that Norma Desmond *is* Hollywood in the most acutely grim way imaginable. Her house, unchanged since the early thirties, her belief that fan letters keep coming in (as they do, though written by her butler and last admirer), her conviction that a script she has written—abominable by even the hack writer's standards—will be produced with her as star: the movie says more about Hollywood than anything Hollywood has ever given us. Indeed, Hollywood takes on a palpable existence in Norma Desmond's phobic mind. Youth *is* all and unchanging for her. In the last scene, when she comes down the steps of her house to the bright lights and whirrings of newsreel cameras, she is on stage again, walking with the delayed grace of a 20-year-old star, smiling with a poignant, beatific smile. Yet the film is discomfitting because we can never at any point totally hate Norma Desmond. Her fantasies, her theatrical style, and her hauteur are so real to her, so integral to her knowledge of what she is, that she seems to have passed the familiar, classifiable forms of schizophrenia and now truly believes she is the greatest of stars, with an enormous public awaiting her comeback. Joe Gillis, the hack writer tells her, "You were a big star once." She is somehow absolutely right in her reply: "I'm still big. It's the pictures that got small."

An American in Paris 1951

THE FIFTIES

The five or six postwar years hardly demonstrated a splurge of new energies on the part of the studios. Indeed, movie production was generally at a lower ebb than it had been in the late thirties. With the fifties, despite the exceptional efforts of the old masters and some newcomers, the industry returned to a system of standardized production and of imitating the latest hit—a system that may have worked in previous years but which now in the days of television, gradually led the studios onto the reefs.

The fifties were largely a decade of genre devices: musicals, bedroom comedies, biblical and historical epics, Westerns, biographies, science fiction. Often a movie would rise above its genre. Just as musicals could offer *An American In Paris*, so Westerns could include *Gunfighter* and *High Noon*. But somehow the creative juices that had made movies in the thirties and forties so promising had dried up in the fifties. Even the best movies (with a few fine exceptions) kept within their genres and promised no new orientation for movies afterwards. It was a decade in which studios clung to older techniques, older devices, older ideas—at the ultimate cost of their own power in filmmaking.

The new "stars" seemed to typify the dilemma. Hollywood had always groomed stars, had always chosen one among many with the idea that this one had *it* (that "it" being some charismatic ability to transcend even the dimensions of the Cinemascope screen). By the fifties, the studios had stopped looking for actors with that secret appeal. Instead, they felt that they could turn anyone into a star overnight by taking just about anyone with a pretty enough face and whipping up enough publicity. And so they did—with an Alan Ladd, an Audie Murphy, a Tab Hunter, a Rock Hudson. Often these men were not bad actors (Rock Hudson has turned in some fine performances, and even Alan Ladd has had his moments), but they were not genuinely the stuff of stars—not fit to follow the footsteps of a Spencer Tracy, a John Wayne, or a Bogart. But the studios, imperious even as their power crumbled, could hardly recognize that. The same was true of the actresses they tried to engineer into stardom: the most tragic of them being, of course, Marilyn Monroe—a girl, potentially a fine actress, unfit for the role Hollywood gave her.

New stars, good stars, did come into being in the fifties. In their appeal could be caught the shifting sensibilities and desires of audiences. Marlon Brando, carefully cast by Elia Kazan in *A Streetcar Named Desire*, became one of the best actors and largest stars of the fifties. His acting reflected the "Method School," a style more notable for its pauses, its cloudy facial expressions and its projection of doubt and uncertainty than the earlier, self-confident Hollywood style.

Had he lived, James Dean—the restless, angry, intense young star of *Giant* and *Rebel Without a Cause*—might easily have become *the* star of the fifties. Moody, capable of an awkward tenderness at one moment and of unfettered rage the next, James Dean captured the sensibilities of the disillusioned young of the fifties much as Bogart had captured the mood of the near-outcast in the thirties and forties. James Dean detested Hollywood, but his death at the age of 24 in an automobile crash was a larger blow to the industry than it could realize.

The fifties was the last era of the stars. By the sixties, the studios realized that stars were no guarantee to a picture's success, and that the biggest money-making movies did not require name stars at all. Nonetheless, throughout the fifties and into the sixties Hollywood continued to breed and publicize its stars, perhaps because it needed them in a way the American public did not.

Throughout the forties and fifties, a number of directors emerged: some very new ones, and older ones who reached a fresh pinnacle of astute filmmaking. This chapter will treat six: Orson Welles, John Huston, Billy Wilder, Elia Kazan, Howard Hawks, and Alfred Hitchcock.

High Noon 1952

Giant 1956

ORSON WELLES

He was radio's "boy wonder," the man who, in his early twenties, organized and directed the famed Mercury Theatre, the most inventive and dramatically successful group of actors and writers radio has ever known. Made even more famous by his *War of the Worlds* broadcast in 1938—a dramatization of H. G. Wells' novel as a news report which terrified millions—Welles was considered the entertainment industry's *enfant terrible*. RKO, a studio at that time in financial trouble, asked him to make a movie. Welles wasn't that interested until RKO offered him total creative control—something never previously given a director by any major studio. With the assistance of veteran scriptwriter Herman Mankiewicz, Welles and his Mercury Theatre troupe made *Citizen Kane*—the greatest of American sound movies.

It was a risky movie, and by that reason all the more exciting to make—for Welles, for his troupe, and for the Hollywood regulars associated with it. It was risky not only in its new techniques—Welles created a fresh form of organization (flashback interpretations by people being interviewed), used camera angles in ways rarely before seen on American screens, and recorded sound in dramatic new ways—but in its subject matter as well: a pseudo-biography of the newspaper magnate William Randolph Hearst. Because of Hearst's intervention, the film was almost destroyed before release.

The French film director François Truffaut said that *Citizen Kane* was probably the movie "that has started the largest number of filmmakers on their careers." The reasons were evident enough: *Citizen Kane* is jammed with invention, innovation, moments of brilliance, and fresh cinematic ideas. As writer and film critic Pauline Kael observed, it is not a particularly profound film; viewers are never led very far beneath the surface, because there is not all that much *beyond* the surface, but also because there is so much *at* the surface.

Citizen Kane is one of those rare films that bears up after not only a few showings, but after a few dozen as well. Little things keep appearing that weren't quite there before—new sounds on the track that give a scene more resonance; cuts that relate shots in surprising new ways, such as a calculated disjunction of mood or the reappearance of an object that takes on a new meaning; habits of the film characters that suggest more than idiosyncrasies, such as Jedediah

Leland's cigar; angular shots that increasingly give Kane the preeminence and physical structure of a statue—leading to his entombment at Xanadu, with all his statues; long, graceful tracking shots that pull us back from our identification with Kane or his associates and suggest a totally different point of view; snatches of humor that relieve the tension, such as Kane's grim obsession with making his wife a major opera singer; Kane's own changing appearance over the years, as if power and wealth turned his body large and rigid and balded his head; the film's incredible ability to shift point of view, both structurally and psychologically, from Bernstein to Leland to Susan Alexander to Kane, without losing the audience and, indeed, while further engrossing it. *Citizen Kane* seems to be one of those movies that teaches us what movies are all about, and what—at their furthest reaches—they can be all about.

Citizen Kane barely broke even at the box office. Because of Hearst, it would be kept from the public showing for another 10 years. Welles, obviously suspect among the studios (who was this *kid* to take on, of all people, the great Hearst?), was able to get another directing assignment, again with

Citizen Kane 1941

Macbeth 1948

RKO, to film the novel *The Magnificent Ambersons*. While Welles was not able to edit the film as we would have liked, it still suggests his power, his experiments with camera angles redolent of the German expressionists, and with psychological innuendo.

Welles' career among the studios was precipitous at best. His films did not make much money, and his genius served largely as a stumbling block for the industry. Eventually Welles moved to Europe, turned to acting as a source of income, and then proceeded to invest most of his earnings in his own productions: *Mr. Arkadin* (1962), *The Trial* (1963), and *Falstaff* (1967) among them. Most of his work after *Citizen Kane* is uneven, dense, capable of shifting from melodrama to pyrotechnic cinematics. Yet it is all proof of a first-rate film genius, perhaps the greatest America has yet produced.

One need only see moments of his films to recognize Welles' range. The mirror sequence, for example, in *The Lady From Shanghai* (1948) in which Welles and actress Rita Hayworth are caught in a hall of mirrors and every action is mirrored in rows —like some great metaphysical symbol of the nature of movies. Or Welles' incredible portrayal in his film *Touch of Evil*: a gruesome, bottom-of-the-barrel sheriff who

moves and speaks with a glutted heaviness, as though all that life has left him with is the sediment, clotted now into his heavy body and brain, stupefying him even as it drives him lower and lower. Or *The Trial*, with its formalist décor and its near-surrealist trappings, one of the most important uses of expressive environment since *The Cabinet of Doctor Caligari*. Or *Macbeth* (1950), an extraordinary rendition of Shakespeare in which lighting and movement become almost as expressive—as wary and as sensitive—as the lines.

The studios have ostracized some of the most creative talents ever to appear in filmmaking—Erich von Stroheim, perhaps, or Robert Flaherty, Jean Renoir, and F. W. Murnau. But probably in no instance has greater damage been done to the movies themselves, to the potential that could emerge from a great director's movies, as in the case of Orson Welles. His style was always thinly disguised stage theatrics, his leading character (himself) bombastic, his settings baroque, his plots convoluted and ultimately hopeless. Yet Welles' movies are a celebration of the art. They pulse and explore and reconnoiter new terrain with a daring and an exuberance that can only be the mark of film genius.

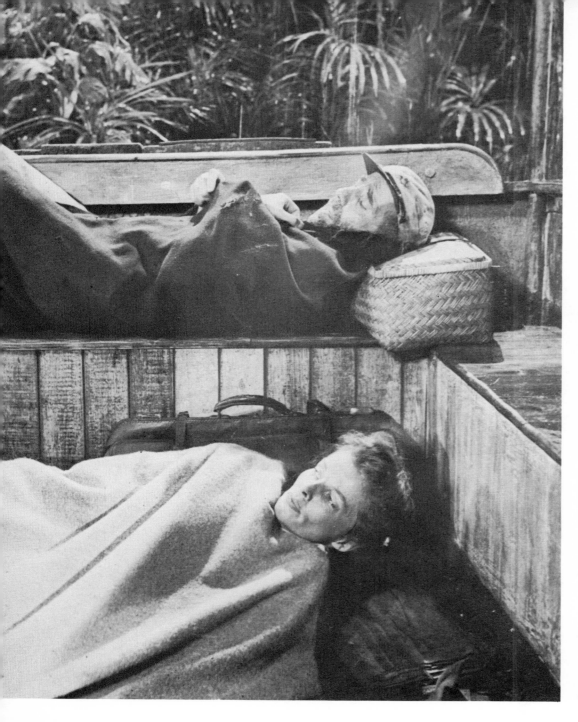

JOHN HUSTON

In 1950, the great critic James Agee published an article in *LIFE* magazine on John Huston, a director he admired and with whom he worked on the film *The African Queen*. Agee wrote of Huston:

Most movies are made in the evident assumption that the audience is passive and wants to remain passive; every effort is made to do all the work—the seeing, the explaining, the understanding, even the feeling. Huston is one of the few movie artists who, without thinking twice about it, honors his audience. His pictures are not acts of seduction or of benign enslavement but of liberation, and they require, of anyone who enjoys them, the responsibilities of liberty. They continually open the eye and require it to work vigorously; and through the eye they awaken curiosity and intelligence. That, by any virile standard, is essential to good entertainment. It is unquestionably essential to good art.

Huston's directing career has been a long and uneasy one—and, unhappily, one that has moved generally away from his better films of the forties and the early fifties. Indeed, Huston's four major films—*The Maltese Falcon* (1941), *The Treasure of the Sierra Madre* (1948), *The Asphalt Jungle*

201

The Treasure of the Sierra Madre 1947

(1950), and *The African Queen* (1952) are such a great remove from his flops (*Freud, The List of Adrian Messenger, The Bible*) that Huston's reputation has suffered lately.

Yet, at his best, Huston could be one of the best: he could illuminate characters through action as few directors knew how; he could bring out performances that were often some of the best of major actors (a case in point is Bogart, among whose best performances Huston directed three); he could give his films a narrative rhythm and a sense of vitality that was all their own.

His first film, one of his best, was *The Maltese Falcon* (1941): it has become the standard to which detective films are compared. Casting Bogart as Dashiell Hammett's tough, cynical Sam Spade, Huston proceeded to establish on the screen an accurate and brilliant visual counterpart to Hammett's lean, astringent prose. The story and the characters were somehow just right for Huston: he could make the room shrink a little around Sidney Greenstreet, and the electricity in the air when Greenstreet meets Bogart is almost palpable. Bogart moves through the film with a droll humor and a bravura that no screen detective has quite caught since (with the possible exception of Bogart again in Howard Hawks' *The Big Sleep*).

After working with the government throughout the war—and producing two of

its finest documentaries, *The Battle of San Pietro* and the unreleased *Let There Be Light*—Huston proceeded to make *The Treasure of the Sierra Madre*, a lean, dark allegory about greed. It is one of the finest films ever made in America. Bogart, Tim Holt, and Walter Huston (John Huston's father) join forces in Mexico to prospect for gold. They find it, spend a couple of months digging it out of the hill, and are threatened at the end by bandits. On one level an unusual adventure story, *The Treasure of the Sierra Madre* reaches its best moments in the deterioration of Fred C. Dobbs, played by Bogart. His rapid progression from neurosis to paranoia to total breakdown is shown smoothly and vividly. Indeed, of all post-war movies to deal with psychological themes, none approaches the quality of Dobbs' breakdown.

The Treasure of the Sierra Madre is rich in one of Huston's best qualities: performances. Bogart is the tough outsider taken to the breaking point—and beyond—as though his roles in all previous movies were to lead ultimately to this. Walter Huston is particularly impressive as the grizzled old prospector. Alfonso Bedoya, as the Mexican bandit leader, is so scary, and grins so wickedly that, as Pauline Kael observed, we tend to be extremely grateful for modern civilization. The film is rich, vigorous, and honest.

Beat the Devil 1953

Apart from one tiny flaw of a dead man's wife's letter sentimentalizing the ending, it is just about as perfect a movie as the postwar period produced.

The Asphalt Jungle is a major film in a minor key. It has been discussed, at greater length, in Chapter Six, under gangster films.

In 1952, Huston made *The African Queen*, based on C. S. Forester's post-Victorian novel of an African missionary woman and a cockney Englishman river pilot in the African jungles. The story had flaws; Huston (as some of his later films would show) was always more comfortable with action and psychosis than with romantic themes. Yet he carried it off beautifully, using the river itself and an impressive length of African footage to keep the two characters balanced against their environment.

Again Agee:

Much that is best in Huston's work comes of his sense of what is natural to the eye and his delicate, simple feeling for space relationships: his camera huddles close to those who huddle to talk, leans back a proportionate distance, relaxing, if they talk casually.

John Huston, like Ford and Hawks, kept his movie in front of the camera. And at his best, he made some of the finest movies to be caught by the postwar camera.

203

Ace in the Hole 1951

BILLY WILDER

There are two kinds of Hollywood cynicism. There is the fast-talking, tough, individualist character, to be found in any score of thirties or forties movies: Claudette Colbert in *It Happened One Night*, or Clark Gable or Bogart in any number of their movies. Then there is the other type of cynicism —namely a Billy Wilder movie.

Wilder's movies are spectacles of decay. In *Ace In the Hole* (retitled *The Big Carnival*) he shows how the entrapment of a miner in a cave becomes the basis for a growing tourist attraction and eventually an insane carnival. *Sunset Boulevard* is a low blow, if ever so accurately placed, to Hollywood—even, in typical Wilder fashion, to its own stars. *The Lost Weekend* never lets up for the audience: we are taken to the very edge of Ray Milland's alcoholism right along with him.

It is not so much that Wilder simply dramatizes the more callous aspects of modern society; he revels in them. In *Carnival,* possibly his most typical movie (though hardly his best), the clever promotion manager who begins the trickle of tourists to the collapsed mine hardly ever reflects on the miner's desperate plight as the tourist stream grows larger and larger—nor, indeed, does anyone. In Wilder's movies, we are all the victims of patterns and behaviors which are intrinsically destructive, but in ways that we are unable to recognize even as the process continues.

There is another type of Wilder movie: a lighter, gentler, comedy of sorts but still loaded with jabs and thrusts and parries.

Movies like *The Seven Year Itch* (1955), *Some Like It Hot* (1959), *The Apartment* (1960), and *The Fortune Cookie* (1966) have shown that the Wilder touch has softened, but has not relented. In *The Apartment*, for example, Jack Lemmon, a rising corporation man, has to play the game of lending-the-boss-the-apartment-for-the-weekend. The consequent complications lead to a sometimes hilariously funny movie, but Wilder isn't just interested in fun. He wants to stab corporate gameplaying and ladder climbing in some of its most vulnerable places, and is generally quite successful.

In typical Wilder movies, the heroes tend to be men who are down on their luck, yet convinced of their innate abilities to become big successes in modern society. It is a toxic combination, and Wilder pushes these men into situations that are often as outrageous as they are ultimately destructive. Not far from the surface of most Wilder movies is the assumption that the only way to get ahead in modern society is by treating other people as fools. And so it is not too surprising that so many of the minor characters in his movies emerge as just that.

Except for *Sunset Boulevard*, Wilder has not made any really great movies. But virtually all his films bear his style, his laconic, dark humor, his fascination for increasing levels of complication that show up the absurdities of so many schemes and devices. No director has tackled the American dream with quite the gusto or the shrewd wit of a Wilder, and his better films remain, to this day, surprisingly fresh and still funny.

The Lost Weekend 1945

Some Like It Hot 1959

205

ELIA KAZAN

Kazan's name was associated, before he got into movies, with the New York theater and the new type of acting being developed there, known as Method Acting. The effect of Method Acting is the creation of a low-key realism: words are not spoken sharply and clearly, but sometimes are muttered half-incoherently, as in real life; gestures and actions are underplayed, rather than overplayed; and the actors are encouraged to rephrase and change lines whenever it seems more natural. Marlon Brando, an actor whom Elia Kazan found, groomed, and placed in several movies, is Hollywood's method actor *par excellence*.

Kazan's films, for the most part, are urban, grimly serious, and—particularly in the earlier ones—heavy with the stuff of natural realism: plenty of exterior shots taken in urban locales; the slow, uncertain, muttered language of the Method School; a use of black and white cinematography that is simple, clean and unpretentious. Films like *A Tree Grows in Brooklyn* (1945), *Boomerang* (1947), *A Streetcar Named Desire* (1951), *Viva Zapata!* (1952), and *On the Waterfront* (1953) made Kazan Hollywood's leading exponent of the "new realism"—a term, and a concept, that has never quite taken with Hollywood since.

Much has been made of the "social implications" in Kazan's films and, indeed, his earlier movies do attack grievous and complex social ills: public apathy and political bosses in *Boomerang*; anti-semitism in *Gentleman's Agreement*; bigotry and racial hate in *Pinky*; the treacheries of revolution in *Viva Zapata!*; dock union gangsterism and violence in *On the Waterfront*. The mistake, however, has been to laud Kazan for his in-cisive social criticism and to miss whether or not he has made good movies. And by and large, his movies have been spotty. Indeed, he has tended to use their social content to buttress their faults—their shaky rhythm, their loosely knit plots, their sometimes facile dialogue.

Yet even Kazan's failures are instructive. In movies like *Splendor in the Grass* (1961), *East of Eden* (1955) and *America, America* (1963), he broke through from constructing skeins of social injustice to making movies which have about them genuine feeling. Kazan, an explorer rather than a finished artist, has given a fresh honesty and integrity to the Hollywood film.

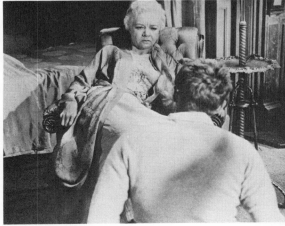

East of Eden 1955

On the Waterfront 1954

On the Waterfront 1954

On the Waterfront 1954

207

Bringing Up Baby 1938

HOWARD HAWKS

The career of Howard Hawks spans almost as much time as that of John Ford: from 1926 to 1970. Hawks has gone largely unrecognized as a major talent in this country until lately, largely because, as Andrew Sarris says, he makes the kind of movies that "Americans do best and appreciate least:" gangster films, Westerns, musicals, adventure films, and wacky comedies. If anything, Hawks' movies are the least pretentious of American films. He breaks no new technical ground; he stresses plot situations that have already become quite familiar to the viewing public; he prefers action over anything that lingers and which might suggest "deeper" dimensions.

Yet if the movies of Howard Hawks are not particularly deep, they are rich. His characters have a life of their own, a life formed largely by Hawks' somewhat Hemingwayesque morality—a morality of courage, of physical prowess in the face of discouraging odds, of a man's destiny being directly linked to his duty. (Hawks and Hemingway were good friends; once they made a bet that Hawks could not salvage on the screen Hemingway's worst book. Two years later, *To Have and Have Not*—based on Hemingway's book—became one of Hawks' best movies.)

Though Hawks had been making movies for half a decade, the film which established him as a major Hollywood director was *Scarface*—the last of a trio of gangster movies to appear in 1931 (the other two were *Little Caesar* and *The Public Enemy*). Considered even today the greatest of gangster movies, *Scarface* followed the career of Al Capone. It is a violent, even barbarous movie, controlled and guided with a sure touch. Paul Muni, in one of his earliest roles, brought suave elegance to the gangster movie —bringing out the idea of the gangster as a new aristocracy and emphasizing, in that sense, the real fascination of the gangster as the darker side of the American dream.

Throughout the thirties, Hawks made a number of adventure films (*Tiger Shark, Viva Villa!, Barbary Coast, Ceiling Zero, The Road to Glory*), but the genre he perfected in that period was the screwball comedy. Movies like *Twentieth Century* (1934), *Come and Get It* (1936), *Bringing Up Baby* (1938), and *His Girl Friday* (1940)—and later, *I Was a Male War Bride* (1949), *Monkey Business* (1952) and *Gentlemen Prefer Blondes* (1953)— established Hawks as *the* director of the shrewd, fast-paced comedy of urbane men and women. It was a species of comedy par-

Gentlemen Prefer Blondes 1953

I Was a Male War Bride 1949

ticularly prevalent in the thirties, sometimes strong in the forties, but waning by the fifties: a comedy of whizzing dialogue, plenty of throwaways, and shrewd, sometimes Machiavellian relationships between men and women.

Hawks' approach to this type of comedy can be glimpsed in an anecdote (which is certainly not the full truth, but a revealing part of the truth) he related in an interview. Asked about the making of *His Girl Friday*, a movie obviously modeled on Lewis Milestone's *The Front Page*, Hawks told interviewer Peter Bogdanovich:

I was going to prove to somebody one night that The Front Page *had the finest modern dialogue that had been written, and I asked a girl to read Hildy's part and I read the editor and I stopped and I said, 'Hell, it's better between a girl and a man than between two men,' and I called Ben Hecht and I said, 'What would you think of changing it so that Hildy is a girl?' and he said, 'I think it's a great idea,' and he came out and we did it.*

In *His Girl Friday*, Hawks not only succeeds in turning one of the best newspaper movies into the best of newspaper comedy

209

Rio Bravo 1959

Monkey Business 1952

Red River 1948

Monkey Business

210

Monkey Business

movies, he gives new life, new vitality, new excitement to the idea and to the characters at every level. Little touches abound—nervous, fidgety reactions; staccato, overlapping dialogue; scenes in which the comedy is heightened by three or four things going on at once.

The funniest and best Hawks comedy, however, is probably *Monkey Business*: a wacky, careening movie built on a clever, explosive idea. Professor Barnaby Fulton (Cary Grant) has discovered a drug which can, he claims, restore youth. (He calls it "B-4," to be advertised as "B-4 and after.") He hasn't quite perfected it—that is, he still doesn't know the right combination of chemicals. Meanwhile, an escaped chimpanzee spills the correct batch in the drinking water. Suddenly Professor Fulton and his wife revert to teenagers. But the reversion is fascinating, because it makes them do exactly what they were too inhibited to do before. In a comedy that is at once a very funny movie and a caustic comment on adult sexual relationships in American culture, Hawks moves smoothly in and out of situations with deft control and timing. He keeps pushing things to their breaking point—in the latter part of the film Professor Fulton and his wife take more of the drug, hoping to be cured. Instead they become children. The earlier inanities suddenly become more inane, less funny, and yet particularly revealing. More so than most Hawks comedies, *Monkey Business* blends laughter with painful recognition. The foibles he depicts are too tightly interwoven with our own predicament in modern society for us *not* to laugh.

Of the Hawks adventure movies, one in particular has barely worn with time and stands beside the greatest films of the Western genre: Ford's *Stagecoach* and *Wagonmaster*, Henry King's *Gunfighter*, Fred Zinnemann's *High Noon*. Hawks' *Red River*, made in 1948, is as beautiful a film as *Wagonmaster*, and morally a far more complex one. As Robin Wood in his study of Hawks notes, John Ford's Westerns stress the pastness of the past; Hawks movies stress the present. Ford summoned nostalgia; he built on the West as a myth and struggled to enlarge that myth. Hawks, in *Red River*, engages the audience in the experience of a lengthy cattle drive from Texas to Oklahoma. We are thoroughly part of the drama and the personal clashes between characters in *Red River*. Not once are we encouraged to look upon the movie nostalgically. As the friendship between Dunson (John Wayne) and Matthew Garth (Montgomery Clift) gradually erodes and finally leads to the climactic fight between them, we become involved in such a way that our own feelings, our own loyalties are at stake. Much in the manner of Hitchcock, Hawks draws us *into* the action, *uses* our identification with characters to make us aware of the stakes involved. We are never simply onlookers in a Hawks movie.

Indeed, the ability to involve the audience in the action, to make action on the screen an *experience* of the audience rather than merely something seen by the audience, is not only Hawks' trademark but his genius as a filmmaker. Whether with racing cars and the men who drive them in *Red Line 7000*, or with the gunfights in *Rio Bravo* and *El Dorado*, or with the cattle drive in *Red River*, Hawks brings us into the world that takes place on the screen; he involves us, implicates us, and, ultimately, by that very process, enlivens us.

ALFRED HITCHCOCK

One problem of looking at movies as a form of art is that one tends to slight those movies which are superlative entertainment. We have driven a wedge deep and tight that separates entertainment from art, and we tend to think that for a thing to be good art it must be a little hard to take, that one has to fight through it, has to accept boredom and uncertainty as the price of art. The idea, of course, is ridiculous: the original audiences of Shakespeare's comedies roared with laughter at *Twelfth Night*, at *As You Like It*, and at the plottings of Falstaff in *Henry IV*. Nonetheless the attitude persists, and it has severely hurt our ability to appreciate one of the greatest directors of the American film, Alfred Hitchcock.

It is ironic that, with those directors and with those types of films so basic to the American movie audience—for example, a Hawks or a Lang, or the western, the musical or the suspense film—recognition has not come from American critics and film scholars but from the French, who seem far more appreciative of the *art* of making a good musical or a chilling suspense thriller. And while American film audiences who are interested in "film as art" catch every Antonioni and Bergman movie, the French audiences who are just as excited about good movies look at all the early Hitchcock movies. Largely, it is the old story of the prophet being without honor in his own land.

Alfred Hitchcock 213

The Birds 1963

Vertigo 1958

Hitchcock began his filmmaking career in England, in the mid-twenties. His silent and early sound films only hint at the talent which would emerge later. Hitchcock's early suspense films—*Blackmail* (1929), *Murder* (1930), *The Man Who Knew Too Much* (1935) and particularly *The Thirty-nine Steps* (1935)—soon established him as the most important director in England and the best director of suspense thrillers in the world. Hollywood was not far away. Between the late thirties and the late forties, Hitchcock moved between Hollywood and London for different productions. All this time his movies were taking on the shape, the mood, the humor, and the style of suspense that we have come to identify with him since. He experimented. Virtually all of *Lifeboat* takes place in a lifeboat. In *Rope*, movie time equals real time, minute for minute. Cross-cutting and new, sophisticated uses of the montage (barely used effectively since the time of Eisenstein) appear in *The Man Who Knew Too Much* (both the 1935 version and the 1955 remake) and in *Strangers On a Train* (1951). By the early fifties, Hitchcock and perfected his form to a degree rare in directors. The result was a group of films remarkable in their expertise, their construction, and their grip on audiences: *Strangers On a Train* (1951), *Rear Window* (1954), *Vertigo* (1958), *North By Northwest* (1959), *Psycho* (1960), and *The Birds* (1963).

Hitchcock is considered, even by those who question his rank as a major director, to be the master technician of the American film. As Andrew Sarris points out, Hitchcock has merged two major technical traditions of filmmaking: the tradition of long tracking shots and exotic, strange angles that comes from Murnau and the tradition of montage and effects through editing that comes from Eisenstein. His films are made with an uncanny kind of precision: one recalls the supple, subtle color hues in

North By Northwest; or the careful, effective tracking and panning shots in *Rear Window*; or the perfect, ominous presence of the feathered demons in *The Birds*; or the brutal, calculated, brilliant shower sequence in *Psycho*; or the suggestive, evocative use of San Francisco locales in *Vertigo*. There is no question but that Hitchcock keeps tight control of every moment in every film he makes.

Indeed, Hitchcock's control is so thorough as to deny a certain plausibility to the characters in his films. Somehow, his characters seem a little *too* exact, their spontaneous outbursts *too* calculated. But Hitchcock is not interested in realism, at least not as an end in itself. He engineers films that give audiences the movie equivalent of a jolting roller coaster ride (his own description), and, in the process, illustrates what sheer visual thrills good movies can be.

Hitchcock is ultimately a filmmaker with supreme visual flair and an almost old-fashioned sense of moralism. The two go hand-in-hand. In *North by Northwest,* we follow Roger Thornhill, a baffled advertising executive caught in a nightmare of espionage, to a flat, naked stretch of farmland where he is supposed to meet the spy with whom he has been mistakenly identified. What he encounters is a low-flying airplane, piloted by spies sent to kill him. The visual quality of the scene is exultant: a man running across a stark horizon, chased by an airplane, the ground chopped by sporadic gunfire coming from the plane.

North by Northwest 1959

The scene is perfect—the tempo, the cutting, the absence of music or movement for the long minutes before the attack as we wait with Thornhill for something to happen.

But the scene works as well as a commentary on Thornhill's moral predicament. The clever self-assured Madison Avenue executive, previously bolstered by the high New York buildings and the bustle and teeming energy of urban life, has been stripped of his familiar environment and identity. Now, he has nothing to sustain him beyond his own slight resources, and the act of rousing those resources and learning to respect them gives Thornhill a purpose and makes him value his integrity.

Hitchcock the shrewd moralist can touch at paradoxes and ambivalences in us through a clever process of making us identify with a character to the point of anticipating and choosing his actions. In *Strangers on a Train*, we are led to identify with Guy, a tennis champ who becomes enmeshed in a typically Hitchcockian nightmare. Guy was approached by a stranger named Bruno who suggested that the two "trade" murders: Bruno was to murder Guy's vapid, small-town wife and Guy was to murder Bruno's detested father. Guy discards the conversation, but Bruno goes ahead and kills the wife—and proceeds to haunt Guy until he reaches a breaking point. Guy slips a gun into his pocket and, late at night, goes to the house where Bruno and his father live. As he walks up the steps, the tension mounts, but it is a curious tension, a moral

Strangers on a Train 1951

tension: we are wondering, will he kill the father, or will he talk to the father? And we are rooting for him to do one of the two things—generally, to kill the father. But we learn that his intention was to talk to the father, despite the loaded gun. Nevertheless, Hitchcock has revealed something about us to ourselves: our capability for murder, our complicity in Bruno's crime. Hitchcock isn't out to *show* us what guilt looks like; he makes us *feel* the green, sickly sensation of guilt.

It is very largely Hitchcock's ability to bring home to us our own guilt, to set us up as surrogate criminals and murderers, that makes his style of suspense so unique and so distinctive. Hitchcock has long abandoned the idea that you can create suspense on the screen simply by having the bad guys chase the good guys. Even in his chase films (*The Thirty-nine Steps*, *Notorious*, *North By Northwest*), the character's identity becomes a critical part of the process, so that the experience itself reveals to him—and to us—a fundamental insecurity, a psychic jungle festering beneath the veneer of modern civilization.

To call Hitchcock a supreme technician of the movies or even the acknowledged master of suspense movies—and let it go at that—is something like calling Chaplin the best laugh-getter of comedians. There may be a calculated air to Hitchcock's movies—maybe even a hint of cynicism—but his movies are so refined, his touch so exact, his images so visually alive, that one cannot deny, finally, his artistry.

A footnote on Hitchcock: in terms of the influence of specific American directors on the films of other countries, Hitchcock is probably the most important American director since D. W. Griffith. Particularly in France, where a generation of younger directors has grown up studying his movies, an admiring kind of imitation can be seen in the work of such directors as Claude Chabrol, François Truffaut, and Costa-Gavras. And whereas other directors in other countries have sought to create their versions of the familiar American genres—the gangster film, the Western, the musical, the monster movie—it is those French directors working (as one of them put it) "in the shadow of Hitchcock" who have made important strides in a new style of French cinema. It is ironically possible that students of the movie 50 years from now might have to discover Hitchcock through his French disciples.

**Chapter Nine
Where the Past Meets the Future**

There is an anecdote about Cecil B. DeMille, the creator of dozens of spectaculars, who was at one time preparing to shoot a scene that cost half a million dollars: the crash-landing of a plane, or the toppling of a building, something of that order. To make sure he got all the proper footage he wanted, he assigned three different cameramen to different locations. Everyone backed away, DeMille called "Roll 'em!" and the clapper was clicked. The scene went as DeMille planned. When it was finished, he went to the first cameraman and asked how it came out. "Gosh, I'm sorry, Mr. DeMille. The lens cap got stuck on the camera." DeMille fumed all the way to the second photographer. "How'd it come out?" he asked. "Well, Mr. DeMille, the footage just ran out only a second or so after we started shooting." DeMille, nervously impatient at this point, called up to the third cameraman —off at a slight distance on a hill. "How'd it go?" he called. The man waved back. "Ready whenever you are, C. B.!"

The phrase suggests something about the entire historical panoply of movies, directors, studios and audiences: "Ready whenever you are, C. B." Ready for what? In the beginning, a Porter, a Sennett, a Griffith. In the twenties, the establishment of a national mecca which would produce our dreams for us—and a place modeled most consciously on that fact. In the thirties, a range of movies from cogent social commentary to the anarchic wit of the Marx Brothers—and yet all revealing a fresh sophisticated vitality. In the forties, the summons to war and a slow, if halting, maturing process. In the fifties, a recognition that the towers were crumbling and scattered efforts to bolster them. And in the sixties?

Sound of Music 1965

The sixties were, in their own way, the most frenetic and exciting period in American movies since the thirties. But, unlike the thirties, the movies tended to wear more rapidly. Studio power, which had been eroding since the war, reached its full breakdown in the late sixties when the major studios were all near-bankrupt—with the significant exceptions of outfits like American-International, which bankrolled independents and owned not a foot of studio, and Disney's studio, which somehow had never lost the magic touch. The studios had never been more paranoid about their position than in the sixties. With the old czars gone, and run mostly by managers trained in law, banking, and business, they became more trend-conscious than at any time before in their history. The astonishing success of Twentieth Century-Fox's *The Sound of Music* (which brought in, between its release in 1965 and 1970, some $72 million) cost the studios far more than they could afford in a time of slipping audiences. Musical spectaculars (*Hello Dolly*, *Paint Your Wagon*), historical spectaculars (*Cleopatra*), war spectaculars (*Tora! Tora! Tora!*, *Catch-22*), and spectaculars of every ilk, cost the studios upwards of $10 million apiece (*Tora! Tora! Tora!* reportedly went over $25 million) and almost alone ran the studios—and their rapport with the banks—aground.

The sixties brought new audiences to the movies, a new consciousness, and a new freedom. But the studios were ill-prepared to deal with these factors. By now the importation of foreign features had reached and helped shape a fresh, young audience that expected more of movies than kisses, gunplay, and a cast of thousands. Indeed, a few foreign films grossed very well in the

Hello, Dolly!

Cleopatra 1963

219

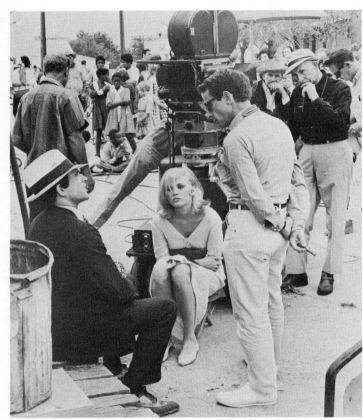
Bonnie and Clyde 1967

larger (not the diminutive "art") theaters: Fellini's *La Dolce Vita*, Richardson's *Tom Jones*, Antonioni's *Blow-Up*, Costa-Gavras' *Z*. Moreover, as the sixties progressed, the studios discovered that well over 70 percent of the country's moviegoers were of high school or college age. The old idea of the "family movie" seemed—with the exception of a thriving anomaly like Disney—defunct.

To the studios, it all added up to repeating the old bandwagon technique—only more so. If one producer gave director Mike Nichols total creative control of an unknown project called *The Graduate*, and if suddenly that film made more money than anything previously released (save the two great standbys *Gone With the Wind* and *The Sound of Music*), then obviously Youth Movies were In. Studios started giving exorbitant contracts to young directors fresh off the street. If a *Bonnie and Clyde* became the most successful movie one year, it was almost a dead certainty that a *Butch Cassidy and the Sundance Kid* was just around the corner. Or, given the success of an *Easy Rider*, expect a *Little Fauss and Big Halsy*.

Hollywood has always played the bandwagon game, but never with such desperate scrambling as in the sixties. For never before had the studios faced a situation that they had no patent answer for. Much of the problem lay in television. TV had usurped the majority of the older, more familiar (and less demanding) movie audience, leaving the theaters to the youth, whose tastes shifted mercurially, and who already had seen about as many movies as their folks—over television.

But it was more than the loss of an audience. The studio technique of production had crested in the thirties, when the studios had had at their disposal some of the most talented writers, directors, and actors in the country. As the forties and fifties progressed, and as the sixties finally

220

The Graduate 1967

proved, factory-made movies were never any the better for being factory-made. But throughout the forties and the fifties, the thirties generation disappeared from Hollywood and was replaced by men better fitted to the organizational and "factory" demands of the studios. Movies lost the excitement, the audacity, the delight they promised so often previously. There were still good movies, of course, but for every one or two really fine movies there might be a dozen potboilers. That hadn't been quite so true in the thirties.

The dominant strain in the movies of the sixties was movement away from the studios —both in geography and in spirit. The major new directors of the decade were not studio men but independents: Stanley Kubrick, Arthur Penn, Frank Perry, Mike Nichols, Sam Peckinpah. The independent producers—and eventually, even the studios —recognized that authentic settings went over better with audiences than the painstaking studio facades. Productions took place in the cities, in the countryside, and— due to spiraling union costs—increasingly abroad where production costs could often be cut in half. The studios were not enthusiastic about having their role reduced to bankrollers and promoters of film, but that seemed to be the direction.

In the sixties, the star system suffered its heaviest blows. Ever since the heyday of Hollywood stars in the late twenties and the thirties, studio front offices and publicity departments had kept careful track of the stars—who were biggest at the box office, who were the newcomers, who were the ones slipping from view. Annual polls determined the most popular male and female stars. The system had gone from a means of promoting movies (when it was begun, about 1913, by some slick promoters of two-reelers) to the central determining factor of every major movie. Suddenly, in the sixties, it backfired. Movies with stars regarded as major box-

Butch Cassidy and the Sundance Kid 1969

office attractions—such as Elizabeth Taylor, Richard Burton, Sidney Poitier, Paul Newman, and Marlon Brando—often failed to make money. Movies that did make big money generally featured names that the public had never heard before: Dustin Hoffman in *The Graduate*, Dennis Hopper in *Easy Rider*. The studios, of course, clung to the system. To discard it would have been like throwing away their own children. But it was obvious, even to them, that the system was no longer working.

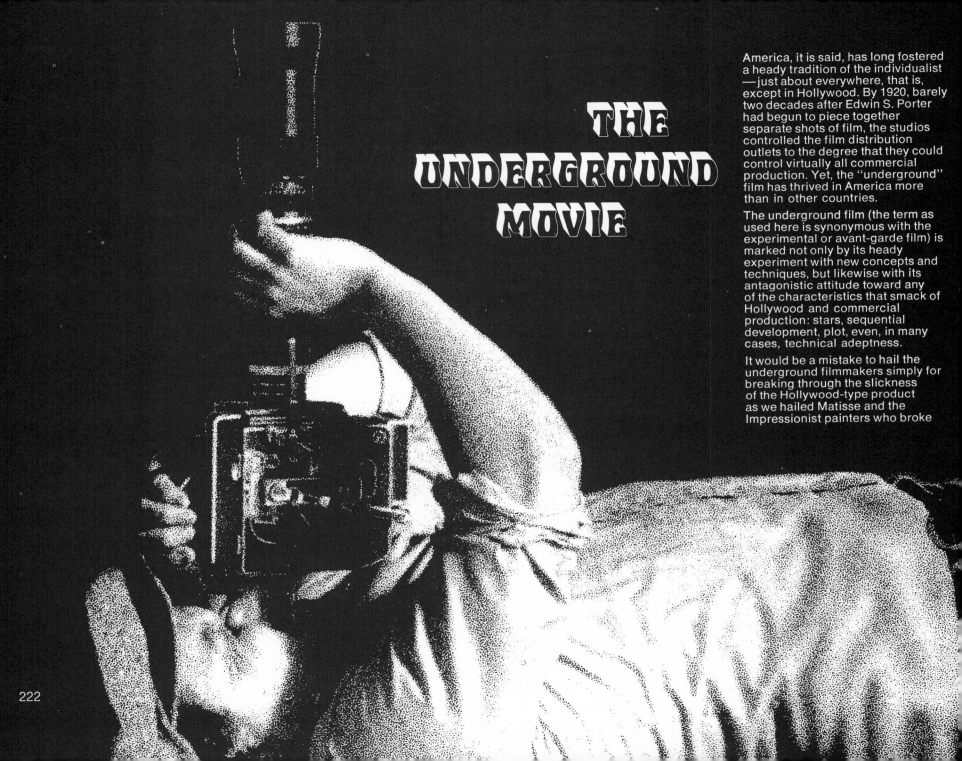

THE UNDERGROUND MOVIE

America, it is said, has long fostered a heady tradition of the individualist —just about everywhere, that is, except in Hollywood. By 1920, barely two decades after Edwin S. Porter had begun to piece together separate shots of film, the studios controlled the film distribution outlets to the degree that they could control virtually all commercial production. Yet, the "underground" film has thrived in America more than in other countries.

The underground film (the term as used here is synonymous with the experimental or avant-garde film) is marked not only by its heady experiment with new concepts and techniques, but likewise with its antagonistic attitude toward any of the characteristics that smack of Hollywood and commercial production: stars, sequential development, plot, even, in many cases, technical adeptness.

It would be a mistake to hail the underground filmmakers simply for breaking through the slickness of the Hollywood-type product as we hailed Matisse and the Impressionist painters who broke through the romanticism of late nineteenth century art. But what the underground filmmakers *have* done is to explore alternate ways of making movies, with varying degrees of success. Without question, the more recent underground films *have* influenced Hollywood. Often this influence has been evidenced in the TV commercial in which experiment-hungry filmmakers like to ape the effects they saw a week ago at an underground screening. The influence extends to other areas of TV and films. The incessantly long panning shot in Ed Emshwiller's *Relativity* is resounded in the "Stargate Corridor" sequence of *2001.* The split-second collages of Stan VanDerBeek's early works have become a standard convention in recent movies and TV; and techniques like color translation through the optical printer and solarization have made their way

from the works of Stan Brakhage to a variety of science fiction and other films.

The tradition of the underground film is too rich to credit it simply for its contributions to the establishment. The "early" underground films, made in the forties and early fifties, showed a heavy bent for surrealism and Freudian nuance. Salvador Dali's and Luis Buñuel's classic *Un Chien Andalou* and the later works of Hans Richter influenced American experimental films of the sixties, such as Kenneth Anger's *Scorpio Rising,* Maya Deren's *Meshes of the Afternoon,* Sidney Peterson's *The Cage,* or Gregory Markopoulos' *Twice a Man.* These films were concerned less with new technique than with complex symbolism, involuted allegory, and rigid images that caught a distorted state of mind.

The underground has since expanded and exploded. With the growing number of filmmakers, the field has become so broad that even the term underground fails to encapsulate it. The films and multimedia experiments of Charles Eames, for example, have contained some brilliantly inventive ideas, but many of them were paid for (perhaps unwittingly) by IBM. Andy Warhol's movies—which make a *virtue* of technical sloppiness—have made enough money to be the envy of many a Hollywood producer. Distinct traditions have emerged. A group of West Coast filmmakers, such as John and James Whitney, and John Stehura (as well as a sporadic Easterner like Stan VanDerBeek) have programmed computers to create graphic effects impossible for the most skilled animator. Filmmaker Jordan Belson has been experimenting with lighting and optical effects since the early sixties to create small, tightly controlled visual masterpieces like *Allures* and *Momentum.* And the films of Bruce Connor, Stan Brakhage and Ed Emshwiller all reflect a passionate concern for mythic images and

rhythms—an attempt to capture, poetically and somewhat abstractedly, rarified moods and states of mind or consciousness.

The most frequent complaints heard by audiences seeing a typical experimental, avant-garde, or underground film for the first time are that it is "boring," or "impossible to follow"—criticisms which tend often to be true of most underground films. But such criticisms are also indicative, to no small extent, of the degree to which we have been conditioned by the Hollywood product. We value narrative, technical slickness, and identifiable characters far more than we should. What a film like Stan Brakhage's *Dog Star Man* or Ed Emshwiller's *Relativity* can do is help us to realize that the film experience can be broader than our expectations for it. Perhaps this is both the lesson and, hopefully, the future of the underground film.

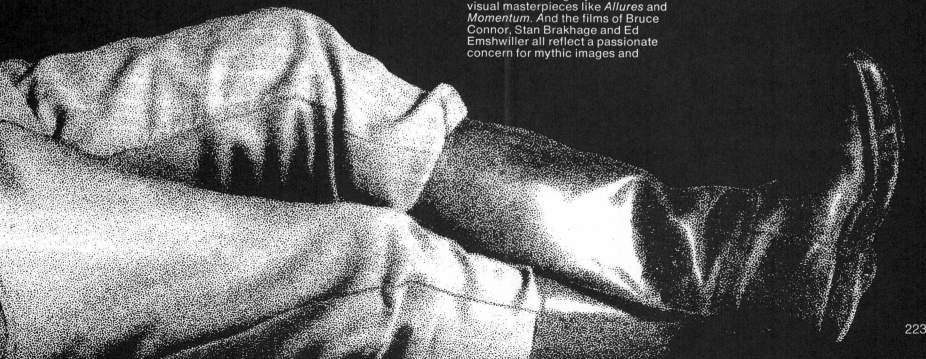

One thing the studios did learn in the sixties was new techniques. There were enough of them to promise a "major breakthrough" in the making of movies—though that promise, at least within the sixties, was never really delivered. Many of the techniques, such as split screen, zoom lens, the long telephoto shot, and the freeze frame were little more than warmed-over gimmicks of earlier years. Some went further. Richard Lester, an American with a background in making commercials, went to England and applied the fast cutting of TV commercials to feature films. The technique worked best when the subject was interesting, such as the Beatles in *Help!* and *A Hard Day's Night*, or the swift, crazed comedy of *The Knack*. But it became more than a little awkward and pretentious with *How I Won the War* and *Petulia*.

Some innovations—in technique and in concept—from Europe found their way into American movies: the breakdown of a plot and temporal progression heralded by the French filmmakers such as Jean-Luc Godard and Alain Resnais found its way into such movies as Arthur Penn's *Mickey One* and Stanley Donen's *Two for the Road*. Andy Warhol at the same time was introducing what seemed to be a counter-trend: making movies with a total *absence* of technique. In Warhol movies, such as *The Chelsea Girls*, a camera would sit relentlessly in front of the subject and never move—just grind on endlessly. In Warhol's "minimal films" there is virtually no cutting, no change in the camera angle—indeed, almost no control over the camera beyond placing it in position and staging something in front of it. The technique—or non-technique, as

The Knack 1965

the case may be—is primitive, harsh, and boring but a distinct and perhaps valid reaction against the super-slick totally engineered products of post-television Hollywood.

In the early sixties, French filmmakers Jean-Luc Godard, Chris Marker, and others developed a style they loosely called *cinéma vérité*. There is no real English equivalent. The phrase has slipped into the vocabulary of American and English film critics as it stands. Roughly it means that the filmmaker has sought an honesty and a realism that come across in the use of actors who don't appear to be acting, in real settings, and in conversations that are not pre-scripted. *Cinéma vérité* has done much to link the once distinctly different forms of the "fiction film" and the documentary. Peter Watkin's *The War Game*, a pseudo-documentary about an event that hopefully will never happen—a nuclear attack on England—is done in such a way that its grim horrors grow larger because they look

so accurate, so real. It is the power of *cinéma vérité* to create credibility where films before had only been able to stifle non-belief. It is the weakness of *cinéma vérité* that the technique (like any technique) will be used for its own sake, and not with any clear conception or purpose. The films by John Cassavetes, *Faces* and *Husbands*, are two remarkable examples of *cinéma vérité* gone slightly awry. While filled with moments of power and revelation, the films suffer because they lack the coherence of more plotted, pre-structured works.

Ultimately, the hallmark of sixties' movies is not new technique or even the much-vaunted "personal style" of the independent filmmakers. Rather it is the search for fresh ways of dealing with images and events on the screen, a quest for a new idiom, a more authentic and involving type of movie. And nowhere can this quest be seen so sharply as in the decade's most inventive and creative directors.

FOUR DIRECTORS

In a sense it is ironic. The sixties, more than any previous decade the period of "the director," introduced dozens of fresh American directors—but few of major consequence. With many, of course, it is hard to tell. A number of talented men have been making films that are slick, tough, well-wrought—but it is difficult to determine to what extent these films have emerged from the talents of the director. In any event, the films have not reached that intensity, or that fresh vitality, that announce a major new director. Some, of course, will emerge as more significant directors than their films have suggested so far. One suspects that there are talents in Don Siegel, Fred Zinnemann, John Frankenheimer, Frank Perry, or in a documentary director like Fred Wiseman, that have not yet reached their peak. Here, at any rate, are four directors who have shown over the sixties more than competence in their approach to moviemaking: Stanley Kubrick, Arthur Penn, Sam Peckinpah, and Robert Altman.

225

Spartacus 1959

STANLEY KUBRICK

Kubrick has become something of a champion to young filmmakers. Both in terms of his art and in his success at the box office, he is easily one of the most successful independent directors in the history of American movies. Kubrick has moved between genres as distant as gangster (*The Killing*), grim comedy (*Dr. Strangelove*), and experimental science fiction (*2001: A Space Odyssey*) with unique facility and flair for achieving new techniques and new effects.

Kubrick's first two films—*Fear and Desire* (1953), and *Killer's Kiss* (1955)—only vaguely hinted at the talents or the sustained virtuosity that would emerge later. His third film, *The Killing* (1957), was not a major attempt by any means, but at least it suggested the presence of a talent who could make a movie that was more than barely competent. *The Killing* is a suspense movie, done in a tough, clipped style and under fine, definite control. It is somewhat redolent of Huston's *The Asphalt Jungle* (both feature Sterling Hayden in his best roles), in that it pulses with a vitality that it has not entirely borrowed from the conventions of the genre.

Neither of Kubrick's next two movies, *Spartacus* (1960) or *Lolita* (1962) are "major" in the sense of *Strangelove* or *2001*. Both, significantly, are studio projects to which Kubrick was not wholeheartedly committed and which he was not entirely free. (He has himself disavowed *Spartacus* and doesn't like to talk about it with interview-

ers.) Yet the two films reveal a development of Kubrick's craft, a sharpening sense of image and character, and in *Lolita* particularly, a play of irony around situations.

In *Dr. Strangelove* (1964), Kubrick added a new chapter to the history of film comedy. Using the nuclear arms race and the American-Russian deadlock of powers as his basic material, Kubrick created what has been regarded since as the "black comedy" masterpiece of the movies. There are no bounds, no restraints, no stylized conventions in the world of Kubrick's imagination. Grotesque farce gives way to scathing satire, and through it all a death's head seems to be grinning with savage delight. The characters, to be sure, were often no more than gross caricatures of the fighting he-men who had taken Iwo Jima in some dozen John Wayne-U.S. Marine movies: General Buck Turgidson is convinced that the Russians are behind fluoridation and are out to destroy our precious bodily fluids; General Jack D. Ripper can't resist a bloody battle even if it's with his own men; Major T. J. "King" Kong rides a falling H-bomb as though it were a rodeo bronc. For dark comedy—perhaps no other genre in recent movies is so cluttered with casualties—*Dr. Strangelove* is a hilariously funny movie. There are moments, such as the time someone shoots into a Coca-Cola machine to rescue a dime to call the President, that reach side-splitting hilarity. Yet that death's head is still there, grinning perversely.

Dr. Strangelove or: How I Learned to Stop Worrying
and Love the Bomb 1963

But it is not only the absurdity and futility of the Cold War that *Strangelove* attacks. Kubrick picks out a wide host of targets. War legislation reveals its nightmare side in the little-known clause that enables General Buck Turgidson to order the bombing mission. The Russian "Doomsday Machine" is a sweetly served corollary to any bureaucracy's tendency to put things beyond the control of men. The final scene, before the bomb falls, reflects the opportunism of politicians and army leaders alike. Who can forget George C. Scott's hungry grin at the thought of being cooped up in a deep bomb shelter for years with a disproportionate number of lovely young girls? Or Dr. Strangelove's uncontrollable hand that keeps rising up, against his will, in the Heil Hitler salute?

Dr. Strangelove is one of those rare movies that creates new ground. It merges satire and farce in a way that is both funny and grimly prophetic. It moves the characters into increasingly inane actions, while never losing control of what is happening. It takes some of the darkest intimidations of recent history and uses them not for suspense or the backdrop to spy escapades, but as the very stuff of comedy. Even the last, closing shots, that montage of nuclear mushrooms, supposedly sprouting throughout the world, is shown against a nightclub rendition of "We'll Meet Again"—a song that is both wildly inappropriate and yet, within the context of the movie, absolutely perfect.

Dr. Strangelove was a hard act for any director to follow, and Kubrick, ever so typically, didn't follow it. Rather he ignored it, not trying at all for comedy but making what has been called "the world's most expensive underground film." For *2001* not only lacked humor, it lacked plot, dialogue, characters of any interest (except maybe the computer Hal). But Kubrick seemed hardly interested in any of these staples of conventional moviemaking. He was out not only to shift around the conventions, the characters, the mode of humor and dialogue, he was after a basic transformation in the experience of movies. Throughout more than three hours of *2001*, we hear very little dialogue, are constantly distracted from

whatever plot there might be by either a kind of lunar travelogue or by the seeming ballet of ships docking in a space port. The only moments of real drama take place when the computer Hal (consciously designed to reflect certain human feelings), turns paranoid and tries to destroy all life on board ship. Even that conflict, resulting in Hal's gradual slippage from memory and computer-consciousness, happens in such a way that we are more fascinated with the process than concerned about the outcome. Kubrick, almost in a perverse way, cast his characters so that we wouldn't become too attached to them, encouraging us *not* to identify, not to care too much—for that, after all, wasn't the point of the movie.

2001: A Space Odyssey is a cosmic movie —-in its dimensions, in its images, in its ambitions. Kubrick is not satisfied with depicting a slice of the life and extra-terrestrial environment in the year 2001; he is more interested in hinting at what movies—and by extension, much of human consciousness—will be like in 2001. Kubrick has not made a movie that we see and feel through a character's eyes; he has given us no story to follow. The movie is less the congruence of people and situation that we have been accustomed to with movies—it is more of a raw datum of images and sounds, with few cues on how to respond to them, and only a semblance of development or progression holding them together. It is a kind of sensory

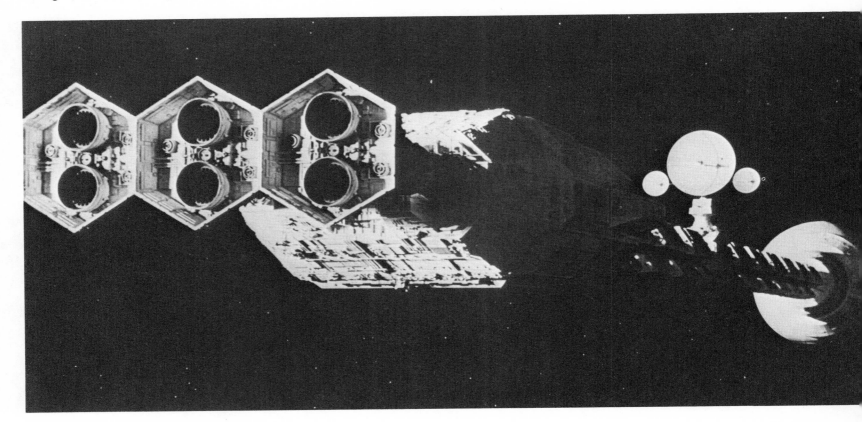

trip, a thrust into the rhythm of the docking ships, the planets, the moons, the stars. Kubrick is using the film medium to say, here is the *experience* of space flight. All else in the movie is largely incidental to that.

A breakthrough in the nature of movies? Actually, Kubrick was anticipated by a score of experimental, or so-called "underground" filmmakers, particularly Maya Deren, Stan Brakhage, Ed Emshwiller, and Bruce Conner. The experimental films of these and other independents had already taken many routes in exploring the potential of movies as ensembles of images and sound. Plot had by and large disappeared from these films. Characters were often little more than parts of the films' visual texture. Audi-

ences were often stymied, bored, or both. Yet such films as Bruce Conner's *Cosmic Ray*, Ed Emshwiller's *Relativity* and Stan Brakhage's *Dog Star Man* had definitely escaped the old idiom of movies—even if they had not yet successfully created a new one. The endless tracking shot in *Relativity* has its parallel in the "Stargate Sequence" in *2001*. The gentle camera rhythms of *Dog Star Man* are not all that distant from the slow eerie camera movements that follow the space docking in *2001*.

What makes *2001* so important—perhaps, if history follows its example, the most important film of the sixties—is that it successfully brings the techniques and appeal of the experimental film into the studio feature-

length movie. There had been moderately successful experimental films before—Warhol's *The Chelsea Girls* only two years earlier—but never on such a grandiose scale, or never so spectacularly successful (by 1971, *2001* had grossed over $21 million in the U.S. and Canada). *2001* promises a new form of movie, one explicitly directed toward a new audience, building on perceptions rather than long-established conventions. It is typical of Kubrick's cosmic ambitions that a movie would break through more than the comfortable genres, but through some of the most basic expectations we have toward what we see on the screen.

2001: A Space Odyssey 1968

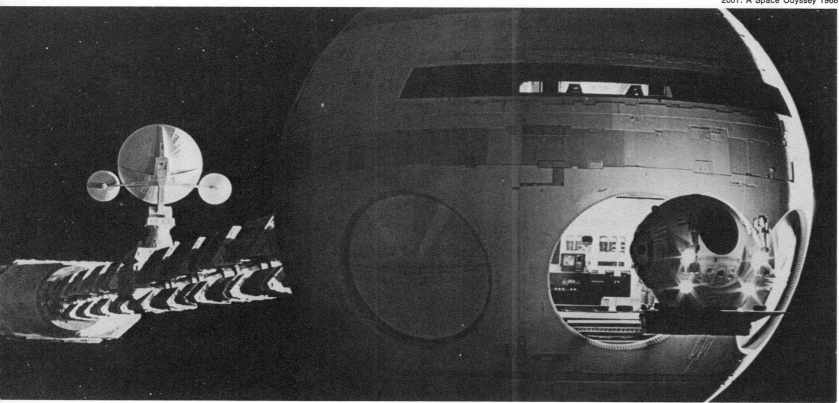

229

The Left Handed Gun 1958

Mickey One 1964

ARTHUR PENN

The stage has always been an uncertain source of directorial talent for the movies. Some stage directors have been able to make the transition and have brought to the movies a dramatic sense uncluttered by unnecessary theatricality. One thinks of Rouben Mamoulian, Elia Kazan, and Orson Welles. But even in these cases—and they represent the best of the stage directors who became film directors—there remains a definite theatricality, a staginess and at least the hint of the proscenium arch. It is to Arthur Penn's credit that his later movies—from *The Chase* onward—reflect not only an escape from the theatrical and the staged but toward a fresh style of moviemaking which, however flawed, is totally impossible in theater but eminently successful as cinema.

Penn is in the uncomfortable position of having made a successful adaptation (*The Miracle Worker*), several not-so-successful experiments (*Mickey One* and *Alice's Restaurant*), two well-wrought but hardly major action pictures (*The Left-Handed Gun* and *The Chase*), an ambitious but sometimes clumsy epic (*Little Big Man*) and what has come to be regarded as a masterpiece of the modern cinema (*Bonnie and Clyde*). Single films that rise far higher than the rest of a director's work are an embarrassment. They provide an awkward incentive for a director to live up to a past performance, and they create in audiences and critics an expectation of style and vitality that become themselves the measure of his future accomplishments.

Much like Kubrick, Penn is an experimenter and innovator. He is attracted to a project less by its "rightness" for his style than by the potential it has for enabling him to try out fresh ideas, fresh modes of narrative, fresh approaches to familiar themes. Indeed, Penn's major failing lies in his eagerness to tackle problems which are patently beyond his full control: the breakdown of temporal narrative in *Mickey One*, the intimate, *cinéma vérité* style of *Alice's Restaurant*, the conjunction of horror and humor in *Little Big Man*.

Throughout Penn's movies, there is a strong sense of the physical as a revelation of subtler relationships and meaning. No director can say quite as much so well in the grip of a hand, the tossing away of an object, the slouch of a body. In *The Miracle Worker*, when Anne Sullivan and the blind and deaf Helen Keller meet, Helen's fingers reach for Anne's face. In closeup, Penn depicts the little girl's fingers searching out Anne's face. It is a poignant moment, capturing what will become the mood and tension of Anne's relationship with Helen. In *Bonnie and Clyde*, there is that classic moment shortly after the two meet when the impotent Clyde shows Bonnie his gun and she strokes it with evident erotic overtones Such moments suggest why Penn's best films are those that deal with relationships and conflicts that are rich in physical expression: the atmosphere of violence in *Bonnie and Clyde* and *The Left-Handed Gun*, the necessarily physical communication between

Annie and Helen in *The Miracle Worker*. It is also not surprising that Penn's most glaring failure, *Mickey One*, results from a conception that depends on staging, lighting, baroque settings, and a confused melodramatic plot—almost Wellesian, in fact—rather than the gestures, movements, and moods of actors.

Penn is a director with supreme confidence in his actors. Ultimately, he is far more concerned with their performances, their movements and nuances, than with exotic camera effects, expressive settings, or complex cutting. (This is not to say that Penn does not use the camera well: indeed the use matures and becomes quite sophisticated in *Bonnie and Clyde*.) But what interests Penn and what he reaches toward consciously is the human, the tragic. There is a psychological vein that runs through Penn's work, a sense of man fighting for a kind of expression which is both personal and freeing. Indeed, the vein is so pronounced as to constitute a motif—Penn's most familiar, his most deeply probed.

Penn's characters are almost all crippled in some way by life, either in a physical, obvious way—as Helen Keller or Anne Sullivan in *The Miracle Worker*, as Clyde Barrow in *Bonnie and Clyde*—or in an emotional way, as Calder and Bubber Reeves in *The Chase*, or as Billy the Kid in *The Left-Handed Gun*. (In the later films, *Alice's Restaurant* and *Little Big Man*, the motif continues but within the context of new themes and without quite the same empha-

The Miracle Worker 1962

sis.) Penn's films thus concentrate on the ways in which these characters fight to find expression and freedom. Most often their expression results not in a successful escape from their condition but in violence—a violence which Penn understands as very few directors ever have. As Robin Wood says in his study of Penn:

Penn in his films to date has given us arguably the most complex and mature treatment of violence in the American cinema. The presentation of violence, the defined attitude to it, differs from film to film. . . . Yet one assumption remains consistent throughout: that violence in all its forms, from Helen's fury at being forced to hold a spoon, through respectable society's vindictive hunting down of Bubber Reeves, to Bonnie and Clyde's armed robbery, is an inevitable outlet for frustrated urges that can find no other.

It is not simply violence which attracts Penn—though violent moments do have a savagery and a pain in his films that they almost never connote anywhere else. Rather he is attracted by the process by which violence comes about, and our involvement in the lives of those who generate it. In *Bonnie and Clyde*, for instance, Penn makes it very easy for us to like these two: they are spontaneous, fun people who enjoy life and live it more thoroughly than anyone else in the film. Yet we are continually torn in our reactions to Clyde Barrow and Bonnie Parker by their obsession for destruction—not only the destruction of others, so vividly depicted in Clyde's smashing the grocer's face through the car window, but in the destruction of themselves and in their growing separation from society and from those around them. True, we are never brought to the point of being thoroughly ambivalent about Bonnie and Clyde, but we are kept from being confident that they will escape. Throughout the film, their fate seems inevitable, and all they possess is a succession of "stays of execution."

Again, Wood: "All Penn's work is concerned with impulses that could be called, in the widest sense, religious: man's blind reaching out towards what lies beyond him, his efforts to break out of the immediate 'reality' which imprisons him: and with the failure of those impulses to find satisfaction." It is a tragic theme and, over and over again, Penn leads us to a tragic ending. Only in *The Miracle Worker,* of all his films, does the ending seem truly cathartic to the characters. Only here is the dark place into which they have plunged themselves really lit by a ray of hope.

This is not to say that Penn's movies are esentially pessimistic—his characters are too alive, too close to us, for us really to think that. Yet Penn refuses an easy truce between the vitality of his characters and the strictures of society. Bonnie and Clyde had to die not only because they were criminals and murderers, but partly because they were more alive, more exuberantly in touch with their own instincts and sensations than anyone else in the film.

Tensions abide in Penn's films, lurking invisibly near the surface as does surrogate guilt in a Hitchcock movie. We are rarely able to respond simply to an act of violence, a fresh character, or a moment of humor. Too many things are going on, that in a sense spoils the single effect of such moments. For example, when Bonnie and Clyde capture the Texas Ranger, that stodgy, righteous fellow, and play games with him. When Bonnie kisses him, it is fun, nothing more. When he responds by spitting at her, we realize it was more than fun—it was a reflection of the different ways in which these people stood toward society. The Texas Ranger was no longer a clown, no longer a hard-breathing bounty hunter. He really does believe in the law, he really does hate both Bonnie and Clyde with a vehemence rooted largely in his own commitment to a social system that Bonnie and Clyde feel outside of.

Penn's last two movies, *Alice's Restaurant* and *Little Big Man*, form a kind of departure from his earlier work, though the earlier themes and style remain. Of the two, *Alice's Restaurant* is the most disparate, as well as the less successful. It lacks the focus, the tightness, and the active quality of other Penn movies. The problem with *Alice's Restaurant* is not that the characters are intrinsically uninteresting, though many lack the vitality Penn usually confers with such sure touch on his supporting players. Rather, the mood of the film—and to some extent its theme—lies in the passivity and listlessness of its characters. They are not, like Bonnie and Clyde, drawn inexplicably into action; they are drawn away from it. Their lives follow a rhythm that Penn captures well enough, but that lacks the basis for the undercurrents and tensions that make Penn's movies so engrossing the second time around.

Arthur Penn is a major director. He is still a relatively young one. His sense of action, character, and motivation is surer than that of most American directors, and generally more complex. He has explored a kind of psychological reality which, while not unfamiliar in American movies, has not been developed with the sophistication that Penn normally brings to it. *Bonnie and Clyde* may be his only unqualified success so far, but it is likewise an indication of a talent and an intelligence that promises more.

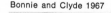
Bonnie and Clyde 1967

Ballad of Cable Hogue 1969

SAM PECKINPAH

Up until the sixties the Western was perhaps the most vital and familiar genre in American movies. Its history has been long and rich. But by the late fifties, its themes seemed depleted, the actions seemed repetitious and stilted, and television had absorbed so much of the genre (in one year in the late fifties over a dozen different Western series were running simultaneously) that the future looked bleak. True, the major directors of Westerns continued into the sixties: John Ford, Howard Hawks, Anthony Mann, Budd Boetticher. But much of the vitality had been leached out and the Western had become little more than the type of movie to get double-billing in drive-ins, and no more.

Sam Peckinpah, a veteran television writer who began making movies in 1961, has almost singlehandedly revitalized an ailing genre. Admittedly, his Westerns are unlike those of Ford or Hawks or Mann. He brings to them themes which seem almost alien—the plight of growing old in a young land; the dour recognition that life has been squandered and misspent; the innate violence and self-destruction of the professional gunfighter.

Peckinpah's films have about them a tough intelligence and an almost Calvinistic sense of the instability of man. His heroes are not fortuitous, gun-happy John Waynes. They are guilt-ridden old men who know they are not far from dying and who have been alienated from the land that they have known all their lives. Throughout Peckinpah's work, even in his warmer *The Ballad* of *Cable Hogue*, there persists a sadness and a sense of loss—as though the loss of the West that Peckinpah's characters have known were mirroring our loss of the mythical West that we have known through so many Hollywood films. Peckinpah, through his characters, through his situations, and through the empty, stark settings he uses, consciously pulls us away from the mythical West and into a world which is too real, too brutal, too disturbing to continue the cherished beliefs that so many thousands of Westerns had long nurtured. Yes, Virginia, the West is dead; but not, thanks to Peckinpah, the Western.

Until 1970 Peckinpah had made five movies, mostly Westerns: *The Deadly Companions* (1961), *Ride the High Country* (1961), *Major Dundee* (1964), *The Wild Bunch* (1969), and *the Ballad of Cable Hogue* (1970). His films have not received the critical attention that Kubrick's or Penn's have drawn, partly because they *are* Westerns and not the major studio projects that tend to attract enormous reviewing and criticism; but partly, too, because Peckinpah prefers to work in a minor key. With the exception of *The Wild Bunch*—possibly the most violent movie yet made—his films lack the obvious intellectual "sex appeal" to those who want to see the latest "in" film, the biggest new attraction around. Like his mentor, the superb action director Don Siegel, Peckinpah makes films which tend to gravitate toward drive-ins and double-billings, not because they belong there, but because

the economics of the industry and the blindness of audiences have not rescued them from that semi-oblivion.

Yet Peckinpah's best films—*Major Dundee*, *The Wild Bunch*, and *The Ballad of Cable Hogue*—are in their own ways muted masterpieces: flawed, certainly, but vitally alive and rich in tensions and complexities that run deeper than the ordinary Western. Peckinpah's storytelling is so dense, his meanings sometimes so subtle, that it might be best to concentrate on one film, *The Wild Bunch*.

It is after the turn of the century, and a gang that has ridden together long and painfully is now in Mexico, looking for that Holy Grail of the "last job"—the only revitalizing hope of the aging outlaw. *The Wild Bunch* opens with a shot that captures immediately the flavor and yet the complexity of the movie: a scorpion swarming with ants, dying in the grip of the tiny yet numberless killers. A gaggle of Mexican children watch, absorbed in the horror. Here life and death are not sheltered from the children, as the movie will go on to show. The children are always there, watching a man dragged to near death by a horse, fascinated by new weapons and even helping in the final massacre. Violence as a way of life engulfs all those who come near it, Peckinpah suggests. It is not simply a contagion, but an extension of our condition, a necessary consequence of men living outside the tight restrictions of civilization.

The gang is led by Pike Bishop (William

Ride the High Country 1961

235

The Wild Bunch 1969

Holden), a tough, laconic man burdened by an unarticulated sense of guilt and lost opportunities. Bishop keeps encountering the past as he might have lived it: the love he has rejected, the respectability he has scorned, the dreams he has ignored. He wants to be insensitive, but can't, and his ambivalence provides the note on which much of the film is sounded: a somber, dying note, not far from the songs of the Mexican villagers.

The film moves forward with an almost palpable dread. Never does Peckinpah suggest that things will somehow not end as they do—in a massacre that is grim, barbaric, and yet in its own way, inevitable. The Americans do not belong in Mexico. They have left their own land because it has become too tight, too constraining. Here they are definitely out of place, in a culture that they haven't the right feelings for, among a people they don't understand. Violence and death seem closer to the Mexicans than to the American gang. What Pike Bishop and his gang fail to understand is how close the joy and celebrations of the Mexicans runs alongside their violence, their nearness to death.

The Wild Bunch is rich in images that suggest man's entrapment between the animalistic and the sublime. A child sucks its mother's breast, the chest-belt of bullets only inches from the baby's head. The Mexican villagers, lined up along the roadside to bid "Adios" to the American gang, chant a song that seems more of a dirge than a celebration. The land itself that Peckinpah has chosen for the exteriors has a quality of isolation and emptiness. It is vast, dry, scorched—hardly the stirring Monument Valley of a Ford film.

Peckinpah is a curious director of Westerns, a master of violence, innuendo, and dialogue that is at once tough and edged with bitterness. Yet he is particularly weak in some of the features that has made the Western traditionally strong—in clear plots, in the heroic possibilities of man, in the fabric of society that holds men together. There is something pessimistic in Peckinpah, something that is most noticeable in *The Wild Bunch*, but which comes through in his other films as well: a sense that men cannot shake off the evil that is in them, much as the scorpion could not shake off the ants. As a result, their death cannot really be a form of salvation—it is simply an end.

236

THE SPLINTERED SCREEN

THE SPLINTERED SCREEN □ Moviemakers have always been looking for ways to give the movie screen more visual power: with color, wider and wider screens, even such gimmickry as the illusion of three dimensions. One of the lately popular techniques—and perhaps one of the more promising—is multi-screen or split-screen: breaking the screen image into a combination of juxtaposed and interlocking images, instead of the single continuous image.

Some of the best uses of multi-screen techniques have not, curiously, been movies. At Expo 67 in Montreal, the Czechs used a 112-screen display in which two slide-projectors were located behind each screen. Programmed by a computer, the slide projectors switched images to create vivid forms and independent images that interlocked graphically at eye-dazzling, split-second pacing.

Hollywood has been both reticent and awkward about the use of multi-screen techniques in its films, in part because: it is difficult to use multi-screen; the masking and laboratory work required for multi-screen is very expensive; and multi-screen tends to interfere with the traditional method of storytelling. Yet, used with ingenuity, the splintered screen can do a number of things: it can reorganize various actions to create fresh interpretations of what is happening; it can present—if only in purely visual terms—several related things occurring simultaneously; and, theoretically, it can create a kind of spatial editing in which contrasting or related images are presented not only one right after another, but next to one another.

So far Hollywood's most impressive demonstration of multi-screen has been certain moments in Norman Jewison's *The Thomas Crown Affair*. But even here the screens that slide beside one another are used often to break up large single images—like Steve McQueen's face. In this instance, the multi-screen is used more for slickness than for function. It's unlikely the split-screen will be explored to create a truly new type of movie—for some time, at least. Rather, it's more probable that multi-screen usage will remain in exhibitions and in movies oriented solely toward being visually impressive.

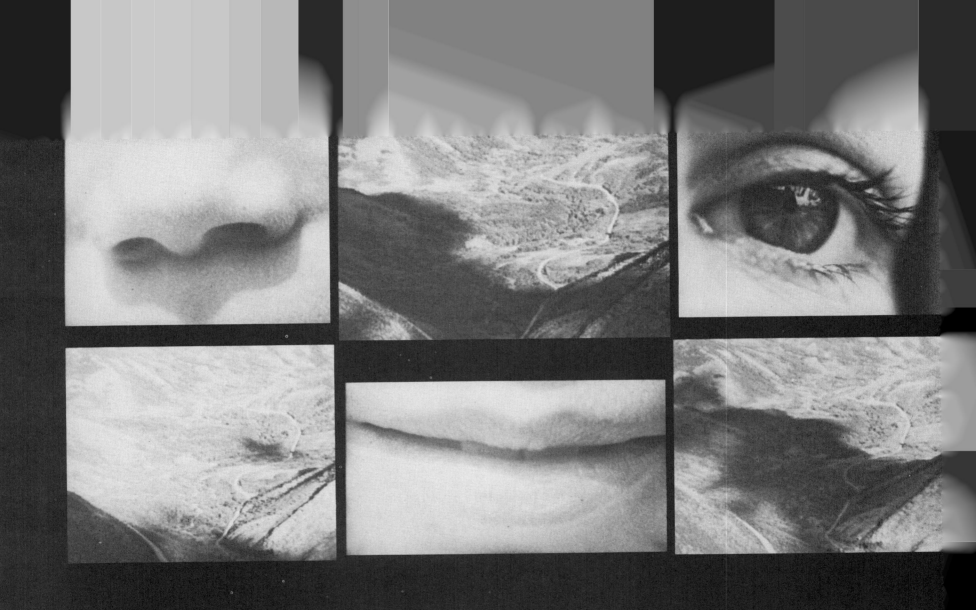

M*A*S*H 1969

ROBERT ALTMAN

Of the directors discussed in this chapter, Altman is the newest and, in terms of the number of films he has made, the least accomplished. Like Peckinpah a veteran television director, Altman moved into movies with *The Delinquents*, followed by *The James Dean Story* and *A Cold Day in the Park*. None of these, however, began to suggest the talents of a fiery, ribald and absolutely unflappable director of a savage new mode of comedy that would be seen in *M*A*S*H* and *Brewster McCloud*.

Really good comedy directors have always been a rarity in Hollywood. Men like Preston Sturges, Frank Capra, Leo McCarey, and Howard Hawks made some brilliant, wacky, and funny movies in the thirties and early forties. But there have been no real comedy directors of any sizable talent since. Robert Altman promises not only movies that are genuinely funny, but which are funny in a vein that is particularly contemporary.

One suspects that in the hands of someone less in control of his material than Altman, the script for *M*A*S*H* would have led to a foundering movie. The script for *Brewster McCloud* would have resulted in total disaster. Altman revels in the absurd, and by adding just the right touches, by catching inflections and moods and facial innuendos, can make an absurd, preposterous situation real, vital, and hilarious. For example, there is the "Last Supper" sequence in *M*A*S*H* when the dentist, who has come to doubt his heterosexual drive and therefore the meaning of his existence, decides to commit suicide. Everything is laid out in advance and the trick of getting him to swallow what he thinks to be a death pill is structured as a formal ritual: the pill is a kind of dark Eucharist. A long shot conveys the horizontal presence of the entire group, an obvious visual spoof of DeVinci's "Last Supper." Once the dentist has been laid into his bed, he is visited by a nurse who provides more than enough reassurance that he is still alive—and will enjoy staying that way. What is striking about the entire sequence is how smoothly and how successfully Altman manages to blend wildly divergent elements to create scenes that are at once somber and rollicking.

Altman's comedy cuts with a scalpel just as sharp as those used by the playboy surgeons in the M*A*S*H* hospital tents. One of the oldest established conventions in movie comedy is that idea of the underdog confounding authority: Sennett, Chaplin, Fields, the Marx Brothers all used it. Here Altman adds a variation by making the surgeons so important to the army that any discipline measures would be costlier than the army can afford. The Japanese sequence (one of the few sequences that strays from the base camp, and which is definitely weakened by that fact) underscores the theme and develops it brilliantly.

The cutting edge of Altman's comedy is more apparent and more incisive, however, in Brewster McCloud, a comedy with a premise at once fantastic and shrewd. The plot, like that in M*A*S*H*, is held together by slivers. What interests Altman is the texture of the moment, the effect of a specific action or line, the enormous possibilities for satire, invective, gags. The characterizations are perversely disparate: the grubby old Houston millionaire who jams money from old age home rentals into his little box; the celebrated San Francisco detective with his dozen turtleneck sweaters. Brewster McCloud aims at Houston, at movie myths, at teenyboppers, at law enforcement. Like the bird droppings that keep appearing throughout the film, the movie is usually just about on target.

Much of Altman's skill lies in his editing. Both M*A*S*H* and Brewster McCloud move with a disjunction of sequences, yet are held together by a rhythm that keeps them from falling apart. In a sense, both comedies are little more than small, nearly self-sufficient episodes, linked together in a kind of sausage fashion. The comedy does not build with uncomfortable situations rising toward the incredulous as with Chaplin. But it does familiarize us with tone, mood, and characters enough to savor each episode as it takes place. It is possible that Altman has hit upon the only way of capturing a truly comic sensibility in depressing times.

Altman's skill is impressive. His comedy still lacks the force of more savage satire— that of a Billy Wilder, for instance—but it rarely lacks for vitality, freshness, or invention. And Altman is the first to know that there is more to good movie comedy than fun.

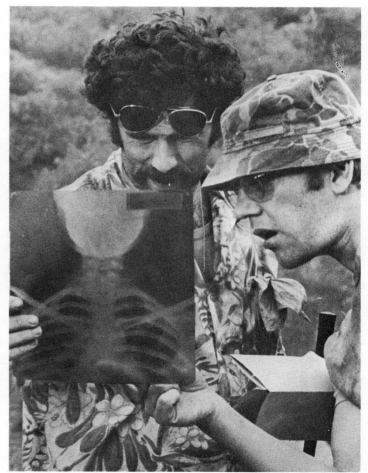

M*A*S*H 1969

241

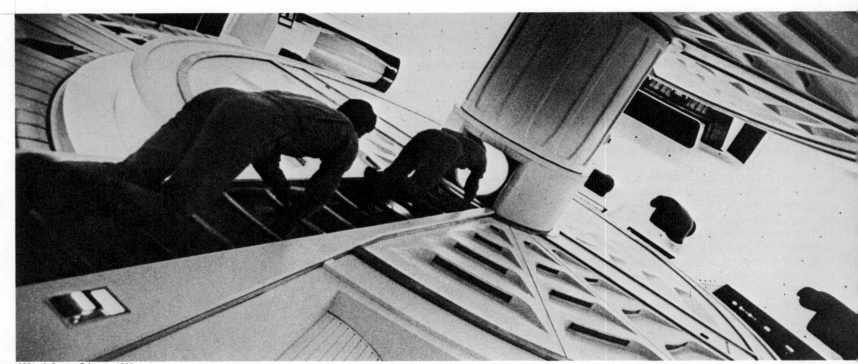

2001: A Space Odyssey 1968

BEYOND THE SCREEN

There is no ending to a history—only a pause. In the early 1970s, movies stand poised between a dying past and an uncertain future. The new communication technologies, particularly cartridge and cable television, promise to change the way in which we see movies, and the access we will have to older movies. Industry officials claim that soon we can stock a library of movie cartridges, much as we stock a library of books—though perhaps not at the same expense.

Further in the future loom even larger changes in the way we see movies. Will a wall-sized television screen, for example, lead to the end of theaters and the viewing of movies (presumably paid) at home? And what of laser holography, a system which enables one to take and show what are, in effect, three-dimensional movies?

But the technologies are only one aspect. What of the studios? Will the rise of the independent producer and the independent director in the sixties lead to a form of filmmaking in which the studios become no more than bankrollers and distributors? And what of film forms which, largely due to the studio monopoly in this country, have never been able to reach a large audience: the short film, the experimental film, the documentary?

Several trends that might suggest what is to come are apparent now. Movies and television have already become inextricably intertwined with one another, and, particularly with declining theater audiences, seem likely to become even more intermeshed in the future. Movies that don't fare too well in theaters may appear on television shortly afterwards. Indeed, the whole distinction between "movies for TV" and "movies" has, in terms of production and often production quality, come to mean almost nothing.

Another trend lies in the changing character of the theater audience. Most moviegoers are young, a fact which has led to a proliferation of some really horrendous films on the part of studios. There is a difference between pandering to the young, jamming movies with themes of sexual liberation, revolution, and identity crisis because they are presumed to be "in," and in making movies that take advantage of the openness and willingness to look at something new that characterizes the best of the young audience. Film producers, directors, and writers are in a better position now than they have been in years to make the best kinds of movies they can make. Not surprisingly, all but a few are ruining the opportunity. One suspects that studio discipline is not all that bad a requirement for many writers and directors.

But regardless of which way they go, movies have a future—if only because they have blazed such a deep trail into our consciousness over the past. It is hard to imagine modern culture without movies, hard to imagine the options of spending an evening without the newspaper's movie page figuring in somehow. Movies have become an undeniable and profound feature of our culture. The myth has been battered and beaten and crippled, but it lives.

BIBLIOGRAPHY

EARLY YEARS

Blesh, Rudi. **Keaton.** 1966, Macmillan. The authoritative biography by an old friend, including material given the author by Keaton.

Brownlow, Kevin. **The Parade's Gone By.** 1969, Knopf; Ballantine paperback. Oral history. Interviews with the old stars, directors, technicians and essays built around interviews. Primary source material lavishly produced.

Eisenstein, Sergei. **Film Form.** 1949, Harcourt, Brace paperback. The two directors who influenced world cinema were Griffith and Eisenstein. This is an explanation of his theories by the man who made *Strike, Ten Days that Shook the World,* and *Ivan the Terrible.*

Geduld, Harry M. **Focus On D.W. Griffith.** 1971, Prentice-Hall paperback. One of the "Focus On" books by the co-author of **Guidebook to Film.** Much material by Griffith himself and essays and reminiscences by those who knew him, including Erich von Stroheim and Lillian Gish.

Gish, Lillian. **The Movies, Mr. Griffith and Me.** Written with Ann Pinchot. 1969, Prentice-Hall; Avon paperback. Lillian Gish, one of the most famous stars of the silent screen, was discovered by Griffith. She starred in *Birth of a Nation.* She writes about the early days and her mentor in a very readable contribution to the history of American cinema.

McCaffrey, Donald W. **Four Great Comedians.** A.S. Barnes paperback. The careers of Chaplin, Lloyd, Keaton and Langdon.

*Robinson, David. **Buster Keaton.** 1969, Indiana University Press Cinema One

Series in association with **Sight and Sound,** a distinguished British film journal, and the Education division of the British Film Institute. (Books in this series, published by various American publishers but with the same format, are marked with *). Critical biography with filmography.

GENERAL FILM HISTORY

Clarens, Carlos. **An Illustrated History of the Horror Film.** 1967, Capricorn paperbacks. Concise history of one of the most popular genres.

Fenin, George and Everson, William. **The Western.** 1962, Orion Press. A comprehensive, illustrated history of the genre the authors maintain is the most representative form of American cinema.

Griffith, Richard and Mayer, Arthur. **The Movies.** 1957, Simon and Schuster. Big, lavishly produced book that is a general history of U.S. film to 1956.

Jacobs, Lewis. **The Rise of American Film.** 1939, Harcourt and Brace; Teacher's College paperback. Scholarly book on U.S. film up to 1939, with supplement on experimental cinema to 1947. A must for the beginner.

Knight, Arthur. **The Liveliest Art.** 1957, Macmillan; Mentor paperbacks. Good general history of the movies up to 1956.

DIRECTORS, ACTORS, PRODUCERS, CAMERAMEN

Bogdanovich, Peter. **John Ford.** 1968, U. of Calif. Press paperback. This book is an interview conducted by Bogdanovich. Very little criticism, but the

meeting of two artists to talk about their craft is always satisfying.

Gottesman, Ronald. **Focus on Citizen Kane.** 1971, Prentice Hall paperback. Another "Focus On" book, this one on one of the milestones in U.S. film made by one of our greatest directors.

*Higham, Charles. **Hollywood Cameramen.** 1970, Indiana University Press. Covers Shamroy, Garmes, Daniels, Miller, Howe, Cortez, Struss. A look at a long-neglected group of artists.

*Madsen, Axel. **Billy Wilder.** 1969, Indiana University Press. Critical biography of the Austrian-born director whose films include *Double Indemnity,* 1944; *The Lost Weekend,* 1945; *Sunset Boulevard,* 1950; *Irma La Douce,* 1963.

Maltin, Leonard. **Behind the Camera.** 1971, Signet paperback. Fine general history of American cinematography. Includes interviews.

Schickel, Richard. **The Disney Version.** 1968. Simon and Schuster. A long look at the Disney industry.

Weinberg, Joseph. **The Lubitsch Touch.** 1968, E.P. Dutton paperback. A long look at a director of highly polished, sophisticated movies about society, usually based on European plays. Lubitsch's art is discussed in eight essays.

Weinberg, Joseph. **Josef von Sternberg.** 1967, E.P. Dutton paperback. Critical biography of one of the giants of the Twenties and Thirties.

Wood, Robin. **Hitchcock's Films.** 1969, A.S. Barnes; Paperback Library. *The* book on Hitchcock, with a full filmography up to *Torn Curtain,* 1966.

Wood, Robin. **Howard Hawks.** 1968, Doubleday. Classic study of the maker of

The Dawn Patrol, 1930; *Viva Villa!* 1934; *The Big Sleep,* 1946.

Zierold, Norman. **The Moguls.** 1969, Howard McCann; Avon paperbacks. And, at the end of this list, a book about the men who were always first in Hollywood: Zanuck, Fox, DeMille, Lasky, the Warners, Goldwyn, Zukor.

THEORY AND CRITICISM

Agee, James. **Agee on Film.** 1958, Ivan Obolensky; 1964, Beacon paperbacks. The most perceptive critic in the Forties was James Agee, an enormously talented man about whom W.H. Auden said "his articles belong in that very select class...of newspaper work which has permanent literary value."

Bazin, André. **What Is Cinema?** Vol. 1, 1967, paperback; Vol. 2, 1971. U. of Calif. Press. Theory by one of the most influential critics in Europe. Excellent.

Kael, Pauline. **I Lost It at the Movies.** 1965, Little, Brown; Bantam. The most important book of criticism since Agee.

Kael, Pauline, **Going Steady.** 1970, Little, Brown, Bantam. Best book of criticism since **I Lost It at the Movies.**

MacDonald, Dwight. **On Movies.** 1968, Prentice-Hall; Berkeley Medallion paperback. Movie criticism 1933-1967, by a respected literary critic.

Powdermaker, Hortense. **Hollywood, the Dream Factory.** 1950, Little, Brown; Grosset paperback. An anthropologist takes a look at movie-making. Great.

Robinson, William and Garrett, George. **Man and the Movies.** 1967, LSU Press; LSU paperback. Good essays: author

Larry McMurtry on Westerns (he was nominated for an Oscar for scripting *Last Picture Show*), Richard Dillard on horror, Garrett on screen writing, Leslie Fiedler on writers and the movies.

Sarris, Andrew. **Confessions of a Cultist: On the Cinema, 1955/1969.** 1970, Simon and Schuster. Essays by one of the best American critics.

Simon, John. **Private Screenings.** 1967, Macmillan; Berkeley Medallion paperback. Simon, 1963-1966. A critic with intelligence, wit, taste and the requisite amount of acid.

Talbot, Daniel. **Film: An Anthology.** 1959, U. of Calif. Press paperback. An anthology of pieces on esthetics, theory, and history, including pieces by Kael, Agee, Hecht and Henry Miller.

REFERENCE

Geduld, Harry M. and Gottesman, Ronald. **Guidebook to Film.** 1972, Holt, Rinehart and Winston. Very useful. Sections include 1) books and periodicals, 2) theses and dissertations, 3) museums and archives, 4) film schools, 5) equipment and supplies, 6) distributors, 7) bookstores, publishers, sources for stills, 8) film organizations and services, 9) festivals and contests, 10) awards, 11) terminology.

Halliwell, Leslie. **The Filmgoer's Companion,** 1967, Hill and Wang. Good general reference, with heavy emphasis on Thirties and Forties.

Sarris, Andrew. **The American Cinema: Directors and Directions 1929-1968.** 1968, E.P. Dutton. Very useful. Encyclopedic in scope.

1930
1940

Volume IV

This Fabulous Century

1930
1940

Volume IV

By the Editors of *TIME-LIFE BOOKS*

Time-Life Books, New York

TIME-LIFE BOOKS

FOUNDER: Henry R. Luce 1898-1967

Editor-in-Chief: Hedley Donovan
Chairman of the Board: Andrew Heiskell
President: James R. Shepley
Chairman, Executive Committee: James A. Linen
Editorial Director: Louis Banks

Vice Chairman: Roy E. Larsen

EDITOR: Jerry Korn
Executive Editor: A. B. C. Whipple
Planning Director: Oliver E. Allen
Text Director: Martin Mann
Art Director: Sheldon Cotler
Chief of Research: Beatrice T. Dobie
Director of Photography: Melvin L. Scott
Assistant Text Directors: Ogden Tanner, Diana Hirsh
Assistant Art Director: Arnold C. Holeywell

PUBLISHER: Joan D. Manley
General Manager: John D. McSweeney
Business Manager: John Steven Maxwell
Sales Director: Carl G. Jaeger
Promotion Director: Paul R. Stewart
Public Relations Director: Nicholas Benton

THIS FABULOUS CENTURY

SERIES EDITOR: Ezra Bowen
Picture Editor: Mary Y. Steinbauer
Designer: John R. Martinez
Assistant Designer: Jean Lindsay Morein
Staff Writers: Tony Chiu, Sam Halper, Anne Horan,
Lucille Schulberg, Gerald Simons, Bryce S. Walker,
Edmund White
Researchers: Alice Baker, Terry Drucker, Marcia A. Gillespie,
Helen Greenway, Helen M. Hinkle, Carol Isenberg,
Nancy J. Jacobsen, Mary Kay Moran, Nancy C. Shappelle,
Victoria Winterer, Johanna Zacharias
Design Assistant: Anne B. Landry

EDITORIAL PRODUCTION
Production Editor: Douglas B. Graham
Quality Director: Robert L. Young
Assistant: James J. Cox
Copy Staff: Rosalind Stubenberg,
Susan B. Galloway, Florence Keith
Picture Department: Dolores A. Littles,
Barbara S. Simon

The following departments and individuals of Time Inc. gave
valuable aid in the preparation of this book: Editorial Produc-
tion, Norman Airey, Nicholas Costino Jr.; Library, Peter
Draz; Picture Collection, Doris O'Neil; Photographic Labora-
tory, George Karas; TIME-LIFE News Service, Murray J.
Gart; Correspondents J. Patrick Barker (Oklahoma City),
Jane Beatty (Philadelphia), Pam Burke (Los Angeles), Patri-
cia Chandler (New Orleans), Jane Estes (Seattle), Juliane
Greenwalt (Detroit), Blanche Hardin (Denver), Ned Judge
(Albuquerque), Lucille Larkin (Washington, D.C.), Frank
Leeming Jr. (St. Louis), Joyce Leviton (Atlanta), Holland Mc-
Combs (Dallas), Jerry Madden (Helena), Jane Rieker (Mi-
ami), William Roberts (Indianapolis), Gayle Rosenberg (Los
Angeles), Rod Van Every (Milwaukee), Nelson Wadsworth
(Salt Lake City), Earl Zarbin (Phoenix).

Contents

Bathing beauties at Catalina Island, California, 1932

Public tour of America's first streamlined train, Lincoln, Nebraska, 1934.

Midwest newsstand, November 1938.

Celebrating the repeal of Prohibition, December 1933.

15

Shop owner in New York's Bowery, 1935.

17   *"Dollar Day" sale at Filene's Department Store, Boston, 1938.*

18

Afternoon dance at a Miami, Florida, trailer camp, 1938.

21

Bedroom suite, Hollywood, California, about 1937.

A poster urged Americans to help the economy. "How'd they expect us to buy autos when we can't buy food?" a tinsmith asked.

Journey through the Lean Years

We are the first nation in the history of the world
to go to the poor house in an automobile.

WILL ROGERS

Herbert Hoover stumbled out of bed at six o'clock on the chill, gray morning of March 4, 1933, to be told that on his last day as President the banking system of the United States had collapsed. The news was the final defeat in a disastrous term of office, and the weary President answered, "We are at the end of our string. There is nothing more we can do." His mournful words echoed the spirit of the nation and concluded the frantic but unavailing course it had taken under the outgoing President.

Not quite three and a half years had passed since the stock market crash had plunged the United States, and most of the world, into the worst economic debacle in Western memory. Industrial output was now less than half the 1929 figure. The number of unemployed, although difficult to count accurately, had mounted to something between 13 and 15 million, or a record high of 25 per cent of the labor force—and the unemployed had 30 million mouths to feed besides their own. Hourly wages had dropped 60 per cent since 1929, white-collar salaries 40 per cent. Farmers were getting five cents a pound for cotton and less than 50 cents a bushel for wheat.

The stark statistics gave no real picture of the situation —of the pitiful men who sold apples on city street corners; of the long lines of haggard men and women who waited for dry bread or thin soup, meager sustenance dispensed by private and municipal charities; of the bloated bellies of starving children; of distraught farmers blocking roads to dump milk cans in a desperate effort to force up the price of milk. "They say blockading the highway's illegal," said an Iowa farmer. "I says, 'Seems to me there was a Tea Party in Boston that was illegal too.'"

Everywhere there was hunger. "We saw a crowd of some 50 men fighting over a barrel of garbage which had been set outside the back door of a restaurant," said an observer in Chicago. "American citizens fighting for scraps of food like animals!" As though they had not troubles enough, millions of workless, hungry and beaten people lacked even the Constitutional right to vote. In September 1932 the city officials of Lewiston, Maine, voted to bar all welfare recipients from the polls; at least 10 states from Massachusetts to Oregon had poll tax and property requirements beyond the reach of Depression victims; and a million or more nomads, wandering about the country, lacked the residency requirements for voting.

For all that, scores of the surviving rich and far too many of those in public office seemed blind to the mis-

Annual Earnings: 1932 to 1934

AIRLINE PILOT	$8,000.00
AIRLINE STEWARDESS	$1,500.00
APARTMENT HOUSE SUPERINTENDENT	$1,500.00
BITUMINOUS COAL MINER	$723.00
BUS DRIVER	$1,373.00
CHAUFFEUR	$624.00
CIVIL SERVICE EMPLOYEE	$1,284.00
COLLEGE TEACHER	$3,111.00
CONSTRUCTION WORKER	$907.00
DENTIST	$2,391.00
DEPARTMENT STORE MODEL	$936.00
DOCTOR	$3,382.00
DRESSMAKER	$780.00
ELECTRICAL WORKER	$1,559.00
ENGINEER	$2,520.00
FIRE CHIEF (city of 30,000 to 50,000)	$2,075.00
HIRED FARM HAND	$216.00
HOUSEMOTHER–BOYS' SCHOOL	$780.00
LAWYER	$4,218.00
LIVE-IN MAID	$260.00
MAYOR (city of 30,000 to 50,000)	$2,317.00
PHARMACEUTICAL SALESMAN	$1,500.00
POLICE CHIEF (city of 30,000 to 50,000)	$2,636.00
PRIEST	$831.00
PUBLIC SCHOOL TEACHER	$1,227.00
PUBLICITY AGENT	$1,800.00
RAILROAD EXECUTIVE	$5,064.00
RAILROAD CONDUCTOR	$2,729.00
REGISTERED NURSE	$936.00
SECRETARY	$1,040.00
STATISTICIAN	$1,820.00
STEELWORKER	$422.87
STENOGRAPHER-BOOKKEEPER	$936.00
TEXTILE WORKER	$435.00
TYPIST	$624.00
UNITED STATES CONGRESSMAN	$8,663.00
WAITRESS	$520.00

erable realities of the Depression. "I do not believe in any quick or spectacular remedies for the ills from which the world is suffering, nor do I share the belief that there is fundamentally anything wrong with the social system," said multimillionaire Andrew Mellon, former Secretary of the Treasury.

"There is something about too much prosperity that ruins the fiber of the people," said diplomat Dwight Morrow when he was running for governor of New Jersey. "People are growing more courteous in business, and often more reasonable at home, thoughtless women especially," editorialized *The Literary Digest*, adding: "Unappreciative wives who were indifferent to their husbands and neglected their homes have become tame and cautious." The Metropolitan Life Insurance Company had a grimmer observation. It reported that 20,000 persons committed suicide in 1931, a figure that far exceeded the legendary suicides of the months following the Crash.

Hoover himself plugged away with firm-jawed righteousness that won him no thanks from the hopeless millions. "Economic depression cannot be cured by legislative action or executive pronouncement," he said. Anxiously seeking some other solution, he was at his desk from 8:30 in the morning till late at night, with 15 minutes off for lunch, drafting proposals, breaking dozens of pencil points in his urgency. He pumped two billion dollars into the banks and investment houses of Wall Street through the Reconstruction Finance Corporation. But what was that to the white-collar worker whose life savings had been wiped out in the failure of his local bank? He proposed the appropriation of money "for the purpose of seed and feed for animals" in the drought-stricken farm belt. But the farmer's children went hungry and Hoover denounced as a "dole" the granting of money and food to human beings. He spent hours on the telephone picking brains and seeking support for this idea and that, and called meeting after meeting of industrial and financial moguls. The latter habit moved the Baltimore *Evening Sun* to deride one such gathering as the President's "new panel of honorary pallbearers" and Representative George

Huddleston of Alabama to growl: "In the White House we have a man more interested in the pocketbooks of the rich than in the bellies of the poor."

Hoover's stand against the concept of the "dole" was shared by thousands. But otherwise he was scorned and derided by most Americans, and his administration was

so bitterly blamed for the Depression that his name became an adjective for all the manifestations of the blight.

There were Hoover blankets, old newspapers used for warmth by park-bench tenants. Hoover flags were empty pocket linings turned inside out. In the country there were Hoover hogs, the jack rabbits that impoverished farmers caught for food, and Hoover wagons, broken-down cars restored to locomotion with the help of mules.

In cities all over the country there were Hoovervilles, squalid villages that sprang up in the vacant lots where the homeless sheltered themselves in sheds made of packing boxes and scrap metal while they foraged about the city for food; New York had at least two Hoovervilles, one below Riverside Drive and the other in Central Park.

The biggest Hooverville of all sprang up on the President's doorstep in Washington, and from it emanated one of the sorest incidents of Hoover's luckless administration. Veterans of World War I had for some time been pleading for advance payment of a war bonus they were due to receive in 1945. In the spring of 1932 an unemployed Oregon canner, Walter W. Waters, conceived the idea of staging a sort of one-shot veterans' lobby in Congress. All through the month of June, war veterans and their families streamed into Washington, by freight car, by truck and on foot, until they numbered 20,000.

The Bonus Expeditionary Force, as the veterans called themselves, found a hostile city; the only official who made them welcome was Brigadier General Pelham D. Glassford, chief of the Washington police. He provided them with makeshift housing in empty government build-

ings, and when those ran out he allowed them to camp in a swampy area across the Potomac. He persuaded the Army to lend them tents and cots, and rigged up an Army field kitchen to provide them with food. He ordered his own men to treat them humanely, and he himself rode from site to site on a motorcycle, giving smiles and encouragement, calling the hopeful veterans "my boys."

Predictably, the Senate voted against the bonus, and most of the veterans left Washington to go home. But some 8,600 with no homes to go to stayed on in their Washington Hoovervilles, jarring the nerves of the President, who was by then engaged in a doomed campaign for reelection. Chains went up on the White House gates, guards patrolled the grounds night and day, and the streets were closed to traffic. On the morning of July 28, Glassford got word from the "highest authority" that the bonus marchers must quit the government buildings.

Glassford's cordial treatment of the men now stood him in good stead. He paid the veterans another visit and persuaded them to move out of their own accord, a request they set out to obey in return for his favors to them.

The evacuation proceeded all through the day, but the "highest authority" was not satisfied. Late in the afternoon General Douglas MacArthur, Chief of Staff of the United States Army, marched up Pennsylvania Avenue, with a major named Dwight D. Eisenhower at his side.

They headed a parade of infantry, cavalry, machine guns, tanks and trucks. That formidable array of weaponry, abetted by tear gas bombs and sabers, scattered the few who remained. Not content with routing the squatters from the empty government buildings, the troops pursued fleeing women, children and even a few legless veterans across the river to the swamp, where they burned the shacks that had been home to the pitiful ragtags for more than a month. In the last burst of gas bombs at midnight, an 11-month-old baby reportedly died, and the remnants of the veterans' march joined the throngs of Americans whom the Depression had already turned into nomads.

"A challenge to the authority of the United States Government has been met," said Hoover. But the episode cost him dear. The marchers never forgave him; neither did hundreds of thousands of sympathizers, who helped to vote Hoover out of office three months later.

The following year a second veterans' army assembled in Washington. Though it too failed to get the bonus payment, it received a far gentler White House recognition, in the form of an appearance by Eleanor Roosevelt, the new President's wife, who walked among the men, listening to their songs and tasting their humble chow. Mrs. Roosevelt's visit was not only humanitarian; it was excellent politics. "Hoover sent the Army," cried the second crop of bonus marchers; "Roosevelt sent his wife."

That shrewd combination of practical politics and instinct for the common touch was to be the hallmark of the new administration, the one that was to leave its

I can go down to the market here and buy a parrot for $2. And in one day I can teach it to say "Dole, Dole, Dole." But that parrot would never understand an economic problem.

FIORELLO H. LA GUARDIA

stamp on the nation and its government as the hard-times generation climbed out of the Depression. During the first 100 days of the new administration, Roosevelt's own sure-handed brand of personal leadership *(pages 114-141)* stirred the country out of its apathy and into effective action. In scarcely three months' time the government gave $500 million for cash, food and shelter to the destitute, for the first time providing federal money for relief (the feared "dole") at the very bottom of the economic ladder. A series of other programs drawn up during this same period put the government squarely into the business of economic planning on a national scale.

Roosevelt called his startling array of legislation a "New Deal" for the nation. And indeed it seemed to be. The Federal Reserve Board's index of industrial production shot up from 59 in March 1933, the month that Roosevelt took office, to 66 in April, 78 in May, 91 in June and 100 in July, just 25 points short of the 125 high registered in the boom year of 1929. When in 1936 Roosevelt campaigned across the country for re-election, he looked out over the crowds that massed to meet him, flashed his brilliant, confident smile and said with the air of a friend, "You look much better than you did four years ago," and the people cried in answer, "God bless you, Mr. President!"

Despite a business setback in 1937-1938, by 1939 the gross national product had climbed to $91 billion, an increase of more than 60 per cent over the black days of 1933. As one bright promise of new prosperity, in October of 1939 the Du Pont Company put on sale in Wilmington 4,000 pairs of stockings made of a new fabric called nylon. It was the first fully man-made fiber and represented an endeavor of such potential that even in the Depression Du Pont was willing to spend $27 million developing it. Some wag claimed that the odd name for the new creation was an acronym made up from the words "Now You Lousy Old Nipponese," a slap at the increasingly unpopular nation of Japan, which bred the silkworms for the silk stockings that nylon would soon make obsolete. The new fabric was also a herald of dozens of wonder products that would someday be spread before millions of Americans—lightweight metal alloys, TV, synthetic detergents and frozen foods. But most Americans would have to wait to make regular use of these new inventions, for the decade that had opened with the reverberations of the financial crash was to close to the rumble of distant gunfire. In 1939 German tanks rolled into Poland; England and France declared war on Germany; and before the decade was out, the United States was tooling up for its own defense. But through the travail of the Depression that lay between the two landmarks of the crash and the Second World War, America had managed to keep its political balance, regain its economic health and reassess some of the old habits and values that had helped to lead it to the brink of these embracing cataclysms.

Depression Shopping List: 1932 to 1934

Automobiles

NEW

Pontiac coupé	$585.00
Chrysler sedan	995.00
Dodge	595.00
Studebaker	840.00
Packard	2,150.00
Chevrolet half-ton pickup truck	650.00

USED

Lincoln '27	125.00
Studebaker '30	200.00
Ford '29	57.50

Clothing

WOMEN'S

Mink coat	$585.00
Leopard coat	92.00
Cloth coat	6.98
Raincoat	2.69
Wool dress	1.95
Wool suit	3.98
Wool sweater	1.69
Silk stockings	.69
Leather shoes	1.79
Reptile leather shoes	6.00

MEN'S

Overcoat	11.00
Wool suit	10.50
Trousers	2.00
Shirt	.47
Pullover sweater	1.95
Silk necktie	.55
Suede hunting shirt	2.94
Calfskin riding boots	9.50
Golf suit	20.00
Tuxedo	25.00
Stetson hat	5.00
Shoes	3.85

Household Items

Silver plate flatware, 26-piece	$4.98
Double-bed sheets	.67
Bath towel	.24
Wool blanket	1.00
Linen tablecloth	1.00
Wool rug (9' x 12')	5.85

Appliances

Electric iron	$2.00
Electric coffee percolator	1.39
Electric mixer	9.95
Vacuum cleaner	18.75
Electric washing machine	47.95
Gas stove	23.95
Electric portable sewing machine	24.95
Copper lamp	1.95

Furniture

Dining room set, 8-piece	$46.50
Bedroom set, 3-piece	49.95
Lounge chair	19.95
Double bed and spring mattress	14.95
Bridge table	1.00
Colonial walnut secretary	54.00
Mahogany coffee table	10.75
Chippendale mahogany sofa	135.00
Louis XV walnut dining table	124.00
Wing chair	39.00
Grand piano	395.00

Miscellaneous

Dental filling	$1.00
Tooth paste (large)	.25
Coty face powder	1.50
L'Aimant perfume, ¼ oz.	1.00
Cultivated Oriental pearls	35.00
Razor blades (10)	.49
Cigarettes	.15
Cigarette lighter	.39
Pipe	.83
Alarm clock	2.00
Fountain pen	1.00
Briefcase	1.00
Console radio	49.95
Electric shaver	15.00
Desk typewriter	19.75
Movie camera, 8 mm.	29.50
Kodak Box Brownie	2.50
Automobile tire	6.20
Gasoline (per gallon)	.18

Toys

Doll carriage	$4.98
Sled	1.45
Tricycle	3.98
Two-wheeled bike	10.95
Fielder's glove and ball	1.25
Catcher's mitt	1.19
Leather basketball	1.00
BB air rifle	.79

Food

Sirloin steak (per lb.)	$0.29
Round steak (per lb.)	.26
Rib roast (per lb.)	.22
Bacon (per lb.)	.22
Ham (per lb.)	.31
Leg of lamb (per lb.)	.22
Chicken (per lb.)	.22
Pork chops (per lb.)	.20
Salmon (16 oz. can)	.19
Milk (per qt.)	.10
Butter (per lb.)	.28
Margarine (per lb.)	.13
Eggs (per doz.)	.29
Cheese (per lb.)	.24
Bread (20 oz. loaf)	.05
Coffee (per lb.)	.26
Sugar (per lb.)	.05
Rice (per lb.)	.06
Potatoes (per lb.)	.02
Tomatoes (16 oz. can)	.09
Oranges (per doz.)	.27
Bananas (per lb.)	.07
Onions (per lb.)	.03
Cornflakes (8 oz. package)	.08

Real Estate

Modern house, 6 rooms 2-car garage, Detroit	$2,800.00
English cottage, 8 rooms, 3 baths, 1 ballroom, Seattle	4,250.00
Italian villa, 12 rooms, Westchester, N.Y.	17,000.00
Spanish stucco, 7 rooms, Beverly Hills	5,000.00

Travel

AIR

New York to Chicago, round trip	$86.31
Chicago to Los Angeles, round trip	207.00

RAIL

Chicago to San Francisco round trip, 16 days in San Francisco	80.50
New York City to Scarsdale, N.Y., monthly commuter ticket	10.39

SEA

Tour of Europe, 60 days, 11 countries	495.00
Bermuda-Havana-Nassau, cruise, 10 days	110.00
Around the world, 85 days, 14 countries	749.00
San Francisco to Hawaii, round trip	220.00
New York to California via Panama Canal	120.00

Radio

The cast of "Gangbusters" blasts away to open a new episode.

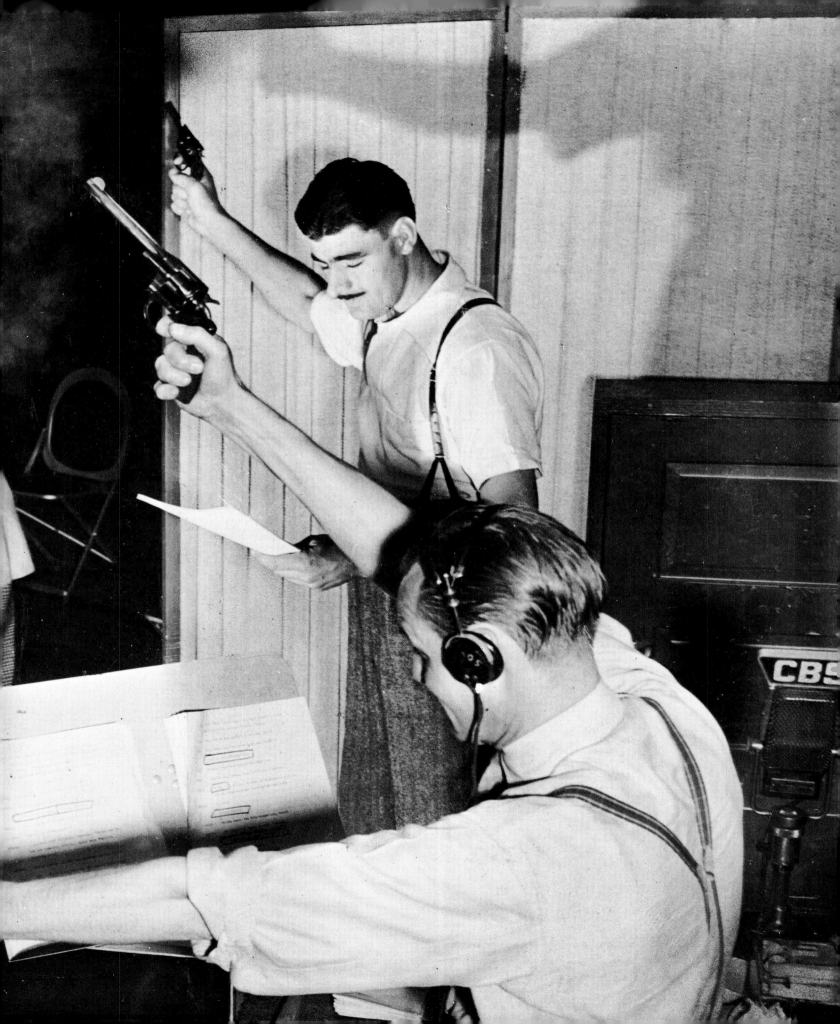

On the Air

There are three things which I shall never forget about America—the Rocky Mountains, the Statue of Liberty and Amos 'n' Andy.   GEORGE BERNARD SHAW, 1933

Every weekday evening from 7:00 to 7:15 p.m., telephone use all over the country dropped 50 per cent, car thieves had an easy time on empty streets, and many movie theaters shut off their projectors to pipe in pure radio while some 30 million Americans—including President Roosevelt—tuned in to *Amos 'n' Andy (page 38)*. Such devotion to a comedy serial—created in black-voice by a pair of white vaudevillians, Freeman Gosden and Charles Correll—was typical of radio audiences in the '30s. The big box in the living room was everybody's ticket to adventure, laughter, sweet music and romance.

People listened for the openers of their favorite shows the way little children listened for the sound of father's car in the driveway. Starting not long after breakfast each morning, serial dramas kept housewives intrigued all day: "Can this girl from a mining town in the West find happiness as the wife of a wealthy and titled Englishman?" the announcer asked at the beginning of *Our Gal Sunday*. Everyone hoped so but no one knew for sure.

During supper the family listened to the news, and then sat back to a marvelous, manufactured world in which you supplied the pictures while the radio brought in the sound. Millions of meek men joined the cops to patrol the dangerous streets of *Gangbusters*. Folksy types eased down in their armchairs when Kate Smith belted out her theme song, "When the Moon Comes Over the Mountain." And comedy fans giggled at Edgar Bergen and Charlie McCarthy. Never mind that Charlie was a ventriloquist's dummy. He seemed so real that the King of Sweden, Winston Churchill and Hollywood's Louis B. Mayer all extended their hands to him upon being introduced.

Real drama came into homes, too. Radio reporters put their shiny, wagon-wheel microphones before the lips of newsmakers and let listeners hear Lou Gehrig when the great ballplayer, dying of amyotrophic lateral sclerosis, said in a low, clear voice before 60,000 at Yankee Stadium, "I consider myself the luckiest man on the face of the earth." Other tears fell when Edward VIII of England renounced his throne for the Baltimore divorcée Wally Simpson, "the woman I love." Americans stayed glued to their radios while commentator H.V. Kaltenborn told of the dying days of peace in Europe during his marathon news broadcast *(page 39)*. But when actor Orson Welles simulated a news broadcast of a fictional invasion by men from Mars, thousands of Americans poured into the streets in panic, sure the end of the world had come.

Kate Smith, the hefty "Songbird of the South," with her cheery "Hello everybody!" was heard by some 16 million fans every Thursday at eight.

31

Highlights of the Six-Day Week

OZZIE NELSON AND HARRIET HILLIARD

GEORGE BURNS AND GRACIE ALLEN

FIBBER MCGEE AND MOLLY

	Sunday	Monday	Tuesday
7:00	NBC–*Red*: JELL-O PROGRAM—Jack Benny, Mary Livingstone, Kenny Baker, Don Wilson, Andy Devine, Phil Harris' orchestra NBC–*Blue*: POPULAR CLASSICS—H. Leopold Spitalny CBS: JOAN AND KERMIT—dramatic serial MBS: HAWAII CALLS	NBC–*Red*: AMOS 'N' ANDY—sketch NBC–*Blue*: MUSIC IS MY HOBBY—guests CBS: JUST ENTERTAINMENT MBS: FULTON LEWIS, JR.—Washington news commentator NBC–*Red*: UNCLE EZRA'S RADIO STATION (7:15)— Pat Barrett	NBC–*Red*: AMOS 'N' ANDY—sketch NBC–*Blue*: EASY ACES—comedy sketch CBS: JUST ENTERTAINMENT MBS: FULTON LEWIS, JR.—Washington news commentator NBC–*Blue*: MR. KEEN, TRACER OF LOST PERSONS (7:15)— dramatic serial. Bennett Kilpatrick
7:30	NBC–*Red*: INTERESTING NEIGHBORS—Jerry Belcher, interviewer NBC–*Blue*: BAKERS' BROADCAST—Feg Murray, Harriet Hilliard, Ozzie Nelson's orchestra CBS: PHIL BAKER—Beetle and Bottle, Bradley's orchestra MBS: HOLLYWOOD WHISPERS—George Fischer	NBC–*Red*: SOLOIST NBC–*Blue*: ROSE MARIE—song stylist CBS: EDDIE CANTOR'S CAMEL CARAVAN—Benny Goodman's Quartet, Bert Gordon, Walter King, Fairchild's orchestra	NBC–*Red*: BY CANDLELIGHT CBS: SECOND HUSBAND—serial, Helen Menken MBS: HEADLINES—news dramatization
8:00	NBC–*Red*: CHASE AND SANBORN PROGRAM—Don Ameche, Edgar Bergen, John Carter, Dorothy Lamour, Stroud Twins, Armbruster's orchestra NBC–*Blue*: SPY AT LARGE—dramatic serial CBS: ST. LOUIS BLUES MBS: THE WOR FORUM—S. Theodore Granik	NBC–*Red*: BURNS AND ALLEN—Tony Martin, Garber's orchestra NBC–*Blue*: RUBY NEWMAN'S ORCHESTRA CBS: YOU SAID IT!—Connie Boswell, Ted Husing, Himber's orchestra MBS: ORCHESTRA	NBC–*Red*: JOHNNY PRESENTS RUSS MORGAN AND HIS ORCHESTRA—Jack Johnstone's "Thrill of the Week" NBC–*Blue*: ENRIC MADRIGUERA AND HIS ORCHESTRA CBS: BIG TOWN—Edward G. Robinson, Claire Trevor, dramatization MBS: ORCHESTRA
8:30	NBC–*Blue*: SONGS WE REMEMBER—Gill's orchestra CBS: LYN MURRAY'S MUSICAL GAZETTE MBS: CHARIOTEERS MBS: NEWS TESTERS (8:45)—Leonard M. Leonard	NBC–*Red*: VOICE OF FIRESTONE—Richard Crooks, Margaret Speaks, Wallenstein's orchestra, guests NBC–*Blue*: THOSE WE LOVE—dramatic serial, Nan Gray, Owen Davis, Jr., Richard Cromwell, Donald Woods CBS: PICK AND PAT—comedy and music MBS: RAYMOND GRAM SWING—commentator	NBC–*Red*: LADY ESTHER SERENADE—Wayne King's orchestra NBC–*Blue*: INFORMATION PLEASE—Clifton Fadiman, John Erskine, John Kiernan and others CBS: AL JOLSON—Martha Raye, Parkyakarkus, Victor Young's orchestra, guests MBS: THE GREEN HORNET—dramatization
9:00	NBC–*Red*: MANHATTAN MERRY-GO-ROUND—Rachel Carlay, Pierre Le Kreeun, Donnie's orchestra NBC–*Blue*: HOLLYWOOD PLAYHOUSE—Tyrone Power, guests CBS: FORD SUNDAY EVENING HOUR	NBC–*Red*: MUSIC FOR MODERNS NBC–*Blue*: NOW AND THEN—orchestra CBS: LUX RADIO THEATRE—Cecil B. De Mille, guests, drama MBS: ORCHESTRA	NBC–*Red*: VOX POP—Parks Johnson, Wallace Butterworth NBC–*Blue*: HORACE HEIDT AND HIS ALEMITE BRIGADIERS— Lysbeth Hughes, Yvonne King CBS: WATCH THE FUN GO BY—Al Pearce, Nick Lucas, Hoff's orchestra MBS: ORCHESTRA
9:30	NBC–*Red*: AMERICAN ALBUM OF FAMILIAR MUSIC—Frank Munn, Jean Dickenson, Haenschen's orchestra NBC–*Blue*: JERGENS PROGRAM—Walter Winchell, news commentator MBS: ORCHESTRA NBC–*Blue*: WELCH PRESENTS IRENE RICH (9:45)— dramatization	NBC–*Red*: TALES OF GREAT RIVERS NBC–*Blue*: PAUL MARTIN AND HIS MUSIC MBS: THE WITCH'S TALE—Alonzo Deen Cole, Marie O'Flynn	NBC–*Red*: FIBBER MCGEE AND MOLLY—Jim Jordan, Clark Dennis, Betty Winkler, Mills' orchestra NBC–*Blue*: NBC JAMBOREE—Don McNeill, Sylvia Clark, Fran Allison, Little Jackie Heller, Bill Thompson CBS: BENNY GOODMAN'S SWING SCHOOL MBS: MUSIC BY—guest artists
10:00	NBC–*Red*: HOUR OF CHARM—Phil Spitalny's All Girl orchestra NBC–*Blue*: NORMAN CLOTIER'S ORCHESTRA CBS: GRAND CENTRAL STATION—dramatic sketch	NBC–*Red*: CONTENTED PROGRAM—Opal Craven, Marek Weber's orchestra NBC–*Blue*: MAGNOLIA BLOSSOMS—Fisk Jubilee Choir CBS: WAYNE KING'S ORCHESTRA	NBC–*Red*: BELIEVE IT OR NOT—Robert L. Ripley, Rolfe's orchestra CBS: TIME TO SHINE—Hal Kemp's orchestra, Judy Starr, Bob Allen
10:30	NBC–*Red*: SYMPHONIC VARIATIONS—Walter Logan's orchestra NBC–*Blue*: CHEERIO—talk and music CBS: HEADLINES AND BYLINES—H. V. Kaltenborn, Bob Trout, Erwin Canham— news commentators	NBC–*Red*: FOR MEN ONLY NBC–*Blue*: NATIONAL RADIO FORUM—guest speaker CBS: LET FREEDOM RING—dramatizations MBS: HENRY WEBER'S PAGEANT OF MELODY	NBC–*Red*: JIMMIE FIDLER'S HOLLYWOOD GOSSIP CBS: RAY HEATHERTON—songs MBS: ORCHESTRA NBC–*Red*: DALE CARNEGIE (10:45)— How To Win Friends and Influence People
11:00	NBC–*Red*: DANCE MUSIC NBC–*Blue*: PRESS-RADIO NEWS; ORCHESTRA CBS: ORCHESTRA MBS: ORCHESTRA	NETWORK SIGN OFF (Local programming only)	NBC–*Red*: DANCE MUSIC NBC–*Blue*: DANCE MUSIC CBS: DANCE MUSIC MBS: DEVELOPMENT OF MUSIC

As this schedule for the week of June 5, 1938, indicates, the big evening shows of radio's week ran from Sunday through Friday on four networks (two

 KAY KYSER

 MAJOR BOWES

 MR. FIRST NIGHTER

Wednesday

NBC-*Red*: AMOS 'N' ANDY—sketch
NBC-*Blue*: EASY ACES—comedy sketch
NBC-*Red*: UNCLE EZRA'S RADIO STATION (7:15)—Pat Barrett
NBC-*Blue*: MR. KEEN, TRACER OF LOST PERSONS (7:15)—dramatic serial, Bennett Kilpatrick

NBC-*Red*: TALES BY EDWIN C. HILL
NBC-*Blue*: ROSE MARIE—song stylist
NBC-*Red*: HAPPY JACK (7:45)—songs
NBC-*Blue*: SCIENCE ON THE MARCH (7:45)
CBS: HISTORY'S HEADLINES (7:45)

NBC-*Red*: ONE MAN'S FAMILY—sketch
NBC-*Blue*: ROY SHIELD'S REVUE
CBS: CAVALCADE OF AMERICA—guests, Voorhees' orchestra
MBS: ORCHESTRA

NBC-*Red*: RALEIGH AND KOOL SHOW—Tommy Dorsey's orchestra, Edythe Wright, Jack Leonard, Paul Stewart
NBC-*Blue*: HARRIET PARSONS—Hollywood commentator
CBS: BEN BERNIE—Lew Lehr, Buddy Clark
MBS: LET'S VISIT—Dave Driscoll, Jerry Danzig

NBC-*Red*: TOWN HALL TONIGHT—Fred Allen, Portland Hoffa, Van Steeden's orchestra
NBC-*Blue*: TUNE TYPES—variety program
CBS: ANDRE KOSTELANETZ—Deems Taylor, guests
MBS: ORCHESTRA
MBS: JOHNSON FAMILY (9:15)—sketch, with Jimmy Scribner

NBC-*Blue*: BOSTON "POP" CONCERT
CBS: THE WORD GAME—Max Eastman
MBS: JAZZ NOCTURNE—Helene Daniels, Stanley's orchestra

NBC-*Red*: KAY KYSER'S MUSICAL CLASS AND DANCE
NBC-*Blue*: CHOIR SYMPHONETTE
CBS: GANGBUSTERS—crime dramatizations, Col. H. Norman Schwartzkopf
MBS: ORCHESTRA

NBC-*Blue*: NBC MINSTREL SHOW—Gene Arnold, orchestra
CBS: EDGAR GUEST IN "IT CAN BE DONE"—Marion Francis Masters' orchestra
MBS: MELODIES FROM THE SKY

NBC-*Red*: DANCE MUSIC
NBC-*Blue*: DANCE MUSIC
CBS: DANCE MUSIC
MBS: ORCHESTRA

Thursday

NBC-*Red*: AMOS 'N' ANDY—sketch
NBC-*Blue*: EASY ACES—comedy sketch
NBC-*Blue*: MR. KEEN, TRACER OF LOST PERSONS (7:15)—dramatic serial
CBS: HOLLYWOOD SCREEN SCOOPS (7:15)—George McCall
MBS: OUTDOORS WITH BOB EDGE (7:15)

NBC-*Red*: VOCALIST
NBC-*Blue*: VOCALIST
CBS: ST. LOUIS BLUES
MBS: HEADLINES—news dramatization

NBC-*Red*: ROYAL GELATIN PROGRAM—Rudy Vallee, guests
NBC-*Blue*: MARCH OF TIME—news dramatizations
CBS: KATE SMITH—Ted Collins, Miller's orchestra
MBS: ALFRED WALLENSTEIN'S SINFONIETTA

MBS: THE GREEN HORNET—dramatization
NBC-*Blue*: PIANO DUO (8:45)

NBC-*Red*: GOOD NEWS OF 1938—Robert Taylor, Fannie Brice, Frank Morgan, Willson's orchestra
NBC-*Blue*: TORONTO PROMENADE CONCERT
CBS: MAJOR BOWES' AMATEUR HOUR
MBS: THE HARMONAIRES

MBS: RAY SINATRA'S MOONLIGHT RHYTHMS—Sylvia Froos, Jack Arthur

NBC-*Red*: KRAFT MUSIC HALL—Bing Crosby, Bob Burns, Trotter's orchestra, guests
NBC-*Blue*: UNDER WESTERN SKIES
CBS: ESSAYS IN MUSIC—Victor Bay's orchestra, Margaret Daum, Ruth Carhart, David Ross
MBS: DRAMATIZATION

NBC-*Blue*: NBC PROMENADE CONCERT
CBS: AMERICANS AT WORK
MBS: HENRY WEBER'S CONCERT REVUE

NBC-*Red*: SPORTS QUESTION BOX
NBC-*Blue*: ORCHESTRA
CBS: DUKE ELLINGTON'S ORCHESTRA
NBC-*Blue*: ELZA SCHALLERT REVIEWS (11:15)—previews, guests
MBS: THEATRE DIGEST (11:15)

Friday

NBC-*Red*: AMOS 'N' ANDY—sketch
NBC-*Blue*: THE FOUR OF US
CBS: JUST ENTERTAINMENT
MBS: FULTON LEWIS, JR.—Washington news commentator
NBC-*Blue*: STORY BEHIND THE HEADLINES (7:15)—Cesar Saerchinger

NBC-*Blue*: TALES OF EDWIN C. HILL
CBS: VOCALIST
NBC-*Red*: THREE ROMEOS (7:45)
NBC-*Blue*: VOCALIST (7:45)
CBS: SCIENCE AND SOCIETY (7:45)

NBC-*Red*: CITIES SERVICE CONCERT—Lucille Manners, Frank Black's orchestra
NBC-*Blue*: MAURICE SPITALNY'S ORCHESTRA
CBS: THE GHOST OF BENJAMIN SWEET—dramatic serial

NBC-*Blue*: DEATH VALLEY DAYS—dramatization
CBS: PAUL WHITEMAN'S ORCHESTRA—Joan Edwards
MBS: TOPICS OF THE DAY—speaker

NBC-*Red*: WALTZ TIME—Frank Munn, Lyman's orchestra
NBC-*Blue*: ROYAL CROWN REVUE—Tim and Irene, Uncle Happy, Graham McNamee, Fredda Gibson, George Olsen's orchestra
CBS: HOLLYWOOD HOTEL—Louella Parsons, Frances Langford, Frank Parker, Ken Murray
MBS: ORCHESTRA

NBC-*Red*: A. L. ALEXANDER'S TRUE STORIES—dramatization
NBC-*Blue*: NBC SPELLING BEE—Paul Wing
MBS: WLW OPERETTA

NBC-*Red*: FIRST NIGHTER—dramatization, Les Tremayne, Barbara Luddy
NBC-*Blue*: PAUL MARTIN'S ORCHESTRA
CBS: COLUMBIA SQUARE
MBS: BAMBERGER SYMPHONY ORCHESTRA

NBC-*Red*: JIMMIE FIDLER'S HOLLYWOOD GOSSIP
MBS: CURTAIN TIME—dramatization
CBS: AMERICAN VIEWPOINT (10:45)

NBC-*Red*: DANCE MUSIC
NBC-*Blue*: ORCHESTRA
CBS: DANCE MUSIC
MBS: DANCE MUSIC

longed to NBC and were code-named Red and Blue). Saturday night most people went to the movies; a few stayed home to hear "Your Hit Parade."

33

Orson Welles narrated "War of the Worlds" on Halloween, 1938. Newspapers the next day reported a "tidal wave of terror that swept the nation."

Great Moments from Great Programs

From the abundant schedule of radio programs, certain moments lingered in the minds of everyone who heard them. Among the most memorable programs, some of them shown on these pages, was one that began as a Halloween joke but wound up scaring the nation half to death. On October 30, 1938, a 23-year-old producer named Orson Welles presented the radio play "Invasion from Mars," written by Howard Koch but mistakenly credited to H.G. Wells, from whose *War of the Worlds* the original idea had sprung. To make the fantasy seem credible the script simulated news broadcasts announcing that invasion forces from Mars had landed in New Jersey and were devastating the countryside with death rays. The show was brilliant radio—and America panicked.

As Welles and his cast went through the script *(excerpted below)*, thousands of people phoned their newspapers and local police to ask what they should do to avoid the invaders. In New Jersey, families tied wet cloths over their faces to escape "gas attack," piled into their cars and clogged traffic for miles. A woman in Pittsburgh, screaming "I'd rather die this way," was barely prevented from taking poison. At the end of the show, most listeners were apparently too frightened to hear Welles, chuckling, sign off by saying, "If your doorbell rings and nobody's there, that was no Martian . . . it's Halloween."

Belatedly realizing the commotion that the show had caused, CBS peppered the airwaves with reassurances that the play had been a spoof. But it took days before the last vestiges of terror had disappeared. How was it that so much of the nation went into shock at a Halloween joke? Explained one social scientist wryly: "All the intelligent people were listening to Charlie McCarthy."

MERCURY THEATRE ON THE AIR
SUNDAY, 8:00 E.S.T., CBS

ANNOUNCER: The Columbia Broadcasting System and its affiliated stations present Orson Welles and the Mercury Theatre on the Air in *War of the Worlds* by H.G. Wells.

SYNOPSIS: As the program opens, narrator Orson Welles explains, from an undetermined year in the future, that the smug people of the early 20th Century did not know about the existence of "superior intelligences" on other planets. They learned, he says, on the evening of October 30, 1938, as they were listening to their radios.

ANNOUNCER CUE
We now take you to the Meridian Room in the Hotel Park Plaza in downtown New York, where you will be entertained by the music of Ramon Raquello and his orchestra. *(Spanish theme song . . . fades)*

ANNOUNCER THREE
Good evening, ladies and gentlemen. From the Meridian Room in the Park Plaza in New York City, we bring you the music of Ramon Raquello and his orchestra. With a touch of the Spanish, Ramon Raquello leads off with "La Cumparsita." *(Piece starts playing)*

ANNOUNCER TWO
Ladies and gentlemen, we interrupt our program of dance music to bring you a special bulletin from the Intercontinental Radio News. At twenty minutes before eight, central time, Professor Farrell of the Mount Jennings Observatory, Chicago, Illinois, reports observing several explosions of incandescent gas, occurring at regular intervals on the planet Mars.

The spectroscope indicates the gas to be hydrogen and moving towards the earth with enormous velocity. Professor Pierson of the observatory at Princeton confirms Farrell's observation, and describes the phenomenon as *(Quote)* like a jet of blue flame shot from a gun. *(Unquote)* We now return you to the music of Ramon Raquello, playing for you in the Meridian Room of the Park Plaza Hotel, situated in downtown New York. *(Music plays for a few moments until piece ends . . . sound of applause)*

Now a tune that never loses favor, the ever-popular "Star Dust." Ramon Raquello and his orchestra . . . *(Music)*

ANNOUNCER TWO
Ladies and gentlemen, following on the news given in our bulletin a moment ago, the Government Meteorological Bureau has requested the large observatories of the country to keep an astronomical watch on any further disturbances occurring on the planet Mars. . . .

Ladies and gentlemen, here is the latest bulletin from the Intercontinental Radio News. Toronto, Canada: Professor Morse of Macmillan University reports observing a total of three explosions on the planet Mars, between the hours of 7:45 p.m. and 9:20 p.m., eastern standard time. This confirms earlier reports received from American observatories. Now, nearer home, comes a special announcement from Trenton, New Jersey. It is reported that at 8:50 p.m. a huge, flaming object, believed to be a meteorite, fell on a farm in the neighborhood of Grovers Mill, New Jersey, twenty-two miles from Trenton. The flash in the sky was visible within a radius of several hundred miles and the noise of the impact was heard as far north as Elizabeth.

We have dispatched a special mobile unit to the scene, and will have our commentator, Mr. Phillips, give you a word description as soon as he reaches there from Princeton. In the meantime, we take you to the Hotel Martinet in Brooklyn, where Bobby Millette and his orchestra are offering a program of dance music. (*Swing band for 20 seconds . . . then cut*)

ANNOUNCER TWO

We take you now to Grovers Mill, New Jersey. (*Crowd noises . . . police sirens*)

PHILLIPS

I wish I could convey the atmosphere . . . the background of this . . . fantastic scene. Hundreds of cars are parked in a field in back of us. Police are trying to rope off the roadway leading into the farm. But it's no use. They're breaking right through. Their headlights throw an enormous spot on the pit where the object's half-buried. Some of the more daring souls are venturing near the edge. Their silhouettes stand out. (*Faint humming sound*)

One man wants to touch the thing . . . he's having an argument with a policeman. The policeman wins. . . . Now, ladies and gentlemen, there's something I haven't mentioned in all this excitement, but it's becoming more distinct. Perhaps you've caught it already on your radio. Listen: (*Long pause*) . . . Do you hear it? It's a curious humming sound that seems to come from inside the object. I'll move the microphone nearer. Here. (*Pause*) Now we're not more than twenty-five feet away. Can you hear it now? Oh, Professor Pierson!

PIERSON

Yes, Mr. Phillips?

PHILLIPS

Can you tell us the meaning of that scraping noise inside the thing?

PIERSON

Possibly the unequal cooling of its surface.

PHILLIPS

Do you still think it's a meteor, Professor?

PIERSON

I don't know what to think. The metal casing is definitely extra-terrestrial . . . not found on this earth. Friction with the earth's atmosphere usually tears holes in a meteorite. This thing is smooth and, as you can see, of cylindrical shape.

PHILLIPS

Just a minute! Something's happening! Ladies and gentlemen, this is terrific! This end of the thing is beginning to flake off! The top is beginning to rotate like a screw! The thing must be hollow!

VOICES

She's a movin'!
Look, the darn thing's unscrewing!
Keep back, there! Keep back, I tell you.
Maybe there's men in it trying to escape!
It's red hot, they'll burn to a cinder!
Keep back there! Keep those idiots back!
(*Suddenly the clanking sound of a huge piece of falling metal*)

VOICES

She's off! The top's loose!
Look out there! Stand back!

PHILLIPS

Ladies and gentlemen, this is the most terrifying thing I have ever witnessed. . . . Wait a minute! Someone's *crawling out of the hollow top*. Some one or . . . something. I can see peering out of that black hole two luminous disks . . . are they eyes? It might be a face. It might . . . (*Shout of awe from the crowd*)

Good heavens, something's wriggling out of the shadow like a grey snake. Now it's another one, and another. They look like tentacles to me. There, I can see the thing's body. It's large as a bear and it glistens like wet leather. But that face. It . . . it's indescribable. I can hardly force myself to keep looking at it. The eyes are black and gleam like a serpent. The mouth is V-shaped with saliva dripping from its rimless lips that seem to quiver and pulsate. The monster or whatever it is can hardly move. It seems weighed down by . . . possibly gravity or something. The thing's raising up. The crowd falls back. They've seen enough. This is the most extraordinary experience. I can't find words. . . . I'm pulling this microphone with me as I talk. I'll have to stop the description until I've taken a new position. Hold on, will you please, I'll be back in a minute. (*Fade into piano*)

ANNOUNCER TWO

We are bringing you an eyewitness account of what's happening on the Wilmuth farm, Grovers Mill, New Jersey. (*More piano*)

We now return you to Carl Phillips at Grovers Mill.

PHILLIPS

Ladies and gentlemen (Am I on?). Ladies and gentlemen, here I am, back of a stone wall that adjoins Mr. Wilmuth's garden. From here I get a sweep of the whole scene. I'll give you every detail as long as I can talk. As long as I can see. More state police have arrived. They're drawing up a cordon in front of the pit, about thirty of them. No need to push the crowd back now.

They're willing to keep their distance. The captain is conferring with someone. We can't quite see who. Oh yes, I believe it's Professor Pierson. Yes, it is. Now they've parted. The professor moves around one side, studying the object, while the captain and two policemen advance with something in their hands. I can see it now. It's a white handkerchief tied to a pole . . . a flag of truce. If those creatures know what that means . . . what anything means! . . . *Wait!* Something's happening! (*Hissing sound followed by a humming that increases in intensity*)

A humped shape is rising out of the pit. I can make out a small beam of light against a mirror. What's that? There's a jet of flame springing from that mirror, and it leaps right at the advancing men. It strikes them head on! Good Lord, they're turning into flame! (*Screams and unearthly shrieks*)

Now the whole field's caught fire. (*Explosion*) The woods . . . the barns . . . the gas tanks of automobiles . . . it's spreading everywhere. It's coming this way. About twenty yards to my right. . . . (*Crash of microphone . . . then dead silence . . .*)

ANNOUNCER TWO

Ladies and gentlemen, due to circumstances beyond our control, we are unable to continue the broadcast from Grovers Mill. Evidently there's some difficulty with our field transmission. . . .

Ladies and gentlemen, I have a grave announcement to make. Incredible as it may seem, both the observations of science and the evidence of our eyes lead to the inescapable assumption that those strange beings who landed in the Jersey farmlands tonight are the vanguard of an invading army from the planet Mars. The battle which took place tonight at Grovers Mill has ended in one of the most startling defeats ever suffered by an army in modern times; seven thousand men armed with rifles and machine guns pitted against a single fighting machine of the invaders from Mars. One hundred and twenty known survivors. The rest strewn over the battle area from Grovers Mill to Plainsboro crushed and trampled to death under the metal feet of the monster, or burned to cinders by its heat-ray. The monster is now in control of the middle section of New Jersey and has effectively cut the state through its center. Communication lines are down from Pennsylvania to the Atlantic Ocean. Railroad tracks are torn and service from New York to Philadelphia discontinued except routing some of the trains through Allentown and Phoenixville. Highways to the north, south, and west are clogged with frantic human traffic. Police and army reserves are unable to control the mad flight. By morning the fugitives will have swelled Philadelphia, Camden and Trenton, it is estimated, to twice their normal population. . . .

OPERATOR THREE

This is Newark, New Jersey. . . .
This is Newark, New Jersey. . . .

Warning! Poisonous black smoke pouring in from Jersey marshes. Reaches South Street. Gas masks useless. Urge population to move into open spaces . . . automobiles use routes 7, 23, 24. . . . Avoid congested areas. Smoke now spreading over Raymond Boulevard. . . .

ANNOUNCER

I'm speaking from the roof of Broadcasting Building, New York City. The bells you hear are ringing to warn the people to evacuate the city as the Martians approach. Estimated in last two hours three million people have moved out along the roads to the north, Hutchison River Parkway still kept open for motor traffic. Avoid bridges to Long Island . . . hopelessly jammed. All communication with Jersey shore closed ten minutes ago. No more defenses. Our army wiped out . . . artillery, air force, everything wiped out. This may be the last broadcast. We'll stay here to the end.

ANNOUNCER

You are listening to a CBS presentation of Orson Welles and the Mercury Theatre on the Air in an original dramatization of *War of the Worlds* by H.G. Wells. The performance will continue after a brief intermission.

(The program resumes as Professor Pierson—a Princeton astronomer—gives his account of the denouement of the Martian invasion. He has wandered north, he reports, through devastated New Jersey, obsessed by the thought that he is the last living man on earth. On the third day of his journey he reaches Newark, which lay undemolished but seemingly devoid of life.)

PIERSON

Presently, with an odd feeling of being watched, I caught sight of something crouching in a doorway. I made a step towards it, and it rose up and became a man —a man, armed with a large knife.

STRANGER

Stop . . . Where did you come from?

PIERSON

I come from . . . many places. . . .

STRANGER

There's no food here. This is my country . . . all this end of town down to the river.

There's only food for one. . . . Which way are you going?

PIERSON

I don't know. I guess I'm looking for—for people. . . . You're in uniform.

STRANGER

What's left of it. I was in the militia—national guard. . . .

PIERSON

You and I and others . . . where are we to live when the Martians own the earth?

STRANGER

I've got it all figured out. We'll live under ground. I've been thinking about the sewers. Under New York are miles and miles of 'em. The main ones are big enough for anybody. . . . And we'll get a bunch of strong men together. No weak ones, that rubbish, out. . . .

PIERSON

Go on.

STRANGER

And we've got to make safe places for us to stay in, see; and get all the books we can —science books. That's where men like you come in, see? We'll even spy on the Martians. It may not be so much we have to learn before—just imagine this: four or five of their own fighting machines suddenly start off—heat-rays right and left and not a Martian in 'em. Not a Martian in 'em! But *men*—men who have learned the way how. It may even be in our time. Gee! Imagine having one of them lovely things with its heat-ray wide and free! We'd turn it on the Martians, we'd turn it on men. We'd bring everybody down to their knees.

PIERSON

That's your plan?

STRANGER

You and me and a few more of us we'd own the world.

PIERSON

I see.

STRANGER

Say, what's the matter? Where are you going?

PIERSON

Not to *your* world. . . . Good-bye, Stranger.

PIERSON

After parting with the artilleryman, I came at last to the Holland Tunnel. I entered that silent tube anxious to know the fate of the great city on the other side of the Hudson. Cautiously I came out of the tunnel and made my way up Canal Street.

I reached Fourteenth Street, and there again were black powder and several bodies, and an evil ominous smell from the gratings of the cellars of some of the houses. I wandered up through the thirties and

forties; I stood alone on Times Square. I caught sight of a lean dog running down Seventh Avenue with a piece of dark brown meat in his jaws, and a pack of starving mongrels at his heels. He made a wide circle around me, as though he feared I might prove a fresh competitor. I walked up Broadway in the direction of that strange powder—past silent shop windows, displaying their mute wares to empty sidewalks —past the Capitol Theatre, silent, dark —past a shooting gallery, where a row of empty guns faced an arrested line of wooden ducks. Near Columbus Circle I noticed models of 1939 motor cars in the showrooms facing empty streets. From over the top of the General Motors Building I watched a flock of black birds circling in the sky. I hurried on. I caught sight of the hood of a Martian machine, standing somewhere in Central Park, gleaming in the late afternoon sun. An insane idea! I rushed recklessly across Columbus Circle and into the Park. I climbed a small hill above the pond at Sixtieth Street. From there I could see, standing in a silent row along the Mall, nineteen of those great metal Titans, their cowls empty, their steel arms hanging listlessly by their sides. I looked in vain for the monsters that inhabit those machines.

Suddenly, my eyes were attracted to the immense flock of black birds that hovered directly below me. They circled to the ground, and there before my eyes, stark and silent, lay the Martians, with the hungry birds pecking and tearing brown shreds of flesh from their dead bodies. Later when their bodies were examined in laboratories, it was found that they were killed by the putrefactive and disease bacteria against which their systems were unprepared . . . slain after all man's defenses had failed, by the humblest thing that God in His wisdom put upon this earth. . . .

Strange it now seems to sit in my peaceful study at Princeton writing down this last chapter of the record begun at a deserted farm at Grovers Mill. Strange to see from my window the university spires dim and blue through an April haze. Strange to watch children playing in the streets. Strange to see young people strolling on the green, where the new spring grass heals the last black scars of a bruised earth. Strange to watch the sightseers enter the museum where the dissembled parts of a Martian machine are kept on public view. Strange when I recall the time when I first saw it, bright and clean-cut, hard and silent, under the dawn of that last great day.

Writers as well as leading actors for the most popular serial of the decade, Freeman Gosden, left, played "Amos" to Charles Correll's "Andy."

Comics in "Black-Voice"

AMOS 'N' ANDY
MONDAY to FRIDAY, 7:00 E.S.T., NBC-*Red*

ANNOUNCER: Here they are:—

SYNOPSIS: The Amos 'n' Andy show was loaded with stereotyped Negro comedy roles —many of them played by Correll and Gosden—nearly as important as the title characters and just as popular with the audience. Two particular favorites were the Kingfish, top man in a fictitious Harlem lodge called the Mystic Knights of the Sea, and Lightnin', clean-up man of the lodge. As the sequence opens, the raffish Kingfish is practicing his customary wiles on the meek Lightnin'.

LIGHTNIN'
De fashion show was a financh success?

KINGFISH
Oh, yeh, it was great all right. Made close to a hundred dollars fo' de lodge, an' we is done paid our rent wid dat, an' light bill an' phone bill—all de utiliries.

LIGHTNIN'
Yessah—dat's good.

KINGFISH
Den it was voted last night to send some money oveh to de Harlem Boys' Club, oveh on 134th Street, on account o' de openin' today.

LIGHTNIN'
Yessah—dat's a big thing oveh dere fo' de chillun.

KINGFISH
Where's Amos 'n' Andy?

LIGHTNIN'
I seed Mr. Amos' taxicab, an' I was oveh talkin' to Mr. Andy dis mornin'—he was goin' home to bed. He didn't feel good.

KINGFISH
Too bad. Now, Lightnin', de reason I ast yo' to pay some o' yo' dues dat yo' is back in. De record show dat yo' ain't paid but thirty-five cents in de last two years, an' dat's a disregrace to de lodge dat's puttectin' yo' like it is.

LIGHTNIN'
Yessah, well, I is behind wid ev'rything; my coffin money's even back now. Insurance man come oveh dis mornin' lookin' fo' ten cents—I had to duck de man—I think dat's done lapsed on me.

KINGFISH
Wait a minute heah, don't fo'git dat dis lodge is givin' yo' puttection.

LIGHTNIN'
Well, I just ain't got it. If yo' would lend me some money, I would pay the lodge.

KINGFISH
Whut yo' mean, *me* lend yo' some money? I is flat as a pancake. I got about fifteen cents, an' I gotta git a dollar by tonight somewhere. We goin' have comp'ny fo' supper. De butcher done tighten up on me. I gotta git a couple o' po'k chops in dat house some way. Yo' can't ast de people comin' to supper to eat gravy *all* de time. . . .

LIGHTNIN'
Yessah.

KINGFISH
Can't you go to some friend?

LIGHTNIN'
I ain't got no money friends—all my friends is sympathy friends—dey listens an' feels sorry fo' me, but den dey's gone.

H. V. Kaltenborn stays with the microphone during a marathon newscast as assistants hand him the latest teletype reports of the Munich crisis.

War in Our Time

H. V. KALTENBORN
WEDNESDAY, 9:30 E.S.T. CBS

ANNOUNCER: H.V. Kaltenborn, dean of radio commentators . . . is going to tell you what he thinks about the headlines.

SYNOPSIS: On September 14, 1938, with the world watching hopefully, Britain's Prime Minister Chamberlain left London to negotiate with Chancellor Adolf Hitler over the German claims on Czechoslovakia. During the 18 days of the crisis, Kaltenborn was on call to make his comments—such as those below—on the fast-breaking news.

KALTENBORN

[Chamberlain] is risking his prestige, risking his position, risking almost everything upon this journey. And the amazing thing to me, is that he's risking it now, before things have actually come to the point where war does seem inevitable.

He has a plan—and perhaps that's the reason that he's going now. He has a plan that's been worked out between Britain and France. What can that plan be? Well, it can't be a plan for the immediate settlement of this problem. I don't believe that it would be possible to settle it as the result of a conversation between Chamberlain and Hitler alone. But, if the British follow the technique in which they are so adept and which they have used successfully in Spain and elsewhere, it will be a plan of postponement. The Czechoslovak delegate from Geneva said today: "Do we go on the butcher's block or have we found a champion who is going forth to battle?" Translated into other terms, that delegate is asking this: Must we Czechs give up to Germany our only dependable frontier, our richest industrial area and our right to exist as an independent nation? . . .

A great deal depends on the personal mood in which Hitler receives Chamberlain. Hitler is a man of moods. I've noticed that each time I've had personal contact with him. Berchtesgaden is one of the loveliest places in all the world. There Hitler has a beautiful Swiss chalet halfway up the green-covered mountainside, where he can stand and look into Austria. I was told that that was one reason why he chose it—because he could look across into his native Austria. I remember that when he invited me to Berchtesgaden he sent his private car with his chauffeur and the head of his Foreign Press service to Munich to meet me. I'm just wondering whether he's going to come to Munich himself to greet the Prime Minister of Britain.

If he does not, I think it will indicate he receives Chamberlain in the mood of a conqueror and that he considers that Chamberlain is coming to bargain. . . .

I am convinced that Chamberlain will not go away empty-handed. He is bound to get something. The Prime Minister of Britain who would visit the leader of Germany won't return completely empty-handed. Chamberlain is skillful enough, and the two men with him are sufficiently skillful in diplomacy, to bring back something. But my own feeling is that it will be little more than a truce. There is grave doubt as to whether or not the visit will bring peace.

Jack Benny's wife Mary, right, restrains Fred Allen and Fred's wife Portland, left, holds Jack back as the comedians act out their famous feud.

Jack's Face-off with Fred Allen

JELL-O PROGRAM
SUNDAY, 7:00 E.S.T., NBC-*Red*

ANNOUNCER: The Jell-O program, coming to you from the Grand Ballroom of the Hotel Pierre, starring Jack Benny, with Mary Livingstone, and Abe Lyman and his Orchestra.

SYNOPSIS: As part of his weekly routine, Jack has created a running feud with Fred Allen, star of Town Hall Tonight. But so far the two mock antagonists have never met. On this particular evening Jack opens the show with a series of anti-Allen jokes. Then he swings into a musical solo praising his own sponsor, Jell-O. He is interrupted by a loud knock on the door.

ALLEN
Whoever's blowing that foghorn . . . has gotta cut it out.

ALL
Fred Allen! (*Crowd: applause*)

BENNY
Well as I live and regret there are no locks on Studio doors . . . if it isn't [Fred] Allen!

. . . What's the idea of breaking in here in the middle of my singing?

ALLEN
Singing? When you set that croup to music and call it singing, you've gone too far!

BENNY
Now look here Allen, I don't care what you say about my singing on your *own* program, but after all, *I've* got listeners!

ALLEN
Keep your family out of this.

BENNY
Well my family likes my singing . . . and my violin playing, too.

ALLEN
Your violin playing! Why I just heard that a horse committed suicide when he found out your violin bow was made from his tail.

BENNY
Another crack like that and Town Hall will be looking for a new janitor.

ALLEN
You lay a hand on me and you'll be hollering Strawberry, Raspberry, Cherry, Orange, Lemon and *Help*.

BENNY
I'm a hard-ridin', two-fisted he-man . . . and if you'll step out in the hallway I'm ready to settle this little affair man to man!

MARY
Next week the Jell-O Program, starring Mary Livingstone! (*Jack and Fred exit, briefly. Then:*)

MARY
Sh, here they come now. (*Door opens, Jack and Allen enter—laughing*)

MARY
What happened to the fight?

JACK
What fight? . . .

ANNOUNCER DON WILSON
Hey fellows, what happened to that fight?

JACK
Why Don, we were never serious about that.

MARY
Then how did you get that black eye?

JACK
Oh, this? Well, I was writing a letter.

ALLEN
And I dotted his eye.

In a battle of quips, comedian W.C. Fields, right, and Charlie McCarthy, left, the dummy of ventriloquist Edgar Bergen, trade wooden glances.

Charlie McCarthy Meets His Match

CHASE & SANBORN HOUR
SUNDAY, 8:00 E.S.T., NBC-*Red*

ANNOUNCER: The makers of Chase and Sanborn Coffee—the blend of the world's choice coffees—now being sold at a very reasonable price—present Constance Bennett, Dorothy Lamour, W.C. Fields, Edgar Bergen and Charlie McCarthy, Ray Middleton, Werner Janssen and Don Ameche!

SYNOPSIS: After chit-chat between actress Constance Bennett and Charlie, W.C. Fields, whom intimates called "Bill," is introduced by announcer Don Ameche. Then:

BERGEN
Excuse me, Don. Am I intruding?

AMECHE
Frankly, Edgar, I'm glad you're here.

BERGEN
I hope I didn't interrupt anything. . . .

FIELDS
Not at all Edwin . . . not at all. . . .

BERGEN
Bill—I just came here to tell you something about Charlie.

FIELDS
I know enough about him already.

CHARLIE
Listen, Mr. Fields . . . I've got a bone to pick with you.

FIELDS
Yeah . . . Pick your head off.

CHARLIE
Aw gee whiz, Mr. Fields.

BERGEN
You've got Charlie all upset, Bill. He's tried all sorts of ways to make friends with you.

CHARLIE
Yes. I've had people intercede for me . . . I brought you a bouquet of flowers. . . .

FIELDS
A nosegay! Go on!

CHARLIE
I don't know where to go or what to do.

FIELDS
I can tell you where to go and also what to do. . . If you want me to go into details.

CHARLIE
I don't know . . . no matter what I say, it seems to be the wrong thing.

FIELDS
Then sew a button on your lip.

BERGEN
Now Bill . . . Charlie doesn't really feel good. Look how pale he is.

FIELDS
He needs a new coat of paint and a little furniture varnish.

CHARLIE
Mr. Fields, my mind is made up. I'm determined to fight fire with fire.

FIELDS
You know what happens to little boys who play with fire?

BERGEN
Don't mind Charlie, Bill. His bark is really worse than his bite.

FIELDS
I'll rip off his bark and bite off his limbs.

CHARLIE
This has gone far enough. I've been a little gentleman up to now. Mr. Fields . . . I'll clip you! So help me . . . I'll mow you down!

FIELDS
Go 'way—or I'll sic a woodpecker on you.

Breakfast with the Barbours

ONE MAN'S FAMILY
WEDNESDAY, 8:00 A.M. E.S.T., NBC-*Red*

ANNOUNCER: *One Man's Family* is dedicated to the Mothers and Fathers of the Younger Generation and to their Bewildering Offspring. Tonight we bring you Chapter Ten, Book Twenty-Three, entitled "Two Million Dollars At Stake." Philip Spencer was killed in a private plane crash, while en route to San Francisco to try to prove that he was the father of David, infant son of his ex-wife Beth Holly. Beth has declared that Spencer was *not* her child's father and was ready to go to any extreme to fight it. Now Spencer is gone and the danger is passed, but circumstances are not willing to let it go at that. *Now* the attorneys for Spencer's estate announce that the deceased has left funds and property to the value of two million dollars; that the only known possible heir is the baby David; and that he will inherit the full amount *providing* Beth can prove that David is Spencer's child. And while Beth faces this new dilemma, Clifford and Ann are walking on air. Father and Mother Barbour have given them a round-trip ticket from San Francisco to Hong Kong on the China Clipper for their honeymoon! This happened last night at the engagement shower for the couple . . . and now the family is at breakfast. . . .

FANNY
(*Coming to Mike*) Now Clifford, eat your breakfast like a normal human being. . . .

CLIFF
But Mom, Dad says the Clipper Ship crosses the Equator on the way to Hong Kong, and it doesn't at all.

HENRY
Certainly you cross the Equator. . . .

CLIFF
No Dad—

FANNY
Are you going to eat your bacon and eggs?

CLAUDIA
What's bacon and eggs in Cliff's young life?

FANNY
Well if I'd known what a goose he was going to be, I'd have put my foot down when your father wanted to buy the tickets. . . .

HAZEL
He hasn't talked about anything else. . . .

CLIFF
But you folks don't *get* it . . . Ann and I are going to *fly the Pacific Ocean* . . . (*Laughter*)

JACK
(*Bored*) Sure we got it . . . You're going to *fly the Pacific* (*Laughter*)

FANNY
Clifford, where are you going?

CLIFF
(*Leaving Mike*) I just want to get the globe.

CLAUDIA
(*Laughs*) Crazy as a loon.

FANNY
Such a business. He's more excited about that trip than about getting married.

HAZEL
(*Amused*) They both are. Ann was so excited before she left last night she was ill. . . .

HENRY
Well their excitement is infectious. . . . I don't know when I've enjoyed giving a present so much. . . .

FANNY
Well it should have worn off a little by this morning. . . . I'm going to be worn to a frazzle if this hilarity keeps up. . . .

CLIFF
(*Coming to Mike*) Here you are Dad. It's just as I said. We don't cross the Equator.

FANNY
Clifford, your breakfast is stone cold. . . .

CLIFF
You see, this is Midway and this is Wake.

FANNY
Humph. . . . Look like fly-specks to *me*. . . . (*Laughter*)

In "One Man's Family," Minetta Ellen, far left, played Fanny (Mother Barbour); and J. Anthony Smythe, far right, was Henry (Father Barbour).

Hard Times

Shacks of Seattle's Hooverville shelter the homeless.

The Hungry Years

I remember lying in bed one night and thinking. All at once I realized something.
We were poor. Lord! It was weeks before I could get over that.

DEPRESSION VICTIM, CHATTANOOGA, TENNESSEE, 1933

In 1930, before the full effect of the Depression was felt across the country, most Americans knew poverty only by reputation. But in the next several years, a large part of the richest nation on earth learned what it meant to be poor; for 40 million people poverty became a way of life.

Misery found its way into every region, group and occupation. Negro factory workers, always the last to be hired in good times, were the first to be fired as production slowed to a painful crawl. Farmers, struggling to keep on their feet amid plummeting crop prices, were knocked down for good by a series of natural disasters—floods, droughts, plagues and dust storms. Businessmen slipped from being home owners to room renters, and even to wandering the street. Experience taught many children to move their dolls about in a game they called Eviction.

"The Depression had pups on our doorstep." So said an Oklahoma farmer whose ill-fortune had multiplied, though he was lucky enough to keep his doorstep. But the luckless were legion, homeless and on the move. Foreclosed farmers became migratory field hands in the West. Sharecroppers drifted north, plodding from city to city in search of a job and a breadline. Ragged bands of youths roamed the country aimlessly, sleeping in hobo jungles.

Naturally, all these wanderers suffered poignantly from cold, hunger and disease. Not so naturally, many were denied relief because they had no legal residence.

Even those fortunate Americans who managed to live out the decade in well-heeled comfort were often shaken by the misery they saw or read about. One *had* to wince at the courage of an Arkansas family that walked 900 miles to apply for work; and then wince again at the bitter humor of a penniless Southerner who announced, "When you gits down to your last bean, your backbone and your navel shakes dice to see which gits it." It was easy to cry at the sacrifice offered by a destitute mother who, after giving birth to her seventh child, told the doctor, "I've never been able to pay you nothin' for deliverin' my other six children; so I'll give you this one."

By 1939, the worst was over; the Depression had made a hero of every sufferer who managed to survive. The names of the poor were largely lost to posterity. But the experience that scourged them survived, recorded with heartbreaking fidelity by photographers, reporters and social workers. The words and pictures gathered by these chroniclers did more than capture the raw emotions of the moment. They captured the soul of the Depression.

Competition was stiff among the apple sellers in New York. Said one peddler, "People mostly hurry by as if they didn't want to look at you."

The Face of Poverty

Before daylight we were on the way to Chevrolet. The police were
already on the job, waving us away from the office.
"Nothin' doin'. Nothin' doin'." Now we were tramping through
falling snow. Dodge employment office. A big
well fed man in a heavy overcoat stood at the door saying, "No, no,"
as we passed before him. On the tramp again. . . .

AN UNEMPLOYED DETROIT AUTO WORKER

Desperate for work, a Detroiter advertises. Others bought jobs; one man paid a $10 fee to earn $13.50.

Jobless New Yorkers haunt the employment agencies on Sixth Avenue. One agency averaged 5,000 applicants daily—and had work for only 300.

A toil-worn California field hand faces an uncertain future. "I have worked hard all my life," said one man, "and all I have now is my broken body."

We had been eating wild greens since January
this year. Violet tops, wild onions, forget-me-not, wild lettuce
and such weeds as cows eat. Our family are in bad
shape childrens need milk women need nurishments food shoes
and dresses—that we cannot get.
A KENTUCKY MINER

A tubercular New York mother still believed she could make it: "Long as I can work, I'll get along somehow."

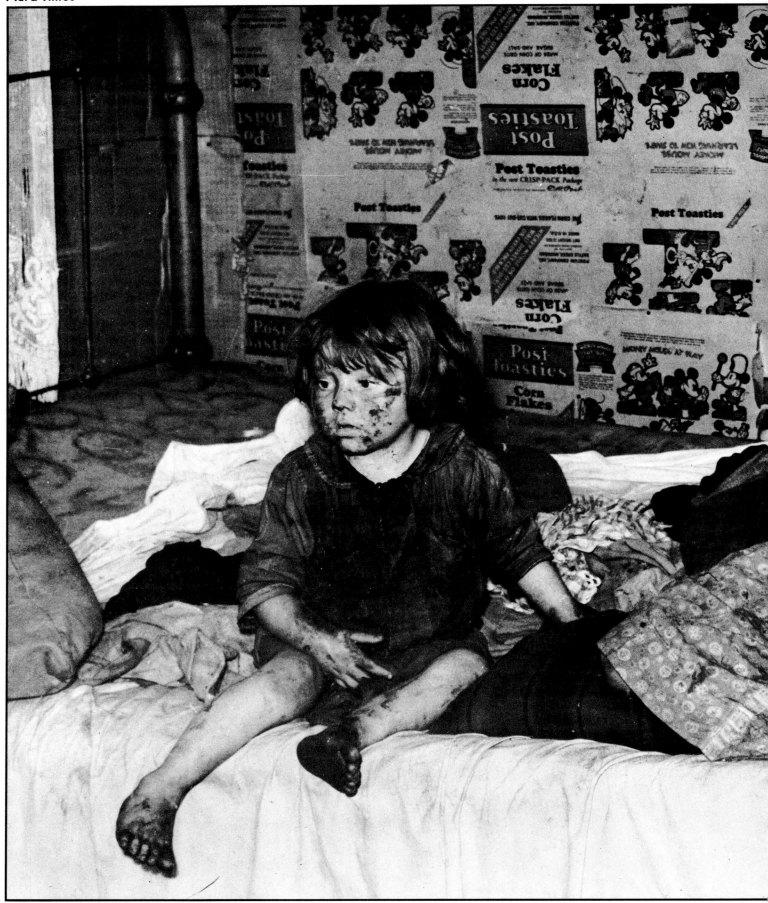

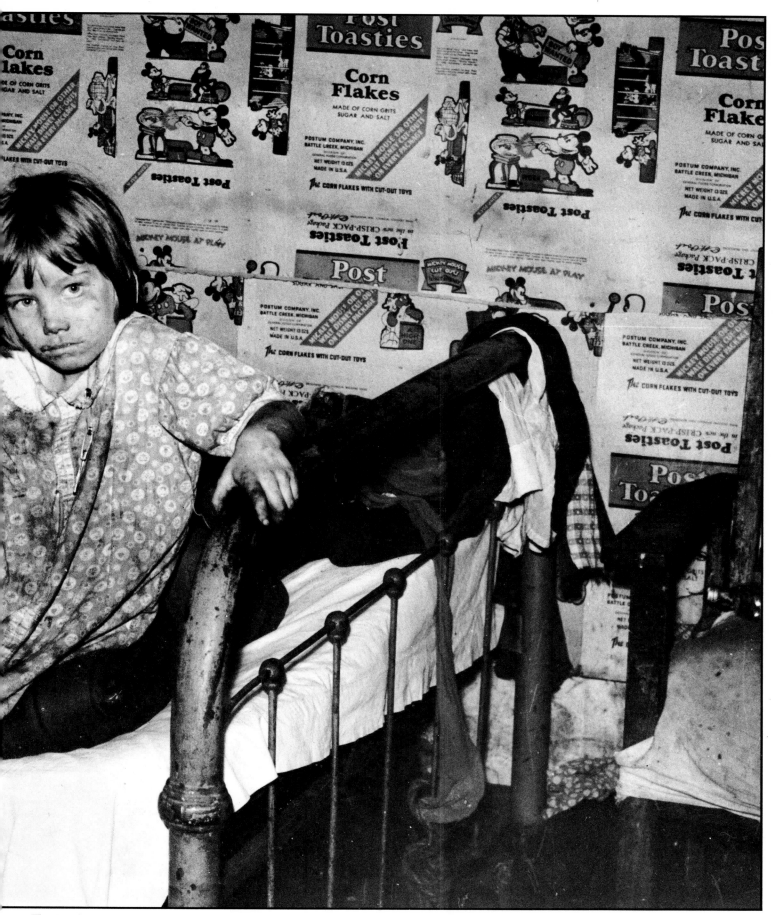

The daughters of a WPA worker and a sick mother are left home unattended. A bitter father said: "A worker's got no right to have kids any more."

Ragged but tough, a South Carolina farm girl remains unintimidated. Many such children worked in the fields from "can see" to "can't see."

If they come to take my farm, I'm going to fight. I'd rather be killed outright than die by starvation. But before I die, I'm going to set fire to my crops, I'm going to burn my house, I'm going to p'izen my cattle.

A DEBT-RIDDEN FARMER

Destitute but steadfast, a miner's family keeps up its spirits during the bitter 1939 strike in the coal fields of West Virginia.

Adding to the burden of the Depression, the Ohio River invades Louisville in 1937. In that year of high water, a million people needed flood relief.

The Hand of Nature

Oh, I tell you I've seen that old river come up.
When it begins to git in the houses,
we take and move everything up on the bank
across the railroad tracks.
Well, city folks come trotting up there with soup
kettles. They's always one saying to
another, "Do you suppose them people's got little
enough sense to go back to them
shacks when the river goes down?" Yes Lord,
we'll always go back to Shanty Town
till the river rises some day and forgits to go down.
A TENNESSEE SQUATTER

The receding flood water leaves mud and wreckage inside an Indiana farmhouse.

Flood victims line up for food and pure water. Said a relief worker: "It ain't going to hurt the government to feed and clothe them that needs it."

After years of drought, the great dust storm of May 21, 1937, strikes Clayton, New Mexico. Despite dust masks, many died of suffocation.

When these winds hit us, we and
our misery were suddenly covered with dust.
Here in the Texas Panhandle
we were hit harder than most anywhere
else. If the wind blew one way,
here came the dark dust from Oklahoma.
Another way and it was the gray
dust from Kansas. Still another way, the
brown dust from Colorado and
New Mexico. Little farms were buried. And
the towns were blackened.
A TEXAS FARMER

These storms were like rolling black
smoke. We had to keep the lights on all day.
We went to school with headlights on,
and with dust masks on. I saw a woman who
thought the world was coming
to an end. She dropped down on her knees in
the middle of Main Street in
Amarillo and prayed out loud: "Dear Lord!
Please give them another chance."
A TEXAS SCHOOLBOY

An abandoned farm lies inundated by dust. Departing farmers reduced the population of Hall County, Texas, from 14,392 to only 7,000.

All that dust made some of the
farmers leave; they became the Okies. We stuck
it out here. We scratched, literally
scratched, to live. We'd come to town to sell
sour cream for nine cents
a pound. If we could find a town big
enough and far enough away
from the dust, we could sell eggs at ten cents
a dozen. Despite all the dust
and the wind, we were putting in crops, but
making no crops and barely
living out of barnyard products only. We
made five crop failures in five years.
AN OKLAHOMA FARMER

"For Sale" signs marked the start of the dust bowlers' migrations.

Heading west, migrants gaze wearily from their car. For them, California, the "Land of Milk and Honey," would offer drudgery and privation.

The Promise of the Road

This is a hard life to swallow, but I just couldn't sit
back there and look to someone to feed us.

A MIGRATORY WORKER

A hapless Okie grimly looks across the desert: "Yessir, we're starved, stalled and stranded."

Too poor to ride, a family from Arkansas walks through Texas to look for work in the Rio Grande cotton fields, a trek of about 900 miles.

October-December 1932. Cut Malaga and muscat grapes

near Fresno. About $40 a month.

December 1932. Left for Imperial Valley, Calif.

February 1933. Picked peas, Imperial Valley. Earned $30 for season.

On account of weather, was fortunate to break even.

March-April 1933. Left for Chicago. Returned to California.

May 1933. Odd jobs on lawns and radios at Fresno.

June 1933. Picked figs near Fresno. Earned $50 in two months.

A MIGRATORY WORKER'S LOG BOOK

Rude cardboard shacks served as winter quarters for migrants in California's Imperial Valley.

A large family, intact despite its migrations, gathers to share a simple meal. "Us people has got to stick together to get by these hard times."

A Tennessee woman succumbs to despondency: "I've wrote back that we're well and such as that, but I never have wrote that we live in a tent."

We make as much as is fitten for such as us runnin'-around

folks. Caint send the children to school we aint got the clothes. By a'savin up we get

so's we can move on to the next place. We haven't had no help no way.

A TEXAS MIGRANT IN CALIFORNIA

When they need us they call us migrants.

When we've picked their crops we're bums and we've got to get out.

A MIGRATORY WORKER

A worker improvises his morning shave. In some camps shaving was a luxury: "You can't waste water when it costs so much to get."

Successful in California, a migrant's wife admires their farm. Said she proudly: "One more piece of pipe and our water tank will be finished."

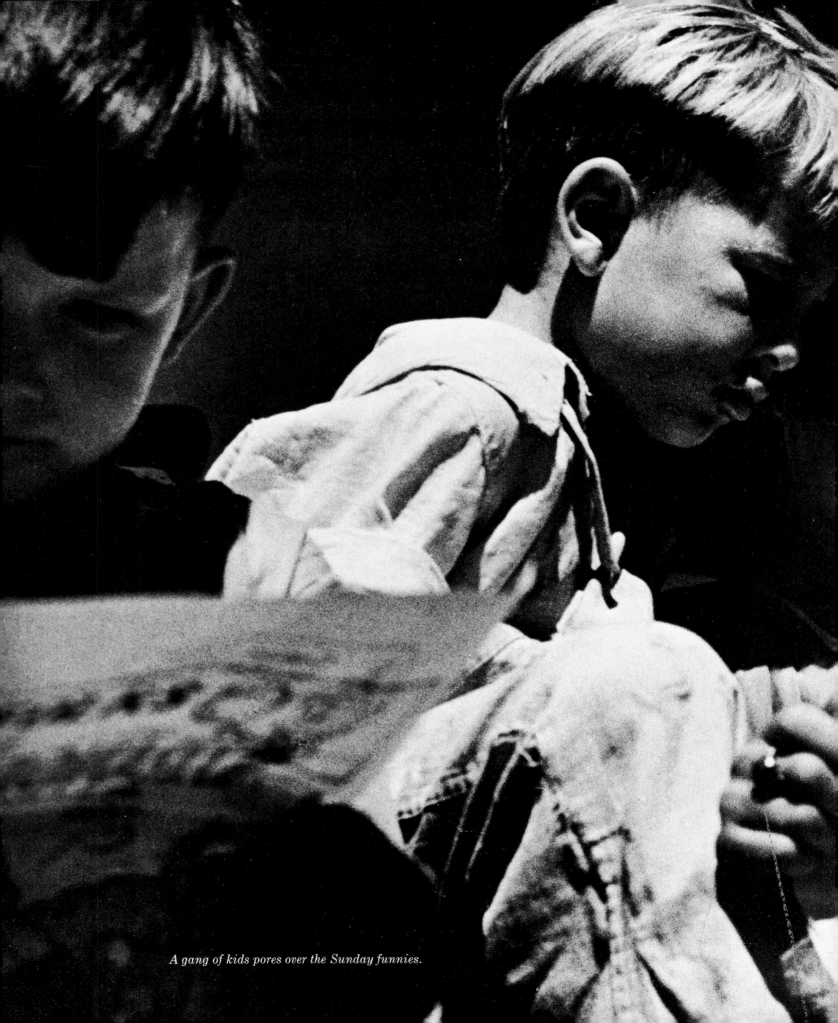

A gang of kids pores over the Sunday funnies.

Dream Factory

The Company of Heroes

Leapin' Lizards! Who says business is bad?
LITTLE ORPHAN ANNIE, 1933

During the '30s, the world of little kids orbited around a set of heroes and heroines whose extravagant lives were chronicled in a rich new range of media. Every Sunday before church, kids all over the country pawed through the funny papers for the latest exploits of Flash Gordon or Little Orphan Annie, whose pet expression "Leapin' Lizards!" was an American standard and whose faith in good old capitalism comforted many a Depression-ridden parent. On weekdays Annie also came booming over the radio, joined by the likes of hard-bitten detective Dick Tracy and Jack Armstrong, a teen-age football hero. Saturday was movie day: four and a half raucous hours of cliff-hanging serials featuring Tarzan or Flash Gordon, animated cartoons, and then perhaps a full-length picture starring that all-time heroine, Shirley Temple. In between times, the kids caught up on back adventures of the same characters through Big Little Books—squat, 400-page cubes of type and pictures that sold for a dime—or amused themselves with pop-up and cut-out books of Shirley, Buck Rogers or a pair of overseas idols, Princesses Elizabeth and Margaret Rose of England.

The kingdoms of these heroes and heroines were even more varied than the media that brought them home to the kids; they ranged from America's playing fields to the slimiest Oriental jungles, from the plains of the Old West to the slums of gangster-ridden cities, from Buckingham Palace to galaxies in the far reaches of outer space. And the idols themselves were just as varied in their makeup; some were real (the Little Princesses), some wholly fabricated (Buck Rogers), others physically real but fictitious in their exploits (Tom Mix and Shirley Temple).

The common ground on which these heroes and heroines stood was virtue, a commodity they sold in heaping portions by proving that good, clean living held unlimited rewards. With the exception of the Little Princesses, the idols also proved awesomely adept at selling commercial products. With each installment of their adventures, they unblushingly fired off a barrage of sales pitches in behalf of various trinkets, toys and breakfast foods. Little Orphan Annie even managed to pitch a chocolate drink called Ovaltine with her left hand while handing out her conservative, pro-business dogma with the right. Despite such blatant salesmanship, however, the most successful product served up by the kids' idols was an inexpensive and wonderful world of make-believe, during hard times when the real world often seemed to be no fun at all.

Moppets, carefully coiffed and rehearsed by would-be movie mothers, participate in a Shirley Temple look-alike contest in Herrin, Illinois.

Little Orphan Annie

When Little Orphan Annie first appeared, she seemed out of place on the funny pages, for the simple reason that she was rarely funny. Rather, cartoonist Harold Gray time and again rallied his never-aging red-haired tyke and her mongrel Sandy to the aid of decent folks who were cowering before treacherous foreigners, mortgage-holders and crimelords. Often Annie's wealthy foster father, Oliver "Daddy" Warbucks, would happen by with his homicidal henchmen Punjab and The Asp to give Annie a hand.

Launched in 1924, the strip's success soon affected *Annie's* story line. Gray, who by 1934 was earning about $100,000 a year, began to color the melodrama with his conservative views on labor leaders and liberal politicians. Only when Annie went on radio did Gray compromise his —and the orphan's—philosophy of "ya hafta earn what ya get"; Annie gave away a glittering array of premiums in exchange for seals from the jars of sponsor Ovaltine's chocolate milk mix. However, $1,000 a week soothed Gray's anguish at the thought of all those free rings, badges, shake-up mugs and those secret-code cards *(right)* that allowed Annie's radio followers to decode such momentous messages as: 8-36-18-28-22/30-44-2-24-40-18-28-10.

ANNIE RINGS

BUTTONS

Radio Orphan Annie's Secret Society

WARNING! Take good care of this book! It is the official Rulebook containing the secrets that only a member of Radio Orphan Annie's Secret Society may know. These secrets are strictly private—only for the eyes of members, and their parents, who are considered as honorary members . . . If it should be accidentally lost, anyone who finds it should return it at once, without reading, to the owner whose name is on the back cover.

Radio Orphan Annie's Secret Code

HERE is a special mystery code that Annie has worked out for broadcasting secret messages over the radio—a code that no one who is not on the inside will be able to understand. And because it's going to be used a lot, you want to learn it right away.

And another thing—always have a pencil and paper with you every night when you listen to Little Orphan Annie. Because you never know when one of these secret messages is going to come over the air. And you always want to be ready to write them down.

And now here's the code itself . . . The idea is simply this: Numbers take the place of letters. And because only the even numbers are used, Annie sometimes calls it the "Even-Number Mystery Code." For example, the number "2" stands for the letter "A"; and the number "4" stands for the letter "B"; the letter "G," etc.

IMPORTANT: Below is a handy chart, showing just how the Mystery Code works.

2 A	4 B	6 C	8 D	10 E	12 F
14 G	16 H	18 I	20 J	22 K	24 L
26 M	28 N	30 O	32 P	34 Q	36 R
38 S	40 T	42 U	44 V	46 W	48 X
50 Y	52 Z	54 &			

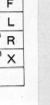

SHAKE-UP MUG

FOR EXTRA PEP 'N' FLAVOR KEEN, DRINK CHOCLATE-FLAVORED OVALTINE!

ARF!

SECRET SOCIETY BADGES AND CODE

Little Orphan Annie's Song

BRACELETS

Who's that little chatterbox?
The one with pretty auburn locks?
Who do you see?
It's Little Orphan Annie. . . .

Bright eyes, cheeks a rosy glow,
There's a store of healthiness handy.
Mite-size, always on the go.
And if you want to know—"Arf!" says Sandy. . . .

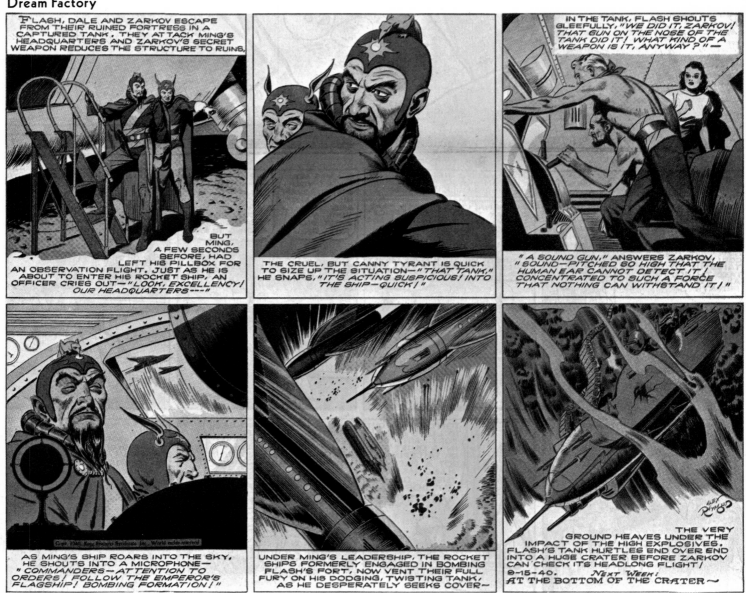

FLASH GORDON

When the planet Mongo threatened to collide with Earth in 1934, Yale-bred polo player Flash Gordon and a beautiful girl named Dale Arden were kidnaped aboard the rocket of crazed genius Hans Zarkov. With that notion for openers, cartoonist Alex Raymond launched the Flash Gordon story, first on the comic pages and eventually on the screen and in Big Little Books.

Guided by Raymond's fertile imagination, Flash, Dale and Dr. Zarkov journeyed from Earth to Mongo; during the trip Zarkov miraculously regained his sanity, having first calculated that the runaway planet would miss

Earth. Though the folks at home were now presumably safe, Flash and his friends were not, for Mongo was ruled by yellow-skinned, almond-eyed Ming the Merciless, who was evil incarnate in the 1930s, when Americans were fretting increasingly over the Yellow Peril of emerging Asia. On Mongo, Flash was ever the target of sensual women and unspeakably foul agents of the wily Ming. Yet he remained true both to Dale and the values of the Yale polo field (as interpreted by Raymond): "This was a Tournament of Death, but it was still to be fought by heroes imbued with the ideals of sportsmanship and fair play."

In films, Olympic swim star Buster Crabbe played a peroxided Flash.

PEDOMETER

Jack Armstrong!

"The All-American Boy!!" As the radio announcer shouted those magic words and a male chorus swung into the "Hudson High Fight Song," millions of kids began to live through the latest adventure of brainy, brawny, awesomely pure-in-heart Jack Armstrong. The All-American Boy's missions were three: to lead Hudson High to athletic glory, to overcome all bad guys and to peddle Wheaties. Naturally Jack broke all scoring records for Hudson High and for Wheaties, in whose behalf he unloaded tons of crispy wheat flakes and scads of premiums. At the same time the show served up heaping portions of fair play and love for America, the latter being shoe-horned into every possible line of script—as witness the dialogue below.

Tell the boys and girls of the United States this world is theirs. If they have hearts of gold, a glorious new golden age awaits us. If they are honest, riches shall be theirs. If they are kind, they shall save the whole world from malice and meanness. Will you take that message to the boys and girls of the United States, Jack Armstrong? TIBETAN MONK TO JACK ARMSTRONG, 1939.

HOVERING DISCS AND GUN

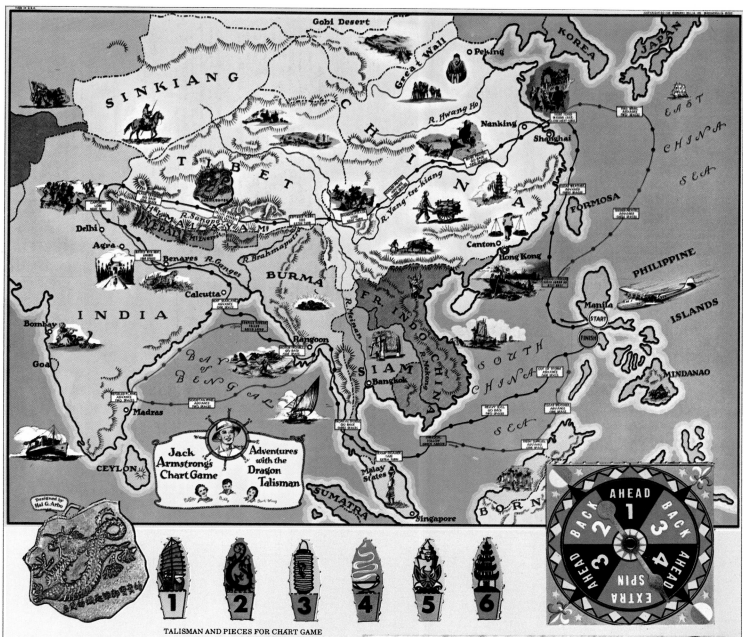

Jack Armstrong's Chart Game — Adventures with the Dragon Talisman

Designed by Hal G. Arbo

TALISMAN AND PIECES FOR CHART GAME

AHEAD 1 — BACK 3 — AHEAD 4 — EXTRA SPIN — AHEAD 3 — BACK 2

THE WHEATIES SONG
Won't you try Wheaties?
They're whole wheat with all of the bran.
Won't you try Wheaties?
For wheat is the best food of man.

HUDSON HIGH FIGHT SONG
Wave the flag for Hudson High, boys,
Show them how we stand!
Ever shall our team be champions,
Known throughout the land!
Rah Rah Boola Boola Boola Boola.

WHISTLE RING

JACK ARMSTRONG'S SECRET WHISTLE CODE

JACK ARMSTRONG

UNCLE JIM

INSTRUCTIONS

One Whistle . . . . (Short) Attention

Two Whistles . . . . (Short) Be on guard for trouble

Three Whistles . . . . . . (One long, two short) In danger, come at once

Four Whistles . . . . . . (Short) We're being watched

Two Whistles . . . . (Two Long) Important news — meet me at once

BETTY

A-1011

BILLY

Tarzan

In 1914 a middle-aged hack writer named Edgar Rice Burroughs collected rejection slips from every major American publisher before he finally sold his first novel: *Tarzan of the Apes*. This bizarre adventure story, set in the jungles of darkest Africa, told of the nurturing of an orphaned year-old boy, scion of the English House of Greystoke, by a fierce she-ape named Kala. In Kala's warm embrace, both Tarzan ("White Skin" in ape language) and Edgar Rice Burroughs grew and prospered.

By the end of the 1930s, Tarzan was the established hero of 21 fast-selling novels, a deftly drawn comic strip *(above)*, a 15-minute daily radio serial and 16 movies. Most popular with Tarzan fans in this decade were the movies, with their "take-me-to-the-elephant-graveyard" plots and their deathless dialogue, the best of it uttered by Olympic swim star Johnny Weissmuller during his incumbency in the title role. In his first film, *Tarzan, the Ape Man (right)*, Weissmuller enlarged the American vocabulary with the line "Me Tarzan, you Jane" and also introduced his fearful jungle yodel, a mixture of five sounds that included his own scream, a soprano singing high C and a recording of a hyena's howl played backwards.

1. *In an early scene in "Tarzan, the Ape Man," ivory-hunters James Parker and Harry Holt quiz natives about the elephant graveyard.*

2. *The safari, including Maureen O'Sullivan as Parker's daughter Jane, hears an unearthly cry and finds its path blocked by Tarzan.*

3. *Infatuated by Jane, Tarzan kidnaps her. At first, she balks at sharing Tarzan's treehouse with either the Ape Man or his chum Cheeta.*

4. *Jane falls in love with Tarzan and teaches him to speak. During a lakeside frolic, he utters the immortal "Me Tarzan, you Jane."*

5. *Conscience-smitten, Jane returns to her father as the safari is captured by Pygmies; Tarzan and his jungle pals swing to the rescue.*

FADEOUT: *The safari over, Jane decides to become the mate of Tarzan, who takes her to the mountain for a view of her new jungle domain.*

COMIC BOOK PREMIUM

MEMBERSHIP OATH

MEMBERSHIP SONG

AUTOGRAPHED PHOTO OF TONY AND TOM

Tom Mix

"Reach for the sky! Lawbreakers always lose, Straight Shooters always win!! It pays to shoot straight!!!" Young radio listeners thrilled to hear cowboy character Tom Mix bark out this instructive battle cry. Naturally, when their hero commanded them to eat his sponsor Ralston's wheat cereal, they hastened to do so; and when Tom said that a few Ralston box tops would yield the treasures shown here, what real Straight Shooter could resist?

Tom's radio fans had plenty of company in their worship of the hard-jawed idol. Long before the radio show began in 1933, Mix had built up an international following that had rooted for him and the Wonder Horse Tony through some 180 feature films.

In real life, the old Straight Shooter was an old roué who ran through three wives and four million dollars. Nevertheless he guarded his public image as a nonsmoking teetotaler. "I want to keep my pictures in such a vein that parents will not object to letting their children see me on the screen," explained Tom solemnly. And all his fans believed him, remaining loyal literally to the end: when he died in 1940, the Tom Mix Club of Lisbon, Portugal, gave up movies for two weeks as a sign of mourning.

SLIDE-WHISTLE RING

SIGNATURE RING

COMPASS AND MAGNIFIER

CLUB BADGE

SIREN RING

MAGNET RING

MIRROR RING

CLUB RING

HORSESHOE NAIL RING

WRANGLER BADGE

DECODER BADGE

COWBOY SPUR

TOM MIX' INJURIES

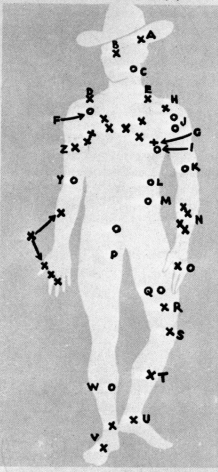

Danger and difficulty have never daunted Tom Mix, nor broken bones stopped him. He has been blown up once, shot 12 times and injured 47 times in movie stunting. The chart shows the location of some of Tom's injuries. (X marks fractures; circles, bullet wounds.)

A. Skull fractured in accident.
B. Nose injured when artillery wagon blew up in China.
C. Shot thru jaw by sniper in Spanish-American War.
D. Shoulder fractured in circus accident.
E. Collar bone broken four times in falls.
F. Shot by bandit in Mix home.
G. Eight broken ribs from movie accidents.
H. Shoulder fractured when horse was shot from under him by bandits in U. S. Marshal days.
I. Shot by cattle rustlers in Texas.
J. Shot twice in left arm by Oklahoma outlaws.
K. Shot below elbow by outlaw.
L. Shot through abdomen by killer he arrested.
M. Wounded in gun fight with rustlers.
N. Left arm broken four times in movie stunting.
O. Hand broken in movie stunt.
P. Shot by bad man while Oklahoma sheriff.
Q. Shot in leg when 14 years old.
R. Leg trampled by horse.
S. Fractured knee in wagon accident.
T. Leg broken while stunting for movies.
U. Fractured ankle breaking wild horses.
V. Foot and ankle broken in wagon accident.
W. Shot through leg by bank robbers.
X. Three broken fingers, hand and arm fractured in screen fights and film stunting.
Y. Shot through elbow in real stage coach hold-up (1902).
Z. Broken arm in film stunting.

NOTE: *Scars from twenty-two knife wounds are not indicated, nor is it possible to show on the diagram the hole four inches square and many inches deep that was blown in Tom's back by a dynamite explosion.*

TOY SIX-SHOOTER

POCKETKNIFE

FLASHLIGHT

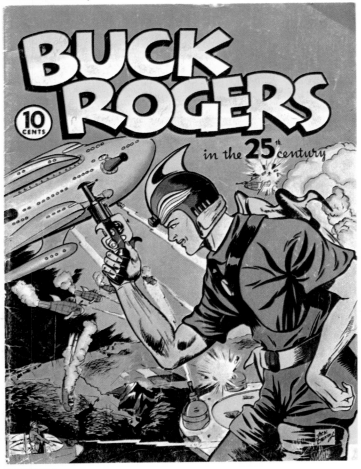

COMIC BOOKS

BUCK ROGERS POCKET WATCH

SOLAR SCOUTS BADGE

"Wilma, does all your equipment check out?" "Yes, Buck, I have my Thermic Radiation Projector, the Electro-cosmic Spectrometer and the Super Radiating Protono-former all set to go!" And so Buck Rogers and his luscious co-pilot Wilma Deering blasted off through the comics and radio on another mission to save "the whole universe."

All of Buck's adventures were marked by this same wild conglomeration of technological prophecy and sheer driv-el, and the climax of each plot was woefully predictable: Buck would capture archvillains Killer Kane and the slinky Ardala and commit them to the intergalactic Re-habilitation Center—from which they invariably escaped.

Killer and Ardala should have stayed put, for they were up against the combined brains and muscle of the Solar Scouts plus an ingenious arsenal of cosmic weapons that included Rocket Pistols, whose discharge introduced to the language the death-sound ZAP, and Atomic Bombs. These weapons of the future were fascinating to Buck's 20th Century fans; when Macy's department store in New York advertised it had toy versions of Buck Rogers Disin-tegrator Guns, the next morning a queue of 20,000 peo-ple—a third-of-a-mile-long—awaited the store's opening.

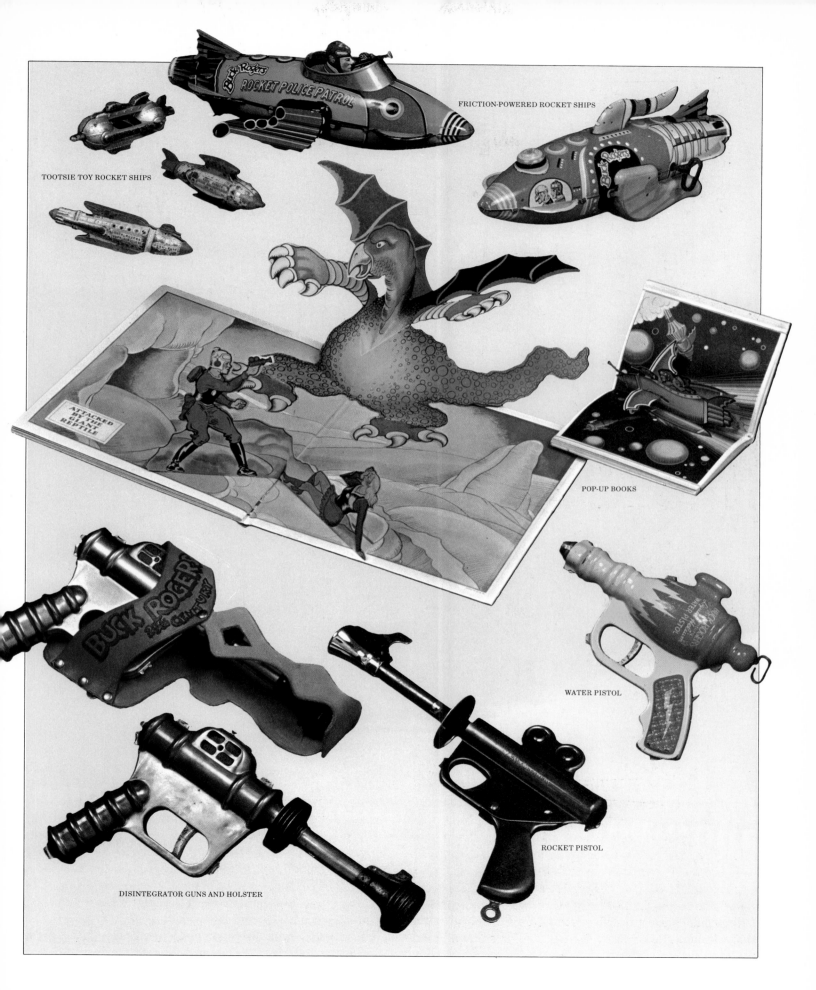

TOOTSIE TOY ROCKET SHIPS

FRICTION-POWERED ROCKET SHIPS

ATTACKED BY THE GIANT REPTILE

POP-UP BOOKS

WATER PISTOL

ROCKET PISTOL

DISINTEGRATOR GUNS AND HOLSTER

89

DETECTIVE BADGE

ROOKIE BADGE

SOPHOMORE BADGE

CLUB BUTTON

OFFICIAL WATCH

SECRET SERVICE PATROL OFFICER BADGES

DICK TRACY

Dick Tracy, the sharp-profiled comic strip detective, was a natural product of the '30s. Describing his cartoon creation, artist Chester Gould said, "Big gangsters were running wild but going to court and getting off scot free. I thought: why not have a guy who doesn't take the gangsters to court but shoots 'em?" So saying, Gould launched a strip loaded with gunfire. In the very first week, the slaying of Jeremiah Trueheart (right) marked the first time anyone had been gunned to death on the funny pages. More, much more, was to follow, for Dick Tracy, fiancé of Trueheart's daughter Tess, was so moved by this foul

deed that he signed on for life with the police force.

Quaker Oats cereal brought the detective to radio and soon devised a diabolically cunning sales gimmick: the Dick Tracy Secret Service Patrol. A boy's rise up the patrol hierarchy was directly proportional to how much Quaker Oats he could cram down, for a sergeant's badge cost five boxtops, a lieutenant's, seven, and so on. The company mercifully stopped the escalation at 15 box tops, but added a fillip for cereal-swelled candidates bucking for the ultimate rank of Inspector-General: they had to come up with a new Quaker Oats-gobbling recruit for the patrol.

Panels selected from the first two weeks of strips show how Dick Tracy's jaw began to jut dangerously after thugs slew his fiancée's father.

ELIZABETH   MARGARET ROSE

The Little Princesses

On the morning of May 12, 1937, two pretty, curly-haired little girls in purple robes and golden coronets stood on a balcony alongside their parents and waved at a cheering throng. On that day Elizabeth and Margaret Rose Windsor of Great Britain *(above)* fulfilled a dream cherished by just about every little girl in the Western world: their daddy was crowned King—of England, no less—and they were going to live in a real palace.

Eleven-year-old Princess Elizabeth and six-year-old Princess Margaret Rose quickly became international heroines and the subjects of a batch of hastily assembled biographies, story books (including one told from the viewpoint of their pet dogs) and paper-doll books. With the latter, a little girl anywhere could cut out dresses, fold the tabs over punch-out figures *(left)* and together with her own two princess pals, dream through a delicious range of royal fantasies, including a private coronation.

93

SHIRLEY TEMPLE

"My first impression of Shirley was a bit of sunshine. She had on a yellow dress and yellow coat and all that golden hair." This loving commentary by Shirley Temple's studio schoolteacher summed up the doting affection of the whole nation for the blonde moppet who swiftly became the child of the decade after she sang and danced, at the age of 5, in the 1934 movie *Stand Up and Cheer*.

In one of the many films that followed, Shirley was "Little Miss Marker"; she might well have been called "Little Miss Mark-Up" in real life. As Hollywood's top box-office draw from 1935 to 1938, her average of four pictures a year grossed five million dollars annually and was credited with keeping her studio solvent. Miss Temple's yearly $300,000 salary was boosted by royalties from a swarm of merchandisers of Shirley-endorsed dolls, doll clothes and accessories, soap, books and ribbons. Her doll manufacturer alone sold some six million toy moppets—at $3 to $30 each—in boxes bearing the star's own childish scrawl *(above)*. Outfits for these dolls *(overleaf)* often cost more than dresses for real girls. Even hairdressers profited from the star's popularity; they were besieged by girls demanding golden, 56-curled hairdos, just like Shirley's.

Dream Factory

Shirley Temple Doll owners were deluged with dresses inspired by the star's movie roles.

Cops and Robbers

The wages of crime for Bonnie and Clyde is death in this bullet-ridden auto.

The Daredevil Crooks

The criminal army in America today is on the march. . . . Crime is today sapping the spiritual and moral strength of America.

J. EDGAR HOOVER

Johnnie's just an ordinary fellow. Of course, he goes out and holds up banks and things, but he's really just like any other fellow, aside from that.

A FRIEND OF JOHN DILLINGER

Hard times brought a marked boom for at least one profession—crime. While legitimate businesses closed and farms lay barren, an alarming number of Americans began looking for easy money through robbery, kidnaping and even murder. Across the Midwest, bands of marauders traveling in fast-moving cars and toting sawed-off shotguns and Tommy guns began knocking over rural banks and Post Offices. In large cities, tightly organized undergrounds were raking in millions of dollars through extortion, prostitution and auto theft rings. By 1935, according to one estimate by the Justice Department, so many Americans had moved to the shady side of the law that crooks outnumbered carpenters by four to one, grocers by six to one and doctors by 20 to one.

The first of the decade's lawbreakers to win real notoriety, and surely the most hated criminal of his time, was an ex-convict from Germany named Bruno Richard Hauptmann. On the night of March 1, 1932, Hauptmann climbed up to a second-story nursery bedroom in Hopewell, New Jersey, and kidnaped the 20-month-old son of aviation hero Charles Lindbergh. The nation was stunned. It was as though Hauptmann had violated every home in America. For Lindy was the country's favorite hero, a modest, tousled-haired symbol of American courage and integrity. Though Lindy paid $50,000 in ransom, the baby was found dead six weeks later, and when Hauptmann was finally caught and executed in the electric chair, the country registered deep satisfaction.

But the country had some strikingly different feelings about other crimes and criminals; many people, impoverished and embittered by the Depression, actually found a certain justice in the mounting number of bank robberies. The most notorious of the bank thieves, John Dillinger, even emerged as a kind of Robin Hood folk hero. "Dillinger did not rob poor people. He robbed those who became rich by robbing the poor," wrote an admirer in Indianapolis. "I am for Johnnie." Indeed, Dillinger projected an image of swashbuckling glamor and generosity. When holding up a bank he would leap the barrier to the teller's cage to grab the loot. Once, when he broke out with two hostages from a supposedly escape-proof Indiana jail, he gave the men four dollars carfare home. In their admiration Dillinger's fans managed to forget that their hero had gunned down 10 men during his career, and that—like the other bandits shown on the following pages—he was basically just a cold-blooded thug.

America's No. 1 desperado, John Dillinger, smiles as he shows off some of the tools of his trade: a Thompson submachine gun and a revolver.

GET·DILLINGER!
$15,000 *Reward*

A PROCLAMATION

WHEREAS, One John Dillinger stands charged officially with numerous felonies including murder in several states and his banditry and depredation stamp him as an outlaw, a fugitive from justice and a vicious menace to life and property;

NOW, THEREFORE, We, Paul McNutt, Governor of Indiana; George White, Governor of Ohio; F. B. Olson, Governor of Minnesota; William A. Comstock, Governor of Michigan; and Henry Horner, Governor of Illinois, do hereby proclaim and offer a reward of Five Thousand Dollars ($5,000.00) to, be paid to the person or persons who apprehend and deliver the said John Dillinger into the custody of any sheriff of any of the above-mentioned states or his duly authorized agent.

THIS IS IN ADDITION TO THE $10,000.00 OFFERED BY THE FEDERAL GOVERNMENT FOR THE ARREST OF JOHN DILLINGER.

HERE IS HIS FINGERPRINT CLASSIFICATION and DESCRIPTION. —— FILE THIS FOR IDENTIFICATION PURPOSES.

John Dillinger. (w) age 30 yrs., 5-8½, 160½ lbs., gray eyes, med. chest, hair, med. comp., med. build. Dayton, O., P. D. No. 10587. O. S. E. No. 559-646.

	M	9	'R	O	O	
F.P.C. (12)						
	S	14	U	OO	8	
13	10	OO	O	O		
u	R	w	w	w		
5	11	15	I	8		
u	U	u	w	u		

FRONT VIEW

Be on the lookout for this desperado. He is heavily armed and usually is protected with bullet-proof vest. Take no unnecessary chances in getting this man. He is thoroughly prepared to shoot his way out of any situation.

GET HIM
DEAD
OR ALIVE

Notify any Sheriff or Chief of Police of Indiana, Ohio, Minnesota, Michigan, Illinois.

or THIS BUREAU

SIDE VIEW

ILLINOIS STATE BUREAU OF CRIMINAL IDENTIFICATION AND INVESTIGATION
J. P. Sullivan, Supt.   Springfield, Illinois

Wanted for murder, robbery and half a dozen other felonies, Dillinger grew a moustache and altered his fingerprints with acid to escape detection.

WANTED

LESTER M. GILLIS,

aliases GEORGE NELSON, "BABY FACE" NELSON, ALEX GILLIS, LESTER GILES,

"BIG GEORGE" NELSON, "JIMMIE", "JIMMY" WILLIAMS.

On June 23, 1934, HOMER S. CUMMINGS, Attorney General of the United States, under the authority vested in him by an Act of Congress approved June 6, 1934, offered a reward of

$5,000.00

for the capture of Lester M. Gillis or a reward of

$2,500.00

for information leading to the arrest of Lester M. Gillis.

DESCRIPTION

Age, 25 years; Height, 5 feet 4-3/4 inches; Weight, 133 pounds; Build, medium; Eyes, yellow and grey slate; Hair, light chestnut; Complexion, light; Occupation, oiler.

All claims to any of the aforesaid rewards and all questions and disputes that may arise as among claimants to the foregoing rewards shall be passed upon by the Attorney General and his decisions shall be final and conclusive. The right is reserved to divide and allocate portions of any of said rewards as between several claimants. No part of the aforesaid rewards shall be paid to any official or employee of the Department of Justice.

If you are in possession of any information concerning the whereabouts of Lester M. Gillis communicate immediately by telephone or telegraph collect to the nearest office of the Division of Investigation, United States Department of Justice, the local offices of which are se forth on the reverse side of this notice.

The apprehension of Lester M. Gillis is sought in connection with the murder of Special Agent W. C. Baum of the Division of Investigation near Rhinelander, Wisconsin on April 23, 1934.

JOHN EDGAR HOOVER, DIRECTOR,
DIVISION OF INVESTIGATION,
UNITED STATES DEPARTMENT OF JUSTICE,
WASHINGTON, D. C.

June 25, 1934

Pint-sized "Baby Face" Nelson, a gunslinger for Dillinger, was sought in 10 states by 5,000 police, 300 infantrymen, the FBI and several airplanes.

George and Kate Kelly, shown both in mug shots and in a cuddly snapshot, were a husband-and-wife team.

Machine Gun Kelly and His Mrs.

George Kelly, who was so hot with a Tommy gun that he could write his name with bullets on a barn door, started out as a small-time bootlegger. He probably would have stayed small had it not been for the ambition of his wife, Kathryn, an ex-manicurist. Kate pressured her husband into moving up to high-powered capers like bank robbery, kidnaping and murder, and enhanced his prestige among fellow crooks by passing out empty shell casings from his machine gun as souvenirs.

Gray-eyed and wavy-haired, Floyd was hunted by the FBI for gunning down four lawmen in Kansas City in 1933.

"Pretty Boy" Floyd

An *enfant terrible* of the underworld, Charles Floyd took up crime at age 18 by robbing a local post office of $350 in pennies. During the next 12 years he was reputed to have robbed more than 30 Midwestern banks; in 1932 his score in Oklahoma alone was so high that the state's bank insurance rates doubled. Floyd was equally adept at shooting people. The latter talent gave him such satisfaction that he filed 10 notches in his pocket watch to remind him of the number of men he had killed.

Key members of the Barker gang included "Dock" (top left), Freddie and "Ma", shown with boyfriend Arthur Dunlop.

"Ma" Barker and Her Boys

Arizona Clark "Ma" Barker, who believed in crime for the whole family, reared her four sons to be God-fearing, obedient thugs. Each Sunday she dragged them off to church; weekdays she schooled them in the finer points of thievery, kidnaping and murder. The Barkers shown here, joined by brothers Herman and Lloyd—and occasionally by other gangland luminaries—pulled off so many audacious capers, that they became the all-time leaders in major crime, family style.

WANTED FOR MURDER
JOPLIN, MISSOURI

F.P.C.29 - MO. 9
26 U 00 6

CLYDE CHAMPION BARROW, age 24, 5'7",130#,hair dark brown and
wavy,eyes hazel,light complexion,home West Dallas,Texas.
This man killed Detective Harry McGinnis and Constable
J.W. Harryman in this city,April 13, 1933.

BONNIE PARKER   CLYDE BARROW   CLYDE BARROW

This man is dangerous and is known to have committed the following
murders: Howard Hall, Sherman, Texas; J.N.Bucher,Hillsboro, Texas;
a deputy sheriff at Atoka, Okla; deputy sheriff at West Dallas,
Texas; also a man at Belden, Texas.
    The above photos are kodaks taken by Barrow and his com-
panions in various poses,and we believe they are better for
identification than regular police pictures.
    Wire or write any information to the

                    Police Department.

The Barrow gang's fondness for hamming in front of a Kodak made identification easier for pursuing lawmen.

Bonnie and Clyde

The most sadistic of the decade's hoods, Clyde Barrow shot down people for the sheer love of killing. He embarked on a murder-and-robbery
spree through Missouri, Texas and Oklahoma with his moll, cigar-
chomping Bonnie Parker, and a succession of young men. Ill-tempered
and somewhat effeminate, Barrow was generally despised by other
Midwestern bandits, who felt that his haphazard killings and frequently bungled robberies lowered the standards of the profession.

Clear-eyed, attentive, all his energies focused on the task at hand, Director J. Edgar Hoover of the FBI pursues a hot lead over the telephone.

The Hero Cop

In the decade's running battle between the law and those who broke it, one man emerged as a living folk hero of law enforcement. He was J. Edgar Hoover, the robust, iron-jawed supersleuth who headed the Federal Bureau of Investigation. "Pick a small boy these days and ask him who of all the people in the world he wants to be like," wrote the New York *World-Telegram* in 1936, "and ten to one he will reply—J. Edgar Hoover."

Hoover was the perfect hero. Nearly six feet tall, sturdily built, with penetrating, coal-black eyes and thick, wiry hair, he seemed the very image of clean-living, hard-driving Americanism. His walk was brisk and military. When he spoke, his words came out in crisp, staccato bursts, like the rattle of a Tommy gun. As he led his crack army of some 600 hand-picked G-men against the underworld, taking on such daredevil outlaws as John Dillinger and "Pretty Boy" Floyd, the nation's top cop seemed far more dashing than the top robbers he was out to catch.

Hoover fought crime with a vitality that was almost compulsive. "The Director," as he liked being called, would tackle a dozen fast-breaking cases at once, shooting a barrage of teletype messages to his 37 field offices about the country, barking orders over his battery of telephones, while at the same time writing his own speeches and reports and handling much of the Bureau's correspondence himself. Sometimes, as when he nabbed Alvin (Old Creepy) Karpis, one-time paramour of the matronly killer "Ma" Barker, the Director would strap on his .45 and charge in at the head of his troops to personally arrest a particularly notorious crook.

The Director's close associates professed themselves to be awed by his energy. "When a big case is on he has often sat at his desk for 72 hours at a stretch," marveled a friend, writer Herbert Corey; and Hoover's boss, Attorney General Homer Cummings, warned him: "You will burn yourself out." But Director Hoover refused to let up. "The job is never done," he would exclaim, in one of the manly clichés that spiced his conversations.

No Boy Scout had fewer vices than the FBI chief. He hardly ever smoked, drank only moderately and was never known to tell an off-color story. His principal diversions were awesomely wholesome and American: baseball and fishing. He had a weakness for boardinghouse gourmandizing, a hearty platter of corned beef and cabbage being his favorite. But he tried to make up for it with a regimen of weight-lifting and light-footed gymnastics at the FBI gym. His only visible eccentricity—a fondness for collecting delicate blown glass and other early American antiques—was itself a model of dedicated patriotism.

On those rare evenings when he was not working late at the Bureau, Hoover would stay at home in his study, reading law enforcement comic strips, such as *Dick Tracy* and *Secret Agent X-9*, or browsing through Jack London's adventure stories. A bachelor, he lived with his elderly mother and pet dog in the same modest frame house in Washington, D.C., where in 1895 he had been born. His few close friends were mostly FBI staffers such as office assistant Clyde Tolson and gun expert Frank Baughman. He had never been known to take a girl on a date. Such fri-

We cannot forget that an army of 200,000 persons who will commit murder before they die roams America.

J. EDGAR HOOVER TO THE HOLY NAME SOCIETY, 1936

volity might give the FBI a bad name; and in any case the Director had little time for romance. For he was wedded to his work, and the FBI was a jealous wife.

Hoover's love affair with the FBI had been a hot item years before the decade began. A George Washington Law School graduate, he became Special Assistant to Attorney General Mitchell A. Palmer in 1919, and two years later he was appointed Assistant Director of the embryo FBI. At that time the Bureau was a relatively obscure branch of the Justice Department. It had been set up in 1908 as the Attorney General's private gumshoe operation, at one point reportedly being used by Teddy Roosevelt to snoop on opposition Senators. By the 1920s, it was still handling only such mundane tasks as uncovering federal bank frauds and pursuing violators of the anti-prostitution Mann Act. When the Directorship fell vacant in 1924, the vigorous 29-year-old Hoover succeeded to the top spot.

The new Director began immediately to throw his weight around. The organization he headed had degenerated into a shambles during the Harding era. In fact, the entire Department of Justice had become known as the Department of Easy Virtue. Harding's Attorney General, Harry M. Daugherty, had used the Bureau to give

I shall continue to direct the attention of the American public toward the filthy mess which sentimentalists, influenced political appointees, persons of inefficiency and others afflicted with an itching palm have made of parole.   HOOVER IN *PERSONS IN HIDING,* 1936

jobs to party hacks, no matter how bizarre their qualifications. One man had been handed an agent's badge for supplying chorus girls to a top administration official, another for singing ribald songs outside the Justice Department building during lunch hour. Many agents had close underworld contacts; some were ex-convicts, others engaged in wholesale graft and bootlegging. One particularly unsavory federal sleuth was Gaston B. Means, an expert at conning rich widows. He had been indicted once, for forging the will of an elderly matron who owned a fortune in timber. Later, during the Lindbergh kidnaping, he scandalized the nation by bilking $100,000 out of a dowager who had hired him to find the missing baby.

Hoover's first major official act was to fire a third of the Bureau, beginning with Means. ("The man had always disgusted me," he said.) "The Bureau must be divorced from politics and not a catch-all for political hacks," Hoover intoned. "Appointments must be made on merit."

He then decreed stiff qualifications for Bureau employees. All agents would need a degree in law or accounting and would have to pass a competitive entrance exam. A character check then scratched all but the "decent, honorable, respectable young men." "We can't afford merely to be right," Hoover said. "We must give every *appearance* of doing right to avoid criticism."

The appearance the new agents did give was unimpeachably clean cut. "One somehow gets an impression that they are just hoping that some ruffian will make a slurring remark about motherhood or some such sacred subject, so that they can toss him into the gutter with a jujitsu flick of the wrist," observed the *New Yorker* in 1937.

Before becoming full-fledged agents, applicants were subjected to a tough, three-month training course in crime-fighting techniques devised by Hoover. They were also handed a code of conduct which, among other strait-laced admonitions, warned against taking a drink on duty. A bit of FBI folklore held that if ever an agent's thirst got too great, he would go to his hotel room, pull the curtains, lock the door and hang his coat over the keyhole. He would then flick out the lights, creep under the bed and take his nip. Having imbibed, he would turn the lights back on, go to the bureau, stare deep into the mirror and say, "You're a liar. I did not."

With the rules laid down, the young Director began to run his Washington office like a military command post. "When he is aroused his voice cracks like a teamster's whip," observed one reporter. His field agents were on call 24 hours a day, and Hoover sent out special inspectors who dropped in unannounced to check on his men. When working on a hot case every G-man was required to phone Washington hourly, so that Hoover could spot their positions with pins on a wall map opposite his desk.

By 1930 the hard-driving Director had turned his Bureau into the most effective crime-fighting machine since the invention of the six-gun. He had gathered a file of some three million fingerprints at a time when most local police forces still identified miscreants by complicated and highly fallible measurements of their skull and arm bones. Another Hoover innovation was a crime laboratory for examining car tracks, expended bullets, blood stains, hair, fabric, and other shreds of evidence.

Despite all this super-organization, in early 1932, hardly anyone outside the government had yet heard of the FBI. Its jurisdiction was still limited by law to substantially the same dreary federal chores, so that Hoover's sleek bloodhounds, like their sleazy predecessors, spent most of their time on the trail of prostitutes, chiselers and violators of such arcane statutes as the Migratory Birds Act. Even in this limited area the G-men could not make arrests, but had to call the local cops for the pinch. Nor were the Feds permitted to carry guns.

Then, quite suddenly, the nation was jolted by a series of spectacular crimes, beginning with the Lindbergh kidnaping *(page 100)*. A whole new race of hoodlums *(pages 101-107)* seemed to rise up, and alarming statistics began to appear in the news: America had the highest homicide rate in the civilized world; the nation's banks were being robbed at the rate of two a day; crime was costing each American $140 a year. And the Justice Department claimed that there were 400,000 hoods loose in America.

Furthermore, state and local police were simply not able to cope with the epidemic of kidnapings, bank robberies, homicides and extortion rackets. Often, while tracking down a gang, the cops would find that the quarry had slipped into the next state and hence out of their jurisdiction. Clearly, something radical needed to be done. The worst alarmists suggested that martial law be declared and the Army called in. J. Edgar Hoover had a better idea: his FBI was ready and able to tackle the job. All he needed was an okay from Congress, removing the limitations on FBI tactics and enlarging the number of federal crimes on which the Bureau could act.

Moving quickly, Congress in mid-1932 passed the "Lindbergh Law" which for all practical purposes made

---

Here is a battle between priceless God-fearing principles on the one hand and pagan ideals and godlessness on the other. . . . In these troubled days, when you strengthen the hand of law enforcement, you add power to the muscles of liberty.

HOOVER TO *TIME* MAGAZINE, 1939

---

snatching a federal crime, thus allowing the G-men to chase kidnapers. Other new laws followed. Robberies of national banks, thefts of more than $5,000 carried out across state lines, illegal use of telephone and telegraph wires, assaults on federal officers and crossing state lines to avoid testifying in court were all made federal offen-

ses. Virtually any other type of crime that crossed a state line became fair game for the G-men. Furthermore, the bans against making arrests and carrying firearms were lifted, and the G-men began to trade shot for shot with the best of the gunslinging hoodlums.

Moving at a full gallop, Hoover's posse of crimebusters began running down desperadoes. They quickly nailed:
- John Dillinger, Public Enemy No. 1. A Chicago brothel-keeper betrayed Dillinger to the Feds and in July of 1934, in front of a Chicago movie house, an attack force led by G-man Melvin Purvis gunned him down.
- "Baby Face" Nelson, a particularly vicious pal of Dillinger's. Nelson was spotted while driving through a Chicago suburb in November 1934. During the ensuing gun battle he was fatally wounded, but he also took the lives of the two federal agents who were arresting him.
- Charles "Pretty Boy" Floyd—shot to death while battling G-men on an Ohio farm in October 1934.
- Arizona Clark "Ma" Barker, who died with her son Freddie while trying to outshoot federal agents besieging her hideout in Oklawaha, Florida, in 1935.
- George "Machine Gun" Kelly, who was responsible for giving the federal investigators their nickname. In 1933 Hoover's agents, seeking Kelly for the kidnaping of Oklahoma City oilman Charles F. Urschel, crashed into his hideout to arrest him. He yelled, "Don't shoot, G-men, don't shoot!" Asked why he had called them "G-men," he said it was short for Government men.

Others, less notorious but no less colorful, fell to the G-men. There was, for one, "Bla Bla the Black Man," who ran a car-theft ring in Brooklyn and shipped so many stolen autos to Europe that at one point he flooded the market, and prices fell. Brooklyn police could pin nothing on him. But the FBI was called in and unearthed the cable address the master car-thief used in his European export business. Bla Bla was hauled in and convicted, and insurance on cars in Brooklyn dropped 15 per cent.

As the record mounted, Hoover and his agents became the heroes of the day. "The nation has waited with the patience of a Job for this hour," extolled the St. Louis *Post*

Dispatch. "In a determined Department of Justice backed by the resources of the national Government, gangsters face an invincible foe." Hollywood got into the act, and in 1935 Warner Brothers premiered *G-Men*, in which James Cagney as the intrepid agent brought to justice the nation's worst public enemy and got the girl as well. (The latter feat was not generally considered part of the job for real live G-men, as the Director's own opinion of women as companions had not thawed.) Meanwhile, small boys all over the country began wearing tin G-man badges, toting toy Tommy guns, wearing G-man underwear and sleeping in G-man pajamas. Hoover himself was showered with honorary degrees from colleges ranging in renown from New York University to Kalamazoo College in Michigan. Other honors bestowed upon him included a Distinguished Service Medal offered by the Boys Clubs of America and the Order of the Star of Romania.

Warming to the glare of the limelight, the tight-lipped Hoover climbed the lecture platform to make pronouncements on virtually anything that occurred to him. For example, he told one audience that mothers who played bridge instead of minding the kids were responsible for a rising tide of juvenile delinquency. The Director hurled rhetorical vitriol at the nation's criminals, calling them "mad dogs with guns in their hands and murder in their hearts," and "scum from the boiling pot of the underworld." "Don't call or refer to the country's outstanding criminals as 'public enemies,'" he warned the graduating class at the University of Maryland in 1936. "I suggest that they be called 'public rats.'"

In the course of his scoldings, the Director summoned up fresh batches of wildly fluctuating scare statistics. In March 1936 he referred to the "armed forces of crime which number more than 3 million." Three months later he set the figure at 500,000, "a whole half-million of armed thugs, murderers, thieves, firebugs, assassins, robbers and hold-up men." Some six months after that, the army of crime had zoomed back up to 3.5 million.

The Director also tried his hand at writing. In 1938 he published *Persons in Hiding*, an account of some of the Bu-

reau's more notable successes. Though the public bought thousands of copies, reviewers gave it a drubbing for its preachy tone and stylistic pomposities. "If he is writing he never calls fishing 'fishing,'" Cal Tinney declared in the New York *Post*. "To him it's 'piscatorial diversion.'"

Undaunted, Hoover intensified his fire in a new broadside of speeches aimed not only at crooks, but at anyone who, he felt, sympathized with them. This included "shyster lawyers and other legal vermin," "sob-sister judges," political liberals and other "sentimental moo-cows" who believed in lightening the sentences of "criminal jackals." He also had some choice words for professional politicians: "The bullets of the underworld are today poisoned by the verdigris of politics."

It was remarks like these that first threatened to trip up the sure-footed Director, who suddenly began to hear indignant voices from sources other than the underworld. Powerful government officials began to feel that Hoover was getting just a bit too big for his breeches. Tennessee's Senator Kenneth McKeller, in a move in 1936 to cut FBI funds, told Hoover: "It seems to me your department is just running wild." Jim Farley, President Roosevelt's Postmaster General and one-time campaign manager, was reported in 1934 by a Washington gossip columnist to have tried to get Hoover fired. Besides eliminating an ir-

Crime is a dangerous, cancerous condition which, if not curbed and beaten down, will soon eat at the very vitals of the country.
HOOVER TO THE UNIVERSITY OF MARYLAND, 1936

ritant, Farley was said to have wanted to use FBI jobs to pay off political debts. Hoover fought back by having the Postmaster General's phone tapped.

Local police officers, who had welcomed the Feds' response to their SOS a few years before, now started to complain that Hoover was grabbing too much limelight. One local news story claimed the Director was nothing but a publicity hound, a "David Belasco in a squad car."

In New York particularly, during the latter half of the decade, the FBI chief was becoming *persona summa non grata.* In December 1936 the city police and the FBI had traced bank robber and kidnaper Harry Brunette to a West Side apartment. The FBI, with Hoover in personal command, charged ahead to make the capture. In the ensuing shoot-'em-up, the G-men set fire to the building with a tear-gas grenade. And when the smoke had all blown away, firemen called to the scene claimed that the G-men had carelessly lobbed a few shots in their direction.

The bad feeling in New York came to a head in 1939, when Hoover managed to get credit for nabbing Louis "Lepke" Buchalter, Manhattan racket czar and boss of Murder, Inc. An ambitious district attorney, Tom Dewey, had been trying to nail Buchalter himself for murder, vice-peddling, and for running a multi-million-dollar extortion racket. In 1939 Dewey announced a $25,000 reward for his capture. Buchalter then became uneasy that one of his pals might turn him in to face Dewey's murder rap. The hoodlum therefore decided to surrender to the FBI, which wanted him only for drug smuggling.

To set up the pinch Buchalter called columnist Walter Winchell, a friend of Hoover's. On the night of August 24, 1939, Winchell picked up Buchalter at Madison Square, and drove him to a spot on Fifth Avenue where a black limousine was idling. The columnist escorted the racketeer to the car and introduced him to the man inside. "Mr. Hoover, this is Lepke," he said. "How do you do," said Hoover, and Buchalter responded, "Glad to meet you."

Naturally the story was splashed all over Winchell's column. And naturally, Dewey was furious at being upstaged.

Quite apart from such personal vendettas, many Americans grew concerned that the zealous Hoover might be encroaching on civil liberties. Senator George Norris of Nebraska expressed the fear in 1940 that the FBI was turning into an "American OGPU," a home-grown version of Soviet Russia's dreaded secret police. Other well-informed people remembered the 1909 rumors of Teddy Roosevelt's Senate snooping. Was it true, now, that the FBI kept secret dossiers on government officials and prominent liberals? Other skeletons were dragged from their tombs: in 1919, under Attorney General Mitchell

Palmer, the Bureau had rounded up thousands of harmless citizens, without warrants, on the suspicion that they might be Communists or anarchists. People also recalled that the man who prosecuted the suspects had been Palmer's eager young assistant—J. Edgar Hoover. Now, toward the end of the '30s, the Justice Department was again in full cry against various radicals. Would there be a repeat of the Palmer raids?

Never, Hoover declared: "The FBI will always strive to preserve the civil liberties of every American citizen.

Intellectual license and debauchery is un-American. In righteous indignation it is time to drive the debauchers of America out in the open.

HOOVER TO THE NATIONAL CONVENTION OF THE AMERICAN LEGION, 1940

We can never become [an OGPU] or a Gestapo." His detractors had "mental halitosis," he claimed, and the campaign to malign him was a Red plot: "Communists at a meeting yesterday in New York have instructed two of their best writers to portray me as a Broadway glamor-boy and particularly to inquire into my affairs with women in New York," he told TIME magazine in 1940.

Aside from such noisily satisfying counterfire, Hoover could take solace from the fact that, in an era when there was still a fairly clear line between the good guys and the bad guys, most ordinary Americans admired him and shared his beliefs about the need for law and order. His hard-handed campaign against the Communists and, of course, fascists—which he called "two twin horrid, spectral growths of alien soil and an alien spirit," seemed justifiable during the uncertain days when a second world war was gathering momentum in Europe. But at the close of the decade the Director maintained that he derived his greatest comfort from a framed text which he kept on top of the radio in his office, and which read in part:

"In every field of human endeavor, he that is first must perpetually live in the white light of publicity. . . . When a man's work becomes a standard for the whole world, it also becomes a target for the shafts of the envious few."

F.D.R.

ABOLISH BREAD LINES
VOTE FOR
ROOSEVELT

F.D.R. campaigns in Indianapolis, October 1932.

That Man in the White House

Never was there such a change in the transfer of a government. The President is the boss, the dynamo, the works.
ARTHUR KROCK IN *THE NEW YORK TIMES*, MARCH 12, 1933

When Franklin D. Roosevelt became the 32nd President of the United States, the country was scared, more scared than ever in its history. That very morning, March 4, 1933, every last bank in the nation had had to close its doors. The old leaders were ashen-faced. "I'm afraid," said the chairman of Bethlehem Steel, Charles Schwab, "every man is afraid."

On the high inaugural platform in front of the Capitol, the 51-year-old President-elect repeated the oath of office in a clear, deliberate voice, looked out over the tense throng covering 10 acres of lawn and pavement and said: "This Nation asks for action, and action now." Entering his car to go to the White House, he clasped his strong hands over his head in the salute of a champion. The next morning, rolling in a wheelchair as he had since he was crippled by polio 12 years before, Roosevelt moved into the oval office of Presidents. He sat alone for a few moments, then gave a great shout for his aides and began to act, starting with a call for a special session of Congress. His emergency banking bill strengthening the nation's financial system roared through the House unchanged in 38 minutes. When the banks reopened four days later, deposits exceeded withdrawals. The immediate panic was over. The nation's confidence was beginning to return.

Sensing opportunity, F.D.R. kept the lawmakers in session. In the next 100 days, riding herd on the uneasy nation with a firmer rein than it had felt since the days of his cousin, Teddy Roosevelt, he permanently altered the conduct of American life. Fifteen major messages streamed from the White House to Capitol Hill. When Congress adjourned on June 16, fifteen new laws assured concerted government action: to employ the jobless, to develop the backward Tennessee Valley, to support crop prices, to repeal Prohibition, to stop home foreclosures, to insure bank deposits, to stabilize the economy, and more.

F.D.R. called the program a "New Deal" for the nation, but others thought it went beyond that. "We have had our revolution," said *Collier's* magazine. "We like it." The people raised their heads; even the well-to-do were at first delighted. As Roosevelt had noted, action, any kind of action, had been their plea. Kansas' Republican governor, Alf Landon, had said: "Even the iron hand of a dictator is in preference to a paralytic stroke." Now industrialist Pierre du Pont sent F.D.R. a friendly letter. And press lord William Randolph Hearst flattered F.D.R.: "I guess at your next election we will make it unanimous."

In 1934 "Vanity Fair" recorded the people's pleasure in another self-assured Rough Rider named Roosevelt who could tame the country.

F.D.R. and his wife, Eleanor, shared an abiding love but both were strong-minded. She believed he might have been happier with a less critical wife.

The Look of the New Family

The second family of Roosevelts to move into the White House within a quarter century was an exciting batch of individualists with lots of verve and offspring *(below)*. Each of F.D.R.'s children tended to go his own way, but Christmas Eve always found the clan gathered. Surrounded by grandchildren, F.D.R. read from Dickens' *A Christmas Carol*, acting out the parts of Scrooge and Tiny Tim with gusto. Next day, at Christmas dinner, he carved paper-thin slices of turkey, boasting "You can almost *read* through it." As the Presidency wore on, however, Roosevelt had less and less time for family matters. One day when a distraught son poured out his troubles, F.D.R. absently handed him a paper, saying: "This is a most important document—I should like to have your opinion on it."

A Spreading Tree

ANNA — JAMES — ELLIOTT — FRANKLIN JR. — JOHN

CURTIS DALL — JOHN BOETTIGER — BETSY CUSHING — ELIZABETH DONNER — RUTH GOOGINS — ETHEL DU PONT — ANNE CLARK

SISTIE — JOHN — SARA — WILLIAM — RUTH — FRANKLIN III

BUZZIE — KATE — ELLIOTT JR.

F.D.R.'s children tended to marry young and to reproduce often. By decade's end the record was: seven marriages, two divorces, nine youngsters.

In old sweater and flannels, F.D.R. takes James sailing on the "Amberjack II." Sailing, he told Harold Ickes, was the only way he could really rest.

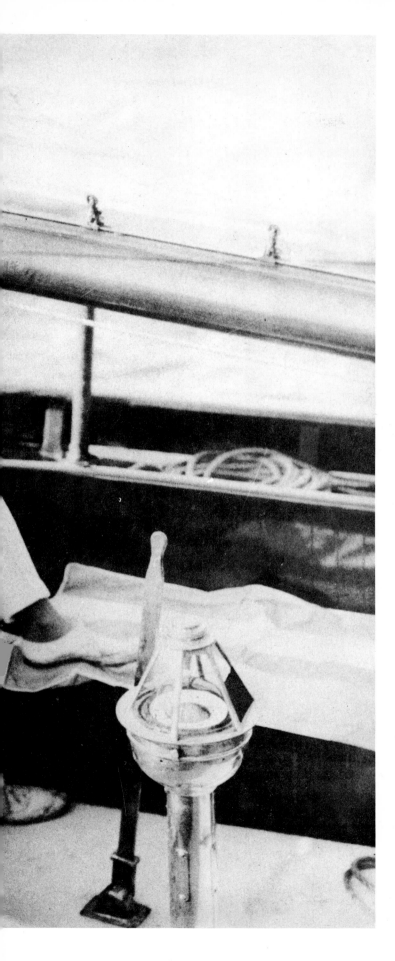

F.D.R. loved the sea. Not only did it restore him after the burdens of office but it gave him a chance to restore his relationships with his children. Joyously he wrote back from a cruise: "The boys are having a grand time and we have one continuous kidding match." In 1934 he took Franklin Jr. and John on a 14,000-mile voyage aboard the cruiser *Houston*. They ranged from Haiti to Hawaii and F.D.R. got another chance, denied him in Washington, to spend lazy hours with his boys. He reported home to his wife, who had long since given up sailing for horseback riding, "The boys are grand and really love it I think."

After a morning ride Mrs. F.D.R. plays with Sistie and Buzzie Dall.

F.D.R. howls along with (from left) son James, William McAdoo and advisor James Farley as Will Rogers gets off a sly introduction in 1932.

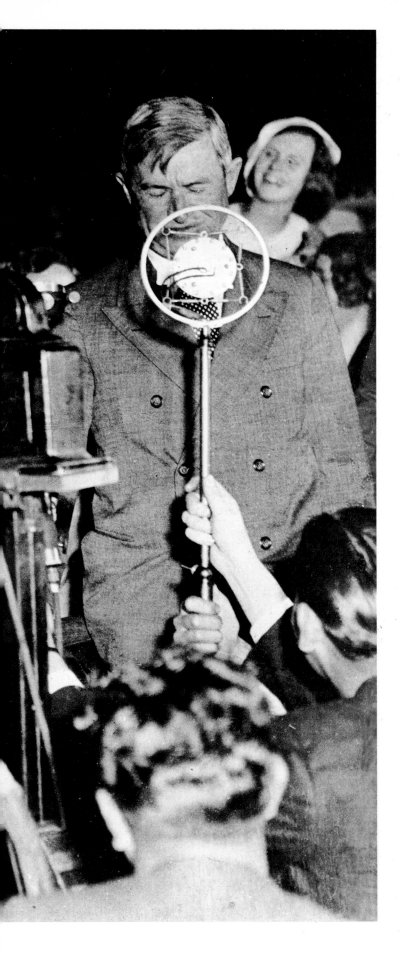

The Style of the New President

The new President surprised a lot of people. Before the election the best thinkers considered him a lightweight —"a pleasant man who, without any important qualifications, would very much like to be President," as pundit Walter Lippmann wrote. But the critics soon realized that F.D.R.'s easy quips and laughter reflected not vacuous amiability but buoyant confidence, that here was a tough-minded man with a quick grasp of what had to be done. Accordingly Lippmann, for one, ate crow: "The nation which had lost confidence in everything and everybody has regained confidence in the government and in itself."

"How do you account for him?" gasped Kansas editor William Allen White. "Was I just fooled before the election, or has he developed?" The quotations below from cowboy entertainer-philosopher Will Rogers expressed the nation's delight at the new man in the White House.

America hasn't been as happy in three years as they are today, no money, no banks, no work, no nothing, but they know they got a man in there who is wise to Congress, wise to our so-called big men. The whole country is with him, just so he does something. If he burned down the capitol, we would cheer and say "well, we at least got a fire started anyhow."

MARCH 5, 1933

Mr. Roosevelt is a terribly plain spoken man. Remember the speech that night about the banks. Long adjectives and nouns he dident mess with 'em at all. He knows what the country wants is relief and not rhetoric. He is the first Harvard man to know enough to drop three syllables when he has something to say. Why compared to me he is almost illiterate.

MAY 7, 1933

I will say one thing for this Administration. It's the only time when the fellow with money is worrying more than the one without it.

OCTOBER 3, 1933

F. D. R.

The Team

LEFT WING

REX TUGWELL	FRANCES PERKINS	HENRY WALLACE	HARRY HOPKINS	HENRY MORGENTHA
Agriculture	Labor	Agriculture	Federal Relief	Treasury

Let's concentrate upon one thing. Save the people and the nation and, if we have to change our minds twice every day to accomplish that end, we should do it.

F.D.R. TO COMMERCE SECRETARY DAN ROPER

If he became convinced tomorrow that coming out for cannibalism would get him the votes he so sorely needs, he would begin fattening a missionary in the White House backyard come Wednesday.

H.L. MENCKEN

It is almost impossible to come to grips with him.

HAROLD ICKES

The New Deal turned Washington from a placid Southern town into an exciting, pulsating seat of power and attracted all sorts of bright, opinionated men with all sorts of new ideas. They came to help F.D.R. remake America, and he reveled in their minds—listening, taking fast decisions, cutting corners. Pragmatism was the game and F.D.R. called the plays: "Take a method and try it. If it fails, try another. But above all, try something."

The team pictured in the *Vanity Fair* montage above represented F.D.R.'s lineup of key players at the end of his first year. Some were quickly benched. The favorite at this time, conservative Lewis Douglas, protested one day that failure to balance the budget meant the end of Western civilization—and was heard of no more. Some

124

RIGHT WING

| CAPTAIN FRANKLIN D. ROOSEVELT President | HUGH JOHNSON NRA | DANIEL ROPER Commerce | GEORGE PEEK Farming Controls | LEWIS DOUGLAS Budget | HAROLD ICKES Interior |

hardy souls lasted: Harold Ickes of Interior, grumpy, incorruptible; Henry Wallace of Agriculture, his farm boots in manure and his head in the clouds; hard-boiled but socially sensitive relief chief Harry Hopkins; Madame Frances Perkins of Labor, the first woman in a U.S. Cabinet.

It was a cocky team, but F.D.R. was captain and if the gang would not arrive at a conclusion, he would say: "Put them in a room and tell them no lunch."

Yet while his men and methods shifted, not so F.D.R.'s motives. As he picked his way, now turning right, now left, not hesitating to be devious when it suited him, he kept moving toward the goals in his mind—and his mind was strong and stubborn. He rammed through such controversial reforms as Social Security. As the country

began to regain confidence, however, F.D.R. found the going tougher. He suffered more defeats. But even in defeat, F.D.R. managed to keep gaining ground. Thus, though he failed in 1937 to pack the Supreme Court with liberal Justices, within months a majority of the nine-man Court, seeing the handwriting on the wall, upheld both the New Dealing Wagner Labor Act and minimum wage laws. F.D.R. kept on losing occasional yardage to an increasingly contentious Congress. Nevertheless, by the end of the decade the overall game had been won. More people had jobs, the economy was alive and breathing and, though many of the old team had departed Washington, Roosevelt was still a strong captain who had persuaded a revived country to play by his rules.

The Personal Touch

In the '30s George M. Cohan, star of the Broadway musical "I'd Rather Be Right," used to break up the audience by saying: "Bring me another fireside, I'm going on the air." Everyone knew he was joshing F.D.R.'s own personal bit of show biz—the Fireside Chats. These were informal radio talks F.D.R. delivered to the nation as Americans were relaxing after dinner. It was his favorite way of selling his programs and, in the face of Establishment and press hostility, it was indispensable in winning support for the New Deal. When F.D.R.'s calm, resonant voice intoned "My Friends," most Americans felt they were.

Inevitably, the Fireside Chats invited spoofing, some of it nasty, some as gentle as Cohan's wisecrack and the 1935 *Esquire* cartoon at right, showing F.D.R.'s wife Eleanor looking on as he broadcasts while his grandchildren badger him to hurry and get off the air. But the Fireside Chats were deadly serious, both for F.D.R. and for the country. The first one, explaining the bank crisis, was decisive in reversing the panic. Here, in part, is what people heard on their radios that evening of March 12, 1933.

I want to tell you what has been done in the last few days, why it was done, and what the next steps are going to be. First of all, let me state the simple fact that when you deposit money in a bank the bank does not put the money into a safe deposit vault. It invests your money in many different forms of credit—bonds, mortgages. In other words, the bank puts your money to work to keep the wheels turning around. A comparatively small part of the money is kept in currency—sufficient to cover the cash needs of the average citizen. In other words, the total amount of all the currency in the country is only a small fraction of the total deposits in all of the banks. What, then, happened? Because of undermined confidence, there was a general rush to turn bank deposits into currency. On the spur of the moment it was, of course, impossible to sell perfectly sound assets of a bank and convert them into cash except at panic prices far below their real value.

It was then that I issued the proclamation for the nationwide bank holiday. The second step was the legislation passed by the Congress to extend the holiday and lift the ban of that holiday gradually. This law also gave authority to develop a program of rehabilitation of our banking facilities. The new law allows the twelve Federal Reserve Banks to issue additional currency backed by actual, good assets. As a result, we start tomorrow, Monday, opening banks in the twelve Federal Reserve Bank cities—banks which have already been found to be all right. On succeeding days banks in smaller places will resume business, subject, of course, to the Government's physical ability to make common sense checkups. When the banks resume a very few people who have not recovered from their fear may again begin withdrawals. Let me make clear that the banks will take care of all needs—and it is my belief that when the people find that they can get their money the phantom of fear will soon be laid. I assure you that it is safer to keep your money in a reopened bank than under the mattress.

There will be, of course, some banks unable to open without being reorganized. The new law allows the Government to assist in making these reorganizations quickly and effectively. I do not promise you that every bank will be reopened or that individual losses will not be suffered, but there will be no losses that possibly could have been avoided; and there would have been greater losses had we continued to drift. I can even promise you salvation for some at least of the sorely pressed banks. Confidence and courage are the essentials in our plan. You must have faith; you must not be stampeded by rumors. We have provided the machinery to restore our financial system; it is up to you to support and make it work. Together we cannot fail.

AW, GEE, GRAN'POP, YOU'RE RUNNIN' OVER INTO ED WYNN'S PROGRAM!

The Alphabet Agencies: NRA

As F.D.R. put his New Deal into effect, Congress spawned dozens of acts and agencies to carry the government's new burdens. Given long names, these organizations became known by their initials, which, added together, made up an entire alphabet of recovery measures. The office that excited the fiercest partisanship was the NRA (National Recovery Administration), created to regulate wages, working hours and, indirectly, prices.

Most ordinary Americans greeted NRA enthusiastically. Posters with the Blue Eagle symbol were splashed everywhere, and big cities staged monster rallies to show support of the NRA codes. In New York, 250,000 people marched up Fifth Avenue to the music of 200 bands. In Tulsa, the hometown of NRA director Hugh Johnson, his 77-year-old mother led a parade and warned: "People had better obey the NRA because my son will enforce it like lightning, and you can never tell when lightning will strike." As columnist Heywood Broun prophesied, these parades had a lasting issue of new hope and confidence: "When a line forms and your shoulder touches that of a fellow and a comrade, solidarity is about to be born."

Nevertheless, New Deal opponents kept up a barrage of criticism. Businessmen damned NRA as "creeping socialism," while union men called it "business fascism." The Hearst newspapers suggested bitterly that what the initials NRA really stood for was: "No Recovery Allowed."

The NRA emblem appeared on any usable empty space.

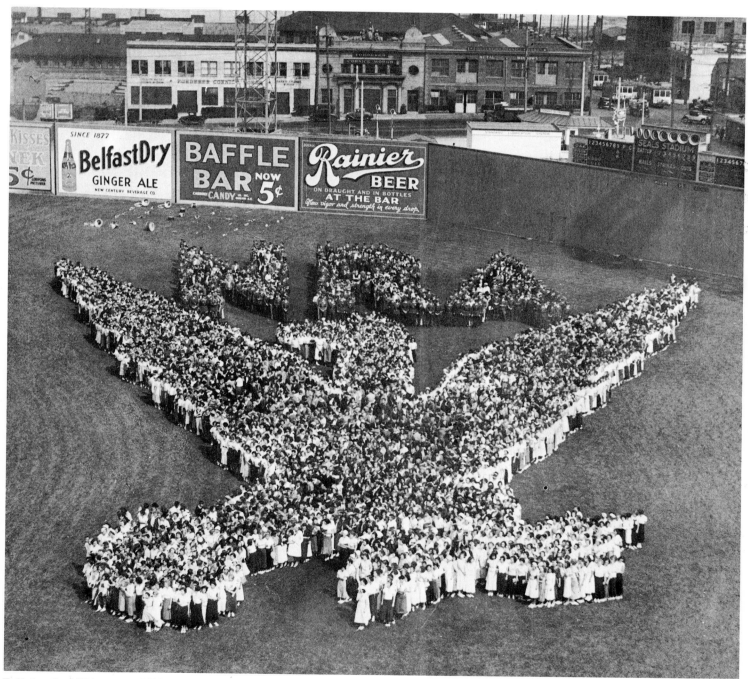

Rallying for NRA, 8,000 children form a giant eagle in a San Francisco ball park. Such public support fostered compliance with NRA codes.

CCC boys give three cheers at Camp Dix, New Jersey, after their first day. The average enlistee was a 20-year-old from a large family on relief.

CCC

Not even the angriest opponents of the New Deal had much to say against the good works initiated by the CCC (Civilian Conservation Corps). In its nine years of existence, the CCC took some 2.5 million young men from the ranks of the unemployed, paid them $30 a month (most of it automatically sent to the home folks) and put them to work planting 200 million trees, fighting pine-twig blight and Dutch elm disease, digging drainage ditches and fish ponds, building firebreaks and reservoirs, clearing beaches and camping grounds, and even restoring historic battlefields. This massive effort of conservation and reforestation benefited not only the nation but the boys themselves. One declared, "It made a man of me all right." Said another man: "If a boy wants to go and get a job after he's been in the C's, he'll know how to work."

The U.S. Army and the Forest Service jointly supervised the CCC.

PWA

To make jobs and stimulate business, F.D.R. in 1933 convinced Congress to create the federally financed PWA (Public Works Administration)—and thereby changed the face of America. Armies of workmen for PWA built a water supply system for Denver; a flood control system for Ohio's Muskingum Valley; a port for Brownsville, Texas; roads and bridges connecting Key West with the Florida mainland. A sampling of other PWA projects appears on these pages—but only a small sampling. Between 1933 and 1939 PWA invested more than six billion dollars and 4.75 billion man-hours of labor in constructing about 10 per cent of all the new transportation facilities built in the United

States during the period, 35 per cent of the new hospitals and health facilities, 65 per cent of the city halls and courthouses and sewage disposal plants, and 70 per cent of all educational buildings.

Because these projects were slow in developing, F.D.R. complemented PWA with a nominally confusing addition to his alphabet soup, the WPA (Works Progress Administration). The main difference between the two agencies was that PWA simply financed the projects, whereas WPA handled the entire operation. In addition, WPA found a new way to use its huge appropriations by making the federal government a big-time patron of the arts (overleaf).

MUNICIPAL FERRYBOAT, NEW YORK CITY

ELECTRIFICATION OF PENNSYLVANIA RAILROAD

PAVILION, HUNTINGTON BEACH, CALIFORNIA

WORK SHED, GRAND CANYON NATIONAL PARK

MENTAL HOSPITAL, CAMARILLO, CALIFORNIA

SAN FRANCISCO FAIR CONSTRUCTION

LINCOLN TUNNEL, NEW YORK—NEW JERSEY

GOLD DEPOSITORY, FORT KNOX, KENTUCKY

TRIBOROUGH BRIDGE, NEW YORK CITY

MALL, WASHINGTON, D.C.

PRISON FARM, TATTNALL COUNTY, GEORGIA

BOULDER DAM, COLORADO RIVER

ZOO, WASHINGTON, D.C.

SWIMMING POOL, WHEELING, WEST VIRGINIA

BAND SHELL, PHOENIX, ARIZONA

WATER TANK, SACRAMENTO, CALIFORNIA

FLORAL CONSERVATORY, ST. LOUIS

FEDERAL TRADE COMMISSION, WASHINGTON, D.C.

WPA

Following the thesis that whenever possible a jobless man should be put in his own line of work, the WPA recruited thousands of unemployed artists and assigned them to projects paying up to $94.90 a month. Composers composed; musical anthropologists toured backwoods America recording folk songs; actors for the Federal Theatre entertained some 30 million people with shows. By decade's end, a whole generation of painters and writers had served its apprenticeship on the WPA. Admittedly, some artists were assigned work of questionable value. One writer made his bread and butter by taking a census of dogs in California's Monterey Peninsula. In 1939 the name of that writer and of his first major novel became household words: John Steinbeck and *The Grapes of Wrath*.

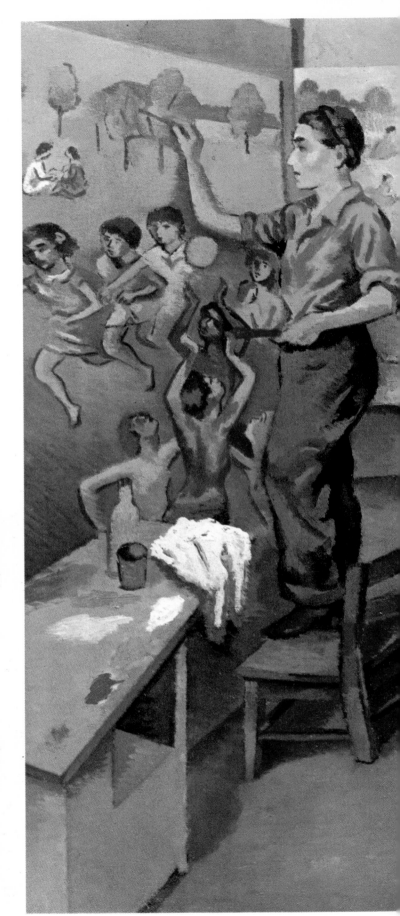

Actors sing in "The Swing Mikado," one of 1,200 WPA productions.

WPA artists are depicted at work by colleague Moses Soyer. Other WPA painters were Jackson Pollock, Willem de Kooning and Ben Shahn.

Cheers and Catcalls

Nobody in the '30s ever said he just guessed F.D.R. was doing okay. People either loved or hated him with a passion. Daily, 5,000 to 8,000 letters, many warmly personal, came flooding into the White House, a tenfold increase over Hoover days. To the little people who wrote these letters, Roosevelt was a personal savior. On the other hand, more prosperous citizens saw Roosevelt as the very devil, and the nation's press, 85 per cent anti-F.D.R., went to absurd lengths to hand the devil what-for. Switchboard operators at the Chicago *Tribune* answered phones before the 1936 election with an ominous: "Do you know there are only -- days to save your country?"

Love him or hate him, the nation was more aware of F.D.R. than of any previous President. This awareness is reflected in the letters excerpted below from the White House mail bag and in the newspaper columns and editorials at right. Some of these anti-F.D.R. comments were pretty rough. A Westbrook Pegler column made Roosevelt's sons so angry they planned literally to horsewhip Pegler until their father calmly talked them out of it. When F.D.R. got their grudging promise to desist, he laughed, saying: "Not that it isn't a grand idea—'in principle'!"

Dear Mr. President:

This is just to tell you that everything is all right now. The man you sent found our house all right, and we went down to the bank with him and the mortgage can go on for a while longer. You remember I wrote you about losing the furniture too. Well, your man got it back for us. I never heard of a President like you.

My dear sir,

It is expensive and a headache to have a playboy as President. Wipe that grin off your face.

Dear President Roosevelt:

I'm proud of our United States and every time I hear the "Star-Spangled Banner" I feel a lump in my throat. There ain't no other nation in the world that would have sense enough to think of WPA and all the other A's.

Mr. President:

If you could get around the country as I have and seen the distress forced upon the American people, you would throw your damn NRA and AAA, and every other God-Damn A into the sea, before you and your crooked crowd are taken out as they are in Germany, and that is just what you and the rest deserve. You are not for the poor nor the middle class, but for the rich, the monopolies, Jewry, and perhaps Communism.

Dear Honored Mr. Roosevelt:

I never saw a President I would write to until youve got in your place, but I have always felt like you and your wife and your children were as common as we were.

Dear Pres. Roosevelt

How's our dandy little quarterback tonight? Our little "planner that wayer", eh? What's become of the "happy days are here again" boys? F. Depression Roosevelt. They tell me that you have no brains or mind of your own—that you are just a "Charlie McCarthy" for a couple of smarties called Cohen and Corcoran or Kelly or something. That's a terrible blow—to find out that our big, noble savior of the common peepul is nothing but a stooge.

The Chief instructs that the phrase Soak the Successful be used in all references to the Administration's tax program instead of the phrase Soak the Thrifty hitherto used, also he wants the words Raw Deal used instead of New Deal.

EXECUTIVE DICTUM TO HEARST EDITORS, 1935

New York, Oct. 28.—Confidence that President Roosevelt will be reelected pervades the headquarters of the communist party. Based on that confidence is the high optimism of communist leaders that another four years of the New Deal will bring them within striking distance of the overthrow of the American form of government and the substitution therefor of a communist state.

ARTHUR SEARS HENNING, CHICAGO *TRIBUNE*, OCTOBER 29, 1936

Mr. Roosevelt himself never spent a day in a public school in all his life. When Mr. Roosevelt had done with nurse and tutors he went to a dude school named Groton, which prepared him for Harvard, and after he had married and taken his bride for a honeymoon tour of England, France, Italy and Germany they returned home for him to go to Columbia Law School. "My mother-in-law," writes Mrs. Roosevelt in her book, "had taken a home for us. She had furnished it and engaged our servants. In summer we visited my mother-in-law at Hyde Park for a time and then went up to stay with her at Campobello. My husband sailed up and down the coast in the little schooner 'Half Moon' and took short cruises." In 1908 the President's mother thought their little house too small and therefore bought a plot in New York and built another for them. Later she also gave to Franklin Roosevelt and his young wife an estate on Campobello Island.

For Mr. Roosevelt to sail his own schooner around Fundy when he had never yet assumed the task of supporting his own wife unassisted was all right, but let some other man cock a funny cap over his eye and toss off such words as "Ahoy!" "Port!" and "Starboard!" on a yacht bought with his own money in enjoyment of his own success and he is not merely ridiculous but an enemy of the great common people of whom the President is paradoxically one. There are those who called Mr. Roosevelt a traitor to his class, but that cry comes from the hereditary rich who grew up endowed and, as he did, looked to their mothers and fathers for support and luxuries long after they had ceased to be children. The class that I have in mind are proud to have taken care of their own parents, and every crack from him about well-fed clubmen and economic royalists evokes from them the soul-satisfying and contemptuous taunt, "mama's boy."

THE DISSENTING OPINIONS OF MISTER WESTBROOK PEGLER, 1938

If the New Deal goes on to the only destination it can have, this may be the last presidential election America will have. It is tragic that America fails to see that the New Deal is to America what the early phase of Nazism was to Germany and the early phase of Fascism to Italy.

MARK SULLIVAN, BUFFALO *EVENING NEWS*, NOVEMBER 16, 1935

The President of the United States has smeared businessmen. His smearing of the newspapers has become one of his confirmed habits, joyously adopted by the radicals in the Cabinet and the pinks among the White House intimates. We have seen the Administration smear the doctors and we have seen it smear the lawyers. There has been a flood of smearing books, ranging from economic volumes revealing the iniquities of our alleged "ruling families" to exaggerated novels calculated to stir the emotions of uninformed and credulous people. The whole smearing game seems to have become a more or less deliberate attempt to destroy respect for the social order and faith in the American economic system by untruth, half-truth and misrepresentation.

FRANK R. KENT, BALTIMORE *SUN*, AUGUST 24, 1939

"*Come along. We're going to the Trans-Lux to hiss Roosevelt.*"

While some of the anti-F.D.R. talk was vicious, most of the protests over the President were reasonably mild and sort of funny. One thing that made them funny was that they erupted among such dignified, genteel people. The mood of disapproval among the gentility was caught beau-tifully by the *New Yorker* magazine both in Peter Arno's cartoon *(left)* and in humorist Frank Sullivan's compila-tion *(excerpted below)* of polite anti-F.D.R. jargon as de-livered by one Mr. Arbuthnot, the Cliché Expert. Note: Mr. Arbuthnot was imaginary, but his clichés were not.

Mr. Arbuthnot: *No sir! Nobody is going to tell ME how to run my business.*

Q: *Mr. Arbuthnot, you sound like a Roosevelt hater.*

A: *I certainly am.*

Q: *Perhaps you could give us an idea of some of the clichés your set is in the habit of using in speaking of Mr. Roosevelt. . . .*

A: *Well, we call him That Madman in the White House, or That Fellow Down in Washington. Sometimes we call him MIS-TER Roosevelt, or Your FRIEND, Franklin D.—like that.*

Q: *Sort of sarcastic, eh?*

A: *And how! Now don't misunderstand me. I'm a liberal. I'm in favor of a lot of the reforms Roosevelt has been trying to put over, but I don't like the way he's going about it.*

Q: *For instance?*

A: *Well, you take the Supreme Court. Where Roosevelt made his big mistake was in attacking the Court.*

Q: *I see.*

A: *And where Roosevelt made his big mistake was in arousing all this class hatred. You know, all this forgotten-man stuff.*

Q: *Yes.*

A: *And where Roosevelt made his big mistake was in all this pump priming. You can't spend your way out of a depression.*

Q: *Really?*

A: *Certainly not. Where's the money coming from to pay for all this—this—*

Q: *Do you mean "orgy of spending"?*

A: *That's just the phrase I was searching for.*

Q: *What about the WPA, Mr. Arbuthnot?*

A: *Oh, the shovel brigade. I'm against the WPA and all this al-phabet-soup stuff. Say, did you hear about the WPA worker and King Solomon? Why is a WPA worker like King Solomon?*

Q: *I heard it. Now then—*

A: *Because he takes his pick and goes to bed. . . .*

Q: *Mr. Arbuthnot, you slay me. Well, go on. Tell us more.*

A: *Well, the trouble with Roosevelt is he's an idealist.*

Q: *Yes?*

A: *And the trouble is he's destroyed individual initiative.*

Q: *Do tell.*

A: *And he's a Communist.*

Q: *I see. Go on.*

A: *The trouble with Roosevelt is he's a Fascist.*

Q: *A Fascist, too?*

A: *Certainly. He wants to be a dictator.*

Q: *Mr. Arbuthnot, your comments have been confined to Mr. Roosevelt's policies. Have you, as an expert in the jargon of the Roosevelt haters, anything to say about his personal life?*

A: *Have I? Oh boy! Why, he's a rich man's son. He never did a tap of work in his life. Where does HE get off, posing as a cham-pion of the people?*

Q: *A traitor to his class, eh?*

A: *Oh, we don't use that chestnut any more. It's out of date.*

FRANK SULLIVAN IN *THE NEW YORKER* MAGAZINE, JUNE 18, 1938

Undismayed by his critics, a relaxed F.D.R. radiates confidence. "He must have been psychoanalyzed by God," declared an awed associate.

Café Society

A Conga line snakes through revelers at New York's Rainbow Room.

Something Old, Something New

I'm established now for '38

With the title of glamor and reprobate.

I've won a position in Vogue and Harper's;

For a hundred bucks I'll advertise garters.

I grit my teeth and smile at my enemies;

I sit at the Stork Club and talk to nonentities.

"GLAMOR GIRL SERENADE" BY BRENDA FRAZIER, 1938

When most of the country hit rock bottom, old-fashioned High Society foundered along with it. Out of the rubble of Newport and Fifth Avenue, however, emerged some survivors who joined a pack of movie stars and gossip columnists and various hangers-on to create something new: a glittering, publicity-mad, indefatigable set called "Café Society." The "cafés" where this group sported were the old speak-easies, which after Prohibition was repealed in 1933 were reborn as chic restaurants: New York's Stork Club, El Morocco, "21," and the like.

The queen of the new gentlefolk was Brenda Frazier, heiress granddaughter of social arbiter Lady Williams-Taylor and so-called Glamor Girl of 1938. On any given night Brenda might be seen dining with her latest beau at the Colony. On such an evening, the table next to Brenda's would be presided over by someone like Grand Duchess Marie, cousin to Russia's last czar and now a commercial photographer. The Duchess, a formidable presence in her own right, usually appeared with a clutch of other deposed Europeans: Prince Serge Obolensky, who ran a restaurant at the St. Regis Hotel; and Princess Ketto Mikeladze, the negligée buyer at Elizabeth Arden's. Occasionally the expatriate crowd would admit into their presence their dear friend, red-hot mama Sophie Tucker.

Such egalitarianism was typical of the new free-for-all, in which Astors, Vanderbilts and Whitneys mixed with popular entertainers, while English titleholders sipped cocktails with advertising executives. Marrying and divorcing were equally indiscriminate: women bore names such as "Mrs. Margaret Emerson-McKim-Vanderbilt-Baker-Amory-Emerson" and "Mrs. Millicent Rogers-Salm-Hoogstraetan-Ramos-Balcom."

The ring-mistress of it all was Elsa Maxwell, a fat nobody from Keokuk, Iowa, who had somehow managed to meet *everybody*. She was also quite adroit at getting instant publicity for favored friends. Thus a socially ambitious new woman in town would wangle an invitation to one of Elsa's bashes. And if that same woman had a good press agent, she might finally win one of Café Society's ultimate accolades—her picture in the new picture magazine LIFE with a caption like the following classic tribute to conspicuous inconsequence: "Mrs. Orson D. Munn, who won fame in a limited circle by wearing a foxtail for a hat at the Colony Restaurant, drops in at El Morocco several times a week, is known for the spirited way she dances the rumba with her remarkably agile husband."

144

Shouting "Oy!" two dancers do the final step of the Lambeth Walk, which originated in England in 1938 and was adopted by Americans.

Sheathed in satin, Brenda Frazier models the gown she wore to her debut. The party made nationwide news; one paper crowed, "Bow's A Wow."

The Ultimate Glamor Girl

The fame of the stars of Café Society went far beyond their own set; at 17, Brenda Frazier was one of the most celebrated personalities in the whole country. Miss Frazier modestly pretended to be astonished by the big fuss: "I don't deserve all this. I haven't done anything at all. I'm just a debutante."

It was true. She hadn't done a thing—except dance every night till five in the morning with scores of men, including Bruce Cabot and Douglas Fairbanks Jr., and pose at the flash of a bulb for any photographer in sight.

Brenda epitomized the Glamor Girl, the idealized woman of the decade. Her extraordinarily pale skin contrasted sharply with her vermilion lipstick, black hair and pencilled eyebrows. She also made the strapless evening gown *(page 150)* a national fad. Although she was due to inherit four million dollars when she was 21, Brenda found it fun to pose for Woodbury Soap ads.

During her big year as 1938's No. 1 Glamor Girl, Brenda worked on 15 charity committees and served as the chairman of an enormous bash called the Velvet Ball. The high point of her brief and spectacular career, however, was really its beginning, her own debut. The description below of that Keystone Kops affair is excerpted from a *New Yorker* profile of Brenda that appeared in June 1939.

The theoretic climax of any debutante's season is her own coming-out party. Brenda happened to have a cold at the time, and the tabloids reported this with all the gravity that might attend the last earthly hours of a dying king or queen. Brenda's ball at the Ritz, despite her indisposition, was a gala affair, disturbed only by uninvited cameramen. Mrs. Watriss [her mother], who had decided that on this one night at least Brenda should remain pictorially unchronicled in the press, barred all photographers but Jay Te Winburn, who was commissioned to record the occasion for Brenda's future entertainment. This was an admirable idea, but Mrs. Watriss underestimated the resourcefulness of the "Daily News," which dressed half a dozen men in tailcoats and supplied them with a room in the Ritz. From there they drifted casually into the ballroom, armed with concealed candid cameras. One, who decided that the chances of taking his own shots without being observed would be slim, sneaked up behind Mr. Winburn and, every time that fast-working gentleman laid down an exposed plate to pick up a fresh one, slipped it under his coat. After a spell he strolled out and sent his collection to the "News." Another stationed himself on the bandstand, disguised as a musician. While waiting for an oppor-

tunity to begin shooting, however, he was recognized by another jealous photographer, a Russian free-lancer, who had managed to get in, but without his camera. The Russian reported the presence of the "News" man to Brenda, who had him thrown out and then had the Russian thrown out too. She just stared blankly at one "News" man who was making faces at her to hold her attention. She took him for one of the thousand guests. By the time the last edition of the "News" went to press, the whole story was ready in pictures—including Brenda being, so the caption read, kissed by an anonymous admirer. Reporters grew hysterical over the food, the music, and the cost (which was reported to have been as high as $60,000), and Elsa Maxwell complained subsequently that she hadn't been able to get a chicken sandwich. The only missing detail was: Who had kissed Brenda? The "News" didn't know, and neither did a society press agent whom the paper called in. Brenda refused to say who he was and maintained that he had only been whispering. That remark got no more attention than Mrs. Watriss's anguished statement, printed in subsequent editions, that the party had cost just under $16,000—which, as deb parties have gone, is neither little nor much.

—E. J. KAHN JR. IN *THE NEW YORKER*, JUNE 9, 1939

A Mother's Pride

*"Certainly in 1939 Cobina, Jr. was the 'most' girl, most photographed,
most publicized, most sought after," announced her mother,
Cobina Wright Sr. To make sure it all kept happening, Mrs. Wright arranged
a screen test for Cobina Jr., hurled the girl into the
unreceptive arms of Britain's Prince Philip and eventually ended up
singing duets with her daughter in a nightclub (both wore Daniel Boone hats).*

A Precocious Spender

*One of the gayest Glamor Girls was Gloria (Mimi) Baker, who came
out in 1937. Ravishingly pretty, by the time she was 15
she had become a habitual nightclubber and frequenter of gambling casinos.
Her debut was so ostentatious that even gossip columnists
condemned her as a decadent aristocrat; her mother denied the charge, saying
that Mimi was "the most democratic person, bar none, I've ever known."*

Debs on the Go

Wherever Brenda, Cobina and Mimi went, whomever they married, whatever they wore, received instant fame. In fact, these "celebutantes," as Walter Winchell called them, were such sure-fire publicity getters that nightclubs sometimes wooed them by giving them the best tables closest to the action and charging them only a dollar for dinner.

In her trend-setting strapless, Brenda Frazier leads the Grand March at the Velvet Ball. At age 14 her clothing allowance was $5,400 a year.

Brenda goes out with an Indian prince. . .   chats with Bill DeRham, a dance instructor. . .   and registers joy at a witty remark.

Cobina Wright Jr. steals a march in Florida by dating Julian Gerard, one of Brenda's beaux.

Cesar Romero ogles Cobina at a premiere.

Mimi Baker wows 'em with "crazyjamas."

Alfred G. Vanderbilt gives away his half-sister Mimi to New York socialite Bob Topping.

Mimi dates the elusive Howard Hughes.

With suave smile and drooping lids, Alfred G. Vanderbilt dances with film star Joan Crawford at the 1937 Screen Actors Guild Ball in Los Angeles.

A light drinker, Vanderbilt has a Coke with starlet K. T. Stevens. *His Saratoga visit with divorced star Joan Bennett stirs gossip.*

Alfred dates actress known as Margo . . .   pretty torch singer Gertrude Niesen . . .   and Manhattan deb Eleanor Young.

Prince of the Glamor Boys

The male counterpart to the Glamor Girl in Café Society was the Man About Town, and for several seasons Alfred Gwynne Vanderbilt led the pack. He had all the qualifications. He was young and handsome, possessed an old name and had inherited millions. When he was 21 (in 1933) he had also inherited his mother's racing stable, Sagamore Farm, and in 1936 his horses earned more money than those of any other American sportsman. As if all those qualifications weren't enough, Alf had as his half-sister Glamor Girl Mimi Baker. Moreover, he had been elected best-dressed man in America by a group of tailors and he was very clever at holding the tablecloth when Ernest Hemingway wanted to play bull to Alf's *torero*. Almost every night he could be seen night-clubbing with a different Glamor Girl or movie star and he never shooed photographers away or bothered to deny gossip columnist rumors that a "romance was brewing." Then, in 1938, he climaxed his gay career as glamor boy and brought an end to all the romantic rumors by marrying another wealthy race-track addict, Manuela (Molly) Hudson.

The Queen from Keokuk

"My social whirl was purely a labor of love in pursuit of pleasure," Elsa Maxwell once announced. Into that pursuit, she poured all her immense energies—disdaining sexual ones. "I wouldn't subject myself to it," she told an interviewer. "I married the world—the world is my husband. That is why I'm so young. No sex. Sex is the most tiring thing in the world."

Elsa was famous for her lavish parties, such as her Pet Hates Ball to which everyone came as his bête noire (she had to limit the number of Franklin and Eleanor Roosevelts). In 1938 Elsa described to gossip columnist Inez Robb the assets she expected of all guests at her parties.

First, I want a woman guest to be beautiful. Second, I want her to be beautifully dressed. Third, I demand animation and vivacity. Fourth, not too many brains. Brains are always awkward at a gay and festive party. Brains are only a requisite when the party is limited to a handful of persons, say six or eight.

And fifth, I expect obedience. It's ruinous if guests refuse to co-operate with a hostess if she asks them to dance, play games, go on a treasure hunt, tell stories, guess riddles or whatever she has planned for the occasion.

Above all things, a man should be good-looking. Then he should boast a tailor who is an artist. Third, he must not be overly married. This is a matter of attitude, which has nothing to do with the fidelity to the wife of his bosom, but with a willingness to make himself charming and a bit flattering to other women.

Fourth, men guests must not only dance well but be willing to dance. You've no idea what a problem that is. Finally, all men should have manner and manners. I want them to reply to invitations which they receive and I don't want them to carry the champagne home under their coats instead of their belts, and I'd rather they didn't throw bottles out of the window.

THE NEW YORK MIRROR, DECEMBER 16, 1938

Elsa toasts suave William Rhinelander Stewart (left) and composer Cole Porter. Porter and Aly Khan were the two men Elsa considered sexy.

Barbara Hutton in 1930

Poor Little Rich Girl

The star-crossed darling of Café Society was Barbara Hutton, an heiress to a $45 million share of the Woolworth fortune. When she was 13, she wrote prophetically: "Why should some have all / And others be without? / Why should men pretend / And women have to doubt?"

The first man to pretend he loved Barbara, and whom she learned to doubt too late, was a self-styled Russian prince, Alexis Mdivani. Mdivani first met Barbara on the Riviera when she was a fat, homely teenager. Although he was honeymooning with his first bride, American heiress Louise Van Alen, Mdivani made a beeline for Barbara and chatted with her all afternoon.

After restraining himself for all of three years while Barbara grew up a little, Mdivani demanded and got a million-dollar settlement out of his first wife. Then the good Prince Alexis moved in for the kill. Barbara's thoroughly alarmed father spirited her off on a world tour; but the intrepid Mdivani pursued her to Bangkok, and in a few weeks the happy couple announced their engagement.

The wedding took place in Paris. Barbara presented the Prince with a string of polo ponies and the Prince presented Barbara with a string of jade beads, which she paid for. Barbara's father gave the groom a token million and the newlyweds took off for India. Soon after the honeymoon, however, Mdivani was reported to have screamed at Barbara, "You're as fat as a pig," and to be devoting most of his time to women more svelte. Barbara endured

1933. Barbara Hutton marries Prince Mdivani in Paris.

1934. Barbara returns to America dieted down 44 pounds.

1935. She marries Count von Haugwitz-Reventlow.

1936. Kurt, Barbara baptize their son Lance in London.

1937. Barbara and Kurt (left) admit they will split.

Barbara Hutton in 1940

two subsequent years of neglect and strenuous dieting, but then called it quits and gave Mdivani another two million toward settlement.

A new European aristocrat was lying in wait, Count Kurt von Haugwitz-Reventlow, and the day after she had stopped being a Georgian princess, Barbara became a Danish countess. "Now at last I have found happiness," Barbara announced. "My search is ended. I know that this is safe and sure." Safe and sure it wasn't, but Bar-

In a foreign land is a very young woman—only 26—who has had a strange life. She is alone, attacked by her husband. She's an American girl fighting alone across the sea. She's made mistakes, been a silly, wild, foolish girl, given in to temptations—but she's still our own. COLUMNIST ADELA ROGERS ST. JOHNS, 1938.

bara spared no expense in trying to make it so. For one thing, she shelled out $4.5 million building a huge mansion in London. During her stay in England, Barbara gave birth to her only child, Lance. A year later, in 1937, the marriage was on the rocks and Barbara commented: "Poor Kurt, I feel sorry for him. It was always, 'I am Count von Haugwitz-Reventlow.' He never forgot it—until one day I said, 'Who cares? Who cares about the Count von Haugwitz-Reventlow today? The world has come a long way from that sort of thing.'"

The world had also come a long way from admiring flighty heiresses. In 1939, when Barbara returned to the U.S., Woolworth clerks picketed her hotel and crowds threatened her. "Why do they hate me?" Barbara asked. "There are other girls as rich, richer, almost as rich."

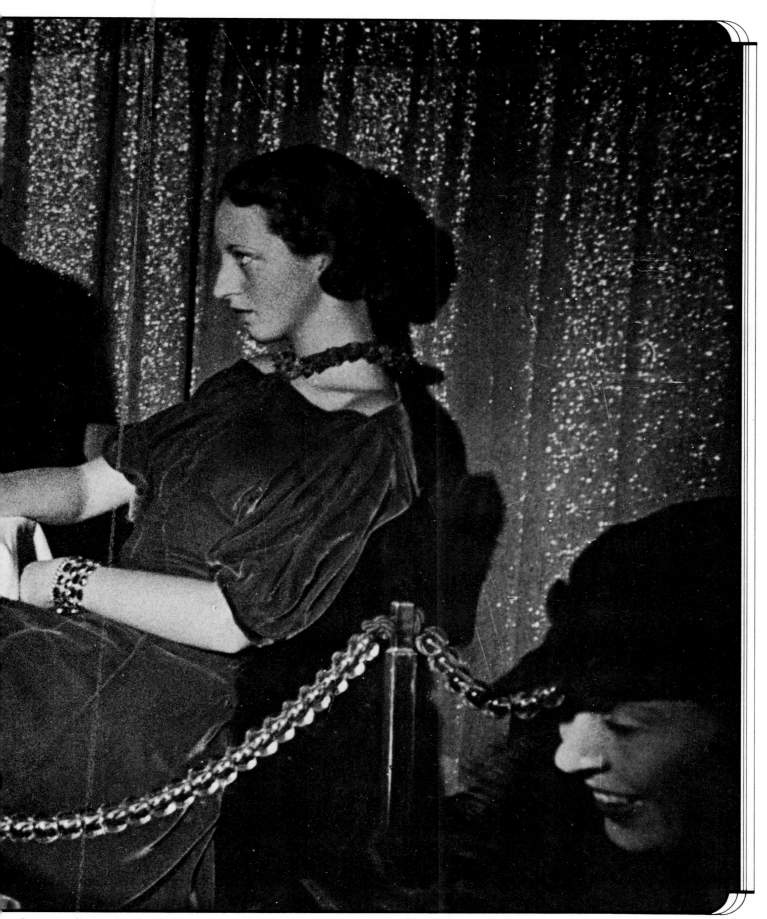

Sensationally bored and cut off from the world by a gold chain, two girls of Café Society sit it out at a supper club with their equally glum escort.

Labor

Cleveland cops move in as strikers overturn a foreman's car.

The Worker Finds a Voice

Labor, like Israel, has many sorrows. Its women keep their fallen and they lament for the future of the children of the race.
JOHN L. LEWIS

By the middle of the 1930s the American workingman was stalking toward a deadly showdown with management. Thanks largely to the shrewd lobbying of bushy-browed John L. Lewis, formidable leader of the United Mine Workers, a federal law was on the books guaranteeing every laborer the right to join a union and use the union to bargain with his bosses. But acknowledging labor's rights by law was easier said than done. In many a big industrial town the only real law was the company's.

In those harsh times, firing was about the mildest punishment given a union organizer. A fair number of U.S. laborers actually worked at gunpoint. Why, a Senate committee had wanted to know in 1928, did the Pittsburgh Coal Company keep machine guns at its coal pits? "You cannot run the mines without them," replied Richard B. Mellon, chairman of the board. In 1935 hired guns still loomed over the toughest of the company towns, where a word for the union could get a man beaten up or killed.

When a strike was brewing in 1935 against the Akron, Ohio, tire manufacturers, the rubber companies had an army of strikebreakers standing by under the direction of one Pearl Bergoff, a king among strikebreakers. Pearl's delicate name mocked his nature (his mother gave him

the name she had picked for the daughter she wanted to have). He ran a multi-million-dollar business, serving various major firms across the country, from an office in New York. His aides daily scanned out-of-town newspapers for hints of brewing strikes, whereupon Pearl dispatched one of his salesmen to peddle the Bergoff services. The deal included shipping a small army of men to fill the struck jobs and fitting them out with weapons from Pearl's armory of machine guns, night sticks and tear gas.

Bergoff was not the only big-time goon for hire. The Pinkerton National Detective Agency, a favorite of the auto companies, earned $1,750,000 for its services to industry between 1933 and 1936. "We must do it," explained Vice President Herman L. Weckler of the Chrysler Corporation, "to obtain the information we need in dealing with our employees." By the mid '30s, however, industrial employees all over the country had long since become fed up with such dealing. And they were rallying behind John L. Lewis, whose tough leadership and political power had brought a new era into view.

They could hardly have had a better man. Lewis had been in the thick of union wars for 25 years. As a teenager with a seventh-grade education, he had gone to work

In 1936, labor czar John L. Lewis blasts Republican Presidential candidate Alf Landon as a "pitiful puppet responsible to the steel industry."

in the coal pits of Iowa with his five kid brothers. His awesome energies, angry convictions and eloquent tongue soon won him a niche of his own in the United Mine Workers. A six-foot-three-inch bull of a man, Lewis had a mind as powerful as his imposing physique. At night and on union organizing trips across the country, he read in their entirety the Bible, the Odyssey and the Iliad, Oswald Spengler and Shakespeare, Karl Marx and Friedrich Engels. By early 1934 this unique mixture of coal miner, labor organizer and reader of classics was entrenched as president of the UMW, and with the backing of the new federal law, he had built the union to 400,000 members and taken the field against intransigent mine owners of Pennsylvania in the first of the decade's climactic labor wars. This occurred in midsummer of 1934, when Lewis called out 70,000 miners to strike.

The companies and their political allies girded for battle. "We're going to meet 'em at the bridge and break their goddam heads," shouted the mayor of Duquesne as the strike spread across the Allegheny Valley. Before it ended, the mine owners had poured some $17,000 into munitions and their henchmen had bombed miners' houses and set crosses ablaze on the hillsides. But in the set-

So I'm a Red? I suppose it makes me a Red because I don't like making time so hard on these goddamned machines. When I get home I'm so tired I can't sleep with my wife.

ASSEMBLY-LINE WORKER, 1935

tlement, the embattled miners won grudging acceptance, and the road toward union recognition was staked out for every man in America's far-flung laboring forces.

With this triumph under his belt, Lewis met with union organizers in Atlantic City, New Jersey, and proposed a drive to pull together all of the country's industrial laborers into an enormous conglomerate. At one point in the maneuvering, Lewis was challenged by a burly trade unionist who called Lewis a "big bastard," to which Lewis replied with a punch in the nose. When the dust of the skirmish had cleared away, a good many of labor's top

Armed with billy clubs and auto parts, Chrysler strikers rally beneath a slogan—borrowed from French soldiers—warning scabs to stay away.

Sit-down strikers take it easy on assembly-line auto seats inside besieged Fisher Body plant in Flint, Michigan, during the crucial strike of 1937.

Ford goons stalk unionists Walter Reuther, Richard Frankensteen.

men had fallen in behind Lewis; the labor conglomerate was formed and subsequently christened the Congress of Industrial Organizations, the CIO. Looking back with a certain pleasure on the imbroglios involved, Lewis crowed: "They smote me hip and thigh, and right merrily did I return their blows."

Then he returned to the war with industrial management, this time in Flint, Michigan, home of several General Motors plants. General Motors was then the third largest corporation in the country. It employed a quarter of a million people, paying its top 20 officials an average of $200,000, its workers scarcely $1,000. It also maintained one of the rankest spy systems in the country; between January 1934 and August 1936 the company paid $994,855.68 to Pinkerton and others.

On December 28, 1936, a thousand workers at one of GM's Cleveland plants, demanding the right to make every GM worker a member of the United Auto Workers, adopted a somewhat new and disconcertingly effective tactic. They laid down their tools and went on a sit-down strike; instead of walking out, as most earlier strikers had done, they remained in the plant. Management was stunned. Two days later the night shift at GM's key Chevrolet plant in Flint sat down too. Fifteen more plants followed, stripping General Motors of 140,000 employees, and bringing all auto production to a halt.

Grabbing Frankensteen, they slug him for handing out union leaflets.

The focal point of the conflict was at Flint. As the sit-down continued, the temperature dropped below zero, and General Motors officials turned off the heat in the plant and directed the Flint police to seize food bound for the shivering strikers. Some 50 policemen sprayed the pickets with buckshot and tear gas and beat them with clubs. "We wanted peace. General Motors chose war. Give it to them!" shouted a voice over a loudspeaker, and the strikers did, with pipes, door hinges, coffee mugs, pop bottles, and an icy blast from the company's fire hose. After an all-night battle in which 14 men were wounded, the strikers succeeded in routing the police.

Governor Frank Murphy, who had given grueling hours to patient mediation and was determined to keep Mich-

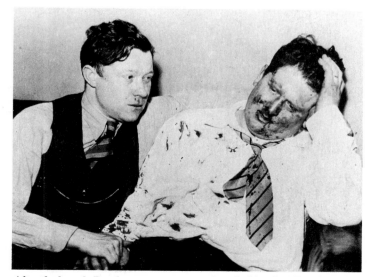
After the brawl, Reuther attempts to comfort the bloodied Frankensteen.

As news of the strikers' victory comes, a jubilant Ladies Auxiliary parades in front of the Chrysler works just before the sit-downers emerge.

igan from further bloodshed, alerted the National Guard. But he decided to consult with Lewis before sending the men into action. What would Lewis do if the Guard tried to evict the strikers, Murphy wanted to know.

"You want my answer, sir?" asked Lewis. "I give it to you. Tomorrow morning, I shall personally enter General Motors plant Chevrolet No. 4. I shall order the men to disregard your order. I shall then walk up to the largest window in the plant, open it, divest myself of my outer raiment, remove my shirt and bare my bosom. Then when you order your troops to fire, mine will be the first those bullets will strike. And as my body falls from that window to the ground, you listen to the voice of your grandfather as he whispers in your ear, 'Frank, are you sure you are doing the right thing?' " Murphy, whose grandfather had been hanged in the Irish rebellion, blanched and tore up his order. He further forbade General Motors to bar the delivery of food to the strikers and with great tact held further violence at bay.

After 44 days of losing profits at the rate of one million dollars a day, General Motors capitulated, agreeing to bargain with the United Automobile Workers in the 17 plants that had been struck. In four months' time the U.A.W. had won its drive for acceptance and organized a majority of General Motors workers. The strikers had scored a monumental triumph against the third mightiest corporation in the country. In the wake of that victory labor's final battles for union recognition got under way (pages 172-177).

> When they tie the can to a union man,
>   *Sit down! Sit down!*
> *When they give him the sack they'll take him back,*
>   *Sit down! Sit down!*
> *When the speed-up comes, just twiddle your thumbs,*
>   *Sit down! Sit down!*
> *When the boss won't talk, don't take a walk,*
>   *Sit down! Sit down!*
>   UNION BALLAD

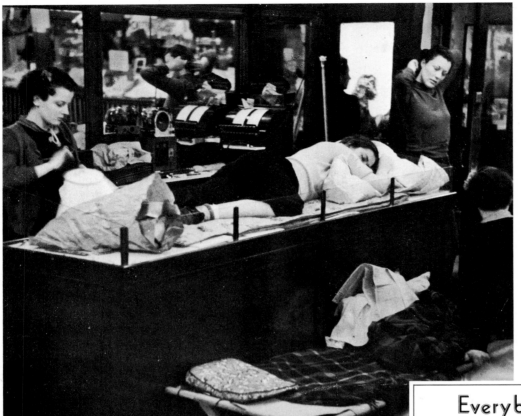

Woolworth clerk naps on a counter during a sit-in at Detroit in 1937.

Everybody Sits

With the success of the big strikes, people all over sat down to protest grievances.

Striking chefs at the Willard Hotel in Washington, D.C., stage their sit-down on top of a cold stove.

An Illinois driver demands the road be fix

ew Jersey barbers sit in a non-union shop.

Philadelphia hosiery makers awaken a sleeping worker with the happy news that their strike is won.

e been stuck here 32 times," he declared.

Striking seamen lounge in deck chairs aboard the S.S. "President Roosevelt" en route to Hamburg.

The Hard Grip of Steel

While the nation's eyes were still fixed on the union coup in the automobile industry at Detroit, labor's eloquent leader, John L. Lewis, got busy elsewhere. He took on, virtually singlehanded, the Goliath of American industry: United States Steel, an antagonist beside which even General Motors seemed comparatively small.

Despite the hard times of the Depression, U.S. Steel, grandly called The Corporation by its officers, reported gross earnings of $35,218,359 in 1934. It turned out more than 53 million tons of iron ore, coal, coke, limestone, pig iron, ingots and finished steel items, and more than a quarter of a million tons of by-products from ammonia to cement. It owned not only mills, but coal and iron mines stretching from Canada to Brazil, a fleet of ships and miles of railroad tracks to move its cargo.

But the view from inside the mills and mines, the view of the common laborer, was grim and hopeless. In 1933, more than half the mill hands were totally unemployed, and by The Corporation's own statement there was not a single full-time worker anywhere on its payroll. Condi-

---

A world without policemen would be like a world without music.
DANIEL J. SHIELDS, MAYOR OF JOHNSTOWN, PENNSYLVANIA

---

tions elsewhere in the steel industry were much the same. That year the average steelworker, with his part-time pickings, earned $369, a sum on which he had to support a family that averaged 5.92 persons. "Work two days a week," said a steelworker in Braddock, Pennsylvania, "loaf around five days, wife sick, one of my girls needs a good doctor, and me with no money, a bunch of rent bills, butcher bills, grocery bills."

Safety conditions were as bad as wages. Occupational diseases such as carbon monoxide poisoning, "hot mill cramps" (from exposure to temperatures up to 220° F. at the furnace mouth) and pneumonia took hundreds of lives every year. Every week, on the average, one man could expect his clothes to catch fire, and if he did not burn to death he had to replace the clothes from his meager earnings. The overseer who went by the title of safety manager at a Jones & Laughlin steel mill in Pittsburgh admitted

to having "a lot of equipment that is out of date, lacks the new safety devices and is liable to break down at any time, causing serious accidents," but he had no plans for improving it. "It still yields a return on investment," he said, "so the company cannot scrap it." Instead the industry scrapped 22,845 human beings in accidents in a single year: 242 were killed, 1,193 permanently disabled and 21,410 temporarily laid up.

As top dog in the industry, U.S. Steel was habitually followed by its pack of friendly competitors in all matters from wage rates to safety measures and, of course, in its attitude toward unions. On that score, Bethlehem, Republic, Youngstown, National and Inland—nicknamed "Little Steel" to differentiate them from the grandiose Corporation—shot down unions with a vigor that would have warmed the hearts of the tough old magnates who laid the foundations of U.S. Steel.

In 1935 Carnegie Steel was paying likely finks about $25 a month to report on union talk among their fellow workers, filing the results of their pickings and firing offenders. Yet Tom M. Girdler, one-time policeman for Jones & Laughlin, now head of Republic Steel, could accuse union organizers of "interference in a man's private affairs." He added: "An ominous fact was repeated in the sketchy facts we had about some of these fellows: They were Communists."

There were some unions in the steel industry, but they were company unions, organizations controlled not by the workers but by management. A Ukrainian mill hand testified at a government investigation of the company union at the Carnegie Steel plant in Duquesne: "Boss say, 'Better you go vote now.' No, I say, I got outside union. I vote in outside union. Boss say then, 'You no like job, huh? No like company? Well, maybe company no like you. Better you go vote now.'"

In all, the steelworkers seemed helpless to improve their lot. But the momentum of the big union victories in coal and autos provided fresh hope; and help was on the way as John L. Lewis, now head of the CIO, stepped forward as the steelworkers' spokesman. By organizing coal,

Cartoonist William Gropper bitterly caricatured the repressions of the Chicago steel magnates against workers who struck in the spring of 1937.

A fallen worker gets a merciless beating as strikers fight scabs during a 1937 strike at Republic Steel in Cleveland. Eighteen workers lost their lives.

he had tied up the source of the fuel on which the steel industry ran; by organizing automobiles, he had tied up steel's major customer. Now he turned to U.S. Steel, certain that if he could move the mighty Corporation its confreres in Little Steel would come along. "If we can organize here," he said, "the rest will follow. If the crouching lion can be routed, it is a safe bet that the hyenas in the adjacent bush may be scattered along the plain."

John L. Lewis was, as a reporter of the day remarked, "a foeman worthy of U.S. Steel." Calling personally on Myron Taylor, the courtly board chairman of The Corporation, he chatted amiably of Gothic tapestries and high finance. Taylor was charmed, and to the nation's astonishment, he signed a contract with the CIO union. After 50 years of losing to clubs and gunfire, the steelworkers

Strikers support a tear-gassed co-worker.

175

seemed to have won the war with Lewis' mellifluous words.

Unhappily, peace in the industry was still some distance away, for the "hyenas in the adjacent bush" were not so easily scattered. Two months after the U.S. Steel settlement, Little Steel had not budged toward any settlement with the CIO. On May 26, seventy thousand workers walked out of 27 plants belonging to Little Steel in seven states, and the companies countered with the bloodiest anti-union battle of the decade.

On Memorial Day some 1,500 workers with their wives and children gathered for a demonstration of solidarity outside the Republic plant in South Chicago. "CIO! Let's go! CIO! Let's go!" they chanted. A corps of 150 Chicago police stormed them with tear gas, night sticks and 200 rounds of gunfire. "Stand back, you son of a bitch," said one of the cops, "or I will fill you full of lead." Over the next

Give me 200 good, tough armed men and I'll clean up them sons of bitches on the picket line.

DISTRICT ATTORNEY, YOUNGSTOWN, OHIO

few minutes, in a bloodbath that came to be called the Memorial Day Massacre, the police killed 10 demonstrators and wounded more than 100 others.

"There can be no pity for a mob," said Republic president Tom M. Girdler later, as if to excuse the violence. "As that artistic brawler, Benvenuto Cellini, said," he went on, " 'blows are not dealt by measure.' Some of the mob were clubbed after they had started to run from the wrath they had aroused. Some women were knocked down. The policemen were there performing a hazardous and harsh duty. What were women doing there?"

The Little Steel strike lasted two months, and this time the laborers lost. Vigilantes lined up against the strikers; the National Guard was called in to back up management; and the various companies in Little Steel maintained a united front. The workers were up against too much. Exhausted and hungry, they went back to work in July without winning their union.

The loss of the Little Steel strike was a bitter blow to workers everywhere after the heady victories that had

gone before it. But it proved to be only a temporary setback. Senator Robert M. La Follette Jr. of Wisconsin launched investigations that exposed the tactics used to crush the Little Steel strike and others, with the result that public opinion began to change and industrial espionage and the sicking of armed guards on factory workers began to disappear. The anti-union shock troops of the Pinkertons turned to private eye work and Pearl Bergoff and his goons went out of business.

As John L. Lewis surveyed the scene when the 1930s drew to a close, he could mark off the worst hurdles as crossed. Despite the stubborn resistance that still lingered in Little Steel, despite confrontations elsewhere in industry, labor in the main had won its quest for recognition. The cost had been heavy; it had entailed the calling of 22,658 strikes in that single decade, the loss of scores of lives and the infliction of uncounted injuries. But by the end of 1937, unions had recruited 7.7 million workers who won contracts guaranteeing wages, hours and safety measures in every kind of company. To the millions of American workers who were mute and hog-tied at the outset of the decade, John L. Lewis' eloquent voice had given the power of speech. At one point Lewis even went so far as to administer a landmark scolding over nationwide radio to the President of the United States. During the Little Steel strike a reporter asked President Roosevelt for his views on the stalemate. "A plague o' both your houses," cried F.D.R. in exasperation, echoing the Shakespearean invocations of labor's champion.

John L. Lewis was not amused. "It ill behooves one who has supped at labor's table and who has been sheltered in labor's house," he roared over a network broadcast, "to curse with equal fervor and fine impartiality both labor and its adversaries when they become locked in deadly embrace."

Franklin D. Roosevelt heard Lewis loud and clear, and so did the rest of the nation. For by the end of this bloody decade American workers, once scattered and beaten by the industrial goons, ignored or opposed by politicians, had assumed their rightful places as first-class citizens.

The long war for union recognition nearly over, a California laborer proudly displays his union membership book after a strike in November 1938.

The Movies

After a Saturday matinee, kids hug their door prizes.

Paradise in Celluloid

The American film has served as propaganda for the emotional monotony, the naive morality, the sham luxury, the haphazard etiquette and the grotesque exaggeration of the comic, the sentimental and the acrobatic that are so common in the United States.

POET AND CRITIC JOHN GOULD FLETCHER

No one who spent his time at the movies during the '30s would ever have known that the nation was down in the dumps. In a typical Hollywood movie of the era, Bette Davis gave up "everything" for the man she loved and moved into a remodeled Vermont farmhouse that one sarcastic critic estimated would cost $12,000 a year just to operate. In other films the vestiges of the real, cruel world of the Depression were replaced by delightful fictions like Walt Disney's 1937 *Snow White and the Seven Dwarfs,* by lurid epics like Cecil B. DeMille's *Sign of the Cross* and *Cleopatra,* and by superspectacular musicals such as the 1933 *Flying Down to Rio,* in which a whole chorus of show girls in gauze uniforms danced on the wings of airplanes in flight.

Hollywood's brand of heaven on earth was a deliberate and enormously successful effort to provide escape. Some 85 million people a week seized on it, commonly paying 25 cents for a ticket (10 cents for kids). Local theaters enhanced the appeal of a night at the movies by offering double and even triple features and by giving away door prizes that ranged from coupons for free hairdos to shiny new automobiles. The religion of escape had its icons; Shirley Temple dolls *(pages 96, 97)* and rubber statuettes

of Disney's dwarfs sold in the millions. The high priestess of Hollywood was gossip Louella Parsons, who divulged her "exclusives" every week on her radio show. Every year thousands of pilgrims journeyed to Hollywood to make reverent tours of the homes of the stars.

Not only were American films devoutly escapist, they were also, after 1934, very clean. In that year America's Roman Catholic bishops banded together to form the National League of Decency and Hollywood cooperated with it by enforcing a long list of taboos. Long kisses, adultery, double beds, words like "damn" and "hell" and even nude babies were banned from films. Criminals could no longer triumph over decent citizens. A hoyden like Mae West could no longer croon "I Like a Man Who Takes His Time." The day of "family movies" was ushered in, featuring adorable youngsters like Shirley Temple, Mickey Rooney and Jane Withers. Jeanette MacDonald and Nelson Eddy—whom Hollywood cynics dubbed "The Iron Butterfly" and "The Singing Capon"—began to turn out a whole series of fluffy white operettas. Even the titles of motion pictures were cleaned up; thus *Good Girls Go to Paris Too* became *Good Girls Go to Paris* and *Infidelity,* by a miraculous transformation, turned into *Fidelity.*

1932	1933	1934	1935	1936	1937	1938	1939	1940
MARIE DRESSLER	MARIE DRESSLER	WILL ROGERS	SHIRLEY TEMPLE	SHIRLEY TEMPLE	SHIRLEY TEMPLE	SHIRLEY TEMPLE	MICKEY ROONEY	MICKEY ROONEY
JANET GAYNOR	WILL ROGERS	CLARK GABLE	WILL ROGERS	CLARK GABLE	CLARK GABLE	CLARK GABLE	TYRONE POWER	SPENCER TRACY
JOAN CRAWFORD	JANET GAYNOR	JANET GAYNOR	CLARK GABLE	ASTAIRE-ROGERS	ROBERT TAYLOR	SONJA HENIE	SPENCER TRACY	CLARK GABLE
CHARLES FARRELL	EDDIE CANTOR	WALLACE BEERY	ASTAIRE-ROGERS	ROBERT TAYLOR	BING CROSBY	MICKEY ROONEY	CLARK GABLE	GENE AUTRY
GRETA GARBO	WALLACE BEERY	MAE WEST	JOAN CRAWFORD	JOE E. BROWN	WILLIAM POWELL	SPENCER TRACY	SHIRLEY TEMPLE	TYRONE POWER
NORMA SHEARER	JEAN HARLOW	JOAN CRAWFORD	CLAUDETTE COLBERT	DICK POWELL	JANE WITHERS	ROBERT TAYLOR	BETTE DAVIS	JAMES CAGNEY
WALLACE BEERY	CLARK GABLE	BING CROSBY	DICK POWELL	JOAN CRAWFORD	ASTAIRE-ROGERS	MYRNA LOY	ALICE FAYE	BING CROSBY
CLARK GABLE	MAE WEST	SHIRLEY TEMPLE	WALLACE BEERY	CLAUDETTE COLBERT	SONJA HENIE	JANE WITHERS	ERROL FLYNN	WALLACE BEERY
WILL ROGERS	NORMA SHEARER	MARIE DRESSLER	JOE E. BROWN	JEANETTE MACDONALD	GARY COOPER	ALICE FAYE	JAMES CAGNEY	BETTE DAVIS
JOE E. BROWN	JOAN CRAWFORD	NORMA SHEARER	JAMES CAGNEY	GARY COOPER	MYRNA LOY	TYRONE POWER	SONJA HENIE	JUDY GARLAND

Year-by-year charts of top 10 box-office stars, begun in 1932 by "Motion Picture Herald," show Gable's durability, Shirley Temple's rise and fall.

Slinky Jean Harlow gazes longingly at herself in "Dinner at Eight." Called the "Blonde Bombshell," she was the sexiest siren of the early '30s.

Sexiest male, by popular acclaim, was Clark Gable, shown here in his costume for the part of Mr. Christian in "Mutiny on the Bounty."

Some connoisseurs of Hollywood beauty preferred the shapely legs of Marlene Dietrich—shown here in "Blonde Venus"—to Harlow's slithery appeal.

Gary Cooper, all done up for his role in the 1935 thriller "Lives of a Bengal Lancer," rivaled Gable at the box-office as Hollywood's top he-man.

JEZEBEL

MARKED WOMAN

PETRIFIED FOREST

The Versatile Vixen

Very likely the most talented star of the decade was a popeyed little dynamo named Bette Davis. Though her own personality was so strong that every screen character she played, from *The Old Maid* to *Jezebel*, was unmistakably Bette Davis, she was nevertheless able to inject a biting realism into a remarkable range of roles. Off-screen she was every bit as strong-willed and sharp-tongued as the characters she played in her films. Her leading man Errol Flynn once commented to her, "I'd love to proposition you, Bette, but I'm afraid you'd laugh at me." Bette responded sweetly, "You're so right, Errol."

OF HUMAN BONDAGE

DARK VICTORY

JUAREZ

THE OLD MAID

Errol Flynn leers at the Virgin Queen in "The Private Lives of Elizabeth and Essex," in which Bette Davis played the 60-year-old monarch.

Sing a Song of Money

In the celluloid paradise created by Hollywood, some of the purest bits of froth were the musicals. These came in several delicious flavors, one fan favorite being the supercolossal productions of Busby Berkeley, which usually were built around love-birds Dick Powell and Ruby Keeler *(page 190)*. Another sticky-sweet variety featured Jeanette MacDonald and Nelson Eddy in schmaltzy operettas.

The biggest money-makers, however, were Fred Astaire and Ginger Rogers. Before they were teamed up, Ginger had played only a few feature parts. The report on Fred's first Hollywood screen test had read: "Can't act. Slightly bald. Can dance a little." But the first film in which they starred, *The Gay Divorcée* in 1934, turned out to be such a smash that RKO insured Fred's legs for a million dollars. By the end of the decade, the team had tapped its way through seven more hits; Astaire was branching out to start a chain of dance studios and Ginger was striking out on her own as an award-winning dramatic actress.

Nelson Eddy sings a duet with Jeanette MacDonald in "Rose Marie."

In the 1938 film "Carefree," Fred Astaire and Ginger Rogers perform a step called the Yam, which one magazine suggested fans learn for home parties.

Dick Powell and his fellow West Point cadets serenade Ruby Keeler and a flock of other innocents in the 1934 musical "Flirtation Walk."

Setting off an orgy of patriotism, Eleanor Powell sings Cole Porter's "Swingin' the Jinx Away," in the 1936 musical "Born to Dance."

Fiddling fairies swirl in "Gold Diggers of 1933." This sequence is typical of the choreography of Busby Berkeley, master of '30s musicals.

The Lovables

In the late '30s a frantic, fumbling, but good-natured towhead name Andy Hardy was everybody's favorite teenager. Ably portrayed by Mickey Rooney, Andy was a romanticized image of the typical American boy; small wonder that though he hailed from the mythical town of Carvel, millions of fans felt that he really lived just down the block. His first movie, *A Family Affair*, convinced MGM that it had a hit; the studio quickly spun out a series of Andy Hardy films that helped make Mickey Rooney the industry's No. 1 box-office attraction in 1939 and 1940.

Always alert to new bonanzas, Hollywood immediately began producing such other groups of films as the hospital tear-jerker *Dr. Kildare*, the comic-strip inspired *Blondie* and the tenement-based *Dead End Kids*. Besides their box-office benefits, these series provided steady work for the squadrons of players the studios had under contract; thus the Hardy series kept busy not only Rooney but also Lewis Stone as paterfamilias Judge Hardy, Fay Holden as Mother Hardy and Cecilia Parker as sister Marian. Because of the simplicity of the roles, the series also were perfect places to allow new talent to gain experience; for example, the 1938 *Love Finds Andy Hardy (below)* showcased ingénues Judy Garland as Betsy, Lana Turner as siren Cynthia and Ann Rutherford as Andy's girl Polly.

1. Would you buy a used car from this man? Andy Hardy, needing some wheels for a big dance, does.

2. Andy's flame, Polly, is so pleased with his buy she accepts the dance date and lets him kiss her.

3. In one bad evening, Andy learns his grandmother is ill and Polly breaks the date to go out of town.

4. Vacation-bound pal Beezy, afraid that his girl Cynthia will stray, hires Andy to "date her up."

5. Smitten by affable Cynthia, Andy forgets Polly and persuades Beezy's girl to go to the big dance.

6. As a favor, Andy dates a neighbor's visiting granddaughter, Betsy, whom he thinks "a mere child."

7. *On a date, Andy swims while Cynthia watches; the lady also eschews tennis and roller skating.*

8. *Cynthia's one sport is smooching—soon, Andy frets that too much kissing will harm his health.*

9. *Meanwhile, car payments are stacking up, and Andy unburdens himself to a stern Judge Hardy.*

10. *The family hears from Mrs. Hardy, who is with her sick mother, that Andy's grandmother is worse.*

11. *Later, they learn by ham radio—Mrs. Hardy is far from a phone—that grandmother is much better.*

12. *Meanwhile, Beezy writes he is through with Cynthia. Betsy, falling for Andy, plots to move in.*

13. *Wily Betsy gets Cynthia to break her date and Polly returns to scold Andy for his brief infidelity.*

14. *Dateless, Andy asks Betsy, who sings so well at the dance she—and Andy—lead the Grand March.*

15. *Happy ending: Betsy goes home, contrite Polly returns to Andy and Judge Hardy finances the car.*

Armed with various gifts, Paul Muni (left) as "Scarface" and a henchman, played by George Raft, prepare to pay a farewell call on a hospitalized rival.

Crime Pays

The 1930 crime film *Little Caesar* taught movie producers that multiple murders meant multiple box-office dollars. *Caesar* set off a spate of gangster films whose swaggering stars were accused of schooling a generation of real-life punks. Hollywood, to duck accusations it was glorifying the underworld, always knocked off the crime lord in the last reel. But censors were unmoved and films glorifying gangsters died of official disapproval and public boredom.

Machine-gun bullets slam into Edward G. Robinson as "Little Caesar."

"Public Enemy" James Cagney persuades a bar owner to buy his booze.

Mae West tries her best to look coy as W.C. Fields offers a few sly suggestions in "My Little Chickadee," a Western spoof larded with Fieldisms.

The Funnymen

My Little Chickadee

During the '30s Hollywood developed the full spectrum of film comedy. The best was the slapstick of the Marx Brothers (overleaf) and the low-key love satires like those excerpted here. In a memorable scene from "My Little Chickadee," snake-oil peddler Cuthbert J. Twillie (W.C. Fields) chances upon a social outcast named Flower Belle Lee (Mae West).

Fields: Nice day.

West: Is it?

Fields: Course it's only one man's opinion. May I present my card?

West: Novelties and notions. What kind of notions you got?

Fields: You'd be surprised. Some are old, some are new. Whom have I the honor of addressing, my lady?

West: Mmmm—they call me Flower Belle.

Fields: Flower Belle. What a euphonious appellation—easy on the ears and a banquet for the eyes.

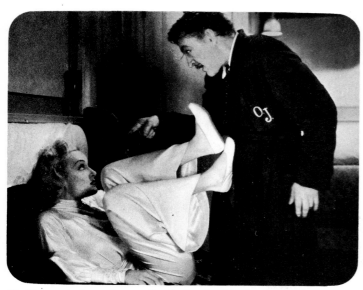

Curling up in her pajamas, Carole Lombard fends off John Barrymore.

Patient Myrna Loy waits for William Powell to finish target practice.

Twentieth Century

*On the famous train, Broadway impresario Barrymore
meets Carole Lombard, an ex-love he had
made a star. He tries to woo her back by outlining a
wild religious play in which she will star.*

Barrymore: *I'm going to have Judas strangle himself with a hair. I want to stagger New York with 100 camels and real sand —brought from the Holy Land—and we'll have a Babylonian banquet where you're covered with emeralds from head to foot and nothing else. You go directly into your snake dance—it's perfect, but it's nothing compared to the finish, where you stand in rags and the Emperor Nero himself offers you half his empire. The last we see of you is as a pathetic little figure selling olives on the—*
Lombard: *You're craaazzzzy!*

The Thin Man

*Having been tagged as a suspect in a murder,
detective Nick Charles (William Powell) swaps bons mots
as he toys with the gun he has received as a
Christmas present from his wife Nora (Myrna Loy).*

Loy: *I'm glad you're not on this case.*
Powell: *The point is, I'm in it. They think I did it.*
Loy: *Well, didn't you?*
(Powell shoots out half a dozen Christmas tree ornaments.)
Loy: *You're not in a shooting gallery.* (Picking up a newspaper) *Finished with this?*
Powell: *Yes, and I know as much about the murder as they do. So I'm a hero; I was shot twice in the "Tribune."*
Loy: *And I read you were shot five times in the tabloid.*
Powell: *It's not true. He didn't come near my tabloid.*

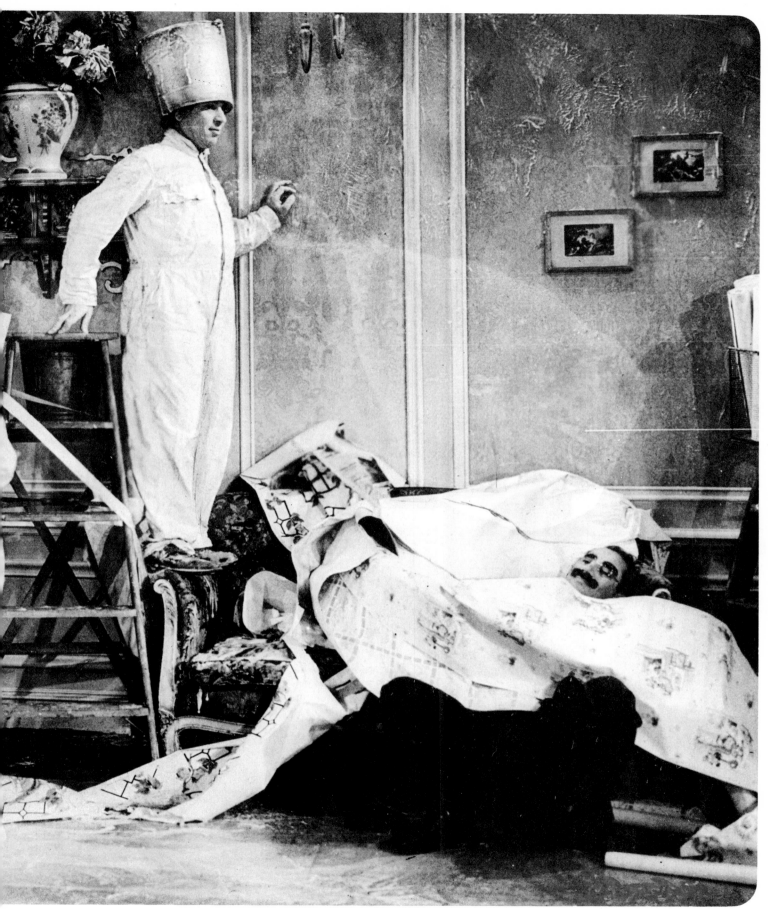

Esther Muir cringes amid the chaos produced by the Marx Brothers—Groucho (right), Harpo (center) and Chico—in "A Day at the Races."

Snow White inspects the dwarfs' hands before dinner. The leader of the dwarfs was Doc (far left); the audience favorite was Dopey (far right).

Animated Fantasy

Hollywood's retreat from reality climaxed in Walt Disney's first feature-length cartoon, *Snow White and the Seven Dwarfs*. Disney and his legion of animators started work on the movie in 1934, and for a long time it seemed they might never make it. Financiers were reluctant to lend them the nearly two million dollars they needed. Friends and enemies warned Disney that the public would never pay to sit through an 80-minute fairy tale.

But when the movie was finally unreeled after three years in production, kids of all ages flocked to watch the amiable cavorting of Disney's dwarfs and to swoon over Prince Charming. The movie quickly broke all previous attendance records, grossed eight million dollars and was translated into 10 languages. Critics, too, were ecstatic, not only about the brilliant animation, but also about the musical score (including "Heigh Ho," "Whistle While You Work," and "Some Day My Prince Will Come"). So vivid were some of the sequences that Radio City Music Hall, according to one legend, had to reupholster all seats after the movie's run; apparently so many children were terrified by Snow White's wicked stepmother that the seats were thoroughly drenched after each performance.

Prince Charming revives Snow White after her stepmother poisons her.

The Movies

Jimmy Stewart, the star of "Mr. Smith Goes to Washington," accuses Claude Rains of corruption.

Great Moments

Everyone who went to the movies left with memories of favorite scenes. Here are a few of the most vivid.

John Wayne leaps for the reins of the "Stagecoach" team after marauding Indians have shot the driver.

Halliwell Hobbs, in toga, and painter Spring Byington play zanies in "You Can't Take It with You."

In "Nothing Sacred," Fredric March socks Carole Lombard, first glamor girl to be hit in the movies.

"Algiers" fugitive Charles Boyer implores girlfriend Hedy Lamarr to run away with him from the Casbah.

An impromptu room divider keeps Clark Gable from Claudette Colbert in "It Happened One Night."

Shirley Temple, star of "Rebecca of Sunnybrook Farm," tap dances with Bill (Bojangles) Robinson.

Atop the Empire State Building "King Kong" swats at attacking planes just before they shoot him down.

Garbo talks: as "Anna Christie," Greta speaks for the first time in the movies: "Gif me a viskey, . . ."

Pouty Jean Harlow is told to shape up or else by angry husband Wallace Beery in "Dinner at Eight."

Charlie Chaplin defiantly gags it up as an enormous machine nearly devours him in "Modern Times."

Lead-slinging Tyrone Power, as "Jesse James," leads his outlaws in a getaway from a bank heist.

As a fisherman in "Captains Courageous," Spencer Tracy croons to castaway Freddy Bartholomew.

Charles Laughton snarls at Clark Gable when trouble starts to simmer in "Mutiny on the Bounty."

Off to see "The Wizard of Oz," Judy Garland chats with Bert Lahr; Jack Haley and Ray Bolger listen.

On the lam, Humphrey Bogart and two armed side-kicks terrorize a roadhouse in "The Petrified Forest."

Gloria Stewart meets "The Invisible Man" (Claude Rains), whose face appears only at the movie's end.

The "Union Pacific" meets the Central Pacific and the first transcontinental rail route is completed.

Bon vivant Melvyn Douglas is so charming that he makes even the dour Garbo laugh in "Ninotchka."

"The Plainsman," Gary Cooper, submits to Indian torture rather than divulge the cavalry's location.

Director Alfred Hitchcock plays a cameo in his film "Rebecca" by eavesdropping on George Sanders.

In a fiery speech, Paul Muni defends the French mar-tyr Alfred Dreyfus in "The Life of Émile Zola."

Bela Lugosi as "Dracula," the Transylvanian vam-pire, closes in on a particularly tempting throat.

As "Captain Blood," swashbuckling Errol Flynn parries Basil Rathbone's attempt to run him through.

Rosalind Russell yanks Paulette Goddard's hair to start a wild female fight scene in "The Women."

British nurse Helen Hayes is smitten by Gary Coo-per, the wounded officer of "A Farewell to Arms."

No beauty herself, Elsa Lanchester recoils at the thought of becoming "The Bride of Frankenstein."

Marlene Dietrich, flashing a famous gam, tries to kick Jimmy Stewart in "Destry Rides Again."

"Public Enemy" James Cagney stops the early-morning nagging of Mae Clarke with a grapefruit.

Margaret Mitchell, the author of "Gone with the Wind," meets Clark Gable, the actor who played her swashbuckling character, Rhett Butler.

Marching through Georgia

OLIVIA DE HAVILLAND AS MELANIE

THOMAS MITCHELL AS MR. O'HARA

SEARCHLIGHTS PLAY ON ATLANTA'S GRAND THEATER ON OPENING NIGHT.

LESLIE HOWARD AS ASHLEY

HATTIE McDANIEL AS MAMMY

The most expensive and most discussed movie of the '30s was *Gone with the Wind*. The picture had its première on December 15, 1939, in Atlanta, Georgia, the city where much of the film's Civil War action was set. For years people had been awaiting the opening night. Producer David O. Selznick had bought the screen rights to Margaret Mitchell's novel in 1936 and then ballyhooed his project by conducting a nationwide hunt for a new face to play the heroine, Scarlett O'Hara. About 1,400 girls were interviewed and the public wrote in thousands of suggestions. When Vivien Leigh was finally chosen, screams of outrage arose because she was English and not American.

Then came the world première. The theater had been rebuilt to resemble a mansion featured in the film, and pretty usherettes wore hoop skirts. And when Miss Leigh appeared on the screen, the old outrage turned to adoration. The feeling quickly spread to the other stars (*above*) and to the show itself. After the show was over, the president-general of the United Daughters of the Confederacy announced: "No one can quarrel now with the selection of Miss Leigh as Scarlett. She is Margaret Mitchell's Scarlett to the life. The whole thing has me overcome."

Vivien Leigh, as Scarlett O'Hara, runs across the lawn of her plantation, Tara, after she learns the man she loves is marrying another girl.

Left, Right & Center

A comrade reads the "Sunday Worker" in Communist headquarters in New York.

The Panacea Seekers

The Nazi salute is the coming salute for the whole United States.
FRITZ KUHN, PRESIDENT OF THE GERMAN-AMERICAN BUND, 1938

With capitalism apparently collapsed around its feet, with its traditional leaders and formulas wiped out, a sizable segment of the country was frantically seeking new ways of doing things. The quest was reflected in the letters full of plans for beating the Depression that poured onto F.D.R.'s desk. A surprising majority of them shared a basic premise: that the United States had a marvelous productive system just aching to create abundance for all. What had to be changed were the financial and political institutions that somehow clogged this horn of plenty.

Thus the search for a remedy to the country's problem started as a kind of innocent democratic exercise, involving a variety of odd people and odd ideas. In Greenwich Village there was leather-coated engineer Howard Scott proposing, in 1932, a social scheme he called Technocracy, that would increase the wealth tenfold by substituting energy units called ergs and joules for dollars and cents. In Royal Oak, Michigan, there was the Reverend Charles E. Coughlin plumping for an inflationary, silver-backed currency; from the Louisiana bayous Huey Long *(overleaf)* was planning to ride into the White House on his "Share Our Wealth" nostrum. In Hollywood and New York there were the earnest intellectuals lapping up, with various de-

grees of innocence, an even more powerful share-the-wealth concept at Communist-run meetings. In California there was Dr. Francis Townsend, an old frontier doctor who would take care of old people—not to mention the whole economy—by giving each citizen over 60 the sum of $200 monthly to be spent within 30 days.

As the decade wore on, however, the innocence began to fade and some of the Messiahs began to appear in very different guises. Coughlin, for one, gradually slid so far to the political right that his lectures dealt less with economics than with Jew-baiting. Many others decided that Adolf Hitler was the real Messiah; and they closed ranks with the Berlin-directed German-American Bund, aping the Nazis' salutes *(right)*, the colored shirts and the broad-gauge racism. As for the Communists, their Soviet idols made a 1939 alliance with Hitler—an ideological turnabout that caused massive disillusionment with people's democracy. By decade's end the seeking after panaceas was about over, for it had become clear that there really weren't any. Furthermore, with the economy alive and progressing, the need seemed no longer urgent, and Americans returned to the practice of leaving politics in the traditional hands of Democratic and Republican politicians.

A German-American Bundist salutes a New Jersey audience at a 1938 Washington's Birthday rally. Bundists called Washington "the first Fascist."

Huey Long, the cocky governor of Louisiana, had few peers as a campaigner. A tireless hand-shaker, he also twisted arms when the need arose.

The Pied Piper of the Bayous

Almost everybody outside of Louisiana saw its governor, Huey Long, as the outrageous demagogue and dictator he was. An unabashed egotist who called himself the Kingfish after a pompous radio character of the day, he ran the state with a capricious will backed by the guns of the police. However, to the poor farmers who made up the state's largest bloc of voters, Long was an infallible friend.

Long's mass appeal was based on a dreamy program, to which he gave the alluring name "Share Our Wealth." Theoretically, Huey would take from the rich and give to the poor. In actual practice, he levied many consumer taxes that, as always, hit the poor the hardest; and he increased the state deficit by almost $100 million.

Long also sold himself a dream—that he would become the President of the Yew-nited States. Huey felt so certain of it that he wrote a wool-gathering book entitled *My First Days in the White House*. This arrogant fantasy appears in excerpt below. Unhappily for the Kingfish, his dream would not come true, for he was shot dead by a constituent who could endure no more of Long's predations.

Soon after I had sent the cabinet names to the Senate, my secretary informed me that Mr. Hoover was trying to get me on the telephone. . . . I heard the voice of that Quaker gentleman say: "Er-r-r, Mr. President—er-r-r, this is Hoover. Is it true that you have tendered me the position of Secretary of Commerce?"

I said I had sent his name to the Senate.

"But, Mr. President, I should have been consulted. This has placed me in a very embarrassing position."

"In what way, Mr. Hoover?" I inquired.

"Why, I am a former President of the United States, and it's a terrible step down for me to be asked to serve in your cabinet," he replied.

"Just what is your position in public life today, Mr. Hoover?"

He hesitated and then: "Well, suppose I decline on the ground that I do not care to be associated with you?"

"All right, Mr. Hoover," I replied. "That is something for you to decide in your own conscience."

Mr. Hoover's voice lost its angry tone. "All right, Mr. President," he replied. "I will consider it."

Some minutes after ten o'clock that night I was called to the telephone. I heard a voice: "Hello, Kingfish!"

It was Franklin D. Roosevelt. "Yes, Mr. President," I answered.

"What in the world do you mean by offering me a cabinet post, after all the things you have said about me as President?"

"I only offered you a position which I thought you were qualified to fill."

"Well, it's a terrible fall from the Presidency to the Secretaryship of the Navy," he replied.

"You sound just like Hoover," I said, "but he couldn't call to mind any position he held just now."

"Well, Huey, I'll have to give this more consideration," the former President told me. "I had a statement all prepared here, declining, but I'll destroy it. Say, suppose I accept and fail to become the best Secretary? What's the penalty then?"

"In that case," I replied, "people will hold me responsible, and they may punish me for your failure."

The former President chuckled: "Well, Huey, that's almost reason enough to accept the position. You'll hear from me later."

My worries about the completion of my cabinet being almost over, I undertook to set in motion my plan for a redistribution of the nation's wealth.

HUEY LONG, *MY FIRST DAYS IN THE WHITE HOUSE*, 1935

Radio's Political Priest

As a political speaker, Father Charles E. Coughlin was second in popularity only to President Roosevelt. Millions listened to the priest's angry tirades and radical schemes for sharing the wealth, broadcast every Sunday from the Shrine of the Little Flower at Royal Oak, Michigan. In 1934, when Coughlin launched his own party, the National Union for Social Justice, more than five million listeners signed up within two months.

Though Coughlin was "for" social justice, among other causes, he was better known by the things he was against.

First and last, he was anti-Communist. He became violently anti-Roosevelt, calling the President a "great betrayer" because the New Deal allegedly had "communistic tendencies." Coughlin made anti-Semitic remarks about "the Jewish bankers," and he also attacked both the labor unions and the industrial capitalists.

These views were met by a rising storm of protest. Under pressure from all quarters, Coughlin slowly curtailed his political activities; and by mid-1940 the air ceased to crackle with fulminations like the excerpts below.

President Roosevelt has both compromised with the money changers and conciliated with monopolistic industry. This spirit of compromise has been the predominant weakness of our present leadership to such an extent that it has not disdained to hold out the olive branch to those whose policies are crimsoned with the theories of sovietism and international socialism.

We cannot applaud a New Deal which, with all its chaotic implications, submits either to the supremacy of a financial overlord more obnoxious than King George III or to the red slavery of an economic Simon Legree.   MARCH 1935

As far as the National Union is concerned, no candidate which is endorsed for Congress can campaign, go electioneering for, or support the great betrayer and liar, Franklin D. Roosevelt, he who promised to drive the money changers from the temple and succeeded in driving the farmers from their homesteads and the citizens from their homes in the cities.

He who promised to drive the money changers from the temple has built up the greatest debt in history, $35,000,000,000, which he permitted the bankers the right, without restriction, to spend, and for which he contracted that you and your children shall repay with seventy billion hours of labor.

I ask you to purge the man who claims to be a Democrat from the Democratic party, and I mean Franklin Double-Crossing Roosevelt.   JULY 1936

When any upstart dictator in the U.S. succeeds in making this a one party form of government, when the ballot is useless, I shall have the courage to stand up and advocate the use of bullets. Mr. Roosevelt is a radical. The Bible commands "increase and multiply," but Mr. Roosevelt says to destroy and devastate. Therefore I call him anti-God.   SEPTEMBER 1936

If we are sincere, we will recall all the Ambassadors and Ministers from the communist countries, from Mexico, from Barcelona, in whose suburbs 300 innocent nuns—the breath of life still in their bodies—were drenched with kerosene and burned.

I say to the good Jews of America, be not indulgent with the irreligious, atheistic Jews and Gentiles who promote the cause of persecution in the land of the Communists, the same ones who promote the cause of atheism in America. Yes, be not lenient with your high financiers and politicians who assisted at the birth of the only . . . system in all civilization that adopted atheism as its religion . . . and slavery as its liberty.   NOVEMBER 1938

Father Charles E. Coughlin carries the political battle to his many enemies. Later he admitted, "It was a horrible mistake to enter politics."

Communist leader "Mother" Bloor, shown with beauty contest winners, was prized by Reds for her deep-dish American look and colonial forebears.

The Very Red-blooded Americans

In the spring of 1937 the New York chapter of the D.A.R. unaccountably failed to celebrate the 162nd anniversary of Paul Revere's ride. On the appointed day, however, hooves clattered along Broadway and into view cantered a horse with a rider attired in Continental costume. He carried a sign: "The DAR forgets but the YCL remembers." The YCL stood for the Young Communist League and the incident stood for the zany fact that during the four years between 1935 and 1939, nobody worked harder at being American than the American Communists. They frenetically tried to build an image of the Party as a native American organization, made up of just plain folks who were anxious to cooperate with other patriots. Explained a YCL leaflet at the University of Wisconsin: "Some people have the idea that a YCLer is politically minded, that nothing outside of politics means anything. Gosh no. We go to shows, parties and all that. The YCL and its members are no different from other people."

The sudden transformation of the local Bolsheviki into 200 per cent Americans began in 1935 in, of all places, Moscow, and for all its absurd contradictions was a serious matter. Realizing that Hitler meant one day to attack Russia, the Soviets shelved their traditional anti-capitalist dogma and ordered Communists the world over to form the widest possible alliances to protect the Red motherland. The new line was called the Popular Front and the U.S. Party skillfully carried it out. Whisking out of sight its bias against capitalism and the American social system, the Party donned a cheerful, homespun exterior and began waving the U.S. flag. Communists trotted out such respectable symbols as Ella Reeves (Mother) Bloor, daughter of a Republican banker, to give themselves a flavor of old-established Americanism and to help woo others with WASP names and Mayflower lineages. New York units joined Negro churches in organizing Mother's Day observances, and the *Daily Worker* inaugurated a super-American sports section.

Different organizations called "fronts" were set up to attract ordinary Americans of every persuasion. Fronts were established to further the interests of medical interns, folksingers, theater buffs, book club joiners and so on. At their peak, the fronts had more than seven million members, represented over 1,000 affiliated organizations, and had acquired a certain respectability. The 1939 congress of the American League against War and Fascism was welcomed in Washington both by the Secretary of the Interior and the Grand Exalted Ruler of the Elks.

Hollywood was where the Popular Front really kicked up dust. After studio hours the chic neighborhoods of Beverly Hills buzzed with activities for a variety of causes, some of enduring value: the Hollywood Anti-Nazi League, the Screen Writers' Guild, the Theatre Committee for the Defense of the Spanish Republic. Stars, many of them unaware of being Red dupes, threw open their hearts, homes and swimming pools so that Hollywood's Popular Front offered an irresistible bargain—an opportunity to combine social climbing with do-gooding. Where else could lowly and lonely liberals rub bosoms and shoulders with the likes of Myrna Loy, Joan Crawford, Franchot Tone, Edward G. Robinson, James Cagney and Melvyn Douglas? The film community welcomed the sensation of being involved with real history and gave generously of time and money. Benefits for the Abraham Lincoln Brigade, a group of Americans who volunteered to fight the Nazi-backed armies of General Francisco Franco in the Spanish Civil War, never yielded less than $5,000 to $8,000. And there was the memorable night when the editor of the Communist magazine *New Masses* appealed for funds at a bigwig's home and came away with $20,000.

It was great fun while it lasted. But on August 23, 1939, in another spectacular about-face, Russia signed with Germany the Nazi-Soviet pact and Stalin toasted Hitler's health: "I know how much the German nation owes to its Fuehrer." At that shocking piece of double-think, the ideological ground beneath the Popular Front gave way, and it soon collapsed. Within a few months the American Communist Party lost thousands of members, especially among the intellectuals; and many thousands of other Americans who had been pursuing good causes under a Red banner awoke to the realization that they'd been had.

The End of a Crusade

When the fascist General Franco, supported by both Hitler and Mussolini, marched to overthrow Spain's Republican Government, idealistic Americans sided strongly with the Republicans. More than 3,000 American men went to Spain to fight in a volunteer unit called the Abraham Lincoln Brigade. Below are excerpts from the letters home of one volunteer, Wilfred Mendelson of Brooklyn, who was killed in action July 28, 1938.

June 3, 1938

I am writing from the training base of the Spanish People's Army. Last night we marched into the nearby town. The older women, careworn faces, thinking of their own sons and husbands at the front, cried. The young girls smiled or raised arms in the popular salute. Our 4,000-mile journey was being understood, appreciated.

June 5, 1938

Sunday in Spain. It is very quiet, almost blissful.

June 22, 1938

About myself, I am doing fine, a good shot really, like a Coney Island range expert. This summer may well seal the fate of world peace. Everybody must be brought to the realization that every day Spain continues in its efforts time is gained for the peace forces all over. In this light Spain is holding the fort for America. If America does not rally it is cutting its own throat.

July 15, 1938

I've seen a magnificent cathedral rising through Barcelona completely stripped of interior and exterior. But that can convey nothing to me. My brain says "Bombers", I know it, I see it, but the terror just isn't there.

July 23, 1938

Looks like any hour now we'll be off. While our forces are tremendously strong and we confidently expect victory, accidents do happen to individuals. Don't show this note to my parents. Take care of them. I love you.

Veterans of the Abraham Lincoln Brigade, back home from Spain, give the Popular Front clenched-fist salute at a 1939 May Day parade.

E.H. Crump, the tough old pol who ran Memphis and dominated much of the rest of Tennessee, styled himself the champion of the "little" man.

Mister Ed Crump, He Runs This Town

When President Franklin D. Roosevelt carried his campaign for re-election into the South in September 1936, his entourage was joined by a big, genial man with a pink puckish face, flowing white hair and eyebrows as bushy as a guardsman's mustachios. This colorful creature was E.H. (Edward Hull) Crump, long-time boss of Memphis. At 61, Ed Crump was at the peak of his power, unbeatable in a fight or a frolic. In this last golden decade for big-city bosses, Crump ruled his bailiwick autocratically. Like his peers in Jersey City, Boston and a dozen other cities, he influenced decisions that affected the whole nation.

F.D.R. greeted the "Boss of Memphis" with the cordiality due one of the President's staunchest backers. But later, F.D.R. expressed concern over a recent bit of Crump pork-barreling, which had brought to Memphis a $15,000 municipal kennel paid for with federal funds.

"Well, Ed," said Roosevelt, "what about that dog house down in Memphis?"

Crump replied confidently, "It will mean a lot of votes for you down there."

The Boss was as good as his word. On election day, his private domain of Memphis and surrounding Shelby County contributed a whopping plurality of almost 60,000 votes to an easy Democratic victory in Tennessee. Only 2,194 voters failed to cast their ballots for Roosevelt.

Crump's delivery of the vote came as no surprise to Tennesseans. For three decades, the Boss and his political organization had been winning elections with monotonous regularity. Though Crump was retired, now, from elective position, he continued to run his machine from the offices of his large, prosperous insurance agency, E.H. Crump & Company; it functioned with such awesome efficiency that one reporter called it "a combined reaper, thresher and binder; a machine that has only one weakness—it's *too* perfect."

Such journalistic judgments irritated Crump but had little effect on his supporters. To most Memphians the Boss was courtly yet earthy, and they treated him with fondness or respect, rather like a fine old Southern landmark. As Crump often declared with a contented smile or a grand wave to passing constituents, "They like me."

But when Crump was at work in his company office, he left no doubt as to who ran the political show. In various meetings, phone calls and letters, he dispensed patronage, deployed his ward leaders, laid down policy guidelines for Crump men in state and national office. Benevolence was his stock-in-trade, ruthlessness his ace-in-the-hole. Any man who needed a loan or a job, and any firm seeking to do business with the city, would get a friendly hearing from the Boss, and they often got more.

Once Ed Crump had bestowed his favors, the recipients showed their appreciation by contributing to his next campaign or by buying insurance from E.H. Crump & Company. They heeded a rumor that Crump kept file cards to enforce voting orthodoxy. As one executive explained it, "He knows how everybody votes, and if a man doesn't

---

I probably have been successful in more elections than any other man in America. I was elected 25 times myself as police commissioner, mayor, congressman, county treasurer, etc., and have assisted in 92 other elections without a single defeat.

EDWARD HULL CRUMP

---

vote right, the machine can hit him through his kinfolks, because everybody has kinfolks at the public trough."

This general principle applied to high officials who owed their posts to Crump. They knew that anyone who departed from the Boss's basic tenets, such as his commitment to public ownership of the utilities, would be defeated in the next election by a more devout believer. Therefore Crump men were inclined to obey his every whim with gusto and alacrity. For example, Crump, a noted bird-lover, once exhorted Memphians to protect their feathered friends, and immediately his county commissioner rushed out to set traps for villainous tomcats.

Crump was, in all, the consummate machine politician. On this point almost everyone agreed, from the fiery minister who called him "the lowest down political boss inside or outside of hell," to the solid businessman who conceded, "He gives us good government." In fact the only notable demurrer was Crump himself. "Who said boss?" he once demanded of a tactless newsman. "I am just an unassuming good citizen working with and for the people."

Crump's angry response to bossism charges was at least understandable. The term "boss" had always implied extravagantly crooked dealings and dictatorial methods. And in the '30s, bosses were scaling new heights of venality and arrogance. Crump had good reason to resent being bracketed with the Vare brothers of Philadelphia

---

If you drive hard, others will hit the same stride. If you hesitate in forcing an organization, those down the line will also hesitate. Don't sit down in the meadow and wait for the cow to back up and be milked—Go after the cow.

CRUMP ON POLITICAL HUSBANDRY

---

or Bill Thompson of Chicago. They were extremely venal men and they were not the worst of the bosses.

In Jersey City, there was Mayor Frank Hague, who had ruled like a feudal baron since 1917. With no visible source of income but a salary of $8,500, he had become a millionaire several times over. Before each election he held a bald-faced shakedown; all municipal and county employees were dunned for contributions on peril of losing their jobs. According to investigators, up to 20 per cent of the Hague vote was cast in the name of people deceased or otherwise unqualified. For those who objected, Hague had a disdainful retort: "I am the law."

Kansas City had Thomas J. Pendergast. In order to afford horse bets of $10,000, Tom opened his town to vice lords and racketeers, from whom he could extort copious payoffs. However, the Internal Revenue bureau discovered that in a single year Tom had neglected to account for $443,550 as income. Sentenced as a tax evader in 1939, Pendergast languished in prison for 12 months; but the locals could not forget his standard promise to his detractors: "I'll break your jaw."

Boston was the stamping ground of James Michael Curley, a charming man who served often as mayor and twice

as a jailbird convicted of fraud. Curley's career was a whirl of patronage, litigation, scandal and gorgeous living. One year Jim was accused of spending $85,206 on cigars, dinners and traveling expenses. To him, and to many of his constituents, it was no crime that he paid for these simple necessities out of public funds.

Compared to such lurid grafters, Ed Crump was painfully honest and decorous. He doted on his wife and three sons; he never smoked and seldom drank anything stronger than Bulgarian buttermilk. In politics, the moral distinctions that he drew seemed esoteric to some, but he held to them. He always returned or paid for the gifts that came his way. He never profited personally by the contributions that lubricated his political machine, and he banished or prosecuted any Crump man who helped himself to the organization's regular collections from business houses, liquor stores and pinball operators. And yet Crump's long career was practically a blueprint for any strong man planning to assume undelegated authority.

Ed Crump was a rawboned farm boy of 19 when, in 1894, he left his home town of Holly Springs, Mississippi, for an office job in Memphis. He arrived with only 25 cents in his pocket. But his assets included a head for figures, consuming ambition and an enormous capacity for sustained labor. Within a decade Crump became owner of a carriage-making company, whose sale made him a budding capitalist. He also plunged into politics, ringing doorbells to get out the vote in Memphis' Fourth Ward. In the next few years he was elected councilman, then police commissioner, and won citywide approval for his aggressive campaigning. "Crump," wrote one reporter, "knows everybody and he shakes hands with everybody. He can cover more territory and be in more places at the same time than any man that entered the political game."

By 1909, Crump had emerged as a tough, smart politician, and, in the context of the times, a reformer. Memphis desperately needed some such man as mayor. The city groaned under a corrupt government; its tawdry streets were an open house for gamblers, sporting girls and violent thugs. Crump leaped into the mayoralty race on just the right platform: law and order, fiscal responsibility and new services for the hard-pressed "little people."

It was a rough, wild contest. Thugs charged Crump's meetings, and he and his boys had to fight them off in pitched battles. But Ed squeaked through by 79 votes, and loomed as the new power of mid-South politics.

In the course of time, Memphians learned that their new mayor was tough enough to keep his campaign promises. His revamped police force drove out the footpads, gamblers and fancy ladies. He broadened city thoroughfares, built schools and hospitals, parks and playgrounds. He accomplished all this partially through frugal contracting and partially by increasing the tax levies on "outside interests" such as utility companies, which had raked in their profits but had paid little more than token taxes.

Crump's whip-cracking leadership was bad news for loafers and other riffraff, and this fact was soon celebrated in two song classics. Down along the Mississippi, Negro dockhands chanted dolefully, "Mister Ed Crump, he runs this town." And on Beale Street in the Negro quarter, a jazz musician named W.C. Handy composed the lament known as "The Memphis Blues":

> Mister Crump don't 'low no easy riders here,
> But we don't care what Mister Crump don't 'low,
> We gonna barrelhouse anyhow,
> 'Cause Mister Crump don't 'low no easy riders here.

Despite the severity of Crump's regime, his policies offered something appealing to almost everyone; and in six years as mayor and eight years as county commissioner he forged a powerful coalition of supporters. As was the case with many other bosses, the city's businessmen liked Crump because he insured the stability they needed for a thriving trade. The farmers not only liked him; they considered him their hero and protector—and a "ring-tailed tooter." And they, along with the low-paid industrial workers, cheered him to the echo whenever he joined a new battle in his righteous war against the "interests."

Crump gave them plenty to cheer about. His pals in Nashville pushed a state law fixing telephone rates, per-

suading the phone company to refund more than $100,000 to local clients. When a railroad failed to meet its contractual obligations, he marched out with a crowbar, tore up a section of track and set policemen to guard the road-

---

We teach people how to vote and urge them to vote. They don't know the candidates they want to vote for, and they don't know where to mark the ballot. If you put Judas Iscariot on the ballot, he'd get 1,000 votes in Shelby County.

CRUMP ON VOTER EDUCATION

---

block until the company capitulated. The locals loved it.

Of course the interests fought back. They hired the Pinkerton Detective Agency to burrow into Crump's dealings. But their best effort, a forced audit of the city's books, gave the Boss's backers yet another chance to cheer. The books were off only three cents—in Crump's favor.

Of all Crump's supporters, the most loyal were Negroes, who constituted about 40 per cent of the population of Shelby County. It seemed to be an anomaly that blacks were voting en masse in Tennessee, while just across the line in Mississippi they were virtually disenfranchised by custom and the poll tax. Crump saw to it that the Memphis Negroes voted, even if his organization had to pay their poll taxes. He gave them a hospital, named a park after the black abolitionist Frederick Douglass, and, above all, he fought the Ku Klux Klan.

Crump's actions were influenced by the fact that he relied heavily on Negro votes; but he was truly an egalitarian of sorts. He retained a Jewish lawyer, Will Gerber, as his trusted aide; and in 1928 he had angrily declared, "The man or woman who votes against Alfred E. Smith because he is a Catholic betrays his American citizenship and violates the letter and spirit of the Constitution." Somehow these attitudes caused little concern among Crump's redneck constituents. After all, the Boss was a dyed-in-the-cotton Southerner who could be counted on to maintain the important facets of the status quo.

In the '20s, Crump became strong enough to move toward statewide mastery. Blocking his way was Luke Lea,

225

the ruthless publisher of the Nashville *Tennessean,* and Crump took him on in a brisk backroom battle in the state capital. As one newspaper put it, "Mr. Crump came to Nashville on Sunday night as the boss of Shelby County. In two days' work, he was elected to the 'boss' of Tennessee politics." That was that.

Thus the opening years of the decade found Ed Crump riding the crest of hard-won success. For three years, he served as U.S. Congressman. But homesickness prompted the Boss to resign and return to his beloved Memphis. Here he fully enjoyed doing what came naturally—i.e., plain and fancy hometown politicking. He added new refinements to his powerful political machine, fought the interests, called for a better and prettier Memphis. Despising unnecessary noise in public places, he even banned horn tooting in traffic—and the city fell strangely silent.

As for those who risked Crump's wrath, they learned at their cost that he was a master of political invective. Indulging his fondness for purple abuse, the Boss said of three rivals, "This trio of mangy bubonic rats are conscienceless liars." Often he added a quotable insult to his famous output of rural wit. He impaled a renegade Crump man with the line, "That man would milk his neighbor's cow through a crack in the fence." When a pompous opponent campaigned on a creditable record made years back, Ed commented, "Even a buzzard is pure white until he is half grown."

Crump's enemies countered with exaggerated charges. They accused the Boss of neglecting to count many anti-Crump votes, of importing Negroes from Arkansas to vote for his candidates. There was a tale that Crump and crony Will Gerber had been seen in a cemetery copying names off tombstones. According to the yarn, Gerber found one inscription illegible, but Crump insisted that he puzzle it out. "We've got to have the right name," said the Boss. "This has got to be an honest election."

In the '30s Crump won the victory that crowned his career. The cause was an old and dear one for him: cheap public power, publicly owned. In 1933 Congress had passed a New Deal measure setting up the Tennessee Valley Authority to provide rural electric power in the mid-South. At once Crump demanded—and Memphians soon endorsed overwhelmingly—a nine-million-dollar bond issue to pipe TVA power into the city.

But then the battle lines hardened. The private power lobby and its conservative allies did all they could to dilute and delay the effect of the TVA; Crump fought the spoilers at every turn and drove recalcitrant officeholders into action. When his current governor, Hill McAlister, was slow in appointing a committee to work with the TVA, Crump wrote him a firm letter, and McAlister nervously replied, "I suppose I had better do it right now."

Never put a sponge on the end of a hammer if you expect to drive a nail. CRUMP ON POLITICAL PERSUASION

With a toss of his hoary head, Crump roared, "I propose to give TVA to all the homes, farms and factories and the Power Trust will not tell me how to do it."

By 1939, TVA was fairly safe. Crump—and the people of Tennessee—had finally won.

The victory came none too soon for old Ed Crump. Within a year, he was staggered by the deaths of his son John and his ancient mother. Afterward, his zest gradually waned, and his bitterness increased as various reporters, ignoring his positive contribution, constantly stigmatized him with the title "Boss." Except to the most loyal of his devoted constituents, he was no more than the best of a bad breed—or the worst product of America's glorious political tradition.

Either way, one thing was certain: before the '30s ended, Crump was a living anachronism. His style of leadership dated back a half-century and more, to a simpler time when politics was an intimate matter between friends, and when an elected official was often the neighbor or drinking companion in whom most people trusted. But by 1940, paternalism and cronyism were losing appeal; the voters, growing sophisticated, often crossed party lines to elect unbossed candidates of their own choosing. The great age of the bosses was drawing to a close.

A big spender, Boss Frank Hague of Jersey City gave himself a $125,000 home, his church a $50,000 altar, his town a $3,000,000 ball park.

Swing

Two swing musicians get top billing on a Broadway marquee.

The Big Bands Break Loose

It makes no diff'rence if it's sweet or hot, Just give that rhythm ev'rything you got. Oh, it don't mean a thing, if it ain't got that swing.

"IT DON'T MEAN A THING" BY IRVING MILLS AND DUKE ELLINGTON

Before dawn one cold day in 1938, hundreds of teenagers started lining up in front of New York City's Paramount Theater, literally spilling out onto the street and stopping traffic. A special squad of cops was called to contain the "riot." The riot outside was nothing compared with the one that soon broke loose inside. When the early morning movie was over, a band on an elevating platform rose out of the orchestra pit; 3,000 adolescents screamed and, as the musicians opened up, began to dance in the aisles. The band was Benny Goodman's, and the music he was playing was "swing."

In the closing years of the decade, all of America was swept by swing fever. In little towns girls in loose skirts and saddle shoes tripped into ice-cream parlors with their boyfriends, plugged nickels into the jukebox and set the place rocking with their intricate jitterbug dance steps. Radio audiences clustered around their sets to hear their favorite bands *(pages 232-233)* on weekly programs, and on Saturdays they tuned in *Your Hit Parade* to learn the top 10 hits of the week. *The New York Times* solemnly suggested that the craze was getting out of hand, quoting a psychologist on the "dangerously hypnotic influence of swing, cunningly devised to a faster tempo than seventy-two bars to the minute—faster than the human pulse."

Actually, swing was nothing more than jazz under a new name. Negro groups in the '20s had developed jazz, which was characterized by a driving rhythm and improvised solos; but few white people heard anything except tame orchestrated versions of it. During the Depression the authentic jazz sound went completely underground. The record industry almost died out. Many jazz musicians found jobs playing bland music in radio studios. Then, in 1934, Benny Goodman, who was only 24 years old, formed a band to play the real jazz to mass audiences. The band's first cross-country tour in 1935 was a string of disasters. By the time the group had reached California, it had returned to playing innocuous dance music. At the end of an evening at the Palomar Ballroom in Hollywood, however, Goodman was so disgusted with syrupy music that he told his sidemen to swing for one set to close the evening. The room was filled with the strong beat of drums, the resonance of brass, the dramatic precision of saxophones and the improvisation of hot soloists. The audience went wild. After that, the swinging sound took the country by storm, and within months this revived form of jazz passed into the mainstream of American culture.

Teenagers jitterbug their way through 1937's popular Big Apple. Such exhibitionistic dancers, showing off for the crowd, were known as shiners.

The Leaders

Big bands became big business in the late '30s and their leaders were as famous as movie stars. In fact, many band leaders made full-length movies. Benny Goodman appeared in *The Big Broadcast of 1937*; Bob Crosby was featured in *Let's Make Music*. As with other celebrities, lives of the big-band leaders became fair game for gossip-mongers. When the hot-tempered musical brothers Tommy and Jimmy Dorsey feuded over the proper tempo for a song in 1935 and split up the Dorsey Brothers Orchestra, the story was big news. Another hot item was the marriage of band-leader Kay Kyser to his svelte blonde vocalist, Georgia Carroll. Equally well-known among musicians and fans was the notorious Goodman "ray," or stare; Benny Goodman was a perfectionist, and if he turned his "ray" on an underrehearsed musician, the man's days with the band were considered numbered.

The most dedicated swing fans followed the exploits of their heroes in *Downbeat* and *Metronome*, the trade journals of the popular band musicians. Every year both magazines asked readers to write in the names of their favorite bands. The two polls made a distinction between "sweet" bands, which played the schmaltzy sound popularized by the likes of Guy Lombardo, and swing bands, those with a hard-driving beat and improvised solos. The men at right were the top 10 swing band leaders of 1939 as selected in *Metronome*.

1. Benny Goodman

"Metronome's" top band leader, the clarinet-playing Goodman was celebrated as "The King of Swing."

2. Artie Shaw

Shaw, though not as hot a clarinetist as Goodman, had a band many fans rated as swinging as Benny's.

3. Tommy Dorsey

After breaking with his brother Jimmy, trombonist Tommy created a new band with a brassier sound.

4. Bob Crosby

Bing's kid brother, Bob Crosby, sang with the Dorseys before he left to lead a popular Dixieland band.

5. Glenn Miller

An excellent arranger, trombonist Glenn Miller played music noted for fast tempos and lead clarinets.

7. Jimmy Dorsey

Playing both alto sax and clarinet, Jimmy wavered between Dixieland and the more modern swing sound.

9. Jimmie Lunceford

Lunceford's group was one of the decade's most dynamic bands, with its showmanship and bouncy beat.

6. Count Basie

Basie's 15-man band featured great vocalists like Jimmy Rushing and the Count's own droll piano style.

8. Harry James

At first a trumpet soloist with Goodman, James started his own group in 1939—with Benny's backing.

10. Duke Ellington

A gifted composer, the Duke created a sophisticated style using a jazz sound he called "jungle music."

Martha Tilton

Known as "Liltin' Martha Tilton," she made "And the Angels Sing" a hit record in 1939 with Benny Goodman.

Helen O'Connell

Famous as Jimmy Dorsey's canary, swing fans voted her the top female vocalist of 1940, when she was twenty.

Billie Holiday

The great jazz vocalist Billie Holiday was almost unknown when she joined the Artie Shaw Orchestra in 1938.

Canaries and Hits

Almost all the big bands, swing and sweet alike, featured vocalists, usually female. The hot voices—or cool looks—of these singers (*aficionados* called them canaries) often outdid the orchestras in putting across hit tunes. Above is a lineup of canaries of the late '30s and at right are box scores from the entertainment newspaper *Variety* of the top 15 tunes from 1936 to 1940. As the charts show, many of the most popular songs of the swing age were not strictly swing.

1936
ALL MY EGGS IN ONE BASKET
ALONE
CHAPEL IN THE MOONLIGHT
DID I REMEMBER?
IS IT TRUE WHAT THEY SAY ABOUT DIXIE?
IT'S A SIN TO TELL A LIE
LIGHTS OUT
MOON OVER MIAMI
THE MUSIC GOES 'ROUND AND 'ROUND
ON THE BEACH AT BALI BALI
PENNIES FROM HEAVEN
RED SAILS IN THE SUNSET
THE WAY YOU LOOK TONIGHT
WHEN DID YOU LEAVE HEAVEN?
WHEN I'M WITH YOU

1937
BOO HOO
CHAPEL IN THE MOONLIGHT
HARBOR LIGHTS
IT LOOKS LIKE RAIN
LITTLE OLD LADY
MOONLIGHT AND SHADOWS
MY CABIN OF DREAMS
ONCE IN A WHILE
SAILBOAT IN THE MOONLIGHT
SEPTEMBER IN THE RAIN
SO RARE
THAT OLD FEELING
VIENI VIENI
WHEN MY DREAMBOAT COMES HOME
YOU CAN'T STOP ME FROM DREAMING

Mildred Bailey

Singing ballads such as "Willow Weep for Me," Mildred was the top attraction for her husband Red Norvo's band.

Marion Hutton

Blonde Marion Hutton was a vocalist for Glenn Miller. At this time her sister, Betty Hutton, was also a singer.

Ella Fitzgerald

Discovered in an amateur show at age 17, Ella joined Chick Webb and dazzled fans with "A-Tisket A-Tasket."

1938
ALEXANDER'S RAGTIME BAND
A-TISKET A-TASKET
BEI MIR BIST DU SCHÖN
CATHEDRAL IN THE PINES
HEIGH-HO
I'VE GOT A POCKETFUL OF DREAMS
LOVE WALKED IN
MUSIC, MAESTRO, PLEASE!
MY REVERIE
ROSALIE
SAYS MY HEART
THANKS FOR THE MEMORY
THERE'S A GOLD MINE IN THE SKY
TI-PI-TIN
WHISTLE WHILE YOU WORK

1939
AND THE ANGELS SING
BEER BARREL POLKA
DEEP IN A DREAM
DEEP PURPLE
JEEPERS CREEPERS
MAN WITH THE MANDOLIN
MOON LOVE
MY PRAYER
OVER THE RAINBOW
PENNY SERENADE
SUNRISE SERENADE
THREE LITTLE FISHIES
UMBRELLA MAN
WISHING
YOU MUST HAVE BEEN A BEAUTIFUL BABY

1940
BLUEBERRY HILL
CARELESS
FERRYBOAT SERENADE
GOD BLESS AMERICA
I'LL NEVER SMILE AGAIN
IN AN OLD DUTCH GARDEN
INDIAN SUMMER
MAKE BELIEVE ISLAND
OH JOHNNY
ONLY FOREVER
PLAYMATES
SCATTERBRAIN
SOUTH OF THE BORDER
WHEN YOU WISH UPON A STAR
WOODPECKER SONG

Completely swept up by the beat of the Big Apple, a hefty adolescent firmly plants her saddle shoes in a spraddle-legged maneuver called Posin'.

Swinging Dance

"Praise Allah, Wiggle, wiggle, wiggle —/ Praise Allah, Wiggle and dance; / Do that stomp with lots of pomp and sweet romance! / Big Apple, Big Apple—" Lee David and John Redmond conjured up these lyrics in 1937 for a swing dance that quickly became a national craze: the Big Apple. Although the Big Apple remained a total mystery to conservative adults, they nonetheless did their solemn best to try to explain it *(excerpt below).*

*D*anced in a circle by a group, the Big Apple is led by one who calls the steps, as in a Virginia reel. Fundamental step is a hop similar to the Lindy Hop. In the words of "Variety," "it requires a lot of floating power and fannying." In groups or singly, the dancers follow the caller and combine such steps as the Black Bottom, "shag," Suzi-Q, Charleston, "truckin'," as well as old square-dance turns like London Bridge, and a formation which resembles an Indian Rain Dance. The Big Apple invariably ends upon a somewhat reverent note, with everybody leaning back and raising his arms heavenward. This movement is called "Praise Allah." Through it all, the "caller" shouts continuously—"Truck to the right . . . Reverse it . . . To the left . . . Stomp that right foot . . . Swing it."

TIME MAGAZINE, 1937

Jive Talk

The fast-moving world of swing gave birth to a language called "jive" that was as free and impressionistic and, to the uninitiated, as confusing as the music itself. Below is an abridged dictionary of this lingo, and at right some of the terms are illustrated.

ALLIGATOR—A devotee of swing.

CANARY—A girl vocalist.

CATS—Musicians in a swing orchestra.

CORN, MICKEY MOUSE, SCHMALTZ, SWEET—Uninspired music good only for sedate dancing.

CUTTIN' THE RUG—Dancing to swing music.

DISC OR PLATTER—A recording.

EIGHTY-EIGHT OR MOTHBOX—A piano.

HEPCAT—A very knowledgeable swing fan.

HIDE OR SKINS—Drums, played by a *skin-beater*.

ICKIE—A person who does not understand swing.

IN THE GROOVE—Carried away by good swing.

JAM SESSION—Informal gathering at which swing musicians play for their own pleasure.

JITTERBUG—A dancer responding to swing music.

KICKING OUT—Being very free, improvising.

KNOCKED OUT—To be so engrossed in the music as to blot out all else; a superlative of *sent*, which means to be aroused by the music.

LICORICE STICK—A clarinet.

LONG HAIR—In general an unaware person, musically one who prefers symphonic music.

ONE NIGHTER—A one-night engagement, often with low, or *coffee-and-cake*, wages.

PAPER MAN—A musician who plays by the *spots* (notes) and is incapable of improvising.

PLUMBING—A trumpet, played by a *liver-lips*.

SCAT SINGER—A vocalist who improvises lyrics, substituting nonsense syllables for words.

SWING—Unrestrained but melodic big-band jazz with a strong element of improvisation.

Lindy hoppers kick out

Fats Waller hits the mothbox

Picking a platter to spin

Canaries all: the Andrews Sisters

Cats jam with Duke Ellington around an eighty-eight

Silly Senders

In the '30s, a spate of nonsense songs swept the country. Some, like the best-sellers below, had lyrics so obscure that many fans never did catch on, and they simply faked the words. Thus *Bei Mir Bist Du Schön* often became "My Mere Bits of Shame."

BEI MIR BIST DU SCHÖN
Bei Mir Bist Du Schön—
Please let me explain,
Bei Mir Bist Du Schön
means that you're grand,
Bei Mir Bist Du Schön—Again I'll explain,
It means you're the fairest in the land. . . .

TUTTI FRUTTI
Be a rooty-tooty;
Find yourself a cutie,
Why should you be snooty.
Just take your cutie, sweet patootie,
While you have a Tut-ti Frut-ti.
Go to the nearest Sugar Bowl,
Do yourself a favor.
Get a taste of what I mean
S'got the mostest, bestest flavor.
Tut-ti Frut-ti Frut-ti
Tut-ti Frut-ti Frut-ti
Tut-ti Frut-ti Frut-ti

THREE LITTLE FISHIES
Down in de meddy in a itty bitty poo,
Fam fee itty fitty and a mama fitty, foo.
"Fim," fed de mama fitty, "Fim if oo tan,"
And dey fam and dey fam all over de dam.
Boop boop dit-tem dat-tem what-tem Chu!
Boop boop dit-tem dat-tem what-tem Chu!
Boop boop dit-tem dat-tem what-tem Chu!
And dey fam all over de dam.

THE FLAT FOOT FLOOGEE
There's a new killer diller
There's a new Harlem thriller
A new way to ruin the rugs
A new dance for Jitter Bugs.
The Flat Foot Floogee with the Floy Floy
The Flat Foot Floogee with the Floy Floy
The Flat Foot Floogee with the Floy Floy
Floy Doy, Floy Doy, Floy Doy, Floy Doy;
The Flat Foot Floogee with the Flou Flou
The Flat Foot Floogee with the Flou Flou
The Flat Foot Floogee with the Flou Flou,
Flou Dow, Flou Dow, Flou Dow, Flow Dow.

©1938, 1966 JEWEL MUSIC

Skin-beater Gene Krupa pounds out the rhythm

A knocked-out alligator

Cuttin' the rug

Schmaltzmen play for ickies

Hepcat in the groove

Jiving it up on their way to class, a bunch of hep high school students in Iowa City practice "truckin'," a finger-waving, hip-tossing walk.

Main Street

Old cronies pass a quiet Saturday afternoon in Versailles, Kentucky.

Two Thirds of a Nation

The big world outside now is so filled with confusion. It seemed to me that hope, in the present muddle, was to try thinking small.   SHERWOOD ANDERSON IN *HOME TOWN*

The most striking quality of life in mid-Depression America was summed up by President Roosevelt in his Second Inaugural Address in 1937: "I see one third of the nation ill-housed, ill-clad, ill-nourished." But for the nation's luckier two thirds, the advent of hard times was not quite so devastating, and many people were able to go on about the business of living pretty much as always.

In thousands of small towns all over America, neither Depression-time blues nor the federal government's massive efforts to shoo those blues away really altered the deep-grained texture of community life. Even in the toughest years, Main Street kept its traditional optimism. "What depression?" asked an Indiana businessman in 1935. "We haven't had a depression here." There was even a brief reverse migration as Americans for the first time in decades moved out of the cities and back to the small towns from which they had originally come.

The bad times made some differences, of course. Fewer people bought houses, washing machines or fancy new clothes. Hard-pressed Americans read more borrowed library books and bought fewer newspapers. And instead of spending money on new cars, people made their old ones last, driving them farther and harder. Partly as a re-

sult, the number of auto repair shops and gasoline stations doubled during the Depression.

Furthermore, as militant labor unions made the five-day week universal, even the people with steady jobs found they had more leisure time. They also discovered that many of the best things in life were indeed free—or nearly so. For example, bridge-playing, stamp-collecting and listening to the radio all saw an upsurge of popularity. So, too, did such venerable arts and crafts as horseshoe pitching and riding a rocking chair on the front porch.

While the lucky two thirds were thus engaged in living, the federal government launched a massive project to record the overall plight of the nation. As part of this effort, the Farm Security Administration sent out a team of crack photographers, primarily to document rural poverty. While the cameramen indeed took the assigned pictures of barren fields and hungry children, they also turned their cameras on the more common scenes—on people going to church, gossiping on the lawn, eating a roadside picnic. Matched with the words of Thomas Wolfe, E.B. White and other commentators on American life, they add up to a powerful testament, shown on these pages, of the enduring qualities of hometown America at ebb tide.

244

*Main Street, like this one in Pennsylvania, seemed
never to change. Thomas Wolfe found
its buildings "all common and familiar as my breath."*

*A Florida man sips a Coke at the sort of hamburger
stand John Steinbeck lovingly described,
with its "pies in wire cages and oranges in pyramids
of four," and its "coffee urns, shiny and
steaming, with glass showing the coffee level."*

In Teton County, Montana, three young members
in good standing of the local Four-H club
show the baby calves that they feed and care for.

An auto repair shop in Atlanta, Georgia: "They
keep the radio going low at the village garage," wrote
E.B. White. "Everything is sort of cozy
and quiet in there, with the music faintly in your ears."

*In Cook, Minnesota, a vacant stool stands
watch beside a nearby empty popcorn machine.*

*Louisiana newsboys fold the local paper, which,
wrote Sherwood Anderson, might tell briefly
of "a revolution in Spain," but "if Mr. Morley's little
girl gets bitten by a dog, it's worth a column."*

"People talking, laughing, streaming out from the dutiful, weekly walnut disinfection of their souls," Wolfe wrote of churchgoers like these in Ohio, people moving "into bright morning-gold of Sunday light again, and standing then in friendly and yet laughing groups upon the lawn outside."

*In Lowell, Vermont, a storekeeper lounging
contentedly in his rocker typifies the
rural New Englanders whom Sinclair Lewis called
"a complicated, reticent, slyly humorous lot."*

*A soda jerk in Corpus Christi, Texas, works
with the sort of panache that prompted Carl Sandburg
to write: "One movie star arches her
eyebrows and refers to 'my public.' One soda-jerker
arches his eyebrows, curves malt-milk
from shaker to glass and speaks of 'my public.'"*

"On Sunday afternoon the small town man gets his car out," observed Sherwood Anderson. Here the family auto
doubles as an al fresco dining room for these visitors to a community sing at Pie Town, New Mexico.

"The sins of Kalamazoo are neither scarlet nor crimson," Carl Sandburg *once said of such city-bred amusements as the local burlesque; this one is in the outskirts of Washington, D.C.*

Hard times or no, a Pennsylvania housewife kept her larder well stocked. "The vision of milk and honey, it comes and goes," wrote E.B. White. "But the odor of cooking goes on forever."

Turned out in their Sunday best, three Louisiana girls try their luck at the bingo tent at that most venerable of rural institutions, the state fair.

*Two boys, clutching books and lunch pails,
come home from school in Hightstown, New Jersey.*

*"These two sat as if formally, or as if sculptured," was
James Agee's description of two small-town
Americans, "all the while communicating thoroughly
with each other by no outward sign of
word or glance or turning, but by emanation."*

*Waving in queasy triumph, the winner of a pie-eating contest in Kansas
identifies himself while the other contestants battle for second place.*

*A coal miner and his wife in West Virginia spend an evening by the radio. As
E.B. White said, when rural people refer to "The Radio," they mean "a
pervading and somewhat godlike presence which has come into their lives and homes."*

An ice cream stand in Connecticut recalls Nathanael West's remark about such architectural fantasies:

"Their desire to startle was so eager and guileless . . . it is easy to sigh."

A sphere and needle dominate the New York World's Fair.

The Big Fair

Merry Days at Mad Meadow

Here is the magnificent spectacle of a luminous world, apparently suspended in space . . .
OFFICIAL FAIR GUIDE BOOK

. . . and your fellow fairgoers trudge on numbed feet with dazed eyes.
LIFE, JULY 3, 1939

The New York World's Fair was the biggest, giddiest, costliest and most ambitious international exposition ever put on. Even before it opened, on April 30, 1939, amid a blaze of fireworks and a blast of windy publicity, it had cost more than $150 million. Its 1,216-acre grounds in Flushing Meadow, Queens, had been made to order by filling in the entire Queens city dump and planting it with 10,000 trees and one million tulips from Holland. Upon this tract had been built 300 massive, futuristic buildings to house the Fair's 1,500 exhibitors. They included 33 states, 58 foreign countries and 1,300 business firms, ranging from the Ford Motor Company to Dr. Scholl's Footease, which maintained an emergency clinic to treat fairgoers whose arches had sagged along the exposition's 65 miles of paved streets and footpaths.

The Fair's president, gardenia-wearing Grover Aloysius Whalen, had christened this gigantic conglomeration "The World of Tomorrow" and dedicated it to both the blessings of democracy and the wonders of technology. The latter included such marvels as television, nylon stockings, a robot named Elektro that could talk and puff a cigarette, nude statues with titles like Freedom of Assembly, and at the Fair's Theme Centre, the 700-foot-tall needlelike Trylon and the 200-foot globe called the Perisphere.

Mixed in with the technological marvels, the Fair's 45 million visitors found a bewildering assortment of promotional gimmicks, side shows and downright corn, which prompted *The New York Times's* Meyer Berger to refer to the Fair as "Mad Meadow." "See me get milked on a merry-go-round!" shouted the poster hawking Elsie, the Borden Cow, and sure enough, at the Borden exhibit you could see 150 of Elsie's sisters being spun on a revolving milking platform. If you were unlucky, you might hit Elsie on her birthday and hear a squad of Western Union boys deliver a singing telegram: "Mooey Birthday to You." At Ford there was a floor show entitled "A Thousand Times Neigh," a horse's-eye view of the automobile, and Life Savers offered a sky dive *(opposite)*. You could even take in a skin show and ogle an innocent (nearly nude) maiden as she wrestled with Oscar the Obscene Octopus in "Twenty Thousand Legs Under the Sea."

In its two-year run, in fact, the Fair provided just about everything for everybody. "It was the paradox of all paradoxes," wrote Sidney M. Shalett in *Harper's* magazine in 1940. "It was good, it was bad; it was the acme of all crazy vulgarity, it was the pinnacle of all inspiration."

High point of the Fair's Amusement Area was the 250-foot parachute jump, which in two years thrilled two million riders.

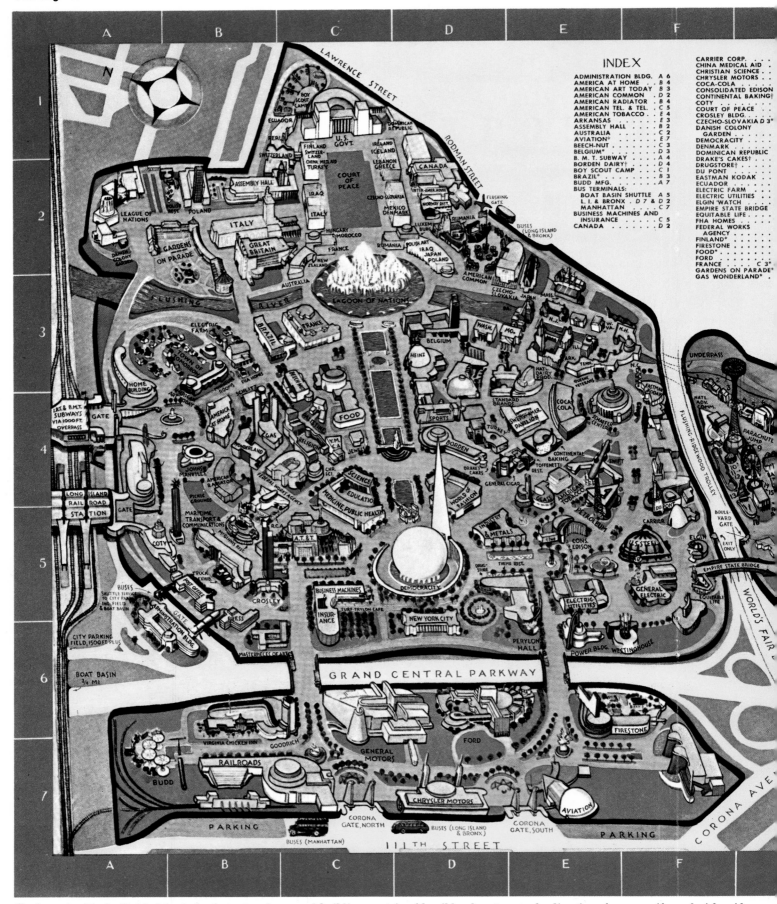

Confronted with the Fair's labyrinth of streets, plazas and buildings, a trio of bewildered matrons asks directions from a uniformed girl guide.

DRAWING BY CARL ROSE: COPR. © 1940, 1968 THE NEW YORKER MAGAZINE, INC.

Atop the modernistic Italian Pavilion, the goddess Roma holds court.

Eighty-foot ships' prows flank the entrance to Marine Transportation.

Beneath Poland's 141-foot tower was a restaurant that served Polish vod

Symbols of Socialism at the Soviet Pavilion included "Big Joe," a 30-ton statue of a worker brandishing a red star.

and 40 different hors d'oeuvre.   *At the National Cash Register Building, a gigantic revolving till rings up the day's attendance at the World's Fair.*

Do-it-yourself glass blowing, which enticed millions of visitors to the Glass Center, usually ended in a scary but harmless pop when the bubble burst.

Gimmicks and Giveaways

Not only was it the biggest fair ever, it was also the most expensive for the patrons. Just getting in cost 50 cents, and dinner at the French Pavilion might run as high as $10 a head. Nevertheless, some of the best things at the Fair were free, beginning with morning coffee at the Silex exhibit and ending with the nightly fireworks at the Lagoon of Nations. Betweentimes, without paying a cent, you could choose from among more than 50 movies, for example, the Petroleum Industry's "Oil Can and Does," or the Planters Nut & Chocolate Company's "Mr. Peanut and His Family Tree." Courtesy of Bell Telephone you could ring up your mother in Seattle. You could also feast on soup and pickles at Heinz, get a shave at Remington Rand, study French at the Linguaphone Institute, ride in a Ford on the Road of Tomorrow and fashion your own Fair souvenir at the Glass Center *(above)*.

In addition, most exhibits handed out prefabricated mementos *(opposite)*. Thus a "Time for Saraka" pin helped you remember an animated cartoon extolling a leading laxative, and a "Where's Elsie?" button meant that you had looked for, and probably found, the famous Borden Cow, in a box stall disguised as a frilly four-poster bed.

JUNGLELAND

G.M. FUTURAMA

HEINZ DOME

SARAKA

CALIFORNIA SOUVENIR

WESTINGHOUSE

BAKELITE

AC SPARK PLUG

PLANTERS NUT CO.

MANUFACTURERS TRUST

FLORIDA PAVILION

TAYLOR HAM

BORDEN

AVIATION SOUVENIR

ADMINISTRATION BUILDING

G.E. BUILDING

SOVIET PAVILION

ITALIAN PAVILION

SWIFT & CO.

SHEFFIELD FARMS

Exhibition souvenirs, either given out free or sold for pennies, helped visitors remember what it was, exactly, that they had seen at the Fair.

A million volts of man-made lightning, accompanied by the crash of synthetic thunder, astounds spectators at the General Electric exhibit.

Wonders of Science

The displays of science-based industry were both dazzling and spooky. Spookiest was the time capsule, designed to preserve for some 50 centuries such items as:

ARTICLES OF COMMON USE
ALARM CLOCK
CAN OPENER
MINIATURE CAMERA
TAPE MEASURE AND SAFETY PIN
TOOTHBRUSH AND TOOTH POWDER
HAT BY LILLY DACHÉ
MICKEY MOUSE PLASTIC CUP
SAFETY RAZOR AND BLADES

MATERIALS OF OUR DAY
FABRICS OF ASBESTOS AND GLASS
CARBON AND STAINLESS STEELS
ANTHRACITE COAL
PLASTIC AIRPLANE CONTROL PULLEY

MISCELLANEOUS ITEMS
SILVER DOLLAR, HALF DOLLAR
 AND OTHER U.S. COINS
ELECTRIC WALL SWITCH AND LAMP SOCKET
THE ALPHABET, IN HANDSET TYPE
SPECIAL MESSAGES FROM SCIENTISTS
 AND WRITERS
VIEWER FOR EXAMINING MICROFILM
 AND NEWSREEL FILM

MICROFILM SEQUENCES
THE LORD'S PRAYER IN 300 LANGUAGES
DICTIONARIES, STANDARD AND SLANG
PHOTOGRAPHS OF FACTORIES
 AND PRODUCTION LINES
ARROWSMITH BY SINCLAIR LEWIS AND *GONE
 WITH THE WIND* BY MARGARET MITCHELL
PHOTOGRAPHS OF POKER PLAYING; A GOLF
 MATCH; A BASEBALL GAME
ASSORTED MAGAZINES
ASSORTED COMIC STRIPS, ATLASES,
 TECHNICAL MANUALS

NEWSREELS
SPEECH BY PRESIDENT
 FRANKLIN D. ROOSEVELT
SCENES FROM HOWARD HUGHES'
 ROUND-THE-WORLD FLIGHT
JESSE OWENS WINNING THE 100-METER DASH IN
 THE OLYMPIC GAMES OF 1936
THE BOMBING OF CANTON IN THE WAR
 BETWEEN CHINA AND JAPAN
THE UNITED STATES NAVY ON MANEUVERS
A FASHION SHOW IN MIAMI, FLORIDA
PREVIEW SCENES OF
 THE NEW YORK WORLD'S FAIR OF 1939

Westinghouse time capsule, to be disinterred in 6939 A.D., hangs between the company's chairman (left) and Fair President Grover Whalen.

Long lines of fairgoers inch their way into General Motors' "Futurama." Despite an hour's wait for admission, 5,100,000 saw the show in one year.

The Shape of Tomorrow

The Fair's "World of Tomorrow" theme received its most spectacular treatment in General Motors' "Futurama." Crowds averaging 28,000 came each day to see the world's largest animated scale model (.8 of an acre), which presented designer Norman Bel Geddes' conception of the American landscape in the year 1960. Each visitor, seated in an armchair on a conveyor belt, was carried over the model on a 15-minute tour, while a sound device in the back of his chair described the scenes he saw below him. The display was so striking that LIFE magazine expanded upon the extravagant GM prophecies in an enthusiastic article excerpted below and on the pages that follow.

America in 1960 is full of a tanned and vigorous people who in 20 years have learned how to have fun. They camp in the forests and hike along the upcountry roads with their handsome wives and children. The college class of 1910 is out there hiking, half its members alive and very fit. These people do not care much for possessions. They are not attached to their own homes and home towns, because trains, express highways (and of course planes) get them across America in 24 hours.

When Americans of 1960 take their two-month vacations, they drive to the great parklands on giant express highways. A two-way skein consists of four 50-m.p.h. lanes on each of the outer edges; two pairs of 75-m.p.h. lanes and in the center, two lanes for 100-m.p.h. express traffic. Cars change from lane to lane at specified intervals, on signal from spaced control towers which can stop and start all traffic by radio. Being out of its driver's control, each car is safe against accident. The cars, built like raindrops, are powered by rear engines that are probably im-

An imagined 1960 airport, serving a small town in the Futurama model, has circular elevators taking airplanes to and from subterranean hangars.

provements of the Diesel. Inside, they are air-conditioned. They cost as low as $200. Off the highway, the driver dawdles again at his own speed and risk.

The highways skirt the great cities. But the happiest people live in one-factory farm-villages producing one small industrial item and their own farm produce. Strip planting protects the valley fields against erosion. The land is really greener than it was in 1939. Federal laws forbid the wanton cutting of wooded hillsides. Dams and canals prevent freshets and floods. Fewer acres, intensively and chemically cultivated, feed all the citizens of the U.S. More of the surface of the land is in forest and park.

Behind this visible America of 1960, hidden in the laboratories, are the inventors and engineers. By the spring of 1939 they had cracked nearly every frontier of progress. Liquid air is by 1960 a potent, mobile source of power. Atomic energy is being used cautiously. Power is transmitted by radio beams, focused by gold reflectors. The Lanova Cell has made all gas-

oline motors Diesels. These great new powers make life in 1960 immensely easier. Such new alloys as heat-treated beryllium bronze give perfect service. Great telescopes show 100 times more of the cosmos than the men of 1939 saw in the sky. Cures for cancer and infantile paralysis have extended man's life span and his wife's skin is still perfect at the age of 75. Architecture and plane construction have been revolutionized by light, noninflammable, strong plastics from soybeans. Houses are light, graceful, easily replaced. Electronic microscopes literally see everything.

On every front America in 1960 knows more about unleashing the best energies in its citizens. Nearly everyone is a high-school graduate. The talented get the best education in the world. More people are interested in life, the world, themselves and in making a better world. Politics and emotion still slow progress. But these obstructions are treated with dwindling patience in 1960.

LIFE, JUNE 5, 1939

In the city of 1960, 1,500-foot-high office buildings and apartment houses form self-sufficient sub-cities set alongside 14-lane superhighways.

The smash hit at the Fair was Billy Rose's Aquacade, where eight million visitors saw a team of "Aquafemmes" splash about to waltz music.

Text Credits

23—Will Rogers quote: Will Rogers, *How We Elect Our Presidents*, Donald Day, ed., Little, Brown and Co., 1952, p. 111. 35-37—"Invasion from Mars" by Howard Koch. Reprinted by permission of author and Manheim Fox Enterprises. 1938, 1940, 1967, 1969 Copyright Howard Koch. 38—"Amos and Andy" script written by Freeman Gosden and Charles Correll, supplied by Jim Harmon, Hollywood, California. Used by permission of Columbia Broadcasting System. 39 —Kaltenborn broadcast from H.V. Kaltenborn, *I Broadcast the Crisis*, New York, Random House, 1938. 48—Auto worker quote adapted from *The New Republic*, March 18, 1931, pp. 118-119. 51—Kentucky miner quote from *The Nation*, June 8, 1932, p. 651. 57—Tennessee squatter quote adapted from *These Are Our Lives*, by the Federal Writers' Project, Works Progress Administration, University of North Carolina Press, 1939, pp. 375-376. 70—Migratory worker's log book adapted from *Brother Can You Spare A Dime?* Milton Meltzer, Alfred A. Knopf, 1969, p. 140. 79—"Little Orphan Annie Song" courtesy of Ovaltine Food Products. 83 —"Have You Tried Wheaties." Lyrics by Donald D. Davis and music by M.K. Jerome. Music copyright 1919 by General Mills, Inc. Copyright renewed 1946. Lyrics copyright 1939 by General Mills, Inc. Used by permission—"Wave the Flag for Hudson High." Lyrics by David Owen and music by Phillip R. Culkin. Copyright 1940 by General Mills, Inc. Used by permission. 123—Walter Lippmann quotes: New York *Herald Tribune*, April 28, 1932; *Review of Reviews*, May 1933 —Will Rogers quotes: *The Autobiography of Will Rogers*, Donald Day, ed., Houghton Mifflin Co., 1949, pp. 312-313; *How We Elect Our Presidents*, Donald Day, ed., Little, Brown and Co., 1952, pp. 143-144, 148-149. 124—F.D.R. to Dan Roper: D.C. Roper, "The New Deal Endorses Profits," *Forum*, Dec. 1934; H.L. Mencken quote: "Three Years of Dr. Roosevelt," *American Mercury*, March 1936. 126

—Fireside Chat: *The Public Papers and Addresses of Franklin D. Roosevelt*, Volume Two, "The Year of Crisis: 1933," Random House, 1938, pp. 61-65. 136, 137—Pro-F.D.R. materials: Richard Harrity & Ralph G. Martin, *The Human Side of F.D.R.*, Duell, Sloan & Pearce, 1960, p. 181; Dixon Wecter, *The Age of the Great Depression*, Macmillan, 1948, p. 96; Ben Whitehurst, *"Dear Mr. President,"* E.P. Dutton & Co., 1937, pp. 17, 34—Anti-F.D.R. materials: Letters, Franklin D. Roosevelt Library, Hyde Park, N.Y.—Message from Hearst executive: James MacGregor Burns, *Roosevelt: The Lion and the Fox*, Harcourt, Brace & World, 1956, p. 241—Pegler quote: Westbrook Pegler, *The Dissenting Opinions of Mister Westbrook Pegler*, Charles Scribner's Sons, 1938, pp. 38-40. 139—"The Cliché Expert Testifies as a Roosevelt Hater," Copyright by Frank Sullivan. Reprinted by permission of the author. 215—Huey Long quotes: Huey P. Long, *My First Days in the White House*, Telegraph Press, Harrisburg, Pa., 1935. 216—Father Coughlin quotes: *New York Times*, March 4, 1935; July 17, 1936; TIME magazine, October 5, 1936; *New York Times*, November 21, 1938. 220—Wilfred Mendelson letters: *Let My People Know*, Joseph Leeds, ed., New York, 1942. 239—"Bei Mir Bist Du Schön," Secunda-Jacobs-Chan-Chaplin. © 1937 by Harms, Inc. Used by permission of Warner Bros.-Seven Arts Music. All rights reserved—"Tutti Frutti," Doris Fisher and Slim Gaillard. Copyright 1938 by Anne-Rachel Music Corporation. Copyright renewed 1965 and assigned to Anne-Rachel Music Corporation and Fred Fisher Music Co., Inc.—"Three Little Fishies," Saxie Dowell. Copyright 1939 by Anne-Rachel Music Corporation. Copyright renewed 1966 and assigned to Anne-Rachel Music Corporation—"The Flat Foot Floogee," Slim Gaillard, Slam Stewart and Bud Green. © 1938, 1966 Jewel Music Publishing Co., Inc. at 1619 Broadway, N.Y., N.Y. 10019.

Picture Credits

The sources for the illustrations which appear in this book are shown below. Credits for the pictures from left to right are separated by semicolons, from top to bottom by dashes.

Cover—Fabric design by John Martinez.

6,7—Historical Collection Security Pacific National Bank. 8,9—Edholm and Blomgren, Lincoln, Nebraska. 10,11—Library of Congress. 12,13—Brown Brothers. 14, 15—Museum of the City of New York. 16,17—Carl Mydans. 18,19—Al P. Burgert. 20,21—Culver Pictures. 22—Courtesy Halbert F. Speer. 28,29—Culver Pictures. 31—Bettmann Archive. 32—Culver Pictures. 33—Irving Settel; John Phillips; Culver Pictures. 34—Culver Pictures. 38—Culver Pictures. 39—CBS. 40—Irving Settel. 41,42,43—Culver Pictures. 44,45—University of Washington Library. 47 —Brown Brothers. 48—*The Detroit News*. 49—Library of Congress. 50 through 55 —Library of Congress except page 51, Library of Congress, Fred Ward from Black Star. 56,57—Margaret Bourke-White; Library of Congress. 58,59—Margaret Bourke-White. 60,61—Mrs. Henry Rhoades. 62 through 73—Library of Congress. 74, 75—Western Ways Features. 77—Wayne State University, Labor History Archives. 78—Chicago Tribune-New York News Syndicate courtesy Woody Gelman and Nostalgia Press. 79—John Savage courtesy Ernest Trova except bottom left courtesy Woody Gelman, Nostalgia Press, and the Wonder Co. 80—Courtesy Al Williamson, © King Features Syndicate—courtesy Woody Gelman and Nostalgia Press, © King Features Syndicate. 81—Culver Pictures—Al Freni courtesy Douglas Steinbauer, © King Features Syndicate, except bottom right courtesy Woody Gelman and Nostalgia Press, © King Features Syndicate. 82—General Mills, Inc. (2); John Savage courtesy Ernest Trova—General Mills, Inc.—Al Freni courtesy General Mills, Inc. 83—General Mills, Inc.—Al Freni courtesy General Mills, Inc.—General Mills, Inc.; John Savage courtesy Ernest Trova. 84 —Courtesy United Features Syndicate. 85—MGM. 86—John Savage courtesy Ernest Trova except bottom left courtesy Ernest Trova and Ralston Purina Co. 87—John Savage courtesy Ernest Trova. 88,89—Al Freni photographed from the Buck Rogers Collection of Tony Goodstone, New York City. 90—John Savage courtesy Ernest Trova except cartoon Walter Daran courtesy Chicago Tribune-New York News Syndicate. 91—Walter Daran courtesy Chicago Tribune-New York News Syndicate. 92—Courtesy Loraine Burdick except top right Marcus Adams, London. 93—Courtesy Loraine Burdick. 94—Al Freni courtesy Ione Wollenzein; courtesy Loraine Burdick; courtesy Ione Wollenzein. 95,96,97 —Al Freni courtesy Ione Wollenzein. 98,99—*Houston Chronicle*. 101—No credit. 102—Collection of Little Bohemia Lodge, Manitowish Waters, Wisconsin. 103 —United Press International. 104—*Daily Oklahoman* (2); No credit. 105—Wide World. 106—United Press International except top left *Daily Oklahoman*. 107 —Charles Moore from Black Star. 108—Brown Brothers. 114,115—Franklin D.

Roosevelt Library, Hyde Park, New York. 117—Reprinted from *Vanity Fair* (now *Vogue* incorporating *Vanity Fair*), copyright © 1934, 1962 by The Condé Nast Publications Inc. 118—Underwood & Underwood. 119—United Press International except second from right Wide World—*The New York Times* and Wide World courtesy Franklin D. Roosevelt Library, Hyde Park, New York; United Press International; Wide World (2); Keystone View; Wide World; Arthur Griffin—United Press International; Wide World; No credit; United Press International; Wide World; United Press International—United Press International; Wide World; Franklin D. Roosevelt Library, Hyde Park, New York. 120,121—Franklin D. Roosevelt Library, Hyde Park, New York; Underwood & Underwood. 122,123—United Press International. 124,125—Reprinted from *Vanity Fair* (now *Vogue* incorporating *Vanity Fair*), copyright © 1934, 1962 by The Condé Nast Publications Inc. (from Culver Pictures). 127—Reproduced by permission of *Esquire Magazine* © 1935 (renewed 1963) by Esquire, Inc. 128 —Culver Pictures; Photo World. 129—United Press International. 130,131 —Underwood & Underwood. 132,133—From "Public Building" by Public Works Administration and Federal Works Agency. 134,135—Culver Pictures; National Collection of Fine Arts copied by Henry B. Beville. 138—Drawing by Peter Arno, copyright © 1936, 1964 The New Yorker Magazine, Inc. 140,141—Tom McAvoy. 142,143—W. Eugene Smith from Black Star. 145—United Press International. 146—Culver Pictures. 148—George Karger-Pix. 149—Jerome Zerbe. 150—Wide World—United Press International; Jerome Zerbe; United Press International. 151—Top Wide World (3)—bottom United Press International (2). 152—United Press International. 153—Photo World (Edward Ozern); Culver Pictures—Stork Club; Wide World; Jerome Zerbe. 154,155—Brown Brothers. 156 —Wide World; Underwood & Underwood—Wide World—United Press International. 157—Underwood & Underwood except top right United Press International. 158,159—Culver Pictures. 160,161—Interphoto. 163—Harris & Ewing from the Gilloon Agency. 164,165—Wayne State University, Labor History Archives. 166—Library of Congress. 167—Wide World except bottom United Press International. 168,169—Wayne State University, Labor History Archives. 170, 171—United Press International except top left William Vandivert and top right the Historical Society of Pennsylvania. 173—Drawing by William Gropper. 174, 175—Wide World; Brown Brothers. 177—Library of Congress. 178,179—Historical Collection, Title Insurance and Trust Company, San Diego, California. 181 —Credits for this page are listed according to amount used from each source: United Press International; Wide World; Culver Pictures; Clarence Sinclair Bull-MGM; Paramount Pictures; Ron Partridge from Black Star; 20th Century-

Fox; Rex Hardy. 182,183—Culver Pictures. 184—Collection Herman G. Weinberg. 185—The Bettmann-Springer Film Archive. 186—Culver Pictures; Photo Files—Photo Files; Culver Pictures—The Academy of Motion Picture Arts and Sciences; Culver Pictures; Warner Bros. 187—Bert Six for Warner Bros. 188, 189—Culver Pictures. 190—No credit. 191—Culver Pictures. 192,193—Brown Brothers. 194,195—MGM except bottom right Culver Pictures. 196,197,198 —Culver Pictures. 199—Culver Pictures; MGM. 200,201—Culver Pictures. 202, 203—© Walt Disney Productions. 204—Columbia Pictures; Walter Wanger Productions—Culver Pictures; R.R. Stuart Collection; Culver Pictures—Culver Pictures; The Bettmann Archive; Larry Edmunds Bookshop, Hollywood, California—The Museum of Modern Art Film Stills Archive; The Academy of Motion Picture Arts and Sciences; United Artists—20th Century-Fox; March of Time-Pix; Photo Files. 205—Culver Pictures; Photo Files; Universal Studios —G.E. Richardson for Paramount; Photo Files; Paramount Pictures—Selznick International Pictures, Inc.; Warner Bros.; The Bettmann Archive—Culver Pictures; The Springer-Bettmann Film Archive; Culver Pictures—Forrest J Ackerman Archives; Sherman Clark for Universal Pictures; Culver Pictures. 206 —George Karger-Pix. 207—Culver Pictures except center Atlanta Historical

Society. 208,209—© Selznick International Pictures, Inc.© renewed 1967 MGM, Inc. 210,211—Alfred Eisenstaedt-Pix. 213—Otto Hagel. 214—Louisiana State Museum. 217—Wide World. 218—Hans Knopf-Pix. 220,221—Wide World. 222 —Robert Capa. 227—Margaret Bourke-White. 228,229—Popsie, New York. 231 —Otto F. Hess. 232—No credit—Brown Brothers; Ernest R. Smith—The Bettmann Archive. 233—Down Beat magazine; Brown Brothers; Photo Files —Photo Files; Duncan P. Schiedt; Photo Files. 234,235—Popsie, New York except left Down Beat magazine. 236,237—Peter Stackpole. 238—New York Daily News; Duncan P. Schiedt—Hansel Mieth; Richard Merrill—Ernest R. Smith. 239—Duncan P. Schiedt—Pete Culross; United Press International—Photo Files; Bernard Hoffman. 240,241—Ken Johnson. 242 through 265—Library of Congress except page 256—Library of Congress, Fred Ward from Black Star. 266,267 and 269—Frank T. Sobeck. 270,271—Drawing by Carl Rose, copyright © 1940, 1968 by The New Yorker Magazine, Inc.; Dave Scherman. 272,273—Museum of the City of New York—Edward J. Orth courtesy Roy R. Mumma; Edward J. Orth—Frank T. Sobeck. 274—Eric Schaal-Pix. 275—J.R. Eyerman. 276 —Eric Schaal-Pix. 277—Underwood & Underwood. 278,279—General Motors. 280—Gjon Mili. 281—Alfred Eisenstaedt-Pix. 282,283—Edward J. Orth.

Bibliography

Amory, Cleveland, *Who Killed Society?* Harper & Row, 1960.
Allen, Frederick Lewis, *Since Yesterday.* Bantam Books, 1965.
Baxter, John, *Hollywood in the Thirties.* A.S. Barnes & Co., 1968.
Bendiner, Robert, *Just Around the Corner.* Harper & Row, 1967.
Bird, Caroline, *The Invisible Scar.* David McKay Co., 1966.
Blum, Daniel, *A New Pictorial History of the Talkies.* G.P. Putnam's Sons, 1968.
Burns, James MacGregor, *Roosevelt: The Lion and the Fox.*
    Harcourt, Brace & Co., 1956.
Clarens, Carlos, *Horror Films.* G.P. Putnam's Sons, 1967.
Coleman, MacAlister, *Men and Coal.* Farrar & Rinehart, Inc., 1943.
Cook, Frederick J., *The F.B.I. Nobody Knows.* The Macmillan Company, 1964.
Daniels, Jonathan, *The Time Between the Wars.* Doubleday & Co., 1966.
Feather, Leonard, *The Encyclopedia of Jazz.* Rev. ed. Horizon Press, 1968.
Federal Writers' Project, Works Progress Administration, *These Are Our Lives.*
    University of North Carolina Press, 1939.
Griffith, Richard, and Arthur Mayer, *The Movies.* Simon & Schuster, 1957.
Gunther, John, *Roosevelt in Retrospect.* Harper & Bros., 1950.
Halliwell, Leslie, *The Filmgoer's Companion.* Hill & Wang, 1967.
Harmon, James, *The Great Radio Heroes.* Ace Books, Inc., 1967.
Hoover, J. Edgar, *Persons in Hiding.* Little, Brown & Co., 1938.
Howe, Irving, and Lewis Coser, *The American Communist Party.*

    Beacon Press, 1957.
Kempton, Murray, *Part of Our Time.* Dell Publishing Co., 1955.
Leonard, Jonathan Norton, *Three Years Down.* Carrick & Evans, 1939.
Leuchtenburg, William E., *Franklin D. Roosevelt and the New Deal.*
    Harper & Row, 1963.
Levinson, Edward, *Labor on the March.* Harper & Bros., 1938.
Maxwell, Elsa, *R.S.V.P.* Little, Brown & Co., 1954.
Meltzer, Milton, *Brother Can You Spare A Dime?* Alfred A. Knopf, 1969.
O'Connor, Harvey, *Steel-Dictator.* The John Day Co., 1935.
Roosevelt, James, and Sidney Shalett, *Affectionately, F.D.R.*
    Harcourt, Brace & Co., 1959.
Schickel, Richard, *The Disney Version.* Simon & Schuster, 1968.
Schlesinger, Arthur M., Jr., *The Age of Roosevelt.* Vol. II: *The Coming of the New Deal.* Vol. III: *The Politics of Upheaval.* Houghton Mifflin Co., 1958, 1960.
Settel, Irving, *A Pictorial History of Radio.* Grosset & Dunlap, 1967.
Simon, George T., *The Big Bands.* The Macmillan Company, 1967.
Taft, Philip, *Organized Labor in American History.* Harper & Row, 1964.
Tanner, Louise, *All the Things We Were.* Doubleday & Co., 1968.
Taylor, Deems, *A Pictorial History of the Movies.* Simon & Schuster, 1949.
Wecter, Dixon, *The Age of the Great Depression.* The Macmillan Company, 1948.
Whitehead, Donald, *The F.B.I. Story.* Random House, 1956.

Acknowledgments

The editors of this book wish to thank the following persons and institutions for their assistance:

Forrest J Ackerman, Forrest J Ackerman Archives, Los Angeles; Atlanta Historical Society; A. K. Baragwanath, Senior Curator, Museum of the City of New York; Busby Berkeley, Los Angeles; Larry Booth, Director of Historical Collection, Title Insurance and Trust Company, San Diego; Mrs. Ruth P. Braun, Chief Librarian, *The Detroit News;* Mrs. Loraine Burdick, Celebrity Doll Club, Puyallup, Washington; Ted Cavagnaro, St. Louis; Mrs. Shirley Clarke, Curator, Audio-Visual Materials, Labor History Archives, Wayne State University, Detroit; Harry Collins, Brown Brothers; Charles Correll and Freeman Gosden, Los Angeles; Patricia Crews, *Daily Oklahoman,* Oklahoma City; Robert Cunningham, Stillwater, Oklahoma; Virginia Daiker, Prints and Photographs Division, Library of Congress; James H. Davis, Western History Division, Denver Public Library; Frank Driggs, New York City; Cam Duane, Institute of Texan Cultures, San Antonio; Moe Fishman, Secretary, Veterans of the Abraham Lincoln Battalion, New York; Woody Gelman, Nostalgia Press, New York; Dorothy Gimmestad, Assistant Curator, Audio-Visual Library, Minnesota Historical Society, St. Paul; Tony Goodstone, New York City; Chester Gould, *The Chicago Tribune;* Martin Herman, *The Philadelphia Bulletin;* The Historical Society of Pennsylvania, Philadelphia; Hoblitzelle Theatre Arts Library, University of Texas, Austin; Roy King, Librarian, *St. Louis Post Dispatch;* Walter Kost, Manager, Consumer and Promotion Services, General Mills Inc., Minneapolis; Joseph W. Marshall, Mrs. Clarice D. Morris, Paul J. McLaughlin,

Franklin D. Roosevelt Library, Hyde Park, New York; Robert D. Monroe, Director of Special Collections, University of Washington Library, Seattle; Dan Morgenstern, *Down Beat,* Chicago; John McCarty, Director, High Plains Art Gallery, Amarillo, Texas; Garnett McCoy, Archivist, Archives of American Art, Detroit; Herbert McLaughlin, Arizona Photographic Associates, Phoenix; Sol Novin, Culver Pictures, New York City; Francis V. O'Connor, University of Maryland; Edward J. Orth, Los Angeles; Margot P. Pearsall, Curator, Social History Division, Detroit Historical Museum; Warner Pflug, Archivist, Labor History Archives, Wayne State University, Detroit; Victor R. Plukas, Security Pacific National Bank, Los Angeles; Henry Raduta, Manager, Chicago Tribune-New York News Syndicate Inc.; Gleason W. Romer, Miami; Marthanne B. Root, Austin; Sy Seidman, New York City; Robert Shipler, Salt Lake City; Mildred Simpson, Librarian, Library of Motion Picture Arts and Sciences, Los Angeles; R. Henderson Shuffler, Director, Institute of Texan Cultures, San Antonio; Ernest Smith, New York City; Paul Smith, President, Johnson Smith Company, Grosse Pointe; Ray Stuart, R. R. Stuart Collection, Los Angeles; Patrick Sullivan, Massachusetts State Library, Boston; Judith Topaz, Assistant, Iconographic Collections, State Historical Society of Wisconsin, Madison; Ernest Trova, St. Louis, Missouri; John Conrad Weiser, New York City; Al Williamson, Callicoon, New York; Mrs. Ione Wollenzein, Waukesha, Wisconsin; Mary Yushak, Museum of Modern Art, New York City; Jerome Zerbe, New York City.

Index

Numbers in italics indicate an illustration of the subject mentioned.

Printed in U.S.A.

✕✕✕✕